"A real public service."—*San Fr*

"This polemical history argues that the U.S. military's role in the development of the Internet indelibly shaped the system into a powerful tool of government surveillance. ... amid increasing dismay about technology's influence on contemporary life, such forceful questioning is salutary."—*New Yorker*

"Provocative history of the internet-equipped security state, implicating key players in the digital economy in the game of espionage.... Levine, a tech-savvy investigative journalist, documents an army of them in his wide-ranging look at the way governments and companies alike spy on ordinary citizens."—*Kirkus*

"This engrossing investigation will find a large audience among those interested in the uses and abuses of technology."—*Library Journal*

"*Surveillance Valley* is perhaps one of the most deeply disturbing books of the year. It leaves no illusions intact ..."—*Scroll.in*

"Yasha Levine's bold and sweeping history of the Internet—from its shadowy inception as a military contrivance for counterinsurgency and domestic surveillance, to its current incarnation as a commercialized tool for everyday communication that turns everyone's life into an open book—tells a gripping story of our algorithmic way of life in the making. Defying common Internet tropes that present a battle between valiant and independent rebels versus omnipresent state and corporate powers, no one comes out of this book looking clean. Whatever your thoughts about our digitized world, this book will challenge them."—Stuart Ewen, Distinguished Professor of History, Sociology and Media Studies at Hunter College and the CUNY Graduate Center

"The Internet will never be the same after you read *Surveillance Valley*. Yasha Levine has done a masterful job of research and reporting about the military origins of the 'world wide web' and how its essential nature has not changed in the years since its creation during the Cold War. I especially applaud his courage in unraveling the connections between the so-called 'deep state' and its economic allies in Silicon Valley with the big guns of the 'privacy' movement, who have scoffed at virtually every attempt at making their operations transparent to the public."—Tim Shorrock, author of *Spies for Hire: The Secret World of Intelligence Outsourcing*

"In this fast-paced, myth busting expose, Yasha Levine documents how a collection of spooks, cybernetic fanatics, and libertarian oligarchs have exploited the internet to promote regime change abroad and establish a totalistic spying network at home. *Surveillance Valley* is an unprecedented journalistic achievement, revealing the untold history of the anti-democratic regime that rules our lives from behind a glossy LED screen."—Max Blumenthal, author of *Goliath: Life and Loathing in Greater Israel*, senior editor of AlterNet's Grayzone Project

"An important history lesson."—*TANK*

"*Surveillance Valley* is a troubling book, but it is an important book. It smashes comforting myths."—*Boundary 2*

SURVEILLANCE VALLEY

SURVEILLANCE VALLEY

THE SECRET MILITARY HISTORY OF THE INTERNET

YASHA LEVINE

ICON

First published in the USA in 2018
by PublicAffairs, an imprint of Perseus Books, LLC,
a subsidiary of Hachette Book Group, Inc
New York

Published in the UK in 2019
by Icon Books Ltd, Omnibus Business Centre,
39–41 North Road, London N7 9DP
email: info@iconbooks.com
www.iconbooks.com

Sold in the UK, Europe and Asia
by Faber & Faber Ltd, Bloomsbury House,
74–77 Great Russell Street,
London WC1B 3DA or their agents

Distributed in the UK, Europe and Asia
by Grantham Book Services,
Trent Road, Grantham NG31 7XQ

Distributed in Australia and New Zealand
by Allen & Unwin Pty Ltd,
PO Box 8500, 83 Alexander Street,
Crows Nest, NSW 2065

Distributed in South Africa by
Jonathan Ball, Office B4, The District,
41 Sir Lowry Road, Woodstock 7925

Distributed in India by Penguin Books India,
7th Floor, Infinity Tower – C, DLF Cyber City,
Gurgaon 122002, Haryana

ISBN: 978-178578-478-1

Print book interior design by Jack Lenzo

Printed and bound in Great Britain
by Clays Ltd, Elcograf S.p.A.

To Nellie and Boris, my parents.
I would be nothing without their love.

Today, everything serves war. There is not one discovery which the military does not study with the aim of applying it to warfare, not one invention which they do not attempt to turn to military use.

—Nikolai Fyodorov, *Philosophy of the Common Cause*, 1891

To fight the bug, we must understand the bug.

—*Starship Troopers*

Contents

Prologue

Oakland, California

t was February 18, 2014, and already dark when I crossed the Bay Bridge from San Francisco and parked my car in downtown Oakland. The streets were deserted, save for a couple of homeless men slumped in a heap against a closed storefront. Two police cruisers raced through a red light, sirens blaring.

I approached Oakland's city hall on foot. Even from a distance, I could see that something unusual was going on. A line of parked police cars ran down the block, and news anchors and TV camera crews scampered about, jockeying for position. A large group of people milled near the entrance, a few of them setting up what looked like a giant papier-mâché rat, presumably intended as a symbol for snitching. But the real action was inside. Several hundred people packed Oakland's ornate high-domed city council chamber. Many of them carried signs. It was an angry crowd, and police officers flanked the sides of the room, ready to push everyone out if things got out of hand.

The commotion was tied to the main agenda item of the night: the city council was scheduled to vote on an ambitious $11 million project to create a citywide police surveillance hub. Its official name was the "Domain Awareness Center"—but everyone called it "the DAC." Design specs called for linking real-time video feeds from thousands of cameras across the city and funneling them into a unified control hub. Police would be able to punch in a location and watch it in real time or wind back the clock. They could turn on face recognition and vehicle tracking systems, plug in social media feeds, and enhance their view with data coming in from other law enforcement agencies—both local and federal.[1]

Plans for this surveillance center had been roiling city politics for months, and the outrage was now making its presence felt. Residents, religious leaders, labor activists, retired politicians, masked "black bloc" anarchists, and reps from the American Civil Liberties Union—they were all in attendance, rubbing shoulder to shoulder with a group of dedicated local activists who had banded together to stop the DAC. A nervous, bespectacled city official in a tan suit took the podium to reassure the agitated crowd that the Domain Awareness Center was designed to protect them—not spy on them. "This is not a fusion center. We have no agreements with the NSA or the CIA or the FBI to access our databases," he said.

The hall blew up in pandemonium. The crowd wasn't buying it. People booed and hissed. "This is all about monitoring protesters," someone screamed from the balcony. A young man, his face obscured by a mask, stalked to the front of the room and menacingly jammed his smartphone in the city official's face and snapped photos. "How does that feel? How do you like that—being surveilled all the time!" he yelled. A middle-aged man—bald, wearing glasses and crumpled khakis—took the podium and tore into the city's political leaders. "You council members somehow believe that the Oakland Police Department, which has an unparalleled history of violating the civil rights of Oaklanders and which cannot even follow its own policies, be it a crowd control policy or a body camera policy, can somehow be trusted to use the DAC?" He left with a bang, yelling: "The only good DAC is a dead DAC!" Wild applause erupted.

Oakland is one of the most diverse cities in the country. It's also home to a violent, often unaccountable police department, which has been operating under federal oversight for over a decade. The police abuse has been playing out against a backdrop of increasing gentrification fueled by the area's Internet boom and the spike in real estate prices that goes along with it. In San Francisco, neighborhoods like the Mission District, historically home to a vibrant Latino community, have turned into condos and lofts and upscale gastro pubs. Teachers, artists, older adults, and anyone else not making a six-figure salary are having a tough time making ends meet. Oakland, which for a time was spared this fate, was now feeling the crush as well. But locals were not going down without a fight. And a lot of their anger was focused on Silicon Valley.

The people gathered at city hall that night saw Oakland's DAC as an extension of the tech-fueled gentrification that was pushing poorer longtime residents out of the city. "We're not stupid. We know that the purpose is to monitor Muslims, black and brown communities and protesters," said a young woman in a headscarf. "This center comes at a time when you're trying to develop Oakland into a playground and bedroom community for San Francisco professionals. These efforts require you to make Oakland quieter, whiter, less scary and wealthier—and that means getting rid of Muslims, black and brown people and protesters. You know this and so do developers. We heard them at meetings. They are scared. They verbally admit it."

She had a point. A few months earlier, a pair of Oakland investigative journalists had obtained a cache of internal city-planning documents dealing with the DAC and found that city officials seemed to be interested more in using the proposed surveillance center to monitor political protests and labor union activity at the Oakland docks than in fighting crime.[2]

There was another wrinkle. Oakland had initially contracted out development of the DAC to the Science Applications International Corporation, a massive California-based military contractor that does so much work for the National Security Agency that it is known in the intelligence business as "NSA West." The company is also a major CIA contractor, involved in everything from monitoring agency employees as part of the agency's "insider threat" programs to running the CIA's drone assassination fleet. Multiple Oakland residents came up to blast the city's decision to partner with a company that was such an integral part of the US military and intelligence apparatus. "SAIC facilitates the telecommunications for the drone program in Afghanistan that's murdered over a thousand innocent civilians, including children," said a man in a black sweater. "And this is the company you chose?"

I looked around the room in amazement. This was the heart of a supposedly progressive San Francisco Bay Area, and yet the city planned on partnering with a powerful intelligence contractor to build a police surveillance center that, if press reports were correct, officials wanted to use to spy on and monitor locals. Something made that scene even stranger to me that night. Thanks to a tip from a local activist, I had gotten wind that Oakland had been in talks with Google about demoing products in what appeared to be an attempt by the company to get a part of the DAC contract.

Google possibly helping Oakland spy on its residents? If true, it would be particularly damning. Many Oaklanders saw Silicon Valley companies such as Google as being the prime drivers of the skyrocketing housing prices, gentrification, and aggressive policing that was making life miserable for poor and low-income residents. Indeed, just a few weeks earlier protesters had picketed outside the local home of a wealthy Google manager who was personally involved in a nearby luxury real estate development.

Google's name never came up during the tumultuous city council meeting that night, but I did manage to get my hands on a brief email exchange between a Google "strategic partnership manager" and an Oakland official spearheading the DAC project that hinted at something in the works.[3]

In the weeks after the city council meeting, I attempted to clarify this relationship. What kinds of services did Google offer Oakland's police surveillance center? How far did the talks progress? Were they fruitful? My requests to Oakland were ignored and Google wasn't talking either—trying to get answers from the company was like talking to a giant rock. My investigation stalled further when Oakland residents temporarily succeeded in getting the city to halt its plans for the DAC.

Though Oakland's police surveillance center was put on hold, the question remained: What could Google, a company obsessed with its progressive "Don't Be Evil" image, offer a controversial police surveillance center?

At the time, I was a reporter for *Pando,* a small but fearless San Francisco magazine that covered the politics and business of Silicon Valley. I knew that Google made most of its money through a sophisticated targeted advertising system that tracked its users and built predictive models of their behavior and interests. The company had a glimpse into the lives of close to two billion people who used its platforms—from email to video to mobile phones—and it performed a strange kind of alchemy, turning people's data into gold: nearly $100 billion in annual revenue and a market capitalization of $600 billion; its cofounders Larry Page and Sergey Brin had a combined personal wealth estimated to be $90 billion.

Google is one of the wealthiest and most powerful corporations in the world, yet it presents itself as one of the good guys: a company on a mission to make the world a better place and a bulwark against corrupt and intrusive governments all around the globe. And yet, as I traced the story and dug into the details of Google's government contracting business, I discovered that the company was already a full-fledged military contractor, selling versions of its consumer data mining and analysis technology to police departments, city governments, and just about every major US intelligence and military agency. Over the years, it had supplied mapping technology used by the US Army in Iraq, hosted data for the Central Intelligence Agency, indexed the National Security Agency's vast intelligence databases, built military robots, colaunched a spy satellite with the Pentagon, and leased its cloud computing platform to help police departments predict crime. And Google is not alone. From Amazon to eBay to Facebook—most of the Internet companies we use every day have also grown into powerful corporations that track and profile their users while pursuing partnerships and business relationships with major US military and intelligence agencies. Some parts of these companies are so thoroughly intertwined with America's security services that it is hard to tell where they end and the US government begins.

Since the start of the personal computer and Internet revolution in the 1990s, we've been told again and again that we are in the grips of a liberating technology, a tool that decentralizes power, topples entrenched bureaucracies, and brings more democracy and equality to the world. Personal computers and information networks were supposed to be the new frontier of freedom—a techno-utopia where authoritarian and repressive structures lost their power, and where the creation of a better world was still possible. And all that we, global netizens, had to do for this new and better world to flower and bloom was to get out of the way and let Internet companies innovate and the market work its magic. This narrative has been planted deep into our culture's collective subconscious and holds a powerful sway over the way we view the Internet today.

But spend time looking at the nitty-gritty business details of the Internet and the story gets darker, less optimistic. If the Internet is truly such a revolutionary break from the past, why are companies like Google in bed with cops and spies?

I tried to answer this seemingly simple question after visiting Oakland that night in February. Little did I know then that this would take me on a deep dive into the history of the Internet and ultimately lead me to write this book. Now, after three years of investigative work, interviews, travel across two continents, and countless hours of correlating and researching historical and declassified records, I know the answer.

Pick up any popular history of the Internet and you will generally find a combination of two narratives describing where this computer networking technology came from. The first narrative is that it emerged out of the military's need for a communication network that could survive a nuclear blast. That led to the development of the early Internet, first known as ARPANET, built by the Pentagon's Advanced Research Projects Agency (known today as the Defense Advanced Research Projects Agency, or DARPA). The network went live in the late 1960s and featured a decentralized design that could route messages even if parts of the network were destroyed by a nuclear blast. The second narrative, which is the most dominant, contends that there was no military application of the early Internet at all. In this version, the ARPANET was built by radical young computer engineers and playful hackers deeply influenced by the acid-drenched counterculture of the San Francisco Bay Area. They cared not a damn about war or surveillance or anything of the sort, but dreamed of computer-mediated utopias that would make militaries obsolete. They built a civilian network to bring this future into reality, and it is this version of the ARPANET that then grew into the Internet we use today. For years, a conflict has raged between these historical interpretations. These days, most histories offer a mix of the two—acknowledging the first, yet leaning much more heavily on the second.

My research reveals a third historical strand in the creation of the early Internet—a strand that has all but disappeared from the history books. Here, the impetus was rooted not so much in the need to survive a nuclear attack but in the dark military arts of counterinsurgency and America's fight against the perceived global spread of communism. In the 1960s, America was a global power overseeing an increasingly volatile world: conflicts and regional insurgencies against US-allied governments from South America to Southeast Asia and the Middle East. These were not traditional wars that involved big armies but guerrilla campaigns and local rebellions, frequently fought in regions where Americans had little previous experience. Who were these people? Why were they rebelling? What could be done to stop them? In military circles, it was believed that these questions were of vital importance to America's pacification efforts, and some argued that the only effective way to answer them was to develop and leverage computer-aided information technology.

The Internet came out of this effort: an attempt to build computer systems that could collect and share intelligence, watch the world in real time, and study and analyze people and political movements with the ultimate goal of predicting and preventing social upheaval. Some even dreamed of creating a sort of early warning radar for human societies: a networked computer system that watched for social and political threats and intercepted them in much the same way that traditional radar did for hostile aircraft. In other words, the Internet was hardwired to be a surveillance tool from the start. No matter what we use the network for today—dating, directions, encrypted chat, email, or just reading the news—it always had a dual-use nature rooted in intelligence gathering and war.

As I traced this forgotten history, I found that I was not so much discovering something new but uncovering something that was plainly obvious to a lot of people not so long ago. Starting in the early 1960s in the United States, a big fear about the proliferation of computer database and networking technologies arose. People worried that these systems would be used by both corporations and governments for surveillance and control. Indeed, the dominant cultural view at the time was that computers and computing technology—including the ARPANET, the military research network that would grow into the Internet we use today—were tools of repression, not liberation.

In the course of my investigation, I was genuinely shocked to discover that as early as 1969, the first year that the ARPANET came online, a group of students at MIT and Harvard attempted to shut down research taking place at their universities under the ARPANET umbrella. They saw this computer network as the start of a hybrid private-public system of surveillance and control—"computerized people-manipulation" they called it—and warned that it would be used to spy on Americans and wage war on progressive political movements. They understood this technology better than we do today. More importantly, they were right. In 1972, almost as soon as the ARPANET was rolled out on a national level, the network was used to help the CIA, the NSA, and the US Army spy on tens of thousands of antiwar and civil rights activists. It was a big scandal at the time, and the ARPANET's role in it was discussed at length on American television, including *NBC Evening News*.

This episode, which took place forty-five years ago, is a vital part of the historical record, important to anyone who wants to understand the network that mediates so much of our lives today. Yet you won't find it mentioned in any recent book or documentary on the origins of the Internet—at least not any that I could find, and I read and watched just about all of them.

Surveillance Valley is an attempt to recover part of this lost history. But it is more than that. The book starts in the past, going back to the development of what we now call the Internet during the Vietnam War. But it quickly moves into the present, looking at the private surveillance business that powers much of Silicon Valley, investigating the ongoing overlap between the Internet and the military-industrial complex that spawned it half a century ago, and uncovering the close ties that exist between US intelligence agencies and the antigovernment privacy movement that has sprung up in the wake of Edward Snowden's leaks. *Surveillance Valley* shows that little has changed over the years: the Internet was developed as a weapon and remains a weapon today. American military interests continue to dominate all parts of the network, even those that supposedly stand in opposition.

Yasha Levine
New York
December 2017

Part I
Lost History

Chapter 1

A New Kind of War

Our hatred for the Americans is as high as the sky.

—North Vietnamese song

On June 8, 1961, a military intelligence officer named William Godel arrived in Saigon from Washington, DC. It was a hot summer's day when he landed in the South Vietnamese capital, and Godel, jetlagged and dripping with sweat, visited several low-slung barracks-style buildings not far from the Saigon River. He walked unevenly, hobbled by the limp he carried from his days fighting Japanese forces in the South Pacific. On the surface, there was nothing special about this excursion. There was little to indicate that these nondescript structures, with their bland white walls and sloping roofs, sat at the center of Project Agile, a top-secret counterinsurgency program that would play a major role in the history of the Vietnam War and the rise of modern computer technology.

From his base in the Pentagon, Godel had been pushing for an initiative like Agile for over a decade. Now, this project had the personal backing of President John F. Kennedy.[1]

The first results were seen on August 10, 1961, when a Sikorsky H-34 helicopter, shaped like a giant guppy, lazily rose above Saigon and made its way toward the impenetrable jungles of Kon Tum, which borders Laos and Cambodia.[2] Once the pilot acquired his target, he signaled, and the crew switched on a special crop duster grafted onto the bottom of the craft. In a slow sweeping motion, they sprayed the jungle below with an experimental mixture of highly toxic defoliation chemicals. Among them was the infamous Agent Orange. Those who smelled it said it resembled perfume.

America was not yet officially at war in Vietnam. Yet for years, the United States had been funneling money and weapons into the region to help the French wage a war against North Vietnam, the communist revolutionary state led by Ho Chi Minh that was fighting to reunify the country and kick out its colonial rulers.[3] Now, as Godel's crew sprayed the jungles below, America was increasing its support in money and weapons. Thousands of military "advisers" were being dispatched to South Vietnam to prop up the puppet government of Ngo Dinh Diem in the hopes of stemming what Americans viewed as a surging global tide of communism.[4]

In the sweltering jungles of Indochina, it was not an easy fight. Dense vegetation cover was a persistent problem. It was one of the rebels' greatest tactical advantages, allowing them to move people and supplies through neighboring Laos and Cambodia undetected and launch deadly raids deep in South Vietnamese territory. With Project Agile, Godel was determined to take that advantage away.

The British Empire had pioneered the use of defoliants as a form of chemical warfare, using them against local movements that opposed colonial rule. In the fight against communist rebels in Malaya, Britain ruthlessly deployed them to destroy food supplies and jungle cover.[5] British military planners described defoliants as "a form of sanction against a recalcitrant nation which would be more speedy than blockade and less repugnant than the atomic bomb."

Godel followed Britain's lead. Under Project Agile, chemists at a secret US Army lab at Fort Detrick, Maryland, had tested and isolated potential defoliant chemicals that could eat away at the dense jungle cover. These were flown to Saigon and tested in the field. They worked with brutal efficiency. Leaves fell several weeks after being sprayed, stripping the canopy bare. A second application increased effectiveness and permanently killed many trees. Bombing the area or lighting it up with napalm also made the defoliation more or less permanent.[6] With the tests a success, Godel drew up ambitious plans to cover half of South Vietnam with chemical defoliants.[7] The idea was not just to destroy tree cover but also to destroy food crops to starve the North Vietnamese into submission.[8]

South Vietnam's President Diem backed the plan. On November 30, 1961, President Kennedy had signed off on it. Thanks to Godel and Project Agile, Operation Ranch Hand was launched.

Ranch Hand got going in 1962 and lasted until the war ended more than a decade later. In that time, American C-123 transport planes doused an area equal in size to half of South Vietnam with twenty million gallons of toxic chemical defoliants. Agent Orange was fortified with other colors of the rainbow: Agent White, Agent Pink, Agent Purple, Agent Blue. The chemicals, produced by American companies like Dow and Monsanto, turned whole swaths of lush jungle into barren moonscapes, causing death and horrible suffering for hundreds of thousands.[9]

Operation Ranch Hand was merciless, and in clear violation of the Geneva Conventions. It remains one of the most shameful episodes of the Vietnam War. Yet the defoliation project is notable for more than just its unimaginable cruelty. The government body at its lead was a Department of Defense outfit called the Advanced Research Projects Agency (ARPA)—better known today by the slightly retooled name of Defense Research Projects Agency (DARPA). Born in 1958 as a crash program to protect the United States from a Soviet nuclear threat from space, it launched several groundbreaking initiatives tasked with developing advanced weapons and military technologies. Among them were Project Agile and Command and Control Research, two overlapping ARPA initiatives that created the Internet.

America Goes Ballistic

In late 1957, Americans watched as the Soviet Union launched the first manmade satellite, *Sputnik 1*. The satellite was tiny, about the size of a volleyball, but it was thrust into orbit by hitching a ride atop the world's first intercontinental ballistic missile. This was both a demonstration and a threat. If the Soviet Union could put a satellite into space, it could also deliver a nuclear warhead to just about any spot in the United States.

Sputnik crashed into America's paranoid politics like a giant meteor. Politicians seized on the event as a sign of US military and technological weakness, and news reports focused on the Soviet victory of being the first in space. How could America fall behind the communists in something so vital? It was an affront to people's sense of exceptionalism.[10]

President Dwight Eisenhower was attacked for being asleep at the wheel. Generals and politicians spun horrific tales of impending Soviet conquest of earth and space and pushed for more defense spending.[11] Even Vice President Richard Nixon criticized Eisenhower in public, telling business leaders that the technology gap between America and the Soviet Union was too great for them to expect a tax cut. The country needed their money to catch up.[12]

As the public reeled from this major defeat in the so-called Space Race, President Eisenhower knew he had to do something big and very public to save face and ease people's fears. Neil McElroy, his newly appointed secretary of defense, had a plan.

Immaculately groomed and with perfectly coiffed hair parted down the middle, McElroy had the looks and manners of a high-flying advertising executive. Which is, in fact, what he was before Eisenhower tapped him to run the Department of Defense. In his previous role as president of Procter and Gamble, McElroy's signature innovation was bankrolling "soap operas"—cheesy daytime dramas tailored to housewives—as pure marketing vehicles for his company's selection of soaps and household detergents. As *Time* magazine, which put McElroy on the cover of its October 1953 issue, put it: "Soap operas get more advertising messages across to the consumer—and sell more soap—simply because the housewife can absorb the messages for hours on end while she goes about her household chores."[13]

In the weeks after the Soviet Union launched *Sputnik*, McElroy cooked up the perfect public relations project to save the day. He called for the creation of the Advanced Research Projects

Agency—ARPA—a new, independent military body whose purpose was to bridge the space gap and to ensure that embarrassing technological defeat like *Sputnik* would never happen again.[14] McElroy was a businessman who believed in the power of business to save the day.[15] In November 1957, he pitched ARPA to Congress as an organization that would cut through government red tape and create a public-private vehicle of pure military science to push the frontiers of military technology and develop "vast weapon systems of the future."[16]

The idea behind ARPA was simple. It would be a civilian-led outfit housed within the Pentagon. It would be lean, with a tiny staff and a big budget. Though it wouldn't build or run its own laboratories and research facilities, it would function like an executive management hub that figured out what needed to be done and then farmed out the actual work to universities, private research institutes, and military contractors.[17]

The plan appealed to President Eisenhower, who distrusted the cynical jockeying for funding and power of various arms of the military—which he believed bloated the budget and burned money on useless projects. The idea of outsourcing research and development to the private sector appealed to the business community as well.[18] The military brass, on the other hand, weren't so pleased. The air force, navy, army, and Joint Chiefs of Staff all balked at the idea of civilians sitting above them and telling them what to do. They feared losing control over technology procurement, a lucrative center of profit and power.

The military pushed back against McElroy's plan. The conflict with the military loomed so large that it made a cameo in Eisenhower's 1958 State of the Union address: "I am not attempting today to pass judgment on the charge of harmful service rivalries. But one thing is sure. Whatever they are, America wants them stopped."[19] He got his way. On February 11, 1958, a month after the State of the Union and just five months after the *Sputnik* launch, Congress wrote ARPA into a US Air Force appropriations bill, giving it $520 million in initial funding and a plan for a gigantic $2 billion budget.[20]

McElroy chose Roy Johnson, an executive at General Electric, to head the new agency. An internal Pentagon report described him as an "utterly confident, calm, strikingly handsome individual who looked every inch like a *Fortune* cover tycoon." It also noted that his only concern with taking the job was potentially losing a lucrative tax loophole: "Johnson was also a very wealthy man, leaving a $158,000 job to accept an $18,000 post at ARPA. For tax reasons, he took the ARPA job on condition that he would be permitted to be physically present in Connecticut for a minimal number of days. This meant he usually left Washington on Friday and returned Monday or Tuesday. He frequently used a private plane." Protecting America against the Soviet Union was important. But a man had to mind his tax bill.[21]

In the first few years of its existence, ARPA took on a range of important projects. It had a space division developing ballistic missiles. It worked on spy and weather satellites as well as satellite tracking systems and did early prep work on putting a man in space. It also helped run nuclear tests like Operation Argus, which involved the detonation of several small nukes in the upper reaches of the atmosphere above the South Atlantic in a radical attempt to create an invisible charged-particle shield that would fry the electronics of any nuclear warhead that flew through it.[22]

With all these projects, it seemed like ARPA was off to a glorious start, but the excitement did not last. Pentagon infighting and the creation of a demilitarized NASA—National Aeronautics and Space Administration—sucked money and prestige out of the agency. Less than a year after it was created, ARPA's budget was slashed to just $150 million—peanuts compared to the $2 billion budget it was promised.[23] Over the next several years, it went through three directors and fought to stay alive. Everyone was convinced that ARPA was on its way to the grave.

Yet one man had a plan to save it: William Godel.

Future War

Five feet ten inches tall, with almond-shaped eyes, a buzz-cut, and a smooth, intellectual manner, William Godel had the manners of a sharply dressed academic or maybe a junior diplomat. He was born in Boulder, Colorado, in 1921, graduated from Georgetown, and got a job doing military intelligence at the War Department. After Japan's attack on Pearl Harbor, he was drafted into the Marine Corps as an officer and saw action in the South Pacific, where he took a bullet in the leg, an injury that left him permanently crippled. After the war, he shot up the ranks of military intelligence, rising to the GS-18 level—the highest pay grade for government employees—before his thirtieth birthday.[24]

Over the years, Godel's clandestine career took a series of sharp and often bizarre turns. He worked at the Office of the Secretary of Defense, where he liaised between the CIA, NSA, and army and became known as an expert in psychological warfare.[25] He negotiated with North Korea to retrieve American soldiers taken prisoner during the Korean War[26], he helped run former Nazi CIA assets in West Germany[27], and he took part in a classified mission to map Antarctica. (For this, he had two glaciers named after him: the Godel Bay and the Godel Iceport.) Part of his storied military intelligence career involved him serving as an assistant to General Graves Erskine, a crusty old retired Marine Corps general with a long history of running counterinsurgency operations. Erskine headed the Pentagon's Office of Special Operations, which handled psychological warfare, intelligence gathering, and black bag ops.[28]

In 1950, Godel joined General Erskine on a clandestine mission to Vietnam. The objective was to evaluate the effectiveness of military tactics the French were using to pacify a growing anticolonial insurgency and to determine what kind of support the United States should provide. The trip got off to a bad start when his team narrowly escaped an assassination attempt: three bombs ripped through the lobby of their hotel in Saigon. It was a nice welcoming ceremony—and no one knew whether the bombs had been placed by the North Vietnamese or by their French hosts to serve as kind of warning that they should mind their own business. Whichever it was, the party plowed ahead. They embedded themselves with French colonial troops and toured their bases. On one outing, Erskine's team accompanied a

French-trained Vietnamese unit on a nighttime ambush. Their objective was to grab a few rebels for interrogation and intelligence gathering, but the intel mission quickly devolved into a rage-filled terror raid. The French-backed Vietnamese soldiers beheaded their prisoners before the rebels could be pumped for information.[29]

There, out in the sweltering jungles, Godel and his team understood that the French had been doing it all wrong. The bulk of French military efforts seemed to focus on protecting their supply convoy lines, which were constantly attacked by massive guerrilla forces that seemed to materialize out of the jungle, deploying up to six thousand men along a three-mile stretch of road. The French were essentially stuck in their fortifications. They had "lost most of their offensive spirit" and were "pinned to their occupied areas," Godel's colleague described.

"The way Godel saw it, the French colonialists were trying to fight the Viet Minh guerrillas according to colonial rules of war. But the South Vietnamese, who were receiving weapons and training from the French forces, were actually fighting a different kind of war, based on different rules," writes Annie Jacobsen, who excavates William Godel's forgotten story in *The Pentagon's Brain,* her history of ARPA.[30]

This "different kind of war" had a name: counterinsurgency.

Godel understood that the United States was on a deliberate collision path with insurgencies all over the world: Southeast Asia, the Middle East, and Latin America. He supported that collision. He also began to understand that the tactics and strategies required in these new wars were not those of World War II. The United States, he realized, had to learn from France's mistakes. It had to fight a different kind of war, a smaller war, a covert war, a psychological war, and a high-tech war—a "war that doesn't have nuclear weapons, doesn't have the North German Plain and doesn't necessarily have Americans," Godel later explained.[31]

Back in the States, he sketched out what this new warfare would look like.

Counterinsurgency theory wasn't particularly new. Earlier in the twentieth century, the United States had conducted brutal counterinsurgency operations in the Philippines and South America. And the CIA was in the midst of running a brutal covert counterinsurgency campaign in North Vietnam and Laos—headed by Godel's future boss, Air Force Col. Edward Lansdale—that included targeted raids, death squads, propaganda, and torture.[32] What made Godel's counterinsurgency vision different was its laser beam focus on the use of technology to bolster effectiveness. Sure, counterinsurgency involved terror and intimidation. It involved coercion and propaganda. But what was equally important was training and equipping fighters—no matter if they were US special operations teams or local forces—with the most cutting-edge military tech available: better weapons, better uniforms, better transportation, better intelligence, and a better understanding of what made the locals tick. "The way Godel saw it, the Pentagon needed to develop advanced weaponry, based on technology that was not just nuclear technology, but that could deal with this coming threat," writes Jacobsen.[33]

Godel proselytized this new vision back in the United States, lecturing and speaking about his counterinsurgency theories at military institutions around the country. In the meantime, the newly created ARPA tapped him to run its vaguely named Office of Foreign Developments, from which he would manage the agency's covert operations. The job was murky, highly secretive, and extremely fluid. Godel would oversee the agency's highly classified missile and satellite projects one moment, then hatch plans to nuke an area on behalf of the National Security Agency the next. One such plan involved ARPA detonating a nuclear bomb on a small island in the Indian Ocean. The idea was to create a perfectly parabolic crater that could fit a giant antenna the NSA wanted to build to catch faint Soviet radio signals that had scattered into space and bounced back off the moon. "ARPA guaranteed a minimum residual radioactivity and the proper shape of the crater in which the antenna subsequently would be placed," an NSA official said. "We never pursued this possibility.

The nuclear moratorium between the US and the USSR was signed somewhat later and this disappeared."[34]

When Godel was not devising plans to blast small tropical islands, he was pursuing his main passion: high-tech counterinsurgency. As Jacobsen recounts in *Pentagon's Brain*: "Godel was now in a position to create and implement the very programs he had been telling war college audiences across the country needed to be created. Through inserting a U.S. military presence into foreign lands threatened by communism—through advanced science and technology—democracy would prevail and communism would fail. This quest would quickly become Godel's obsession."[35]

Meanwhile, in his work for ARPA he traveled to Southeast Asia to assess the growing Viet Minh insurgency and booked a trip to Australia to talk counterinsurgency and scope out a potential polar satellite launch site.[36] All through this time he pushed his main line: the United States needed to establish a counterinsurgency agency to take on the communist threat. In a series of memos to the assistant secretary of defense, Godel argued, "Conventionally trained, conventionally organized and conventionally equipped military organizations are incapable of employment in anti-guerrilla operations." Despite the overwhelming size superiority of the South Vietnamese army, it had not been able to put down a much smaller armed insurrection, he pointed out. He pushed for letting ARPA set up a counterinsurgency research center in the field—first to scientifically study and understand the needs of local anti-insurgency forces and then to use the findings to set up local paramilitaries. "These forces should be provided not with conventional arms and equipment requiring third- and fourth-level maintenance but with a capability to be farmers or taxi drivers during the day and anti-guerrilla forces at night," he wrote.[37]

Godel's vision clashed with the dominant US Army thinking at the time, and his proposals did not generate much enthusiasm with President Eisenhower's people. But they were on their way out, anyway, and he found an eager audience in the incoming administration.

Bugging the Battlefield

John F. Kennedy was sworn in as the thirty-fifth president of the United States on January 20, 1961. Young and dashing, the former Massachusetts senator was progressive on domestic politics and a committed Cold War hawk on foreign policy. His election ushered in a crop of young elite technocrats who truly believed in the power of science and technology to solve the world's problems. And there were a lot of problems to be solved. It wasn't just the Soviet Union. Kennedy faced regional insurgencies against American-allied governments all around the world: Cuba, Algiers, Vietnam and Laos, Nicaragua, Guatemala, and Lebanon. Many of these conflicts came out of local movements, recruited local fighters, and were supported by local populations. Countering them was not something that a traditional big military operation or a tactical nuclear strike could solve.

Two months after taking office, President Kennedy delivered a message to Congress arguing for the need to expand and modernize America's military posture to meet this new threat. "The Free World's security can be endangered not only by a nuclear attack, but also by being slowly nibbled away at the periphery, regardless of our strategic power, by forces of subversion, infiltration, intimidation, indirect or non-overt aggression, internal revolution, diplomatic blackmail, guerrilla warfare or a series of limited wars," he said, forcefully arguing for new methods of dealing with insurgencies and local rebellion. "We need a greater ability to deal with guerrilla forces, insurrections, and subversion. Much of our effort to create guerrilla and anti-guerrilla capabilities has in the past been aimed at general war. We must be ready now to deal with any size of force, including small externally supported bands of men; and we must help train local forces to be equally effective."[38]

The president wanted a better way of countering communism— and ARPA seemed the perfect vehicle for carrying out his vision.

Shortly after the speech, advisers from the CIA, the Pentagon, and the State Department drew up a plan of action for a huge program of covert military, economic, and psychological warfare initiatives to deal with what Kennedy saw as the biggest problem: the growing insurrection in Vietnam and Laos. The plan included William Godel's personal obsession: Project Agile, a high-tech counterinsurgency research and development program.[39] At a National Security Council meeting on April 29, 1961, President Kennedy signed his name to it: "Assist the G.V.N. [Government of Vietnam] to establish a Combat Development and Test Center in South Vietnam to develop, with the help of modern technology, new techniques for use against the Viet Cong forces."[40]

With those few short lines, ARPA's Project Agile was born. Agile was embedded in a much larger military and diplomatic program initiated by President Kennedy and aimed at shoring up the government of South Vietnam against a growing rebel offensive. The program would very quickly escalate into a full-blown and, ultimately, disastrous military campaign. But for ARPA, it was a new lease on life. It made the agency relevant again and put it at the center of the action.

Godel operated Agile with a free hand and reported to Edward Lansdale, a retired air force officer who ran the CIA's covert counterinsurgency operations in Vietnam.[41] Because of a need for secrecy—the United States was not officially involved militarily in Vietnam—a thick fog hung over the project. "Reporting directly to Lansdale, he conducted work so secret that even the heads of ARPA, let alone the rank and file employees, were unaware of specifics," writes Sharon Weinberger in *The Imagineers of War,* her history of ARPA.[42]

The initial focus of activity was ARPA's top-secret Combat Development and Test Center, the cluster of buildings on the bank of the Saigon River that Godel helped set up in the summer of 1961. The program started with a single location and a relatively straightforward mission: to develop weapons and adapt counterinsurgency battlefield gadgets for use in the dense and sweltering jungles of Southeast Asia.[43] But as US military presence increased in Vietnam and finally morphed into a full-on, grinding war, the project grew in scope and ambition.[44] It opened several other large research and development complexes in Thailand as well as smaller outposts in Lebanon and Panama. The agency did not just develop and test weapons technology but also formulated strategy, trained indigenous forces, and took part in counterinsurgency raids and psychological operations missions.[45] More and more, it took on a role that would have felt right at home in the CIA. It also went global, aiming its sights on quelling insurgencies and left-wing or socialist political movements wherever they were—including back home in the United States.

The agency tested light combat arms for the South Vietnamese military, which led to the adoption of the AR-15 and M-16 as standard-issue rifles. It helped develop a light surveillance aircraft that glided silently above the jungle canopy. It formulated field rations and food suited to the hot, wet climate. It bankrolled the creation of sophisticated electronic surveillance systems and funded elaborate efforts to collect all manner of conflict-related intelligence. It worked on improving military communication technology to make it function in dense forest. It developed portable radar installations that could be floated up on a balloon, a technology that was quickly deployed commercially back in the United States to monitor the borders for illegal crossings.[46] It also designed vehicles that could better traverse the boggy landscape, a prototype "mechanical elephant" similar to the four-legged robots that DARPA and Google developed a half-century later.[47]

ARPA frequently pushed way past the boundaries of what was considered technologically possible and pioneered electronic surveillance systems that were decades ahead of their time. It played a big role in some of the most ambitious initiatives. That included Project Igloo White, a multi-billion-dollar computerized surveillance barrier.[48] Operated out of a secret air force base in Thailand, Igloo White involved depositing thousands of radio-controlled seismic sensors, microphones, and heat and urine detectors in the jungle. These eavesdropping devices, shaped like sticks or plants and usually dropped from airplanes, transmitted signals to a centralized computer control center to alert technicians of any movement in the bush.[49] If anything moved, an air strike was called in and the area was blanketed with bombs and napalm. Igloo White was like a giant wireless alarm system that spanned hundreds of miles of jungle. As the US Air Force explained: "We are, in effect, bugging the battlefield."[50]

John T. Halliday, a retired air force pilot, described the Igloo White operation center in Thailand in his memoir. "Remember those huge electronic boards from the movie *Dr. Strangelove* that showed Russian bombers headed for the U.S. and ours headed at them?" he wrote. "Well, Task Force Alpha is a lot like that except with real-time displays in full color, three stories tall—it's the whole goddamned Ho Chi Minh Trail in full, living color."[51]

Halliday was part of a team that flew nighttime bombing raids over the Ho Chi Minh Trail, targeting supply convoys on the basis of intel provided by this electronic fence. He and his unit were amazed by the futuristic nature of it all:

> Step out of the jungle and inside the building, you step back into America—but an America fifteen years from now . . . maybe 1984. It's beautiful . . . gleaming tile floors . . . glass walls everywhere. They have a full cafeteria where you can get anything you want. They even have real milk, not that powdered crap we get at the mess hall. And air-conditioning? The whole damned place is air-conditioned. There's even a bowling alley and a movie theater. I and a whole bunch of civilians who look like IBM guys running around in three-piece suits all wearing glasses . . . it's "Geek Central." We never see them over on our part of the base, so I guess they have everything they need in there.
>
> Then there's this main control room that looks like the one we saw on TV during the Apollo moon shots, or maybe something out of a James Bond movie. There's computer terminals everywhere. But the main feature is this huge, three-story-tall Lucite . . . or maybe it's plastic, I don't know . . . full-color depiction of the whole Ho Chi Minh Trail with a real-time depiction of trucks coming down the trail. It's wild, man.[52]

Igloo White ran for five years with a total cost of somewhere near $5 billion—roughly $30 billion today. Though widely praised at the time, the project was ultimately judged an operational failure. "The guerrillas had simply learned to confuse the American sensors with tape-recorded truck noises, bags of urine, and other decoys, provoking the release of countless tons of bombs onto empty jungle corridors which they then traversed at their leisure," according to historian Paul N. Edwards.[53] Despite the failure, Igloo White's "electronic fence" technology was deployed a few years later along America's border with Mexico.[54]

Project Agile was a huge hit with the South Vietnamese government. President Diem made several visits to the ARPA research center in Saigon and personally met with Godel and the rest of the ARPA team there.[55] The president had one main condition: American involvement must remain secret. Godel was of the same mind. Back home, to justify the need for a new counterinsurgency approach, he frequently trotted out what President Diem told him: "The one way we lose is if the Americans come in here."

Know Your Enemy

To William Godel, high-tech counterinsurgency was about more than just developing modern killing methods. It was also about surveilling, studying, and understanding the people and cultures where the insurrection was taking place. It was all part of his vision for the future of warfare: to use American advanced science to defeat the superior discipline, motivation, and support of local insurgents. The idea was to understand what made them resist and fight, and what it would take to change their minds.[56] The ultimate aim was to find a way to predict local insurgencies and stop them before they had time to mature. The problem in Southeast Asia was that Americans were operating in environments and cultures they did not understand. So how to ensure the military was making the right decisions?

In the early 1960s, defense and foreign policy circles were awash in seminars, meetings, reports, and courses trying to establish proper counterinsurgency policy and doctrine. At one influential multi-agency seminar organized by the US Army and attended by Godel's ARPA colleagues, a military researcher described the difficulty of fighting counterinsurgencies in a very direct manner: "The problem is . . . that we must operate in a strange cultural environment and influence persons with different cultural values, customs, mores, beliefs, and attitudes." He concluded with a stark statement: "The same bullet will kill with just about the same effectiveness whether used against a target in the United States, Africa, or Asia. However, the effectiveness of the counterinsurgency weapon is dependent upon the specific target."[57]

The Pentagon started throwing money at social and behavioral scientists, hiring them to make sure America's "counterinsurgency weapon" always hit its target, regardless of the culture in which it was being fired. Under William Godel, ARPA became one of the main pipelines for these programs, helping to weaponize anthropology, psychology, and sociology and putting them in the service of American counterinsurgency. ARPA doled out millions to studies of Vietnamese peasants, captured North Vietnamese fighters, and rebellious hill tribes of northern Thailand. Swarms of ARPA contractors—anthropologists, political scientists, linguists, and sociologists—passed through poor villages, putting people under a microscope, measuring, gathering data, interviewing, studying, assessing, and reporting.[58] The idea was to understand the enemy, to know their hopes, their fears, their dreams, their social networks, and their relationships to power.[59]

The RAND Corporation, under an ARPA contract, did most of this work. Based out of a building overlooking the wide, tan beaches of Santa Monica, RAND was a powerful military and intelligence contractor that had been created by the US Air Force several decades earlier as a private-public research agency.[60] In the 1950s, RAND was central to formulating America's belligerent nuclear policy. In the 1960s, it added a big counterinsurgency division and became a de facto privatized extension of ARPA's Project Agile. ARPA placed the orders; RAND hired the people and got the job done.

In one major effort, RAND scientists studied the effectiveness of the Strategic Hamlet initiative, a pacification effort that had been developed and pushed by Godel and Project Agile and that involved the forced resettlement of South Vietnamese peasants from their traditional villages into new areas that were walled off and made "safe" from rebel infiltration.[61] In another study commissioned by ARPA, RAND contractors were tasked with answering questions that nagged the Americans: Why were North Vietnamese fighters not defecting to our side? What was it about their cause? Weren't the communists supposed to be brutal to their own people? Don't they want to live like we do in America? Why was their morale so high? And what could be done to undermine their confidence?[62] They conducted twenty-four hundred interviews of North Vietnamese prisoners and defectors and generated tens of thousands of pages of intelligence in pursuit of this goal.[63]

At the same time, ARPA funded multiple projects aimed at studying local populations to pinpoint the social and cultural factors that could be used to predict why and when tribes would go insurgent. One initiative, contracted with RAND, sent a team of political scientists and anthropologists from UCLA and UC Berkeley to Thailand to map out "the religious systems, value systems, group dynamics, civil-military relationships" of Thai hill tribes, focusing in particular on predictive behavior.[64] "The objective of this task is to determine the most likely sources of social conflict in Northeast Thailand, concentrating on those local problems and attitudes which could be exploited by the Communists," reads the report.[65] Another study in Thailand, carried out for ARPA by the CIA-connected American Institutes for Research (AIR), aimed at gauging the effectiveness of applied counterinsurgency techniques against rebellious hill tribes—practices such as assassinating tribal leaders, forcibly relocating villages, and using artificially induced famine to pacify rebellious populations.[66]

A 1970 investigation for *Ramparts* magazine detailed the effects of these brutal concentration camp–style counterinsurgency methods on a rebellious minority Thai hill tribe known as the Meo. "Conditions in the Meo resettlement villages are harsh, strongly reminiscent of the American Indian reservations of the 19th century. The people lack sufficient rice and water, and corrupt local agents pocket the funds appropriated for the Meo in Bangkok." The magazine quoted an eye witness report: "Physical hardship and psychological strain have taken a heavy toll on these people. They are gaunt and sickly; many are in a permanent state of semi-withdrawal stimulated by the shortage of opium to feed lifelong habits. Yet the decay of the Meos' spirit is even more distressing than the deterioration of their bodies. They have lost all semblance of inner strength and independence: they seem to have withered, while assuming the manner of the humbled."[67]

An even more disturbing dimension of the AIR's pacification work in Thailand was that it was supposed to serve as a model for counterinsurgency operations elsewhere in the world—including against black people living in American inner cities, where race riots were breaking out at the time. "The potential applicability of the findings in the United States will also receive special attention. In many of our key domestic programs, especially those directed at disadvantaged sub-cultures, the methodological problems are similar to those described in this proposal," reads the project's proposal. "The application of the Thai findings at home constitutes a potentially most significant project contribution."[68]

That's exactly what happened. After the war, researchers, including a young Charles Murray (author of *The Bell Curve*), who had worked on counterinsurgency programs for ARPA in Southeast Asia, returned to the United States and began to apply the pacification ideas they developed in the jungles to the thorny domestic issues of class, race, and economic inequality.[69] The effects were just as disastrous at home as they were overseas, giving a modern scientific veneer to public policies that reinforced racism and structural poverty.[70]

As the AIR proposal had not so subtly hinted, ARPA's behavioral science programs in Southeast Asia went hand in hand with a bloodier and more traditional counterinsurgency policy: covert programs of murder, terror, and torture that collectively came to be known as the Phoenix Program.

One of the guiding lights of this dark side of counterinsurgency was Edward Lansdale, a former Levi Strauss and Company executive who learned the trade fighting the communist insurgency in the Philippines after World War II.[71] Lansdale's hallmark psychological warfare strategy was using local myths and beliefs to induce primal terror and fear in his targets. A celebrated trick was exploitation of a Filipino belief in the existence of vampires to scare communist guerrillas. "One of Lansdale's counter-terror psy-war tactics was to string a captured Communist guerrilla upside down from a tree, stab him in the neck with a stiletto, and drain his blood," explained Douglas Valentine, a journalist who exposed the Phoenix Program. "The terrorized Commies fled the area and the terrified villagers, who believed in vampires, begged the government for protection."[72] Lansdale, who would become Godel's boss, replicated the Philippine strategy in Vietnam: assassinations, death squads, torture, and the obliteration of entire villages.[73] It was all meant to "deincentivize" peasants from helping the North Vietnamese rebels. Somewhere between forty thousand and eighty thousand Vietnamese were killed in the Phoenix Program's targeted assassinations; the CIA estimates the number closer to twenty thousand.

By the late 1960s, the Vietnam War had turned into a meat grinder. In 1967, 11,363 American soldiers lost their lives. A year later, that number climbed to almost 17,000. By 1970, American soldiers no longer wanted to fight. There was chaos on the battlefield and insubordination back at base. There were hundreds of cases of "fragging," superior officers killed by their own soldiers. Drug use was rampant. Soldiers were wasted—drunk, high on grass and opium. ARPA's Project Agile was not immune to the transformation but connected to it. Indeed, according to a former head of ARPA, William Godel was personally involved with "Air America" missions to supply the CIA's covert war in Laos, an operation that, according to credible reports, involved smuggling heroin to finance anticommunist militias.[74]

As Saigon turned into a military camp full of booze, heroin, prostitution, and cheap thrills, ARPA's research center became a bizarre nexus of stuffy anthropologists, spies, generals, South Vietnamese officials, and sociopathic commandos passing on their way to terror missions deep inside enemy-controlled territory. An old French colonial villa in the city that housed RAND scientists became a social hub for this weird scene, by day a working command center, by night a dinner-and-cocktail-party venue.[75]

A strange pseudoscience emerged. Blending free-market economics and rational choice theory, military planners and scientists viewed the Vietnamese as automatons, nothing more than rational individuals who were acting purely in their own self-interest. They had no bigger guiding values or ideals—no patriotism, no loyalty to their communities or traditions or to some bigger political idea. They were interested in nothing other than maximizing positive outcomes for themselves. The trick would be to peel the Vietnamese away from the insurgency through a mix of marketing, consumer-style incentives, and a bit of tough love when nothing else worked. Cash handouts, jobs, small infrastructure improvements, land privatization schemes, anticommunist propaganda, crop destruction, mutilations, murder, assassinations—all these were legitimate variables to throw into the coercion equation.[76]

Some began to doubt America's mission in Vietnam and questioned the purpose of ARPA's scientific approach to counterinsurgency. Anthony Russo, a RAND contractor who worked on ARPA projects and who would later help Daniel Ellsberg leak the Pentagon Papers, discovered that when results of ARPA studies contradicted military wishes, his bosses simply suppressed and discarded them.[77]

"The more I grew to admire Asian culture—especially Vietnamese," Russo wrote in 1972, "the more I was outraged at the Orwellian horror of the U.S. military machine grinding through Vietnam and destroying everything in its path. Tens of thousands of Vietnamese girls were turned into prostitutes; streets that had been lined with beautiful trees were denuded to make room for the big military trucks. I was fed up with the horror and disgusted by the petulance and pettiness with which the RAND Corporation conducted its business."[78]

He believed that ARPA's entire Project Agile apparatus was a giant racket used by military planners to give scientific cover to whichever existing war policies they were intent on pursuing. This wasn't cutting-edge military science, but a boondoggle and a fraud. The only people benefiting from Project Agile were the private military contracting firms hired to do the work.

Even William Godel, the counterinsurgency star who started the program, got caught up in a petty embezzlement scheme that involved the misappropriation of part of the $18,000 in cash that he had carried to Saigon in 1961 to set up Project Agile.[79] It was a bizarre case that involved an almost insignificant sum of money. Some of his colleagues hinted that it was politically motivated, but it didn't matter. Godel was ultimately convicted of conspiracy to commit embezzlement and sentenced to five years in prison.[80]

Other ARPA contractors had reservations about their work in Vietnam as well, but the mission rolled on. Fraudulent or not, Project Agile turned Southeast Asia, from Thailand to Laos and Vietnam, into a giant laboratory. Every tribe, every jungle path, every captured guerrilla was to be studied and analyzed and monitored and understood. While assassination teams terrorized the rural population of Vietnam, ARPA scientists were there to log and measure program effectiveness. Incentive programs were designed and then monitored, analyzed, tweaked, and monitored again. ARPA didn't just bug the battlefield; it tried to bug entire societies.

Interviews, polls, population counts, detailed anthropological studies of various tribes, maps, available weapons, migration studies, social networks, agricultural practices, dossiers—all this information poured out of ARPA's centers in Vietnam and Thailand. But there was a problem. The agency was drowning in data: typewritten paper reports, punch cards, giant tape reels, index cards, and tons of crude computer printouts. There was so much information coming in that it was effectively useless. What good was all this intel if no one could find what they needed? Something had to be done.

Chapter 2

Command, Control, and Counterinsurgency

What separates military intelligence in the United States from its counter-parts in totalitarian states is not its capabilities, but its intentions. This is a significant distinction, but one which may not wholly reassure many Americans.

—Christopher Pyle, "Army Surveillance of Civilians:
A Documentary Analysis," 1973

Early Monday morning, October 1, 1962, a man named J. C. R. Licklider woke up in an apartment along the Potomac River across from the White House. He ate breakfast, said goodbye to his wife and daughters, and drove the short way to the Pentagon to start his new job as director of ARPA's Behavioral Science and Command and Control Research divisions.

Settling into his modest office, he surveyed the scene. For the past few years, those in defense circles had pushed to upgrade America's military and intelligence communication systems. As soon as he came into office, President Kennedy had complained about the difficulty of effectively exercising command of US military forces. He found himself blind and deaf at the most crucial moments, unable to get real-time intelligence updates or to communicate timely commands to commanders in the field. Believing that military commanders were using the outdated technology as cover to buck his authority and ignore instructions, he pushed Defense Secretary Robert McNamara to investigate solutions. He also harangued Congress about the need to develop "a truly unified, nationwide, indestructible system to insure high-level command, communication and control."[1]

Licklider agreed. America's defense communication systems were indeed pathetically outdated. They simply could not effectively respond to the challenges of the day: dozens of small-scale wars and insurgencies happening in distant places no one knew a damn thing about. All that combined with the ever-present threat of nuclear strikes that could decapitate huge chunks of military command. But what exactly would such a new system look like? What components would it have? What new technologies needed to be invented for it to work? Few people in the Pentagon knew the answers. Licklider was one of the few.

Joseph Carl Robnett Licklider—a ridiculously long name—was simply called "Lick." He wore Coke-bottle glasses and three-piece suits and was known for his Coca-Cola addiction. In rarified military circles, Lick had a reputation as a brilliant psychologist and a computer futurist with some far-out ideas about the coming age of the man-machine.

He was born in 1915 in St. Louis, Missouri. His father, a Baptist minister and the head of the St. Louis Chamber of Commerce, was a God-fearing, business-oriented man. Lick made his dad proud. In 1937, he graduated from Washington University in St. Louis with a triple major in psychology, mathematics, and physics and then moved on to study how animals processed sound, which mostly involved slicing cats' skulls open and zapping their brains with electricity.[2] During World War II, Lick was recruited to work at Harvard's Psycho-Acoustic Laboratory, which was established with lavish funding from the US Air Force to study human speech, hearing, and communication.[3] At this lab he met his future wife, Louise Thomas, who worked as a secretary in a military research center. She considered herself a socialist and even brought her copy of *Socialist Worker* to the office. She'd leave it on the edge of her desk so that the men in the lab could grab it on the way to the bathroom and have something to read while they were on the can.

After the war, Lick left Harvard for the Massachusetts Institute of Technology. There, he came into contact with the world's first networked digital computer surveillance system. It changed the trajectory of his life.

Soviet Nukes

A t precisely 7:00 a.m. on August 29, 1949, engineers sitting in a fortified bunker on the isolated steppes of the Kazakh Soviet Socialist Republic threw a switch and detonated the first Soviet nuclear bomb: First Lightning, codename RDS-1.[4] The bomb was set up on a wooden tower surrounded by mock buildings and industrial and military machinery trucked there to test the effects of the blast: a T-34 tank, brick buildings, a metal bridge, a small section of a railroad complete with railroad cars, automobiles, trucks, field artillery, an airplane, and over a thousand different live animals—dogs, rats, pigs, sheep, guinea pigs, and rabbits—tied down in trenches, behind walls, and inside vehicles.

It was a fairly small bomb, around the size of the one dropped on Nagasaki. In fact, it was almost a one-to-one replica of Fat Man, as that bomb was known. Before and after photos of the site show heavy damage. Many of the animals died instantly. Those that didn't were badly burned and died of radiation exposure. Lavrentiy Beria, the notorious NKVD (People's Commissariat for Internal Affairs, a Soviet secret police organization) chief, was there to observe. He cabled Stalin: the test was a success.[5]

News of the explosion threw America's military establishment into a panicked frenzy. US nuclear dominance was no more. The Soviet Union now had the capability to launch a nuclear strike against the United States; all it needed was a long-range bomber. This posed a serious problem.

America's early warning radar system was sparse and full of holes. The process of tracking airplanes was done by hand: uniformed military men sitting in dark rooms filled with cigarette smoke, watching primitive green radar screens, barking out coordinates and jotting them down on glass boards, and then radioing commands to pilots. The system would be useless in the face of a large, targeted nuclear attack by air.

A report of a special body convened by the US Air Force recommended that the early warning radar system be automated: radar information should be digitized, sent over wires, and processed in real time by computers.[6] In 1950, this recommendation was more than just ambitious—it was a crackpot idea. MIT professor George Valley, who headed the air force study, asked several computer companies if they would be able to build such a real-time computer system. He was laughed out of the room. The technology for real-time data processing, especially from multiple radar installations that were hundreds of miles away from the central computer, just did not exist. Nothing even came close.

If the air force wanted an automated radar system, it would have to invent a computer powerful enough to handle the job. Luckily, the Pentagon was already a prime mover and shaker in this field.

During World War II, the US military played a leading role in advancing the primitive state of digital computer technology. The reasons for this were many, and all of them central to the war effort. One was cryptography. The navy's intelligence division, as well as several other predecessor agencies to the National Security Agency, had long used specialized IBM punch card tabulators to perform cryptographic analysis and code breaking. During the war, they were faced with advanced Nazi encryption techniques and needed machines that could work faster and with much more complicated code. Digital computers were the only thing that could get the job done.

Other services were also desperate for machines that could carry out mathematical calculations at high speeds, but for a slightly different reason. During the war, powerful new cannons and field artillery rolled off production lines and headed out to the European and Pacific theaters. All this firepower was useless if it couldn't be properly aimed. Artillery, big guns that can hit targets a dozen miles away, don't shoot in a straight trajectory but lob shells at a slight angle so that they descend on far-off targets after tracing a parabolic arc. Each gun has a firing table that specifies the angle at which to fire so shells hit their mark. Firing tables aren't simple, one-page sheets but thick booklets with hundreds of variables in the equations. The 155-millimeter "Long Tom" field cannon, one of the most popular big guns used during World War II, incorporates five hundred variables in its firing table.[7] Air temperature, gunpowder temperature, elevation, humidity, wind speed and direction, and even soil type—all are important environmental factors required in the complex calculations.

Not surprisingly, these charts were treacherous to calculate. All the variables in hundreds of permutations had to be plugged in and worked out by hand. Mistakes regularly crept in and calculations restarted from scratch. Just one firing table for one type of gun could take more than a month to complete. And there were surprises: the army discovered that tables calculated to work in Europe didn't work in Africa because the soil variables were different; though the guns were delivered, they were little more than dead weight until the firing data could be recalculated from scratch.[8] Squads of clerks—usually women—worked around the clock using pen, paper, and mechanical adding aids to crunch the numbers. These women were called "computers" before digital computers existed, and they were incredibly important to the war effort.[9] Firing tables were of such vital significance that both the navy and the army funded separate efforts to build automated calculators—all in the service of aiming giant killing machines—and helped develop the first digital computers in the process. Most notable among them was the ENIAC, built for the army by a team of mathematicians and engineers at University of Pennsylvania's Moore School of Electrical Engineering. The computer was an instant sensation.

"Robot Calculator Knocks Out Figures Like Chain Lightning" declared a newspaper headline in 1948 in an article reporting the unveiling of the ENIAC:

> Philadelphia, PA—The war department tonight unveiled "the world's fastest calculating machine" and said the robot possibly opened the mathematical way to better living for every man.
>
> Improved industrial products, better communication and transportation, superior weather forecasting and other advances in science and engineering may be made possible, the army said, from the development of "the first all-electronic general-purpose computer."
>
> The army described the machine as 1,000 times faster than the most advanced calculating machine previously built and declared the apparatus makes it possible "to solve in hours problems which would take years" on any other machine.
>
> Does Everything
>
> The machine, which can add, subtract, multiply, divide and compute square root, as well as do most complex calculations based on those operations, is called the "ENIAC"— short for "electronic numerical integrator and computer." It also has been nicknamed the "mechanical Einstein."[10]

The ENIAC didn't come fast enough to help with the war, but it stayed in operation for nearly a decade, crunching firing tables, running atomic bomb calculations, and building weather models of the Soviet climate, including mapping the potential spread of fallout from a nuclear war.[11] As powerful as it was, the ENIAC wasn't enough.

To develop the computer and networking technology necessary to power a modern radar defense system, a special research division known as the Lincoln Laboratory was created. Attached to the Massachusetts Institute of Technology and based out of a research campus ten miles east of Cambridge, the Lincoln Lab was a joint project of the navy, air force, army, and IBM. Its sole objective was to build a modern air defense system. An astounding number of resources were thrown at the effort. Thousands of civilian contractors and military personnel were involved over a ten-year period. The software itself took about a thousand man-years to program.[12] The entire project cost more than the Manhattan Project, the effort to develop the first atomic weapon.

The Lincoln Lab assembled a monster: the Semi-Automatic Ground Environment, or SAGE. It was the biggest computer system in history and the first real computer network. SAGE was controlled by two dozen "Direction Centers" located strategically around the country. These giant nuclear-proof concrete bunkers housed two IBM computers that together cost $4 billion in today's dollars, weighed six hundred tons, and took up an acre of floor space; one was always on standby in case the other failed.[13] Each control center employed hundreds of people and was connected to land-based and coastal radar arrays, missile silos, and nearby interceptor aircraft bases. The system could track up to four hundred airplanes in real time, scramble fighter jets, launch Nike missiles, and aim antiaircraft cannons.[14] SAGE was the eyes, ears, and brains of a massive weapon. It was also the first nationwide computerized surveillance machine—surveillance in the broader sense: a system that collected information from remote sensors, analyzed it, and allowed the military to act on the intelligence it produced.

SAGE was an incredibly sophisticated machine, but in practice it was outdated before it was ever turned on. It went online in the early 1960s, more than three years after the Soviet Union had launched the *Sputnik* and thereby demonstrated its long-range intercontinental missiles capability. The Soviets could shoot a nuclear payload into space and have it come down anywhere in the United States, and no fancy radar defense system could do anything about it.

On the surface, SAGE was a boondoggle. But in a bigger historical sense it was a phenomenal success. MIT Lincoln Laboratory—with its top-notch engineering talent and nearly limitless resources directed at a narrow set of problems—became more than just a research and development center for a single military project. It turned into a training ground for a new engineering elite: a multidisciplinary group of scientists, academics, government officials, businessmen, and mathematicians who would go on to create the modern computer industry and build the Internet.

And J. C. R. Licklider was at the center of it all. At the Lincoln Laboratory, he worked on the human side of this vast radar computer system and helped develop the system's graphic display, which had to integrate data from multiple radars and to display real-time heading and speed information that could then be used to guide aircraft interceptors. It was a small but vital component of SAGE, and the work opened his eyes to the possibilities of building tools that integrated people and computers into one continuous system: a man-machine that broke through human physical limitations and created powerful new hybrid beings.

Cyborgs and Cybernetics

The Massachusetts Institute of Technology was ground zero for a new science called cybernetics. Developed by MIT professor Norbert Wiener, cybernetics defined the world as a giant computational machine. It offered a conceptual and mathematical framework for thinking about and designing complex information systems.

Wiener was an odd and brilliant man. He was short, pudgy, with a meaty round head and thick glasses. In his later years, he looked a bit like Hans Moleman from *The Simpsons*. He was also a true wunderkind. The son of a strict and ambitious academic and Slavic scholar, Wiener was forced to memorize entire books and recite them from memory and to perform complex algebra and trigonometry in his head.[15] "My father would be doing his homework for Harvard and I had to stand beside him and recite my lessons by memory, even in Greek, at six years old, and he would ignore me until I made the simplest mistake, then he would verbally reduce me to dust," he recalled in his autobiography.[16]

With this kind of training, Wiener went to college at the age of eleven—the "infant prodigy of Boston" one newspaper called him—earned a PhD in mathematics by age eighteen, and, rejected from a job at Harvard, started teaching at MIT. His life of frantic study and pitiless criticism from his father didn't prepare him for the social dimension of life: he was clumsy, couldn't talk to women, had few true friends, was depressive, and could barely take care of himself.

His parents arranged his marriage to Margaret Engemann, an immigrant from Germany who had had trouble finding a husband. They had two normal daughters, and the marriage seemed fine, except for one little detail: Margaret was a steadfast supporter of Adolf Hitler and forced their daughters to read *Mein Kampf.* "One day she told us that the members of her family in Germany had been certified as *Judenrein*— 'free of Jewish taint.' She thought we'd be pleased to know," recalled her daughter. "She said I should not feel sorry for the Jews of Germany because they were not very nice people." During a Christmas party, she tried to convince guests that Aryan lineage stretched back to the son of God himself. "Jesus was the son of a German mercenary stationed in Jerusalem, and this had been scientifically proven." It was an awkward situation given that her husband was a Jew of German descent, and her daughters were thereby half Jewish. But this was no ordinary household.

Wiener's mind was perpetually hungry, devouring everything in its path. He crossed just about every disciplinary boundary, cutting through philosophy, mathematics, engineering, linguistics, physics, psychology, evolutionary biology, neurobiology, and computer science. During World War II, Wiener met a problem that tested the limits of his brilliant multidisciplinary brain. He was recruited to work on a quixotic top-secret venture to build an automatic aiming-targeting mechanism that could increase the effectiveness of ground-to-air antiaircraft cannons. All through the war, he worked on a specialized computer apparatus that used microwave radar to watch, pinpoint, and then predict a plane's future position on the basis of its pilot's actions in order to more effectively blast it out of the sky. It was a machine that studied the actions of a human being and responded dynamically to them. While building it, he had a profound insight about the nature of information. He began to see that the communication of information wasn't just an abstract or ephemeral act but had a powerful physical property to it. Like an invisible force, it could be relied on to trigger a reaction. He also made another simple but profound leap: he realized that communication and transmission of messages were not limited to humans but pervaded all living organisms and could be designed into the mechanical world as well.

Wiener published these ideas in a dense 1948 tract called *Cybernetics: Control and Communication in the Animal and the Machine.* What was cybernetics? The concept was slippery and maddeningly difficult to define. In simple terms, he described cybernetics as the idea that the biological nervous system and the computer or automatic machine were basically the same thing. They were "devices which make decisions on the basis of decisions they have made in the past," he explained.[17] To Wiener, people and the entire living world could be seen as one giant interlocking information machine, everything responding to everything else in an intricate system of cause, effect, and feedback. He predicted that our lives would increasingly be mediated and enhanced by computers and integrated to the point that there would cease to be any difference between us and the larger cybernetic machine in which we lived.

Despite being full of incomprehensible mathematical proofs and jargon, the book excited the public's imagination and became an instant best seller. Military circles received it as a revolutionary work as well. What Karl Marx's *Das Kapital* did for nineteenth-century socialists, Wiener's *Cybernetics* did for America's anticommunist Cold Warriors. On a very basic level, cybernetics posited that human beings, like all living things, were information processing machines. We were all computers—highly complex, but computers nonetheless. That meant that the military could construct machines that could think like people and act like people: scan for enemy planes and ships, transcribe enemy radio communications, spy on subversives, analyze foreign news for hidden meaning and secret messages—all without needing sleep or food or rest. With computer technology like this, America's dominance was guaranteed. *Cybernetics* triggered an elusive decades-long quest by the military to fulfill this particular vision of cybernetics, an effort to create computers with what we now call artificial intelligence.[18]

Cybernetic concepts, backed by huge amounts of military funding, began to pervade academic disciplines: economics, engineering, psychology, political science, biology, and environmental studies. Neoclassical economists integrated cybernetics into their theories and began looking at markets as distributed information machines.[19] Ecologists began to look at the earth itself as a self-regulating computational "bio system," and cognitive psychologists and cognitive scientists approached the study of the human brain as if it were literally a complex digital computer.[20] Political scientists and sociologists began to dream of using cybernetics to create a controlled utopian society, a perfectly well-oiled system where computers and people were integrated into a cohesive whole, managed and controlled to ensure security and prosperity.[21] "Put most clearly: in the 1950s both the military and U.S. industry explicitly advocated a messianic understanding of computing, in which computation was the underlying matter of everything in the social world, and could therefore be brought under state-capitalist military control—centralized, hierarchical control," writes historian David Golumbia in *The Cultural Logic of Computation*, a groundbreaking study of computational ideology.[22]

In a big way, this intermeshing of cybernetics and big power was what caused Norbert Wiener to turn against cybernetics almost as soon as he introduced it to the world. He saw scientists and military men taking the narrowest possible interpretation of cybernetics to create better killing machines and more efficient systems of surveillance and control and exploitation. He saw giant corporations using his ideas to automate production and cut labor in their quest for greater wealth and economic power. He began to see that in a society mediated by computer and information systems those who controlled the infrastructure wielded ultimate power.

Wiener envisioned a bleak future and realized that he himself was culpable, comparing his work on cybernetics to that of the world's greatest scientists who unleashed the destructive power of atomic weapons. In fact, he saw cybernetics in even starker terms than nukes.

"The impact of the thinking machine will be a shock certainly of comparable order to that of the atomic bomb," he said in a 1949 interview. The replacement of human labor with machines—and the social destabilization, mass unemployment, and concentrated economic power, that such change would cause—is what worried Wiener the most.[23] "Let us remember that the automatic machine, whatever we think of any feelings it may have or may not have, is the precise economic equivalent of slave labor. Any labor which competes with slave labor must accept the economic conditions of slave labor. It is perfectly clear that this will produce an unemployment situation, in comparison with which the present recession and even the depression of the thirties will seem a pleasant joke," Wiener wrote in a dark and prescient follow-up book, *The Human Use of Human Beings: Cybernetics and Society.*[24]

The destruction would be political and economic.

After popularizing cybernetics, Wiener became a kind of labor and antiwar activist. He reached out to unions to warn them of the danger of automation and the need to take the threat seriously. He turned down offers from giant corporations that wanted help automating their assembly lines according to his cybernetic principles, and refused to work on military research projects. He was against the massive peacetime arms buildup taking place after World War II and publicly lashed out at colleagues for working to help the military build bigger, more efficient tools of destruction. He increasingly hinted at his insider knowledge that a "colossal state machine" was being constructed by government agencies "for the purposes of combat and domination," a computerized information system that was "sufficiently extensive to include all civilian activities during war, before war and possibly even between wars," as he described it in *The Human Use of Human Beings.*

Wiener's vocal support of labor and his public opposition to corporate and military work made him a pariah among his military contractor–engineer colleagues.[25] It also earned him a spot on J. Edgar Hoover's FBI subversive surveillance list. For years, he was suspected of having communist sympathies, his life documented in a thick FBI file that was closed upon his death in 1964.[26]

Of Mice and Keyboards

J. C. R. Licklider interacted with Norbert Wiener at MIT and participated in conferences and dinner parties where cybernetic ideas were hashed out, debated, and discussed. He was radicalized by Wiener's cybernetic vision. Where Wiener saw danger, Lick saw opportunity. He had no qualms about putting this technology in the service of US corporate and military power.

Though most computer engineers thought of computers as little more than oversized calculators, Lick saw them as extensions of the human mind, and he became obsessed with designing machines that could be seamlessly coupled to human beings. In 1960, he published a paper that outlined his vision for the coming "man-computer symbiosis" and described in simple terms the kinds of computer components that needed to be invented to make it happen. The paper essentially described a modern multipurpose computer, complete with a display, keyboard, speech recognition software, networking capabilities, and applications that could be used in real time for a variety of tasks.[27] It seems obvious to us now, but back then Lick's ideas were visionary. His paper was widely circulated in defense circles and earned him an invitation by the Pentagon to do a series of lectures on the topic.[28]

"My first experience with computers had been listening to a talk by [mathematician John] von Neumann in Chicago back in nineteen forty-eight. It sounded like science fiction then: a machine that could carry out algorithms automatically," recalled Charles Herzfeld, a physicist who would go on to serve as the director of ARPA in the mid-1960s.[29] "But the next big shock was Lick: not only could we use these machines for massive calculations, but we could make them useful in our everyday lives. I listened. I got very excited. And in a very real sense, I became a disciple from then on."

Indeed, Lick's papers and interviews show that he thought almost any problem could be solved with the right application of computers. He even came up with a plan to end poverty and "stimulate young ghetto blacks" by having them tinker with computers. He called the process "dynamations," a 1960s version of an idea that is very popular in Silicon Valley even today, fifty years later: the belief that teaching poor kids to code will somehow magically lift them out of poverty and boost global literacy and education rates.[30] "What is difficult to convey in a few words is the almost messianic view carried by Licklider of the potential for advances in the use of computers, the way people could relate to computers, and the resultant impact on how people would come to make decisions," explained an internal declassified ARPA report.[31] Lick infected everyone with his enthusiasm for the coming computer revolution, including top people at ARPA, who were also on a quest to leverage computers to boost military effectiveness.

In 1962, after a brief job interview at the Pentagon, Lick moved his family from Boston to Washington, DC, and went to work building ARPA's Command and Control Research program from scratch.[32]

At the time, computers were giant metal monsters that occupied entire basements and were attended by multiple technicians. Despite their complexity and size, they were primitive and had less computational power than a 1990s graphic calculator. They also ran one program at a time, and each one had to be fed in by hand using punch cards. "Imagine trying, for example, to direct a battle with the aid of a computer on such a schedule as this," Lick explained in his 1960 paper. "You formulate your problem today. Tomorrow you spend with a programmer. Next week the computer devotes 5 minutes to assembling your program and 47 seconds to calculating the answer to your problem. You get a sheet of paper 20 feet long, full of numbers that, instead of providing a final solution, only suggest a tactic that should be explored by simulation. Obviously, the battle would be over before the second step in its planning was begun."[33]

And networks? They existed. But, like the network that tied SAGE together, they were usually highly specialized and built for a particular purpose and function. A network would have to be designed and custom built to fit every new situation.

The way Lick saw it, this was the wrong way to handle the command and control technology problem. What ARPA needed was to develop a universal and standardized computer and networking platform that could be modified with minimal effort to handle just about any task: missile tracking, behavioral studies, databases, voice communication, intelligence analysis, or simple text processing and mail functions. This computer framework would have a few basic underlying components. It would be easy to use and have an intuitive graphical user interface, feature a universal operating system and programs that could be loaded onto it, and, most important, would move away from the calculator mode of computer operation by allowing users to work in real time in the same way people interact with one another. Though this may sound basic and obvious, these kinds of computer tools did not exist in the early 1960s.

"There was the belief in the heads of a number of people—a small number—that people could become very much more effective in their thinking and decision making if they had the support of a computer system, good displays, and so forth, good data bases, computation at your command. It was the kind of image that we were working toward the realization of," explained Lick in an ARPA report.[34] "It really wasn't a command and control research program. It was an interactive computing program. And my belief was, and still is, you can't really do command and control outside the framework of such a thing."

The crude state of computer technology meant that Lick's goal was still years away, and one thing was for sure: it wouldn't be invented on its own. Someone had to do the work. As Lick saw it, ARPA's primary mission was to throw money at engineers who could build the underlying computer components that a modern command and control system required. At a minimum, ARPA would at least get people working on computer projects that pointed in the right direction. Lick saw his job in historical terms. He would use ARPA's budget and influence to push the computer industry into a new territory, one that aligned with his vision and the needs of the defense establishment.

But first, he wanted to make sure that US intelligence agencies hadn't secretly developed this kind of interactive computing technology already. "I even went over to the CIA and gave them a pitch," said Lick. "I had to tell them, 'Look, I do not know what you're doing about this. I hope you are doing the following. But let me tell you about what I am doing, and then maybe we can figure some way to talk about what the relations are.'" He also arranged a meeting with reps from the NSA and made the same pitch about the beauty of a universal, easy-to-use computer platform. Neither agency was working on interactive computing, but they sure wanted to get their hands on it—"the NSA, they really needed what I wanted," he recalled in an interview years later.[35] Indeed, intelligence agencies were among the first users of the tools ARPA's command and control program produced just a few years later.

ARPA's initial Command and Control Research budget was $10 million. Lick spread that cash through his personal and professional networks in the military-academic-contractor world. He bankrolled projects on interactive computing and time sharing, graphical interface design, networking, and artificial intelligence at MIT, UC Berkeley, UCLA, Harvard, Carnegie Mellon University, Stanford, and the RAND Corporation. At MIT, Lick set up one of his biggest and most important initiatives: Project MAC, short for Machine-Aided Cognition, which evolved into a sophisticated interactive computer environment complete with email, bulletin boards, and multiplayer video games. MIT's Project MAC spawned the first crop of "hackers," ARPA contractors who tinkered with these giant computers in their free time.

At the Stanford Research Institute, which was also doing ARPA contract work on chemical warfare in Vietnam, Lick funded Douglas C. Engelbart's Augmentation Research Center. This team became legendary in computer circles. It developed hypertext links, multiuser real-time word processing, video conferencing, and, most notably, the computer mouse. Lick also jumpstarted a whole range of networking projects, efforts that would lead directly to the creation of the Internet. One of these was a $1.5 million joint UCLA–UC Berkeley initiative to develop software and hardware for a network that connected multiple computers to multiple users.[36] As a funding proposal explained, this research would be used directly to improve military networks, including the National Military Command System, which was then a new communication system linking the military to the president.[37]

Lick worked hard and fast, and his efforts at ARPA were remarkable. Companies like General Electric and IBM did not initially accept his ideas about interactive computing. But with his tenacity and ARPA's funding, his vision gained traction and popularity and ultimately changed the direction of the computer industry. His tenure at ARPA achieved something else as well: computer science became more than just a subdivision of electrical engineering; it developed into a proper field of study of its own.[38] The long-term research contracts the ARPA Command and Control Research division handed out to research teams helped seed the creation of independent computer science departments in universities across the country and tied them closely, through funding and personnel, to the US military establishment.

Networking: The Dark Side

Computer history buffs consider Lick one of the most important personalities in the development of computer science and the Internet. A five-hundred-page biography, called *The Dream Machine* by M. Mitchell Waldrop, chronicles Lick's life and work. What almost never gets reported, but what comes through the pages and pages of released and declassified government files covering Lick's tenure at ARPA, is just how much his computer research efforts were infused with the agency's greater counterinsurgency mission.

Lick died in 1990, a few months shy of turning seventy-five. In interviews, he had made sure to distance his efforts at ARPA from the agency's less wholesome work fighting insurgencies. "There was a kind of a cloak and dagger part of it," he recalled in a 1988 interview.[39] "There was a fellow named Bill Godel who, it seemed to me, was always trying to get control over what I was doing. I could never tell what he was doing, so that part made me nervous. I had one project that I wasn't cleared deeply enough to know what was, and that made me nervous." He readily conceded that he knew something shady was cooking at ARPA, and hinted that he took part in some of it, but claimed that he resisted attempts to involve his command and control project in unsavory Vietnam counterinsurgency efforts. "I sort of stayed out of that as best I could," he explained.

The truth is a bit stickier.

Lick's job was to develop the underlying computer and networking technology necessary to fight modern wars. Naturally, this applied to counterinsurgency in a very general way. But his work was also much more specific and direct.

For instance, documents show that in March 1962, he attended an influential US Army symposium that convened in Washington, DC, to discuss how behavioral science and computer technology could be used to better wage "limited war" and counterinsurgency. There, Lick was part of a working group dedicated to crafting a US Army counterinsurgency research program that could meet a "multidimensional Communist challenge—in paramilitary warfare, in psychological warfare, and in the conventional and nuclear field."[40] The symposium took place just as Lick was starting his job as head of ARPA's Behavioral Science and Command and Control Research divisions. Going forward, his work at ARPA was part of the military's larger counterinsurgency efforts and directly overlapped with William Godel's Project Agile.[41]

Naturally, many of ARPA's programs in Southeast Asia—from remote-control drones to electronic sensor fences and large-scale human intelligence gathering—were all tied in one way or another to data collection and communication, and they ultimately depended on computer technology to organize and automate these tasks. They necessitated tools that could ingest data on people and political movements, compile searchable databases, tie in radio and satellite communications, build models, predict human behavior, and share data quickly and efficiently over great distances between different agencies.. Building the underlying technology that could power all newfangled communication platforms was Lick's job. He certainly never shied away from steering research toward counterinsurgency applications. A glance at the contracts from those days shows him directing funds to projects that used computers for everything from studying and predicting the behavior of people and political systems to modeling human cognitive processes and developing simulations that predicted "the behavior of international systems."[42] Records show that as early as 1963, Lick's Command and Control Research division was sharing and intermingling funds with William Godel's Project Agile.[43]

Indeed, even as Lick started at ARPA, Project Agile was deploying data-driven counterinsurgency initiatives in the field. One of the earliest took place between 1962 and 1963 at ARPA's Combat Development Test Center in Thailand, on the outskirts of Bangkok. It was called Anthropometric Survey of the Royal Thai Armed Forces. On the surface, it was a benign study that sought to measure the body size of several thousand Thai military personnel to aid in the design of equipment and uniforms. It collected fifty-two different data points, everything from sitting height to buttock–knee length to crotch–thigh circumference and seven different measurements of the face and head.

The survey's data points had the unpleasant feel of a eugenic study, but the physical measurements were just the surface level of the study. The deeper purpose was rooted in prediction and control.[44] "Thai participants were also asked a bevy of personal questions—not just where and when they were born, but who their ancestors were, what their religion was, and what they thought of the king of Thailand," explains Annie Jacobsen in *The Pentagon's Brain*. These questions were at the heart of the study's true goal: to create a computer profile of each Thai serviceman and then use it to test predictive models. "ARPA wanted to create a prototype showing how it could monitor third world armies for future use. The information would be saved in computers stored in a secure military facility. In 1962 Thailand was a relatively stable country, but it was surrounded by insurgency and unrest on all sides. If Thailand were to become a battle zone, ARPA would have information on Thai soldiers, each of whom could be tracked. Information—like who deserted the Thai army and became an enemy combatant—could be ascertained. Using computer models, ARPA could create algorithms describing human behavior in remote areas."[45]

The link between counterinsurgency and computers is not that surprising. The first rudimentary computer technology was developed in the United States almost a century before the Vietnam War to count, categorize, and study masses of people. In the late 1880s, an American by the name of Herman Hollerith invented a tabulation machine under contract with the US government to speed the process of counting people for the US Census. Because of a huge immigration influx, the census had become so unwieldy that it took a full decade to finish the count by hand.

Hollerith came up with an elegant electromechanical solution, a contraption that would later become the backbone of International Business Machines, or IBM, the oldest computer company in the world. His design broke down the process of automatic data calculation into two general steps. First, data were digitized, that is, converted into a format that could be understood by a machine, via a series of holes punched in a piece of paper. The second step involved feeding this paper into an apparatus containing electrical pins that tabulated and sorted the punch cards on the basis of position and arrangement of the punched holes. Hollerith initially thought to record the information on a long strip of paper, like a ticker tape. But he quickly abandoned the idea because it made it too difficult to locate and isolate individual records—in a census the machine would process hundreds of thousands and even millions of individuals. "The trouble was that if, for example, you wanted statistics regarding Chinamen, you'd have to run miles of paper to count a few Chinamen," Hollerith explained.[46]

So, he went with a different idea: each person would be represented by a separate punch card. The inspiration came from an observation he made on a train. To prevent people from passing around and reusing train tickets, conductors punched out a passenger's description on a little slip of paper: height, type of hairstyle, eye color, and nose type. It was an elegant and powerful solution. Each person had their own card—and each card had a standardized pattern of holes that corresponded to information collected by the census takers. Each card would encode a person's attributes: age, sex, religion, occupation, place of birth, marital status, criminal history. Once a clerk transferred the data from a census form onto a punch card, the cards would be fed into a machine that could count and arrange them in all sorts of ways. It could provide aggregate totals for each category or find and isolate groups of people in specific categories. Any trait—nationality, employment status, disability—could be singled out and sorted quickly. Hollerith described his system as making "a punch photograph of each person." And, indeed, it did: a first-generation digital dossier of people and their lives.

Used to count the census in 1890, Hollerith's tabulators were a huge success, cutting the time it took to crunch the numbers from years to months. The machines also lent census trackers the ability to slice, dice, and mine the data in ways that had never been possible; for example, to find a particular person or group of people—say, Americans with at least one Japanese parent in California or all orphans living in New York with a felony. This kind of fine-grained analysis on a mass scale was unprecedented. Overnight, Hollerith's tabulators transformed census taking from a simple count into something very different—something that approached an early form of mass surveillance.

Newton Dexter North, a wool industry lobbyist chosen to head the 1900 census, was astounded by the ability of Hollerith's tabulators to so precisely tabulate racial data. Like many upper-class Americans of his day, North worried that the massive influx of immigrants from Europe was destroying the fabric of American society, causing social and political unrest, and threatening the nation's racial purity.[47] This fear of immigration would become intertwined with anticommunist hysteria, leading to repression of workers and labor unions across the country. North saw statisticians like himself as technocratic soldiers: America's last line of defense against a foreign corrupting influence. And he saw the tabulator machine as their most powerful weapon. "This immigration is profoundly affecting our civilization, our institutions, our habits and our ideals. It has transplanted here alien tongues, alien religions, and alien theories of government; it has been a powerful influence in the rapid disappearance of the Puritanical outlook upon life," North warned, but he heaped praise on Hollerith's newfangled computation device. "I cannot detain the reader with a statement of the correlation of the data of individual elements of the population, in combination with other data, beyond the reach of hand tabulation, which this invention opened up," he explained. "Without it we could never hope to lay bare all the truth we must have, if we are to cope successfully with the problems growing out of the heterogeneous commingling of races which our defective immigration laws are forcing upon us."[48]

Two decades after its debut, Hollerith tabulation technology was absorbed into IBM. Improved and refined over the years, the machines became a runaway hit with businesses and government. They were used extensively by the US military during World War II to keep an up-to-date tally of troop numbers and were even dragged onshore during the invasion of Normandy. They were also used to process the internment of Japanese Americans during the war. And, after President Franklin Delano Roosevelt created the Social Society system, IBM and its tabulators functioned as a de facto privatized arm that did all the processing and accounting for America's pension system.[49] Perhaps most infamously, IBM's tabulator machines were employed by Nazi Germany to run death labor camps and to institute a system of racial surveillance by enabling the regime to comb genealogical data to root out people with traces of Jewish blood.[50]

Willy Heidinger, head of IBM operations in Germany and a devout member of the Nazi Party, knew the part he played, with the help of IBM tabulators, in studying a sick German people and helping Adolf Hitler provide the cure: "We are very much like the physician, in that we dissect, cell by cell, the German cultural body. We report every individual characteristic . . . on a little card," he said in a fiery speech dedicating a new IBM factory in Berlin. "We are proud that we may assist in such a task, a task that provides our nation's Physician with the material he needs for his examinations. Our Physician can then determine whether the calculated values are in harmony with the health of our people. It also means that if such is not the case, our Physician can take corrective procedures to correct the sick circumstances. . . . Hail to our German people and der Fuhrer!"[51]

Nazi Germany's use of IBM technology is an extreme example, but it underscores the connection between the development of early computer technology and the study and management of large groups of people. IBM tabulators remained in operation through the 1980s. Indeed, until J. C. R. Licklider and ARPA developed interactive computing systems, tabulators and punch cards were the principal means by which militaries, government agencies, and corporations wrote programs and worked with complex data sets.

There is no doubt that Licklider's computer research at ARPA was intimately bound to the agency's expanding counterinsurgency mission.[52] But in internal discussions with his ARPA contractors— engineers and social scientists at major universities across the country—Lick sought to deemphasize the military applications of his command and control project, instead shifting the focus to the need to build productivity-boosting computer technology for his civilian collaborators and their colleagues.

In a letter to his contractors, Lick wrote:

> The fact is, as I see it, that the military greatly needs solutions to many or most of the problems that will arise if we tried to make good use of the facilities that are coming into existence. I am hoping that there will be, in our individual efforts, enough evident advantage in cooperative programming and operation to lead us to solve the problems and, thus, to bring into being the technology that the military needs. When problems arise clearly in the military context and seem not to

appear in the research context, then ARPA can take steps to
handle them on an ad hoc basis. As I say, however, hopefully,
many of the problems will be essentially the same, and essentially as important, in the research context as in the military
context.[53]

On a fundamental level, the computer technology required to
power active military operations was no different from the tech scientists and researchers used to do their work. Collaboration, real-time
collection and sharing of data, predictive modeling, image analysis,
natural language processing, intuitive controls and displays, and computer graphics—if the tools developed by ARPA contractors worked
for them and their academic buddies, they would also work for the
military with only slight modifications. Today's military takes this
for granted: computer technology is always "dual use," to be used in
both commercial and military applications. Deemphasizing ARPA's
military purpose had the benefit of boosting morale among computer
scientists, who were more eager to work on the technology if they
believed it wasn't going to be used to bomb people.[54]

Two years into his job at ARPA, Lick began to view the various computing projects he had seeded all over the country—from
UCLA to Stanford and MIT—as parts of a larger connected unit:
computer "thinking centers" that at some point in the near future
would be netted together into a single, unified, distributed computing
machine. It mirrored the vision of a networked society he had outlined in 1960: first, you connect the powerful computers via a high-
bandwidth network. Then you connect users to these computers with
telephone lines, satellite dishes, or radio signals—whichever technology was best suited to their particular needs. It would not matter
whether people logged in from home, work, a jeep crawling through
the jungles of Vietnam, or a stealth bomber flying ten miles above the
Soviet Union. "In such a system, the speed of the computers would
be balanced, and the cost of the gigantic memories and the sophisticated programs would be divided by the number of users," he had
written. In 1963, four years after publishing that paper, Lick began

coyly referring to this idea as the "Great Intergalactic Network." Fundamentally, his vision for a distributed interactive computing network is not very different from what the Internet looks like today.[55]

In 1964, two years after coming to ARPA, Lick decided that he had fulfilled his mission of getting the agency's Command and Control Research program up and running. He moved his family to Westchester County, New York, to start a cushy gig running a research division at IBM.[56] Younger and more energetic men would have to finish the job he started.

The ARPANET

Lawrence Roberts was twenty-nine years old when he reported to duty at ARPA's Command and Control Research division inside the Pentagon. The year was 1966, and he was hired for a big and important job: to make Lick's Great Intergalactic Network a reality.

Everything was in place. ARPA had a range of functional overlapping interactive computer projects spread across the country, including at the following centers:

> MIT's Artificial Intelligence Laboratory
> MIT's Project MAC
> Stanford's Artificial Intelligence Laboratory
> Stanford's Research Institute
> Carnegie Mellon University
> University of California, Irvine
> University of California, Los Angeles
> University of California, Berkeley
> University of California, Santa Barbara
> RAND Corporation
> Utah University

It was time to wire all these computer centers together and have them function as one unit. It would be called the ARPANET.

Roberts came from the MIT Lincoln Laboratory, where he had been working on graphics and computer communication systems. Some of his colleagues found the strict atmosphere there stifling. In fact, two of them left in a huff because of the lab's "no pets" policy. "They wanted to bring a cat into the lab. Lincoln would not allow them to bring a cat in. And they decided that was unfair; they would go somewhere where cats were tolerated," he recalled, noting wryly that the cats were not for companionship but for gruesome experimentation. "It was really a fight over having that connection with the brain electrodes and all of that. Lincoln just did not want anything to do with it."[57]

But Roberts had no such problem. He had a broad forehead, big, floppy earlobes, and a stern but calm and measured way of talking. He was a math and theory kind of guy. He thrived at Lincoln Lab, working on moon-shot algorithms, image compression, and data network design. He knew Lick and was inspired by his vision of a universal network that could net all sorts of systems together. Indeed, Roberts was an efficient networker. "Within a few weeks, he had the place—one of the world's largest, most labyrinthine buildings— memorized. Getting around the building was complicated by the fact that certain hallways were blocked off as classified areas. Roberts obtained a stopwatch and began timing various routes to his frequent destinations," write Katie Hafner and Matthew Lyon in their upbeat and zany book about the creation of the Internet, *Where Wizards Stay Up Late*.[58] Inside the Pentagon, people started calling the most efficient path between two points "Larry's Route."

Roberts liked building networks, just not the social kind. He was reserved and extremely socially averse. None of his coworkers, not even the ones closest to him, knew much about him or anything about his personal life. He was obsessed with efficiency and was really into speed reading, studying and improving his technique to the point where he could read thirty thousand words a minute. "He'd pick up a paperback and be through with it in ten minutes. It was typical Larry," one of his friends recalled.

Roberts's task was daunting: connect all of ARPA's far-flung interactive computer projects—with computers made by a half dozen different companies, including a one-of-a-kind ILLIAC supercomputer—into one network. "Almost every conceivable item of computer hardware and software will be in the network. This is the greatest challenge of the system, as well as its greatest ultimate value," said Roberts.[59]

Not long after arriving at ARPA, he convened a series of meetings with a core group of contractors and several outside advisers to hash out the design. The sessions brought together a mix of ideas and people. One of the most important was Paul Baran, who had worked at RAND designing communication systems for the air force that could survive a nuclear attack.[60] Over time, the group came up with a design: key to the network would be what Roberts called interface message processors, or IMPs. These were dedicated computers that would form the connective tissue of the distributed network. Connected by telephone lines leased from AT&T, they would send and receive data, check for errors, and ensure that data successfully reached the destination. If part of the network went down, the IMPs would attempt to retransmit the information using a different pathway. IMPs were the generic gateways to ARPA's network, functioning independently of the computers that used them. Different makes and models of computers did not need to be designed to understand each other—all they needed to do was communicate with the IMPs. In a way, IMPs were the first Internet routers.

Finally, in July 1968, Roberts put out a contract request to over a hundred computer companies and military contractors. Bids came back from some of the biggest names in the business: both IBM and Raytheon were interested, but the contract was ultimately awarded to an influential early computer research firm in Cambridge, Massachusetts, called Bolt, Beranek and Newman, where J. C. R. Licklider was a senior executive.[61]

The very first ARPANET node, powered by the IMPs, went live on October 29, 1969, linking Stanford to UCLA.[62] The first attempt to connect barely worked and dropped after a few seconds, but by the next month, connections to UC Santa Barbara and University of Utah were also made. Six months later, seven more nodes became operational. By the end of 1971, more than fifteen nodes existed. And the network kept growing.[63]

In October 1972, a full demonstration of the ARPANET was carried out at the first International Conference on Computer Communications in Washington, DC. It astounded people. ARPA contractors fit out a hall with dozens of computer terminals that could access computers across the country and even a link in Paris. Software available for demonstration included an air traffic simulation program, weather and meteorological models, chess programs, database systems, and even a robotic psychiatrist program called Eliza that provided mock counseling. Engineers ran around like children at an amusement park, overwhelmed by how all the different parts flawlessly fit together and worked as one interactive machine.[64]

"It was difficult for many experienced professionals at that time to accept the fact that a collection of computers, wide-hand circuits, and minicomputer switching nodes—pieces of equipment totaling well over a hundred—could all function together reliably, but the ARPANET demonstration lasted for three days and clearly displayed its reliable operation in public," Roberts recalled. "The network provided ultra-reliable service to thousands of attendees during the entire length of the conference."[65]

Even so, not everyone was excited by what ARPA was doing.

"The Octoputer: Serves the Ruling Class"

September 26, 1969, was a mild fall day at Harvard University. But all was not well. Several hundred angry students gathered on campus and marched on the office of Harvard's dean. They piled inside and refused to leave. A day earlier, five hundred students had marched through campus, and a small contingent of activists from Students for a Democratic Society had broken into the school's Office of International Affairs and forced the administrators out onto the street.[66]

Similar troubles were afoot just across the river at MIT, where students were holding protests and teach-ins.[67]

Fliers posted on both campuses railed against "computerized people-manipulation" and "the blatant prostitution of social science for the aims of the war machine." One leaflet warned: "Until the military–social science complex is eliminated, social scientists will aid the enslavement, rather than the liberation, of mankind."[68]

What exactly were the students protesting?

The ARPANET.

> Vietnam is the most blatant example of the U.S. attempt to control underdeveloped countries for its own strategic and economic interests. This global policy, that prevents the economic and social developments of the third world, is imperialism.
>
> In serving these policies, the U.S. government has no qualms about setting up a project that ties together MIT, Harvard, Lincoln Labs, and the entire Cambridge research and development complex.[69]

Earlier that year, activists from Students for a Democratic Society got their hands on a confidential ARPA proposal written by none other than J. C. R. Licklider. The document ran to almost a hundred pages and outlined the creation of a joint Harvard-MIT ARPA program that would directly aid the agency's counterinsurgency mission. It was called the Cambridge Project. Once complete, it would allow any intelligence analyst or military planner connected to the ARPANET to upload dossiers, financial transactions, opinion surveys, welfare rolls, criminal record histories, and any other kind of data and to analyze them in all sorts of sophisticated ways: sifting through reams of information to generate predictive models, mapping out social relationships, and running simulations that could predict human behavior. The project emphasized providing analysts with the power to study third-world countries and left-wing movements.

Students saw Cambridge Project, and the bigger ARPANET that plugged into it, as a weapon. A pamphlet handed out at the MIT protest explained: "The whole computer set-up and the ARPA computer network will enable the government, for the first time, to consult relevant survey data rapidly enough to be used in policy decisions. The net result of this will be to make Washington's international policeman more effective in suppressing popular movements around the world. The so-called basic research to be supported by Project CAM will deal with questions like why do peasant movements or student groups become revolutionary. The results of this research will similarly be used to suppress progressive movements."[70] Another booklet featured a mock advertisement that gave a visual representation to these fears. It featured "The Octoputer," a computer shaped like an octopus that had tentacles reaching into every sector of society. "The Octoputer's arms are long and strong," read the mock ad copy. "It sits in the middle of your university, country and reaches helping hands out in all directions. Suddenly your empire works harder. More of your agents use the computer—solving more problems, finding more facts."[71]

To activists, ARPA's Cambridge Project was part of a networked system of surveillance, political control, and military conquest being quietly assembled by diligent researchers and engineers at college campuses around the country. The college kids had a point.

The Cambridge Project—also known as Project CAM—was born out of an idea proposed in 1968 by Licklider and his longtime colleague Ithiel de Sola Pool, an MIT political science professor and expert in propaganda and psychological operations.

As head of ARPA's Command and Control Research project and Behavioral Sciences program, Lick had seen how the agency struggled with the mountains of data generated by its counterinsurgency initiatives in Southeast Asia. A major goal of his work during his brief stint at ARPA was to jump-start a program that would ultimately build the underlying systems that could make computer-aided counterinsurgency and command and control more efficient: tools that ingest and analyze data, create searchable databases, build predictive models, and allow people to share that information across vast distances. Pool was driven by the same passion.

Pool, a descendant of a prominent rabbinical family that traced its roots to medieval Spain, was an MIT professor and renowned expert in communications and propaganda theory. Starting in the late 1950s, he ran MIT's Center for International Studies, a prestigious department for communication studies that was funded by the CIA, and helped set up MIT's Department of Political Science. He was a hardcore anticommunist and a pioneer in the use of opinion polling and computer modeling for political campaigns. With his expertise, he was tapped to guide the messaging for John F. Kennedy's 1960 presidential bid, crunching poll numbers and running simulations on issues and voter groups. Pool's data-driven approach to political campaigning was on the cutting edge of a new wave of electoral technologies that sought to win by pretesting people's preferences and biases and then calibrating a candidate's message to fit them. These new targeted messaging tactics, enabled by rudimentary computers, had a lot of fans in Washington and over the next several decades would come to dominate the way politics were done.[72] They also inspired fear that America's political system was being taken over by manipulative technocrats who cared more about the marketing and selling of ideas than they did about what those ideas actually meant.[73]

Pool was much more than a campaign pollster; he was also an expert in propaganda and psychological operations and had close ties to ARPA's counterinsurgency efforts in Southeast Asia, Latin America, and the Soviet Union.[74] From 1961 through 1968, his company, the Simulmatics Corporation, worked on ARPA counterinsurgency programs in South Vietnam as part of William Godel's Project Agile, including a major contract to study and analyze the motivation of captured Vietnamese rebels and to develop strategies to win the allegiance of South Vietnamese peasants. Pool's work in Vietnam helped further the idea that a purely technical solution could stop the insurgency. "Simulmatics relied heavily on the work of Pool's MIT colleague, Lucian Pye, who had argued since the early 1950s that communism was a psychological disease of transitioning peoples. In his influential *Politics, Personality, and Nation-Building,* he explained that psychological failures lay at the root of stalled nation-building efforts," writes historian Joy Rohde in "The Last Stand of the Psychocultural Cold Warriors." To win the war for hearts and minds, Americans needed to design a psychologically appropriate political infrastructure for the emerging nation—a structure through which peasants would develop the appropriate psychological ties to the state. . . . Military research would write the protocol for a kind of national therapy."[75]

At the same time Simulmatics contractors gathered data in Vietnam's sweltering jungles, Pool's company worked on another ARPA initiative called Project ComCom, short for "Communist Communications." Run out of Pool's home base at MIT, ComCom was an ambitious attempt to build a computer simulation of the internal communications system of the Soviet Union. The objective was to study the effects that foreign news and radio broadcasts were having on Soviet society as well as to model and predict the kind of reaction a particular broadcast—say, a presidential speech or a breaking news program—would have on the Soviet Union.[76] Unsurprisingly, Pool's models showed that covert CIA attempts to influence the Soviet Union by beaming radio propaganda were having a big effect, and that these efforts needed to be stepped up. "Most of the things of a positive character that are happening in the Soviet Union today are explainable only in terms of the influence of the West, for which the most important single channel is radio," Pool said in a speech explaining the results of the ComCom study. "In the long run those who are talking to the Soviet Union are not talking to deaf ears. Their voices will be heard and will make a great deal of difference."[77]

But Pool was never satisfied with ComCom's performance. Even in the late 1960s, the crude state of computer technology meant that it took several months for him and his team to build a model for just one situation.[78] It was painstaking work that clearly required more powerful computer tools—tools that simply did not exist.

Pool saw computers as more than just apparatuses that could speed up social research. His work was infused with a utopian belief in the power of cybernetic systems to manage societies. He was among a group of Cold War technocrats who envisioned computer technology and networked systems deployed in a way that directly intervened in people's lives, creating a kind of safety net that spanned the world and helped run societies in a harmonious manner, managing strife and conflict out of existence. This system wouldn't be messy or wishy-washy or open to interpretation; nor would it involve socialist economic theories. In fact, it wouldn't involve politics at all but would be an applied science based on math, "a kind of engineering."

In 1964, at the same time his company was doing counterinsurgency work for ARPA in Vietnam, Pool became a vocal supporter of Project Camelot, a different counterinsurgency effort funded by the US Army and backed in part by ARPA.[79] "Camelot" was just a code name. The project's full official title was "Methods for Predicting and Influencing Social Change and Internal War Potential." Its ultimate goal: to build a radar system for left-wing revolutions—a computerized early warning system that could predict and prevent political movements before they ever got off the ground.[80] "One of the project's anticipated end products was an automated 'information collection and handling system' into which social researchers could feed facts for quick analysis. Essentially, the computer system would check up-to-date intelligence information against a list of precipitants and preconditions," writes historian Joy Rohde. "Revolution could be stopped before its initiators even knew they were headed down the path to political violence."[81]

Project Camelot was a big undertaking that involved dozens of leading American academics. It was very dear to Pool personally, but it never got very far.[82] Chilean academics who were invited to participate in Project Camelot blew the whistle on its military intelligence ties and accused the United States of trying to build a computer-assisted coup machine. The affair blew up into a huge scandal. A special session of the Chilean Senate was convened to investigate the allegations, and politicians denounced the initiative as "a plan of Yankee espionage."[83] With all this international attention and negative publicity, Project Camelot was shut down in 1965.

In 1968, Lick's Cambridge Project at MIT picked up where Camelot left off.[84]

To Lick, the Cambridge Project was the realization of the interactive computer technology he had been pushing for. Finally, after nearly a decade, computing technology had advanced to a point where it could help the military use data to fight insurgencies. The Cambridge Project included several components. It ran a common operating system and a suite of standard programs custom-tailored to the military's "behavioral science mission" that could be accessed from any computer with an ARPANET connection. It was a kind of stripped-down 1960s version of Palantir, the powerful data mining, surveillance, and prediction software the military and intelligence planners use today. The project also funded various efforts to use these programs in ways that were beneficial to the military, including compiling various intelligence databases. As a bonus, the Cambridge Project served as a training ground for a new cadre of data scientists and military planners who learned to be proficient in data mining on it.

The Cambridge Project had another, less menacing side. Financial analysts, psychologists, sociologists, CIA agents—the Cambridge Project was useful to anyone interested in working with large and complex data sets. The technology was universal and dual use. So, on one level, the goal of the Cambridge Project was generic. Still, the project was customized to the military's needs, with particular focus on fighting insurgencies and rolling back communism. A big part of the proposal Lick submitted to ARPA in 1968 focused on the various types of "data banks" the Cambridge Project would compile and make available to military analysts and behavioral scientists connected through the ARPANET:[85]

- Public opinion polls from all countries
- Cultural patterns of all the tribes and peoples of the world
- Archives on comparative communism . . . files on the contemporary world communist movements
- Political participation of various countries. . . . This includes such variables as voting, membership in associations, activity of political parties, etc.

- Youth movements
- Mass unrest and political movements under conditions of rapid social change
- Data on national integration, particularly in "plural" societies; the integration of ethnic, racial and religious minorities; the merging or splitting of present political units
- International propaganda output
- Peasant attitudes and behavior
- International armament expenditures and trends

It was clear that the Cambridge Project wasn't just a tool for research, it was counterinsurgency technology.

In the late 1960s and early 1970s, huge antiwar protests erupted on university campuses across the country. Activists occupied buildings, stole documents, published newsletters, staged sit-ins and marches, clashed with police, and became increasingly violent. At the University of Michigan, students attempted to block campus recruitment by Dow Chemical, which produced the napalm that rained down on Vietnam.[86] Someone blew up the Army Mathematics Research Center at the University of Wisconsin.[87] The Weather Underground set off a bomb inside Harvard's Center for International Affairs.[88] They wanted to stop the Vietnam War. They also wanted to halt the cooptation of academic research by the military-industrial complex.

ARPA programs were a constant target. Students protested against the ILLIAC-IV, the massive ARPA supercomputer housed at the University of Illinois.[89] They targeted the Stanford Research Institute, an important ARPA contractor involved in everything from chemical weapons research to counterinsurgency work and development of the ARPANET. Students occupied the building, shouting, "Get SRI out!" and "Down with SRI!" A few brave contractors stayed behind to protect ARPA's computers from the angry mob,[90] telling protesters that computers were "politically neutral."[91] But are they?

The student demonstrations against the Cambridge Project were part of this wave of protests sweeping the country. The common belief among students at MIT and Harvard was that the Cambridge Project, and the bigger ARPA network it was tied to, was essentially a front for the CIA. Even some professors began turning on it.[92] The language of Licklider's proposal—talk about propaganda and monitoring political movements—was so direct and so obvious that it could not be ignored. It confirmed students' and activists' fears about computers and computer networks and gave them a glimpse into how military planners wanted to use these technologies as tools for surveillance and social control.

A crew of activists from Students for a Democratic Society produced a small but informative booklet that laid out the group's opposition to the initiative: *The Cambridge Project: Social Science for Social Control*. It sold for a quarter. The cover featured a series of punch cards being fed into a computer that transformed "Black Militancy," "Student Protest," "Strikes," and "Welfare Struggles" into "Counter-insurgency," "Ghetto Pacification," and "Strike Breaking."[93] At one point, the pamphlet's producers gathered on Technology Square at the edge of the MIT campus. They obtained a copy of Lick's Cambridge Project proposal and set fire to it. Lick, ever enthusiastic and confident in his ability to sway people to his way of thinking, met the protesting students outside and attempted to reassure them that everything was okay—that this ARPA project wasn't some nefarious initiative cooked up by spies and generals. But students would have none of it.

"The group was hostile," Douwe Yntema, the director of the Cambridge Project, told M. Waldrop.[94] "But he [Licklider] was pretty cool about it. At one point, in fact, they had a copy of the proposal and tried to set fire to it—not very successfully. Well, after a few minutes Lick said, 'Look, if you want to burn a stack of paper, don't just try to light it. Spread the pages out first.' So he showed them how, and it really did burn much better!"

But the students gathered there had a deep understanding of the political and economic dimensions of ARPA's military research, and they were not going to be dismissed like petulant schoolchildren. They persisted. Lick tried to be a good sport about it, but he was disappointed.[95] Not in the project. No, he was down on the kids. He believed the protesters did not understand the project and completely misread its intentions and military ties. Why couldn't young people understand that this technology was completely neutral? Why did they have to politicize everything? Why did they think America was always the enemy and would use technology for political control? He saw the whole thing as a symptom of the degradation of American youth culture.

The demonstrations against the Cambridge Project involved hundreds of people. They were ultimately a part of the larger anti-war movement at MIT and Harvard that attracted the leading lights of the antiwar movement, including Howard Zinn. Noam Chomsky showed up to lambast academics, accusing them of running cover for violent imperialism by "investing it with the aura of science."[96] But in the end, the protests didn't have much of an effect. The Cambridge Project proceeded as planned. The only change: further proposals and internal discussions for funding omitted overt references to military applications and the study of communism and third world societies, and project contractors simply referred to what they were doing as "behavioral science."

But behind the scenes, the military and intelligence dimension of the project remained foremost. Indeed, a classified guide from 1973 commissioned by ARPA for the Central Intelligence Agency noted that, although the Cambridge Project was still experimental, it was nonetheless "one of the most flexible" tools available for complex data and statistical analysis in existence, and recommended that the CIA's international security analysts learn how to use it.[97]

The Cambridge Project ran for a total of five years. As time would prove, the kids were right to fear it.

Chapter 3

Spying on Americans

Historical mythmaking is made possible only by forgetting.

—Nancy Isenberg, *White Trash*

On June 2, 1975, NBC correspondent Ford Rowan appeared on the evening news to report a stunning exposé. Baby-faced with light blue eyes, he spoke straight into the camera and told viewers that the military was building a sophisticated computer communications network and was using it to spy on Americans and share surveillance data with the CIA and NSA.[1] He was talking about the ARPANET.

"Our sources say, the Army's information on thousands of American protesters has been given to the CIA, and some of it is in CIA computers now. We don't know who gave the order to copy and keep the files. What we do know is that once the files are computerized, the Defense Department's new technology makes it incredibly easy to move information from one computer to another," Rowan reported. "This network links computers at the CIA, the Defense Intelligence Agency, the National Security Agency, more than 20 universities, and a dozen research centers, like the RAND Corporation."

Rowan had spent months piecing the story together from several "reluctant whistleblowers"—including ARPA contractors who were alarmed at how the technology they were building was being used. For three days after the initial story, he and his colleagues at NBC evening news aired several more reports looking more closely at this mysterious surveillance network and the shadowy agency that had built it.

> The key breakthrough in the new computer technology was made at a little known unit of the Defense Department—the Advanced Research Projects Agency, ARPA.
>
> ARPA scientists created something new in computer communications with this device, it's known as the IMP, the interface message processor. Different computers communicate in different computer languages. Before the IMP it was enormously difficult, in many cases impossible, to link the various computers. The IMP, in effect, translates all computer messages into a common language. That makes it very very easy to tie them into a network.
>
> The government is now using this new technology in a secret computer network that gives the White House, the CIA, and the Defense Department access to FBI and Treasury Department computer files on 5 million Americans.
>
> The network, and it is referred to as "the network," is now in operation. . . . This means that from computer terminals now in place at the White House, the CIA, or the Pentagon, an official can push a button and get whatever information there might be on you in the FBI's vast computer files. Those files include records from local police agencies which are hooked to the FBI by computer.[2]

Rowan's exposé was phenomenal. It was based on solid sources from the Pentagon, the CIA, and the Secret Service, as well as key ARPANET insiders, some of whom were concerned about the creation of a network that could so seamlessly link multiple government surveillance systems. In the 1970s, the historical significance of the ARPANET was not yet apparent; what Rowan uncovered has become only more relevant in hindsight. It would take more than twenty years for the Internet to spread into most American homes, and four decades would pass before Edward Snowden's leaks made the world aware of the massive amount of government surveillance happening over the Internet. Today, people still think that surveillance is something foreign to the Internet—something imposed on it from the outside by paranoid government agencies. Rowan's reporting from forty years ago tells a different story. It shows how military and intelligence agencies used the network technology to spy on Americans in the first version of the Internet. Surveillance was baked in from the very beginning.

This is an important fact in the history of the Internet. Yet it has vanished down the collective memory hole. Crack any popular history of the Internet and there is no mention of it. Even today's foremost historians do not seem to know it occurred.[3]

Counterinsurgency Comes Home

In the late 1960s, as engineers at MIT, UCLA, and Stanford diligently worked to build a unified military computer network, the country convulsed with violence and radical politics—much of it directed at the militarization of American society, the very thing that the ARPANET represented. These were some of the most violent years in American history. Race riots, militant black activism, powerful left-wing student movements, and almost daily bombings in cities across the country.[4] The United States was a pressure cooker, and the heat kept building. In 1968, Robert Kennedy and Martin Luther King Jr. were assassinated, the latter's death triggering riots across the nation. Antiwar protests swept American university campuses. In November 1969, three hundred thousand people descended on Washington, DC, for the largest antiwar protest in the history of the United States.[5] In May 1970, the Ohio National Guard fired on protesters at Kent State University, killing four students—called "Nixon's Massacre" by Hunter S. Thompson.

To many, it seemed that America was about to explode. In January 1970, a former military intelligence officer by the name of Christopher Pyle tossed more wood on the blaze.

Pyle was political science PhD student at Columbia University. He wore glasses, had a mop of hair parted on the side, and carried himself with the thoughtful and meticulous manner of an academic. He had been an instructor at the US Army Intelligence School in Fort Holabird outside Baltimore and saw something there that concerned him enough that he had to blow the whistle.[6]

In early 1970, he published an exposé in the *Washington Monthly* that revealed a massive domestic surveillance and counterinsurgency operation run by the US Army Intelligence Command. Known as "CONUS Intel"—Continental United States Intelligence—the program involved thousands of undercover agents. They infiltrated domestic antiwar political groups and movements, spied on left-wing activists, and filed reports in a centralized intelligence database on millions of Americans.[7] "When this program began in the summer of 1965, its purpose was to provide early warning of civil disorders which the Army might be called upon to quell in the summer of 1967," reported Pyle. "Today, the Army maintains files on the membership, ideology, programs, and practices of virtually every activist political group in the country."

CONUS Intel was masterminded in part by General William P. Yarborough, the army's top intelligence officer at the time. He had a long, distinguished career in counterinsurgency and psychological operations, from World War II to the Korea and Vietnam conflicts. In 1962, General Yarborough took part in the influential US Army "limited war" counterinsurgency symposium held in Washington, DC, which J. C. R. Licklider also attended.[8] Fear of a domestic insurgency was swirling in military circles, and the general was not immune. He came to believe that there existed a growing communist conspiracy to foment unrest and to overthrow the United States government from within. His evidence? The burgeoning civil rights movement and the surging popularity of Martin Luther King Jr.

Yarborough looked at the masses of people agitating for racial equality and didn't see Americans getting politically involved because of legitimate grievances and concerns. He saw dupes and foreign agents who, whether they realized it or not, were part of a sophisticated insurgency operation financed and directed by the Soviet Union. This was not the view of a lone conspiracy nut but was shared by many of Yarborough's peers in the army.[9]

When race riots broke out in Detroit in 1967 a few months after Martin Luther King delivered a speech trying to unite the civil rights and antiwar movements, Yarborough told his subordinates at the US Army Intelligence Command: "Men, get out your counterinsurgency manuals. We have an insurgency on our hands."[10]

William Godel had set up ARPA's Project Agile to fight insurgencies abroad. General Yarborough focused on an extension of that same mission: fighting what he saw as a foreign insurgency on American soil. Just as in Vietnam, his first order of business was to take out the insurgents' base of local support. But before he could start clearing the weeds, his men needed information. Who were these insurgents? What motivated them? Who called the shots? Who were their domestic allies? Among what groups did they hide?

To root out the enemy, General Yarborough oversaw the creation of CONUS Intel. Priests, elected officials, charities, after-school programs, civil rights groups, antiwar protesters, labor leaders, and right-wing groups like the Ku Klux Klan and the John Birch Society were targeted, but it seemed the primary focus of CONUS Intel was the Left: anyone perceived to be sympathetic to the cause of economic and social justice. It didn't matter if they were clergy, senators, judges, governors, long-haired radicals from Students for a Democratic Society, or members of the Black Panthers—all were fair game.[11]

By the late 1960s, CONUS Intel involved thousands of agents. They attended and reported on even the smallest protest at a time when protests were as common as PTA bake sales. They monitored labor strikes and kept note of groups and individuals who supported unions. They bugged the phone of Senator Eugene McCarthy, a critic of the Vietnam War, at the 1968 Democratic National Convention. They noted that the senator had taken a call from a "known radical group" to discuss providing medical assistance to protesters who had been injured by Chicago police. That same year, agents infiltrated a meeting of Catholic priests who protested the church's ban on birth control. They spied on Martin Luther King's funeral, mixing with mourners and recording what was talked about. They infiltrated the 1970 Earth Day festival and took photographs and filed reports on what antipollution activists were discussing and doing.[12]

Some of their surveillance targets were downright comical. A young army recruit from the Fifth Military Intelligence Detachment at Fort Carson, Colorado, spied on the Young Adults Project, which was established by church groups and a ski club to provide recreation for "emotionally disturbed young people."[13] The reason it was targeted? Apparently, local clergy did not like the project's hippie associations and thought its leaders were leading these young adults to "drugs, loud music, sex, and radicalism."[14] The damning evidence proving that this group was part of a nefarious plot to take down the United States? One of its founders had attended an antiwar rally outside the Fort Carson military base.[15] Then in 1968, agents were ordered to report on the Poor People's March on Washington—and to pay particular attention to the mules' buttocks. The pack animals were used to pull covered wagons from the rural South, and the army wanted its spies to look for sores or abrasions on the animals' hides that could show signs of abuse. The idea was to accuse and charge protesters with animal cruelty.[16]

Much of the justification for the surveillance on suspected "foreign agents" was weak or nonexistent, but it did not matter. When army agents failed to find evidence of communist orchestration, their commanders told them to get back out there and try harder: "You haven't looked hard enough. It must be there."[17]

CONUS Intel agents used all sorts of tactics to spy on and infiltrate groups considered to be threats to America. Agents grew out their hair, joined groups, and marched in movements. They even created a "legitimate" news media front: Mid-West News. Wearing press accreditation passes, agents posed as reporters and attended protests, photographed attendees, and secured interviews with participants and organizers. The army even had its own sound and TV truck to videotape demonstrations.[18]

In an interview forty-five years after he blew the whistle on this surveillance program, Christopher Pyle told me:

> The generals wanted to be consumers of the latest hot information. During the Chicago riots of 1968, the army had a unit called Mid-West News with army agents in civilian clothes and they went around and interviewed all the antiwar protesters. They shipped the film footage to Washington every night on an airliner so the generals could see movies of what was going on in Chicago when they got to work in the morning. That made them so happy. It was a complete waste of time. You could pick up the same thing on TV for far less, but they felt they needed their own film crew. The main thing they were going after was a pig named Pigasus, who was the Yippies' candidate for president. They were really excited about Pigasus.[19]

Surveillance of left-wing activists and political groups was nothing new. Going back to the nineteenth century, law enforcement agencies, both local and federal, kept files on labor and union leaders, socialists, civil rights activists, and anyone suspected of having left-wing sympathies. The Los Angeles Police Department maintained a huge file on suspected communists, labor organizers, black leaders, civil rights groups, and celebrities. Every other major city in America had its own "Red Squad" and extensive files.[20] Private companies and right-wing vigilante groups like the John Birch Society also maintained their own files on Americans. In the 1960s, private security contractor Wackenhut boasted of having two million Americans under surveillance.[21] This information was shared freely with the FBI and police departments but was usually stored the old-fashioned way: on paper in filing cabinets. The US Army database was different. It had the backing of an unlimited Pentagon budget and access to the latest computer technology.

Pyle's reporting revealed that CONUS Intel's surveillance data were encoded onto IBM punch cards and fed into a digital computer located at the Army Counter Intelligence Corps center at Fort Holabird, which was equipped with a terminal link that could be used to access almost a hundred different information categories as well as print out reports on individual people. "The personality reports—to be extracted from the incident reports—will be used to supplement the Army's seven million individual security clearance dossiers and to generate new files on the political activities of civilians wholly unassociated with the military," he wrote in the *Washington Monthly*.[22] "In this respect, the Army's data bank promises to be unique. Unlike similar computers now in use at the FBI's National Crime Information Center in Washington and New York State's Identification and Intelligence System in Albany, it will not be restricted to the storage of case histories of persons arrested for, or convicted of, crimes. Rather it will specialize in files devoted exclusively to the descriptions of the lawful political activity of civilians."

Big Data Totalitarianism

The late 1960s was the beginning of America's computerization gold rush, a time when police departments, federal government agencies, military and intelligence services, and large corporations began to digitize their operations. They bought and installed computers, ran databases, crunched numbers, automated services, and linked computers via communication networks. Everyone was in a hurry to digitize, link up, and join the glorious computer revolution.[23]

Digital government databases popped up across the country.[24] Naturally, the Federal Bureau of Investigation led the pack. It began building out a centralized digital database in 1967, by order of J. Edgar Hoover. Called the National Crime Information Center, it spanned all fifty states and was available to state and local law enforcement agencies. It contained information on arrest warrants, stolen vehicles and property, and gun registrations and was accessible via a dispatcher service. By the mid-1970s, the system was expanded to support keyboard terminals mounted in police cruisers for immediate data search and retrieval.[25]

As the FBI database grew, it interfaced and plugged into local law enforcement databases that were sprouting up around the country, systems like the one built in Bergen County, New Jersey, in the early 1970s. There, the sheriff and local police departments pooled resources to create the Regional Enforcement Information Network, a county-wide computerized database system that digitized and centralized law enforcement records of arrests, indictments, warrants, suspects, and stolen property information. The database was run on an IBM 360/40, and participating agencies could access it on local computer terminals. The system was linked to state police and FBI databases, which allowed local agencies to quickly call up county, state, and federal records.[26]

At the same time, multiple attempts were made to set up national data banks that would tie in and centralize all sorts of disparate data. They had names like "National Data Bank" and FEDNET.[27] In 1967, the Bureau of the Budget wanted to build the National Data Center, a centralized federal database that would pull together, among other things, income tax and arrest records, health data, military draft status, social security information, and banking transactions and combine this information with a unique number that would serve both as a person's lifelong identification number and permanent telephone number.[28]

Not just the cops and the feds rushed to computerize. Corporate America was an enthusiastic adopter of digital databases and networked computers to increase efficiency and bring down labor costs. Credit card companies, banks, credit rating bureaus, and airlines all began to digitize their operations, utilize centralized computer databases, and tap into the information via remote terminals.[29]

In 1964, American Airlines rolled out its first fully computerized registration and booking system, which was built by IBM and modeled after SAGE, America's first early warning and air defense system, meant to guard against a sneak nuclear bombing raid by the Soviet Union. The airline's system even had a similar name.[30] SAGE stood for "Semi-Automatic Ground Environment"; the American Airlines system was called SABRE, which stood for "Semi-Automated Business-Related Environment." Unlike SAGE, which was outdated the moment it came online because it could not intercept Soviet ballistic missiles, SABRE was a huge success. It connected more than a thousand Teletype machines to the company's centralized computer located just north of New York City.[31] The system not only promised to help American Airlines fill empty seats but also to "supply management with abundant information on day-to-day operations." And that it did.

"From its first day of operation SABRE began accumulating reels of information, the most detailed information ever compiled on the travel patterns emanating from every major city—by destination, by month, by season, by day of the week, by hour of the day—information that in the right hands would become exceedingly valuable in the industry that American sought to dominate," writes Thomas Petzinger Jr. in *Hard Landing*.[32] With SABRE, American Airlines set up a monopoly on computerized bookings, and it later leveraged that power to crush its competition.[33] Eventually, American Airlines spun the system off as a standalone company. Today, SABRE is still the number one travel booking system in the world, with ten thousand employees and revenues of $3 billion.[34]

The growth of all these databases did not go unnoticed. The dominant public fear at the time was that proliferation of corporate and government databases and networked computers would create a surveillance society—a place where every person was monitored and tracked, and where political dissent was crushed. Not just left-wing activists and student protesters worried.[35] These concerns pervaded almost every layer of society. People feared government surveillance and corporate surveillance as well.

A 1967 cover story for the *Atlantic Monthly* exemplifies these fears. Written by a University of Michigan law professor named

Arthur R. Miller, it mounts an attack on the push by both businesses and government agencies to centralize and computerize data collection. The story includes amazing cover art, showing Uncle Sam going berserk at the controls of a giant computer. It focuses on one proposed federal database in particular: the National Data Center, which would centralize personal information and connect it to a unique identification number for every person in the system.

Miller warned that such a database was a grave threat to political freedom. Once it was put in place, it would invariably grow to encompass every part of people's lives:

> The modern computer is more than a sophisticated indexing or adding machine, or a miniaturized library; it is the keystone for a new communications medium whose capacities and implications we are only beginning to realize. In the foreseeable future, computer systems will be tied together by television, satellites, and lasers, and we will move large quantities of information over vast distances in imperceptible units of time. . . .
>
> The very existence of a National Data Center may encourage certain federal officials to engage in questionable surveillance tactics. For example, optical scanners—devices with the capacity to read a variety of type fonts or handwriting at fantastic rates of speed—could be used to monitor our mail. By linking scanners with a computer system, the information drawn in by the scanner would be converted into machine-readable form and transferred into the subject's file in the National Data Center.
>
> Then, with sophisticated programming, the dossiers of all of the surveillance subject's correspondents could be produced at the touch of a button, and an appropriate entry—perhaps "associates with known criminals"—could be added to all of them. As a result, someone who simply exchanges Christmas cards with a person whose mail is being monitored might find himself under surveillance or might be turned down when he

applies for a job with the government or requests a government grant or applies for some other governmental benefit. An untested, impersonal, and erroneous computer entry such as "associates with known criminals" has marked him, and he is helpless to rectify the situation. Indeed, it is likely that he would not even be aware that the entry existed.[36]

The *Atlantic* wasn't alone. Newspapers, magazines, and television news programs of that time are filled with alarming reports about the growth of centralized databases—or "data banks," as they were called back then—and the danger they posed to a democratic society.

In this fearful time, Christopher Pyle's exposé exploded like a nuclear bomb. CONUS Intel was front-page news. Protests and outraged editorials followed, as did cover stories in just about every major news magazine in America. Television networks followed up on his reporting and carried out their own in-depth investigations. There were congressional queries to get to the bottom of the accusations.[37]

The most forceful investigation was led by Senator Sam Ervin, a North Carolina Democrat with a bald head, thick bushy eyebrows, and fleshy bulldog jowls. Ervin was known as a moderate Southern Democrat, which meant that he consistently defended Jim Crow laws and the segregation of housing and schools and fought against attempts to secure equal rights for women. He was frequently called a racist, but he saw himself as a strict constitutionalist. He hated the federal government, which also meant he hated domestic surveillance programs.[38]

In 1971, Senator Ervin convened a series of hearings on Pyle's revelations and recruited Pyle to help with the effort. Initially, the investigation focused narrowly on the army's CONUS Intel program, but it quickly expanded to encompass a much bigger issue: the proliferation of government and corporate computer databases and surveillance systems.[39] "These hearings were called because it is clear from the complaints being received by Congress that Americans in every walk of life are concerned about the growth of government and private records on individuals," Senator Ervin said before the Senate in the dramatic opening statement for his investigation. "They are concerned about the growing collection of information about them which is none of the business of the collectors. A great telecommunications network is being created by the computer transmissions which crisscross our country every day. . . . Led on by the systems analysts, State and local governments are pondering ways of hooking their data banks and computers onto their Federal counter-parts, while Federal officials attempt to 'capture' or incorporate State and local data in their own data systems."[40]

The first day of the hearings—which were titled "Federal Data Banks, Computers, and the Bill of Rights"—attracted a huge amount of news media coverage. "Senators Hear of Threat of a 'Dossier Dictatorship,'" declared a front-page *New York Times* headline; the story shared space with one about the South Vietnamese bombing offensive into Laos.[41] "The private life of the average American is the subject of 10 to 20 dossiers of personal information in the files and computer data banks of Government and private agencies . . . most Americans are only vaguely aware of the extent to which they are watched."

Over the next several months Senator Ervin grilled Pentagon brass about the program, but he met stiff resistance. Defense officials stalled, ignored requests to provide witnesses, and refused to declassify evidence.[42] The confrontations grew from a minor annoyance into a full-blown scandal, and Senator Ervin threatened to publicly denounce the army's surveillance program as unconstitutional and use his power to subpoena the necessary evidence and legally compel testimony if Pentagon representatives continued to be uncooperative. In the end, Senator Ervin's efforts succeeded in shedding light on the scope of the military's computerized domestic surveillance apparatus. His committee established that the US Army had amassed a powerful domestic intelligence presence and had "developed a massive system for monitoring virtually all political protest in the United States." There were over 300 regional "records centers" nationwide, with many containing more than 100,000 cards on "personalities of interest." By the end of 1970, a national defense intelligence center had 25 million files on individuals and 760,000 files on "organizations and incidents." These files were full of lurid details—sexual preferences, extramarital affairs, and a particular emphasis on alleged homosexuality—things that had nothing to do with the task at hand: gathering evidence on people's supposed ties to foreign governments and their participation in criminal plots.[43] And, as the committee established, the Army Intelligence Command had several databases that could cross-reference this information and map out relationships between people and organizations.

Senator Sam Ervin's committee confirmed something else as well: the army surveillance program was a direct extension of America's bigger counterinsurgency strategy, which had been developed for use in foreign conflicts but which was immediately brought back and used on the home front. "The men who ran the domestic war room kept records not unlike those maintained by their counterparts in the computerized war rooms in Saigon," noted a final report on Senator Ervin's investigations.[44]

Indeed, the army referred to activists and protesters as if they were organized enemy combatants embedded with the indigenous population. They "billeted," planned assaults on "targets and objectives," and even had an "organized sniper element." The army used standard war game colors: blue for "friendly forces" and red for "Negro neighborhoods." Yet, as the report made very clear, the people being watched were not combatants, but regular people: "Army intelligence was not just reconnoitering cities for bivouac sites, approach routes and Black Panther arsenals. It was collecting, disseminating, and storing amounts of data on the private and personal affairs of law-abiding citizens. Comments about the financial affairs, sex lives, and psychiatric histories of persons unaffiliated with the armed forces appear throughout the various records systems." That is, the army was spying on a huge swath of American society for no good reason.

"The hypothesis that revolutionary groups might be behind the civil rights and anti-war movements became a presumption which infected the entire operation," explained Senator Ervin in a final report his staff produced based on his investigation. "Demonstrators and rioters were not regarded as American citizens with possibly legitimate grievances, but as 'dissident forces' deployed against the established order. Given this conception of dissent, it is not surprising that army intelligence would collect information on the political and private lives of the dissenters. The military doctrines governing counterintelligence, counterinsurgency, and civil affairs operations demanded it."[45]

Senator Ervin's hearings drew a lot of attention and shone a light on the proliferation of federal surveillance databases being assembled in the background unchecked. The army promised to destroy the surveillance files, but the Senate could not obtain definitive proof that the files were ever fully expunged. On the contrary, evidence mounted that the army had deliberately hidden and continued to use the surveillance data it collected.[46] Indeed, even as army generals were making promises to destroy files that they had amassed on hundreds of thousands of Americans, ARPA contractors fed them into a new real-time data analysis and retrieval system hooked up to the ARPANET.[47]

ARPANET Surveillance

It was 1975 when NBC aired Ford Rowan's reporting that the ARPANET was being used to spy on Americans. Three years had passed since Senator Ervin's investigation of the army's CONUS Intel spying operation, and the scandal had long become old news, eclipsed by the Watergate investigation that brought down President Richard Nixon. But Rowan's reporting dragged the sordid CONUS Intel affair back into the spotlight.[48]

"In the late 1960's at the height of the demonstrations against the war, President Johnson ordered the CIA, the FBI, and the Army to find out who was behind the protests. What followed was a major campaign of infiltration and surveillance of antiwar groups," Rowan told NBC viewers on June 2, 1975. "In 1970, Senator Sam Ervin exposed the extent of Army spying. He got the Pentagon to promise to stop its surveillance program and to destroy the files. But four years after the promise to Sam Ervin, the Army's domestic surveillance files still exist. NBC News has learned that a new computer technology developed by the Defense Department enabled the Pentagon to copy, distribute, and secretly update the Army files."

Two days later, Rowan delivered a follow-up segment:

> The secret computer network was made possible by dramatic breakthroughs in the technique of hooking different makes and models of computers together so they can talk to one another and share information. It's a whole new technology that not many people know about. If you pay taxes, or use a credit card, if you drive a car, or have ever served in the military, if you've ever been arrested, or even investigated by a police agency, if you've had major medical expenses or contributed to a national political party, there is information on you somewhere in some computer. Congress has always been afraid that computers, if all linked together, could turn the government into "big brother" with the computers making it dangerously easy to keep tabs on everyone.

He then got specific about what happened to those surveillance files that the army was supposed to destroy: "According to confidential sources, much of the material that was computerized has been copied and transferred, and much of it has been shared with other agencies where it has been integrated into other intelligence files. . . . In January 1972, at least part of the computerized Army domestic surveillance files were stored in the NSA's Harvest computer at Fort Meade, Maryland. Through the use of a defense department computer network, the materials were transmitted and copied in Massachusetts at MIT, and were stored at the Army's Natick Research Center."

The first ARPANET node between UCLA and Stanford went online in 1969 and the network expanded nationally that same year. Now, with Rowan's exposé six years later, this groundbreaking military network had its first big moment in the public spotlight.

When I finally tracked down Rowan, he was surprised to hear me bring up that old NBC transmission. No one had discussed it with him in decades. "I haven't heard anyone who talked about this in a long time. I'm honored that you dug it all out," he said.

He then told me how he broke the story.[49] In the early 1970s, he was working the Washington beat. He covered Watergate and the Church Committee Hearings run by Senator Frank Church, which remain the most thorough and damning government investigation into the illegal activities of American intelligence agencies, including the CIA, NSA, and FBI. It was during the Church Committee that he first stumbled on the ARPANET story and began piecing it together. "This was post-Watergate, post-Vietnam. This was also the time when they were investigating the assassinations of Kennedy, the assassination of Martin Luther King and later the assassination of Robert Kennedy. Then stories came out about massive domestic spying by the FBI and DoD on antiwar protesters. These investigations were things I was covering and so I would speak to people who were living in that world—the FBI and CIA and the Department of Defense," Rowan explained. The ARPANET surveillance operation was closely connected to the political upheavals taking place in America at the time, and he learned of its existence in bits and pieces while pursuing other stories. "It was not something that was very easy to find. There was no Deep Throat. No one person that knew it all. You had to really dig."

His ARPANET investigation took months to complete. Most sources would not go on the record, but one of them did.[50] He was an MIT computer technician named Richard Ferguson, who was there in 1972 when the Pentagon transferred the surveillance data to his lab. He decided to come forward with the information and personally appeared on NBC to make the accusation. He explained that the files were in fact dossiers containing personal information as well as political beliefs. "I've seen the data structure that they've used and it concerns a person's occupation, their politics, their name," he told NBC. He explained that he got fired from his job for objecting to the program.

Multiple intelligence sources and people involved with the spy file transfer corroborated Ferguson's claims, but not on the record. In time, other journalists verified Rowan's reporting.[51] There was no doubt: the ARPANET was being used to monitor domestic political activity. "They stressed that the system did not perform any actual surveillance, but rather was designed to use data which had been collected in 'the real world' to help build predictive models which might warn when civil disturbances were imminent," he later wrote in *Technospies,* a little-known book that expanded on his investigation into the network surveillance technology built by ARPA.[52] At least part of the work of writing the database "maintenance program" for the army's illegal surveillance files appeared to have been carried out at MIT through the Cambridge Project, J. C. R. Licklider's grand initiative to build computer counterinsurgency data tools.[53] They were possibly transferred to other ARPANET sites.

Harvard and MIT students who protested ARPA's Cambridge Project back in 1969 saw the ARPANET as a surveillance weapon and a tool of social and political control. They were right. Just a few years after their protests failed to stop the project, this new technology was turned against them and the American people.

Ford Rowan's reporting, and the revelations that the army had not destroyed its illegal surveillance files, triggered another round of congressional investigations. Senator John Tunney, a Democrat from California, led the biggest one. On June 23, 1975, he convened a special session of the Committee on the Judiciary to investigate surveillance technology and to specifically address the role that ARPA's networking technology played in disseminating the army's domestic surveillance files.

Senator Tunney opened the hearings with a condemnation: "We have just gone through a period in American history called Watergate where we saw certain individuals who were prepared to use any kind of information, classified or otherwise, for their own political purposes, in a way that was most detrimental to the interests of the

United States and individual citizens," he said. "We know that the Department of Defense and the Army violated their statutory powers. We know that the CIA violated its statutory power as it related to the collecting of information on private citizens and putting it on computers."

He vowed to get to the bottom of the current surveillance scandal to prevent this kind of abuse from happening again and again. For three days, Senator Tunney grilled top defense officials. But just like Senator Sam Ervin, he ran into resistance.[54]

Deputy Assistant Secretary of Defense David Cooke, a portly man with a clean-shaven head and slick manner, was one of the main officials representing the Pentagon. He had served under Secretary of Defense Neil McElroy, the man who created ARPA, and he commanded respect and authority. In his testimony, Cooke denied that the army's domestic surveillance data banks were still in existence, and he doubly denied that the ARPANET had anything to do with transferring or utilizing these nonexistent surveillance files. "Officials at MIT and ARPA state that no transmission of civil disturbance data over ARPANET was ever authorized and they have no evidence it ever occurred," he testified. He also did his best to convince Senator Tunney that the Pentagon had no operational need for the ARPANET, which he described as a pure research and academic network. "The ARPANET itself is a totally unclassified system, which was developed by and is widely utilized by the scientific and technological community throughout the United States," he told the committee. "Neither the White House nor any of the intelligence agencies has a computer connected to the ARPANET."

As Cooke explained it, the military did not need the ARPANET because it already had its own secure database and network for communication and intelligence files: the Community Online Intelligence System, known simply as COINS. "It is a secure system, connecting selected data banks of three intelligence agencies, the Defense Intelligence Agency, National Security Agency, and the National Photo Interpretation Center. It is designed to exchange classified and highly sensitive foreign intelligence data among these intelligence agencies and within the Department of Defense. The Central Intelligence Agency and Department of State can access the system," he explained, and then added emphatically: "COINS and the ARPANET are not linked, and will not be linked."

He was either misinformed or stretching the truth.

Four years earlier, in 1971, ARPA director Stephen Lukasik, who had run the agency during the build-out of the ARPANET, very clearly explained in his testimony to the Senate that the whole point of the ARPANET was to integrate government networks—both classified (like COINS) and unclassified—into a unified tele-communications system.[55] "Our objective is to design, build, test and evaluate a high-performance, low-cost, reliable computer network to meet the growing DoD requirements for computer-to-computer communications," he said. He added that the military had just started testing the ARPANET as a way to connect operational computer systems.[56]

According to Lukasik, the beauty of the ARPANET was that, although it was technically an unclassified network, it could be used for classified purposes because data could be digitally encrypted and sent over the wire without the need to physically secure actual lines and equipment. It was a general-purpose computer network that could connect to public networks and be used for classified and non-classified tasks.[57]

Lukasik was right. Between 1972 and 1975, multiple military and intelligence agencies not only connected directly to the ARPANET but also began to build their own operational subnetworks that were based on the ARPANET design and that could interconnect with it. The navy had multiple air bases tied to the network. The army used the ARPANET to link supercomputer centers. In 1972, the NSA had commissioned Bolt, Beranek and Newman—J. C. R. Licklider's company and major ARPANET contractor—to build an upgraded ARPANET version of its COINS intelligence system, the very system that Cooke promised three years later would never be plugged into the ARPANET. This system ended up being connected to the ARPANET to provide operational data communication services for the NSA and the Pentagon for many years afterward.[58]

Even as Cooke denied to Senator Tunney that the ARPANET was used for military communications, the network featured multiple connections from the army, navy, NSA, and air force—and very likely contained unlisted nodes maintained by intelligence agencies such as the CIA.[59] But the issue soon became moot. A few weeks after Cooke's testimony, the ARPANET was officially absorbed by the Defense Communications Agency, which ran the communications systems for the entire Pentagon. In other words, even if still somewhat experimental, the ARPANET was the definition of an operational military network.[60]

Military Internet

In the summer of 1973, Robert Kahn and Vint Cerf locked themselves in a conference room at the upscale Hyatt Cabana El Camino Real just a mile south of Stanford. The Cabana was the most glamorous hotel in Palo Alto, having hosted the Beatles in 1965, among other celebrities. Kahn was stocky and had thick black hair and sideburns. Cerf was tall and lanky, with an unkempt beard. The two could have been a folk music duo passing through on tour. But Kahn and Cerf weren't there to play or socialize or party. They didn't have any booze or drugs. They didn't have much more than a few pencils and pads of paper. For the past several months, they had been trying to create a protocol that could connect three different types of experimental military networks. At the Cabana, their mission was to finally get their thoughts on paper and hash out the final technical design of an "inter-net."[61]

"Do you want to start or shall I?" asked Kahn.

"No, I'll be happy to begin," Cerf replied, and then sat there staring at a blank piece of paper. After about five minutes, he gave up: "I don't know where to start."[62]

Kahn took over and scribbled away, jotting out thirty pages of diagrams and theoretical network designs. Both Cerf and Kahn had been involved in building the ARPANET: Cerf had been part of a UCLA team responsible for writing the operating system for the routers that formed ARPANET's backbone, while Kahn had worked at Bolt, Beranek and Newman helping to design the network's routing protocols. Now they were about to take it to a new level: ARPANET 2.0, a network of networks, the architecture of what we now call the "Internet."

In 1972, after Kahn was hired to head ARPA's command and control division, he had convinced Cerf to leave a job he had just taken teaching at Stanford and work for ARPA again.[63] A major goal for Kahn was to expand the ARPANET's usefulness in real-world military situations. That meant, first and foremost, extending the packet-based networking design to wireless data networks, radio, and satellite. Wireless data networks were crucial to the future of military command and control because they would allow traffic to be transmitted over huge distances: naval vessels, aircraft, and mobile field units could all connect to computer resources on the mainland through portable wireless units. It was a mandatory component of the global command and control system ARPA was charged with developing.[64]

Kahn directed the effort to build several experimental wireless networks. One was called PRNET, short for "packet radio network." It had the ability to transmit data via mobile computers installed in vans using a network of antennas located in the mountain ranges around San Bruno, Berkeley, San Jose, and Palo Alto. The effort was run out of the Stanford Research Institute. At the same time, Kahn pushed into packet satellite networking, setting up an experimental network called SATNET that linked Maryland, West Virginia, England, and Norway; the system was initially designed to carry seismic data from remote installations set up to detect Soviet nuclear tests. ARPANET's data packet technology worked remarkably well in a wireless setting. But there was one problem: although they were based on the same fundamental data-packet-switching designs, PRNET, SATNET, and ARPANET all used slightly different protocols to run and so could not connect to each other. For all practical purposes, they were standalone networks, which went against the whole concept of networking and minimized their usefulness to the military.

ARPA needed all three networks to function as one.[65] The question was: How to bring them all together in a simple way? That's what Kahn and Cerf were trying to figure out in the Cabana conference room. Eventually, they settled on a basic plan for a flexible networking language that could connect multiple types of networks. It was called TCP/IP—Transmission Control Protocol/Internet Protocol, the same basic network language that powers the Internet today.[66]

In a 1990 oral history interview, Cerf, who now works as Google's Chief Evangelist, described how his and Kahn's efforts to devise an internetwork protocol were entirely rooted in the needs of the military:

> There were lots of ramifications for the military. For example, we absolutely wanted to bring data communications to the field, which is what the packet radio project and the packet satellite projects were about; how to reach wide areas, how to reach people on the oceans. Can't do it by dragging fiber, can't do it very well with terrestrial store-and-forward radio because line-of-site doesn't work very well on a wide ocean. So you need satellites for that. So the whole effort was very strongly motivated by bringing computers into the field in the military and then making it possible for them to communicate with each other in the field and to assets that were in the rear of the theatre of operations. So all of the demonstrations that we did had military counterparts.[67]

Even the first successful test of the Internet-grade TCP/IP network, which took place on November 22, 1977, simulated a military scenario: using radio, satellite, and wired networks to communicate with an active mobile unit battling a Soviet invasion of Europe. An old GMC delivery van outfitted by SRI with a bunch of radio gear played the role of a motorized NATO division, driving up and down the freeway near Stanford and beaming data over ARPA's radio network. The data were then forwarded over ARPA's satellite network to

Europe—by way of Sweden and London—and then sent back to the United States to UCLA via satellite and wired ARPA connections.[68] "So what we were simulating was a situation where somebody was in a mobile unit in the field, let's say in Europe, in the middle of some kind of action trying to communicate through a satellite network to the United States, and then going across the US to get to some strategic computing asset that was in the United States," recalled Cerf. "And there were a number of such simulations or demonstrations like that, some of which were extremely ambitious. They involved the Strategic Air Command at one point where we put airborne packet radios in the field communicating with each other and to the ground using the airborne systems to sew together fragments of Internet that had been segregated by a simulated nuclear attack."

Cerf described working very closely with the military every step of the way and in many cases helping find solutions to specific needs. "We deployed a whole bunch of packet radio gear and computer terminals and small processors to Fort Bragg with the 18th Airborne Corps and for several years did a whole bunch of field exercises. We also deployed them to the Strategic Air Command in Omaha, Nebraska, and did a series of exercises with them. In some cases, the outcome of the applications that we used were so good that they became part of the normal everyday operation."

Of course, Vint Cerf wasn't the only one working out practical military applications for the ARPANET. Congressional reports and internal ARPA documents from the 1970s are full of examples of the armed services putting the network to use in a variety of ways, from wirelessly transmitting submarine locator sensor data, to providing portable communication in the field, teleconferencing, remote maintenance of computer equipment, and military supply chain and logistics management.[69] And, of course, all of this was intertwined with ARPA's work on "intelligent systems"—building the data analysis and predictive technologies Godel and Licklider initiated a decade earlier.[70]

This was the great thing about ARPANET technology: it was a general-purpose network that could carry all sorts of traffic. It was useful to everyone involved.

It turned out I was correct," Ford Rowan told me forty-one years after he broke the ARPANET army surveillance story on NBC. "The concerns that a lot of people had were largely that the federal government was making one big computer that would have everything. One of the new things that came out was that you did not need one big computer. You could link a lot of computers together. That was the leap that occurred in the early 1970s as they were doing this research. We could figure out a way to share info across the network without having to actually have one big computer that knows everything."[71]

Part II
False Promises

Chapter 4

Utopia and Privatization

Ready or not, computers are coming to the people. That's
good news, maybe the best since psychedelics.

—Stewart Brand, "SPACEWAR," 1972

I f you got hit by a bus and fell into a coma in 1975, and then woke
up two decades later, you would have thought Americans had gone
crazy or had joined a millennial cult en masse. Probably both.

In the 1990s the country was ablaze with sweeping religious
proclamations about the Internet. People talked of a great leveling—
an unstoppable wildfire that would rip through the world, consum-
ing bureaucracies, corrupt governments, coddled business elites, and
stodgy ideologies, clearing the way for a new global society that was
more prosperous and freer in every possible way. It was as if the End
Times had arrived. Utopia was at hand.

Louis Rossetto, the founder of a new, hip tech magazine called
Wired, compared computer engineers to Prometheus: they brought
gifts of the gods to us mortals that spurred "social changes so profound their only parallel is probably the discovery of fire," he wrote
in his magazine's inaugural issue.[1] Kevin Kelly, a bearded evangelical Christian and *Wired* editor, agreed with his boss: "No one can
escape the transforming fire of machines. Technology, which once

progressed at the periphery of culture, now engulfs our minds as well as our lives. As each realm is overtaken by complex techniques, the usual order is inverted, and new rules established. The mighty tumble, the once confident are left desperate for guidance, and the nimble are given a chance to prevail."[2]

It wasn't just the tech kids pushing these visions. It did not matter who you were—Republican, Democrat, liberal, or libertarian—everyone seemed to share this single, unflinching conviction: the world was on the cusp of a technology revolution that would change everything, and change it for the better.

Few embodied the early years of this new Great Awakening more than George Gilder, an old-school Reaganomics pundit who in the early 1990s reinvented himself as a techno prophet and investment guru. In his book *Telecosm,* he explained how computer networks combined with the power of American capitalism were about to create a paradise on earth. He even came up with a name for this utopia: the Telecosm. "All of the monopolies and hierarchies and pyramids and power grids of industrial society are going to dissolve before the constant pressure of distributing intelligence to the fringes of all the networks," he wrote, predicting that the power of the Internet would destroy the physical structure of society. "The telecosm can destroy cities because then you can get all the diversity, all the serendipity, all the exuberant variety that you can find in a city in your own living room."[3] Vice President Al Gore agreed, telling anyone who'd listen that the world was in the grips of a "revolution as sweeping and powerful as any revolution in history."[4]

Indeed, something was happening. People were buying personal computers and hooking them up with screeching modems to a strange new place: the World Wide Web. A labyrinth of chat rooms, forums, corporate and government networks, and an endless collection of webpages. In 1994, a start-up called Netscape appeared with an exciting new product, a web browser. A year later, the company went public and surged to a market value of $2.2 billion by the end of the first day of trading. It was the start of a new gold rush in the San Francisco Bay Area. People cheered as obscure tech companies went public on the stock market, the price of their shares doubling, even tripling on the first day. What did these companies do? What did they make? How did they make money? Few investors really knew. More importantly: no one cared! They were innovating. They were driving us forward into the future! Stocks were booming, with no end in sight. From 1995 to 2000, the NASDAQ spiked from 1,000 to 5,000, quintupling before crashing down on itself.

I was still a kid, but I remember these times well. My family had just emigrated from the Soviet Union to the United States. We left Leningrad in 1989 and spent six months bouncing around a series of refugee camps in Austria and Italy until we finally made it to New York, and then quickly relocated to San Francisco, where my father, Boris, used his incredible talent for languages to land a job as a Japanese translator. My mother, Nellie, retooled her Soviet pedagogical PhD and began to teach physics in Galileo High School, while my brother Eli and I tried to acclimate and fit in as best we could. By the time we got our bearings, the Bay Area was in peak dot-com hysteria. Everyone I knew was getting into tech and seemed to be making out like a bandit. The city was full of pimply kids driving convertibles, buying homes, and throwing lavish techno raves. My friend Leo traded his kiddie hacker skills into a high five-figure salary— real money for a teenager. Another immigrant kid I knew made a small fortune speculating on domain names. My older brother got a great job with a great salary at a mystifying start-up that pivoted half a dozen times in the span of a few years and then folded without putting out a viable product. "We had some investors from the Midwest who had no idea what the Internet was, they just heard that you needed to invest in it," he recalls. Computer games, the Internet, webpages, never-ending porn, remote commuting, distance learning, streaming movies, and music on demand: the future was here. I enrolled in community college and transferred to UC Berkeley, intent on pursuing a computer science degree.

Two decades earlier, Americans had feared computers. People, especially the young, saw them as a technocratic tool of surveillance and social control. But everything changed in the 1990s. The hippies who protested computers and the early Internet now said that this tool of oppression would liberate us from oppression! Computers were the great equalizer! They would make the world freer, fairer, more democratic and egalitarian.

It was impossible not to believe the hype. Looking back on it now, with full knowledge of the history of the Internet, I can't help but marvel at the transformation. It's as weird as waking up and seeing hippies marching for the military draft.

So, what happened? How did a technology so deeply connected to war and counterinsurgency suddenly become a one-way ticket to global utopia? It's an important question. Without it, we can't begin to understand the cultural forces that have shaped the way we view the Internet today.

In a way, it all started with a disillusioned entrepreneur named Stewart Brand.[5]

Hippies at ARPA

October 1972. It's evening, and Stewart Brand, a young, lanky free-lance journalist and photographer, is hanging out at the Stanford Artificial Intelligence Laboratory, an ARPA contractor located in the Santa Cruz mountains above the campus. And he is having a lot of fun.

He's on assignment for *Rolling Stone*, the edgy house magazine of America's counterculture, partying with a bunch of computer programmers and math geeks on ARPA's payroll. Brand is not there to inspect computerized dossiers or to press engineers about their surveillance data subroutines. He is there for fun and frivolity: to play SpaceWar, something called a "computer video game."

> Two dozen of us are jammed in a semi-dark console room just off the main hall containing AI's huge PDP-10 computer. AI's Head System Programmer and most avid Spacewar nut, Ralph Gorin, faces a display screen. Players seize the five sets of control buttons, find their spaceship persona on the screen, and

simultaneously: turn and fire toward any nearby still-helpless spaceships, hit the thrust button to initiate orbit before being slurped by the killer sun, and evade or shoot down any incoming enemy torpedoes or orbiting mines. After two torpedoes are fired, each ship has a three-second unarmed reloading time.[6]

Playing a video game against other people in real time? Back then, this was wild stuff, something most people only saw in science fiction films. Brand was transfixed. He had never heard of or experienced anything like that before. It was a mind-expanding experience. Thrilling, like taking a gigantic hit of acid.

He looked at his fellow players squeezed into that tiny, drab office and had a vision. The people around him—their bodies were stuck on earth, but their minds had been teleported to another dimension, "effectively out of their bodies, computer-projected onto cathode ray tube display screens, locked in life-or-death space combat for hours at a time, ruining their eyes, numbing their fingers in frenzied mashing of control buttons, joyously slaying their friends and wasting their employer's valuable computer time."[7]

The rest of Stanford's Artificial Intelligence Laboratory was straight out of science fiction, too. While Brand and his new buddies obsessively played the video game, one-eyed robots wandered autonomously on wheels in the background. Computer-generated music filled the air, and weird lights projected on the walls. Was this a military-funded Stanford computer lab or a psychedelic Jefferson Airplane concert? To Brand, it was both, and much more. He marveled at "a fifteen-ring circus in ten different directions" going on around him. It was "the most bzz-bzz-busy scene I've been around since Merry Prankster Acid Tests."[8]

At the time, the atmosphere around Stanford was charged with anti-ARPA sentiment. The university had just come off a wave of violent antiwar protests against military research and recruitment on campus. Activists from Students for a Democratic Society specifically targeted the Stanford Research Institute—a major ARPA contractor deeply involved in everything from the ARPANET to chemical weapons and counterinsurgency—and forced the university to cut official ties.

To many on campus, ARPA was the enemy. Brand disagreed.

In a long article he filed for *Rolling Stone,* he set out to convince the magazine's young and trend-setting readership that ARPA was not some big bureaucratic bummer connected to America's war machine but instead was part of an "astonishingly enlightened research program" that just happened to be run by the Pentagon. The people he was hanging with at the Stanford AI lab were not soulless computer engineers working for a military contractor. They were hippies and rebels, counterculture types with long hair and beards. They decorated their cubicles with psychedelic art posters and leaflets against the Vietnam War. They read Tolkien and smoked pot. They were "hackers" and "computer bums . . . full of freedom and weirdness. . . . These are heads, most of them," wrote Brand.[9]

They were cool, they were passionate, they had ideas, they were doing something, and they wanted to change the world. They might be stuck in a computer lab on a Pentagon salary, but they were not there to serve the military. They were there to bring peace to the world, not through protest or political action but through technology. He was ecstatic. "Ready or not, computers are coming to the people. That's good news, maybe the best since psychedelics," he told *Rolling Stone* readers.

And video games, as out-of-this-world cool as they were, just scratched the surface of what these groovy scientists were cooking up. With help from ARPA, they were revolutionizing computers, transforming them from giant mainframes operated by technicians into accessible tools that any person could afford and use at home. And then there was something called the ARPANET, a newfangled computer network that promised to connect people and institutions all around the world, make real-time communication and collaboration across vast distances a cinch, deliver news instantaneously, and even play music on demand. The Grateful Dead on demand? Imagine that. "So much for record stores," Stewart Brand predicted.

The way he described it, you'd think that working for ARPA was the most subversive thing a person could do.

Cults and Cybernetics

Brand was thirty-four and already a counterculture celebrity when he visited Stanford's AI Lab. He had been the publisher of the *Whole Earth Catalog*, a wildly popular lifestyle magazine for the commune movement. He ran with Ken Kesey and his LSD-dropping Merry Pranksters, and he had played a central role in setting up and promoting the psychedelic concert where the Grateful Dead debuted and rang in San Francisco's Summer of Love.[10] Brand was deeply embedded in California's counterculture and appeared as a major character in Tom Wolfe's *The Electric Kool-Aid Acid Test*. Yet there he was, acting as a pitch man for ARPA, a military agency that had in its short existence already racked up a bloody reputation—from chemical warfare to counterinsurgency and surveillance. It didn't seem to make any sense.[11]

Stewart Brand was born in Rockford, Illinois. His mother was a homemaker; his father, a successful advertising man. After graduating from an elite boarding school, Brand attended Stanford University. His diaries from the time show a young man deeply attached to his individuality and fearful of the Soviet Union. His nightmare scenario was that America would be invaded by the Red Army and that communism would take away his free will to think and do whatever he wanted. "That my mind would no longer be my own, but a tool carefully shaped by the descendants of Pavlov," he wrote in one diary entry.[12] "If there's a fight, then, I will fight. And fight with a purpose. I will not fight for America, nor for home, nor for President Eisenhower, nor for capitalism, nor even for democracy. I will fight for individualism and personal liberty. If I must be a fool, I want to be my own particular brand of fool—utterly unlike other fools. I will fight to avoid becoming a number—to others and to myself."[13]

After college, Brand enrolled in the US Army and trained as a parachutist and a photographer. In 1962, after finishing his service, he moved to the Bay Area and drifted toward the growing counterculture. He hooked up with Kesey and the Merry Pranksters, took a lot of psychedelic drugs, partied, made art, and participated in an experimental program to test the effects of LSD that, unknown to him, was secretly being conducted by the Central Intelligence Agency as part of its MK-ULTRA program.[14]

While the New Left protested against the war, joined the civil rights movement, and pushed for women's rights, Brand took a different path. He belonged to the libertarian wing of the counterculture, which tended to look down on traditional political activism and viewed all politics with skepticism and scorn. Ken Kesey, author of *One Flew Over the Cuckoo's Nest* and a spiritual leader of the hippie-libertarian movement, channeled this sensibility when he told thousands of people assembled at an anti–Vietnam War rally at UC Berkeley that their attempt to use politics to stop the war was doomed to failure. "Do you want to know how to stop the war?" he screamed. "Just turn your backs on it, fuck it!"[15]

Many did exactly that. They turned their backs, said "fuck it!" and moved out of the cities to rural America: upstate New York, New Mexico, Oregon, Vermont, western Massachusetts. They blended eastern spirituality, romantic notions of self-sufficiency, and the cybernetic ideas of Norbert Wiener. Many tended to see politics and social hierarchical structures as fundamental enemies to human harmony, and they sought to build communities free of top-down control. They did not want to reform or engage with what they saw as a corrupt old system, so they fled to the countryside and founded communes, hoping to create from scratch a new world based on a better set of ideals. They saw themselves as a new generation of pioneers settling the American frontier.

Stanford University historian Fred Turner called this wing of the counterculture the "New Communalists" and wrote a book that traced the cultural origins of this movement and the pivotal role that Stewart Brand and cybernetic ideology came to play in it. "If mainstream America had become a culture of conflict, with riots at home and war abroad, the commune world would be one of harmony. If the American state deployed massive weapons systems in order to destroy faraway peoples, the New Communalists would deploy small-scale technologies—ranging from axes and hoes to amplifiers, strobe lights, slide projectors, and LSD—to bring people together and allow them to experience their common humanity," he wrote in *From Counterculture to Cyberculture.*[16]

The commune kids were moving to the wilderness and striking out on their own. For that they needed more than just ideas. They needed tools and the most cutting-edge survival gear they could get. Brand saw opportunity. After taking an extended tour of the communes with his wife, Lious, he cashed in a part of his inheritance to launch a consumer and lifestyle guide marketed to that world. He called it the *Whole Earth Catalog.* It highlighted tools, featured discussions about science and technology, gave farming and building tips, ran letters and articles from commune members all across the country, and suggested books and literature, mixing pop libertarian titles like Ayn Rand's *Atlas Shrugged* with Wiener's *Cybernetics.*[17] "It was sort of like Google in paperback form, 35 years before Google came along," was how Steve Jobs, a young fan of the magazine, later described it. "It was idealistic, overflowing with neat tools and great notions."[18]

The mail-order L.L. Bean catalogue was what inspired Brand to create the *Whole Earth Catalog.* But it was not just about commerce. Like other New Communalists, Brand was enamored with cybernetics ideas—the notion that all life on earth was one big, harmonious interlocking information machine appealed to his sensibilities. He saw his fellow New Communalists as the start of a new society that fit into a larger global ecosystem. He wanted the *Whole Earth Catalog* to be the connective tissue that held all these isolated communes together, a kind of print magazine–based information network that everyone read and contributed to and that bound them into one collective organism.[19]

The *Whole Earth Catalog* was a huge success, and not just with the hippies. In 1971, a special issue of the magazine topped best-seller book lists and won a National Book Award. Yet, despite the cultural and financial success, Brand faced an identity crisis. By the time *Whole Earth* won the National Book Award, the commune movement it served and celebrated lay in ruins.

Years later, filmmaker Adam Curtis interviewed former members of communes in his BBC documentary *All Watched Over by*

Machines of Loving Grace. He discovered that the cybernetic structures that these groups imposed on themselves, rules that were supposed to flatten and equalize power relations among members and lead to a harmonious new society, produced the opposite result and, ultimately, ripped many of the communities apart.[20]

"We were trying to create a society based on understanding eco-systems, a society based on interrelationships and balance—a man machine biological system working in combination," recalled Randall Gibson, a member of the Synergia commune in New Mexico that ran on a cybernetic notion he called eco-technics.[21] The community had strict rules against collective action or organization. Members had to resolve problems and conflicts through "connection sessions," where two people carried out one-on-one discussions in full view of the commune but could not solicit support or backing from anyone else. "The idea of eco-technics is simply that you are part of the system in which there would be less, if not no hierarchy at all," Gibson said. Ultimately, these connection sessions descended into something darker: exercises in shaming, bullying, and control, where dominant members took advantage of weaker and meeker members. "In practice these would be 20-and 30-minute hazing sessions and were usually met by silence with the rest of one's peers."[22]

Other communes went through similar transformations, morphing from upbeat youthful experiments into repressive environments and, often, straight-up personality cults. "There was fear actually because the people who were more dominating—there was anger. There was constantly a background of fear in the house—like a virus running in the background. Like spyware. You know it's there but you don't know how to get rid of it," said Molly Hollenback, a member of a commune called The Family in Taos, New Mexico.[23] Formed by students from UC Berkeley in 1967, The Family quickly transformed into a rigid hierarchy, with men addressed with titles like "sir" and "Lord," and women forced to wear skirts and assigned conservative gender-based work: cooking, child care, and washing. A founding member who called himself Lord Byron presided over the group and reserved the right to have sex with any woman in the commune.[24]

Most communes lasted only a few years, and some less than that. "What tore them all apart was the very thing that they were supposed to have banished: power," explained Adam Curtis. "Strong personality came to dominate the weaker members of the group, but the rules of a self-organizing system refused to allow any organized opposition to this oppression." In the end, what were supposed to be experiments in freedom and new utopian societies simply replicated and magnified the structural inequality of the outside world that people brought with them.

But Stewart Brand did not admit defeat, nor did he try to understand why the cybernetic-libertarian ideology underpinning the experiment failed so spectacularly. He simply transferred the utopian ideas of the mythical commune into something that had long fascinated him: the rapidly growing computer industry.

Rebranding Stewart Brand

On the surface, the worlds of ARPA and military computer research and the drugged-out hippie commune scene of the 1960s could not be more different. Indeed, they seemed to occupy different solar systems. One had uniforms, stuffy suits, pocket protectors, thoughts of war, punch cards, and rigid hierarchies. The other had long hair, free love, drugs, far-out music, hostility to authority, and a scrappy and ragged existence.

But the differences were superficial. On a deeper level, the two scenes operated on the same cybernetic wavelength and overlapped on multiple fronts. J. C. R Licklider, Ithiel de Sola Pool, and other ARPA and military engineers were deploying cybernetic ideas to build computer networks, while dreaming of building prediction technology to run the world and manage political strife out of existence. The hippies were doing the same with their cybernetic communes. Except, where ARPA and the military were industrial and global, communes were small-scale, boutique.

There were direct connections as well. Take the Stanford

Research Institute (SRI), a major ARPA contractor working on everything from counterinsurgency and chemical warfare to running an important ARPANET node and research center. Several SRI staffers were close friends of Stewart Brand and active contributors to the *Whole Earth Catalog*.[25] Brand frequently hung around at SRI and even consulted for the institute on a 1968 demonstration of the interactive computer technology Douglas Englebart's Augmentation Research Center had developed under an ARPA contract.[26] The event featured real-time video conferencing and collaborative document editing carried over the ARPANET, which was then only two months old.[27] And then there was Engelbart himself. The engineer and interactive computing guru was a favorite of Licklider's and received millions in ARPA funding. At the same time, he experimented with LSD and dosed other computer engineers with acid to see whether it made them more efficient and creative. He also went on a tour of various communes and was highly supportive of the movement's attempt to create new forms of decentralized societies.[28]

The feeling was mutual. The Bay Area hippie counterculture scene lived and breathed the cybernetic ideas pumped out by America's military-industrial complex. Richard Brautigan, a shaggy-haired writer with a droopy mustache who lived in San Francisco, composed an ode to the coming cybernetic utopia that demonstrates the spiritual closeness of these two seemingly contradictory worlds. Published in 1967 and titled "All Watched Over by Machines of Loving Grace," the poem describes a world in which computers merge with nature to create a kind of altruistic god-like being that would take care of us all—a world "where mammals and computers / live together in mutually / programming harmony / like pure water / touching clear sky."[29] Brautigan handed his poem out on Height Street, the epicenter of the counterculture movement. Naturally, Brand was a fan of Brautigan and published his work in the *Whole Earth Catalog*. "Richard could not code. I'm not sure he knew any computers personally," Brand would later recall. You didn't need to be a programmer to believe.

There was deep sympathy and close ties between the two worlds, and Stewart Brand took it further. In the early 1980s, after the commune dream collapsed, he cashed in his counterculture cred and turned the utopian ideals of the New Communalists into a marketing vehicle for the sprouting consumer computer industry. He was instrumental to the cause. Like an experienced midwife, he guided the birth of this industry's growing sense of self-importance and cultural relevance. He was shrewd. He understood that the Bay Area sat atop a major economic and cultural fault line. The tectonic plates were shifting and trembling and sending off shockwaves. The whole place felt overdue for a monster quake that would restructure society in a major way, spawning new industries, new businesses, a new politics, and a radically new culture. He really believed it, and he helped a new class of computer entrepreneurs see themselves as he saw them— as counterculture rebels and heroes. He then helped them sell that image to the rest of the world.

In this new role, Brand was still a utopian idealist, but he was also an entrepreneur. "I'm a small-business man who is hit with the same kind of problems that face any small entrepreneur," he told *Newsweek* magazine.[30] Over the coming years, as personal computers gained traction, he gathered around himself a crew of journalists, marketing types, industry insiders, and other hippies-turned-entrepreneurs. Together, they replicated the marketing and aesthetics that Brand had used during his *Whole Earth Catalog* days and sold computers the same way he once sold communes and psychedelics: as liberation technologies and tools of personal empowerment. This group would spin this mythology through the 1980s and 1990s, helping obfuscate the military origins of computer and networking technologies by dressing them up in the language of 1960s acid-dropping counterculture. In this rebranded world, computers were the new communes: a digital frontier where the creation of a better world was still possible.

In the parlance of today's Silicon Valley, Brand "pivoted." He transformed the *Whole Earth Catalog* into the *Whole Earth Software Catalog* and *Whole Earth Review*—magazines billed as "tools and ideas for the computer age." He also launched the Good Business Network, a corporate consulting company that applied his counterculture public relations strategies to problems faced by clients such as Shell Oil, Morgan Stanley, Bechtel, and DARPA.[31] He also organized an influential computer conference that brought together leading computer engineers and journalists.[32] It was called, simply, "Hackers' Conference" and was held in Marin County in 1984. About 150 of the country's top computer geniuses attended, including Apple's Steve Wozniak. Brand cleverly stage-managed the event to give the group maximum cultural cachet. To hear him and other believers tell it, the event was the "Woodstock of the computer elite!" Newspaper accounts regaled readers with tales of strange nerds with fantastical visions of the future. "Giving a computer self-hood. The greatest hack is artificial consciousness," one attendee told a *Washington Post* reporter. "My vision of hacking is a fuzzy little intelligent creature growing inside each machine," quipped another.[33]

A PBS film crew was on site to shoot a documentary and capture Brand's role in bringing these hackers together. He was not the young man who launched *Whole Earth Catalog* two decades earlier. His face showed his age and he sported a shiny, bald pate, but he still had the fire in him. He wore a black-and-white plaid shirt under a sheepskin vest and waxed lyrical about the rebellious nature of those gathered there in Marin.[34] "They are shy, sweet, incredibly brilliant and I think more effective in pushing the culture around in good ways than almost any group I can think of." Off camera, he took to the pages of his *Whole Earth Review* to further expound on the rebel nature of computer programmers. "I think hackers—innovative, irreverent computer programmers—are the most interesting and effective body of intellectuals since the framers of the U.S. Constitution," he wrote in an introduction to a photo spread of the 1984 Hackers' Conference. "No other group that I know of has set out to liberate a technology and succeeded. . . . High tech is now something that mass consumers do, rather than just have done to them, and that's a hot item in the world." He added, "The quietest of the '60s sub-subcultures has emerged as the most innovative and most powerful—and most suspicious of power."[35]

The Hackers' Conference was a big moment in the cultural history of Silicon Valley. It helped introduce computer programmers to the public in a totally different way. These were no longer engineers working for big corporations and military contractors but "hackers"—geniuses and rebels bucking the system. Although Brand was an important figure driving this change of perception, he was not operating in isolation but represented a bigger cultural sea change.

The year 1984 was a big and symbolic one for the computer industry beyond Brand's Hackers' Conference. That year, William Gibson published *Neuromancer,* a science fiction novel about a drug-addled hacker battling his way through a dangerous virtual reality cybernetic world run by frightening corporations and their godlike supercomputers. It was a world of no rules, no laws, only power and cleverness. Gibson meant it to be a metaphor for the growth of unrestrained corporate power at a time when poverty and inequality spiked under President Ronald Reagan—a science fiction experiment of what would happen if this trend ran to its natural conclusion. *Neuromancer* coined the term *cyberspace.* It also launched the cyberpunk movement, which responded to Gibson's political critique in a cardinally different manner: it cheered the coming of this cyber dystopia. Computers and hackers were countercultural rebels taking on power. They were cool.

That same year, Apple Computer released its "1984" ad for the Macintosh. Directed by Ridley Scott, who had just wowed audiences with the dystopian hit *Blade Runner,* and aired during the Super Bowl, Apple's message could not have been more clear: forget what you know about IBM or corporate mainframes or military computer systems. With Apple at the helm, personal computers are the opposite of what they used to be: they are not about domination and control but about individual rebellion and empowerment. "In a striking departure from the direct, buy-this-product approach of most American corporations, Apple Computer introduced its new line of personal computers with the provocative claim that Macintosh would help save the world from the lockstep society of George

Orwell's novel," reported the *New York Times*.[36] Interestingly, the paper pointed out that the "1984" ad had grown out of another campaign that the company had abandoned but that had explicitly talked about the ability to misuse computers. A draft of that campaign read: "True enough, there are monster computers lurking in big business and big government that know everything from what motels you've stayed at to how much money you have in the bank. But at Apple we're trying to balance the scales by giving individuals the kind of computer power once reserved for corporations."

Apple cofounder and CEO Steve Jobs was a huge Stewart Brand fan.[37] He was just a kid in the late 1960s when the magazine and commune culture were at their peak of popularity and power, but he read the *Whole Earth Catalog* and absorbed its culture into his own worldview. So it wasn't surprising that the original Apple ad campaign that hinted at computers as corporate and government monsters was left in the Dumpster while Brand's view of personal computers as a technology of freedom prevailed.

Stewart Brand offered a powerful vision that was planted deep in the American psyche. His push to rebrand military computer technology as liberation coincided with a less visible force: the gradual privatization of the ARPANET and the creation of a global commercial Internet.

The Man Who Privatized the Internet

It was sometime in 1986 when Stephen Wolff walked into the offices of the National Science Foundation on 1800 G Street in Washington, DC, just two blocks from the White House..

Like most people involved in the early Internet, Wolff was a military man. Tall and skinny, with a calm, reassuring voice, he spent the 1970s working on the ARPANET at the US Army Ballistic Research Lab at the Aberdeen Proving Ground, a chunk of lush marshland and forest jutting into the Chesapeake Bay about thirty-five miles north of Baltimore. Aberdeen, now closed, enjoyed a long and storied history. It was established during World War I and tasked with developing and testing field artillery and heavy weapons: cannons, air defense guns, ammunition, trench mortars, and bombs. Norbert Wiener served there as a precomputer human calculator, working out ballistic trajectories for the massive guns being developed. During World War II, it was the birthplace of America's first fully digital and electronic computer, the ENIAC. In the 1960s, Aberdeen was connected to something a bit spookier: a series of "limited war laboratory" experiments in which the US Army Chemical Corps deployed mind-bending drugs—including LSD and the nightmare super-hallucinogen known as BZ, which could put a person into a hallucinatory coma lasting days—as chemical weapons.[38]

Stephen Wolff's job at Aberdeen in the 1970s involved working on the ARPANET and linking it with the US Army's network of supercomputers.[39] In 1986, the National Science Foundation's Networking Office hired him to do the same thing, but with a major twist: he was to build a government-funded network that extended the ARPANET design into the civilian world, and then spin this network off to the private sector.[40] In the end, Wolff oversaw the creation and privatization of the Internet.

When I spoke to Wolff, I asked, "Is it right to call you the man who privatized the Internet?"

"Yes, that is a fair assessment," he replied.[41]

Even before Stephen Wolff arrived at the National Science Foundation, it was clear ARPANET's days were numbered. In 1975, the Pentagon had officially relieved ARPA of its responsibilities for running the network and placed it under the direct control of the Defense Communication Agency. The army, navy, air force, and National Security Agency had all started building out their own networks based on ARPANET technology. They maintained links to the original ARPANET infrastructure, but the physical network, with its limited 56K modem speeds, was beginning to show its age. The experiment had been a success, but as the 1980s approached, it looked as if the original ARPANET was going to be dumped in the trash.

The network had become obsolete, but the technology and framework on which it ran were only getting started. Many of the original ARPANET architects and designers cashed in on their ARPA experience in trade for lucrative private sector jobs in the rapidly growing computer networking industry; others remained at the Pentagon, pushing and evangelizing for a wider adoption of the ARPANET network design. Many were eager to see the original ARPANET grow beyond military circles and into a commercial network that everyone could use.[42] The National Science Foundation (NSF), a federal agency created by Congress in 1950 with a mission to "promote the progress of science" and "secure the national defense," was the vehicle that would ultimately get the job done.

In the early 1980s, the NSF ran a small network that connected a handful of university computer science departments to the ARPANET. By 1985, administrators wanted to expand the project into a bigger, faster network that would connect a larger pool of universities, extending the ARPANET out of purely military and computer science circles and making it available to all academic and educational users.[43] On the basis of his decade of experience connecting US Army supercomputers to the ARPANET at Aberdeen, Wolff was brought on to build and manage this new educational network project—called the NSFNET.

The first version of the NSFNET came online in 1986. It was a modest effort, connecting supercomputer centers at five universities funded by the NSF, wiring them together so they could share data, and plugging them into a wider set of universities connected to the old military ARPANET. The network was limited in scope, but demand for it was so high that it crashed the system. Its puny leased lines had the combined throughput of a slow modem and could not handle the swell of users. Clearly, the NSFNET needed a major upgrade and more bandwidth. The question was: What would this new network look like?

The answer came quickly.

"Starting with the inauguration of the NSFNET program in 1985, we had the hope that it would grow to include every college and university in the country," recalled Wolff in an interview.[44] "But the notion of trying to administer a three-thousand-node network from Washington—well, there wasn't that much hubris inside the Beltway."

Hubris, indeed. This was the height of the Reagan era, a time of privatization and deregulation, when public ownership of vital infrastructure was considered a barbaric relic that had no place in the modern world; if anything, it needed to be lanced like a boil. Everything was being deregulated and privatized—from the banking sector to telecommunications and broadcast industries. Wolff and his team at the NSF, like the obedient public servants that they were, toed the line.

In early 1987, he and his team finally hashed out a design for an improved and upgraded NFSNET. This new network, a government project created with public money, would connect universities and be designed to eventually function as a privatized telecommunications system. That was the implicit understanding everyone at NSF agreed on. They viewed the public nature of the NSFNET as a transitory state: a small government pollywog that would transition into a commercial bullfrog. According to specs, the new NSFNET would be built as a two-tier network. The top layer would be a national network, a high-speed "backbone" that spanned the entire country. The second layer would be made up of smaller "regional networks" that would connect universities to the backbone. Instead of building and managing the network itself, the NSF would outsource the network to a handful of private companies. The plan was to fund and nurture these network providers until they could become self-sufficient, at which point they would be cut loose and allowed to privatize the network infrastructure they built for the NSFNET.

Later in 1987, the NSF awarded contracts for its upgraded NSF-NET design. The most important part of the system, the backbone, was run by a new nonprofit corporation, a consortium including IBM, MCI, and the state of Michigan.[45] The second-tier regional networks were farmed out to a dozen other newly created private consortiums. With names like BARRNET, MIDNET, NYSERNET, WEST-NET, and CERFNET, they were run by a mix of universities, research institutions, and military contractors.[46]

In July 1988, the NSFNET backbone went online, connecting thirteen regional networks and over 170 different campuses across the country.[47] The physical network ran on MCI's T-1 lines capable of transmitting 1.54 megabits per second and was routed through data switches built by IBM. The network stretched from San Diego to Princeton—snaking through regional network exchange points in Salt Lake City, Houston, Boulder, Lincoln, Champaign, Ann Arbor, Atlanta, Pittsburgh, and Ithaca and throwing out an international transatlantic line to the European Organization for Nuclear Research in Geneva.[48] The network was a huge success in the academic community.[49]

Even as demand surged, NSF managers began the privatization process. "We told them: 'You guys will eventually have to go out and find other customers. We don't have enough money to support the regionals forever.' So they did," Wolff explained. "We tried . . . to ensure that the regionals kept their books straight and to make sure that the taxpayers weren't directly subsidizing commercial activities. But out of necessity, we forced the regionals to become general-purpose network providers."[50]

Telling NSFNET providers to diversify their client base by seeking commercial clients—it seems like a minor decision. Yet, it is a crucial detail that had a huge impact, allowing the agency a few years later to quietly and quickly privatize the Internet while making it seem like the transition was inevitable and even natural. People on the inside understood the gravity of what Wolff and the NSF were doing. They saw it as a kind of clever trick, a sleight of hand.

Vinton Cerf, who in 1982 had left his job at ARPA to head up MCI's networking division, described Wolff's private-public network provider scheme as "brilliant." He said, "The creation of those regional nets and the requirement that they become self-funding was the key to the evolution of the current Internet."[51]

Cerf is right. The Internet is perhaps one of the most valuable public inventions of the twentieth century, and decisions made by a few key unelected officials in the federal bureaucracy set the Internet on the certain path to privatization. There was no real public debate, no discussion, no dissension, and no oversight. It was just given away, before anyone outside this bureaucratic bubble realized what was at stake.

The privatization of the Internet—its transformation from a military network to the privatized telecommunications system we use today—is a convoluted story. Wade in deep enough and you find yourself in a swamp of three-letter federal agencies, network protocol acronyms, government initiatives, and congressional hearings filled with technical jargon and mind-numbing details. But on a fundamental level, it was all very simple: after two decades of lavish funding and research and development inside the Pentagon system, the Internet was transformed into a consumer profit center. Businesses wanted a cut, and a small crew of government managers were all too happy to oblige. To do that, with public funds the federal government created a dozen network providers out of thin air and then spun them off to the private sector, building companies that in the space of a decade would become integral parts of the media and telecommunications conglomerates we all know and use today—Verizon, Time-Warner, AT&T, Comcast.

But how did it happen exactly? Unravelling the tale requires looking at the first privatized NSFNET provider: a consortium led by IBM and MCI.[52]

The National Science Foundation functioned on an educational mandate and could support only initiatives that had an education dimension. Legally, NSFNET contractors were not allowed to route their commercial traffic through the government-funded network. These terms were baked into the federal agency's "Acceptable Use Policy" contract, and they were quite clear. How could the network be privatized if it couldn't route commercial traffic? Later, the NSF managers claimed that NSFNET providers didn't violate these terms and that they routed commercial traffic through separate, privately built network infrastructure. But a backroom deal the NSF made with its backbone operator shows that the truth is a bit murkier.

In 1990, the MCI-IBM consortium, with approval from NSF, split into two corporate entities: a nonprofit called Advanced Network Services and a for-profit confusingly named ANS CO+RE Systems. Advanced Network Services—ANS—continued to contract with the NSF to maintain and run the physical NSFNET backbone. Meanwhile, its for-profit division, ANS CO+RE, sold commercial network services to business clients on a new network it called the ANSNET.[53] Of course, this new ANSNET ran on the exact same physical network infrastructure that powered the NSFNET. Legally, though, the two—NSFNET and ANSNET—were treated as completely separate entities by the National Science Foundation, which meant that despite the Acceptable Use Policy that forbade commercial traffic on the NSFNET, the IBM-MCI consortium had a green light to do just that for profit.[54] It was a clever maneuver. On a basic level, it allowed the MCI-IBM consortium to double book the same asset, pocketing government money to run the NSFNET and then selling this same network to commercial clients. More fundamentally, it allowed a corporate entity with a direct stake in the business of computer networking to privatize a government asset without doing so explicitly. That's exactly how executives at MCI-IBM's newly formed ANS division saw it: "[We] have privatized the NSFNET," the president of ANS bragged at a networking industry workshop at Harvard in 1990.[55]

This public-private flip was not announced to the public, and it was also hidden from other NSFNET providers. When they finally discovered the existence of this sly deal a year later, they raised alarm and accused the agency of privatizing the network to a favored corporate insider. Some called for a congressional investigation into what they saw as mismanagement and possibly fraud. "It's like taking a Federal park and giving it to K Mart. It's not right," a manager of a large NSFNET provider told the *New York Times*.[56]

They had a right to be upset. This backbone privatization deal gave a powerful company a privileged position that allowed it to quickly dominate the budding commercial networking market, frequently at the expense of other regional NSFNET providers.[57] The key to this advantage was the NSFNET backbone itself. Built and sustained with government funds, the network spanned the width of the United States and had connections to more than thirty other countries. Regional networks, on the other hand, were smaller, usually restricted to geographic areas like Greater New York, the Midwest, or northern California. Those that expanded into the national commercial market could not route commercial traffic through the NSFNET backbone but had to build their own private networks without government funding. In short, the NSF directly subsidized the MCI-IBM consortium's national business expansion. The company used its privileged position to attract commercial clients, telling them that its service was better and faster because it had direct access to the national high-speed backbone.[58]

Stephen Wolff understood that backing a telecommunications company like MCI could lead to a situation where a handful of powerful corporations controlled the newly created Internet, but he brushed those dangers aside. As Wolff explained in an interview at the time, his main objective was to bring a viable commercial Internet into existence. Regulating fairness and competitive practices was someone else's job.[59] On a very basic level, he was right. His objective was just to build a network, not regulate it. The problem was that by building a privatized network, he was also building an industry and, by extension, laying down the basic rules that governed and regulated this industry. These were intertwined.[60]

Wolff's laissez-faire management style triggered an outcry among the smaller regional NSFNET providers. There were accusations of conflict of interest, insider dealings, favoritism. William Schrader, president of a New York area provider called PSINET, charged the NSF pointblank with granting a monopoly over government assets to a single privileged corporation. "The Government has privatized the ownership of a federal resource," he said at a 1992 congressional hearing held to investigate possible government mismanagement of the NSFNET. "The privatization unnecessarily provided the contractor [IBM-MCI] with an exclusive monopoly position to use Federal resources paid by taxpayer funds."[61]

Schrader's PSINET banded together with other regional NSF-NET providers to push the government to end MCI-IBM's privilege and to finally open the network to unrestricted commercial traffic. "A level playing field can only be built by changing current NSF policies which favor one competitor," Schrader told Congress.[62]

Schrader wasn't contesting the privatization itself. Why would he? His own company, PSINET, had also been spun off from a regional NSFNET provider seeded with federal money as a for-profit entity.[63] Like IBM-MCI's ANS, PSINET represented a de facto privatization of a government-subsidized asset by a few privileged insiders who happened to be at the right place at the right time. Schrader didn't challenge that. What he opposed was the NSF giving a different—and perhaps more powerful—group of privileged insiders more privilege than his company had received. This was a spat between competing government-subsidized networking companies in an industry created by the government. It was not a fight about privatization. It was a scrabble over how to divvy up the future profits in an emerging market worth billions.

In the mid-1980s, while Stephen Wolff was planning the NSFNET upgrade, the United States was in the grips of two closely related computer technology booms: the explosion of cheap personal computers and easy access to computer networking. First, IBM released a powerful personal computer and licensed the design so that any computer manufacturer could make compatible IBM computer components. A few years later, in 1984, Apple released the Macintosh, complete with a graphical user interface and mouse. Microsoft's text-based DOS operating system for IBM computers was followed by a crude version of Windows. Computers were suddenly easy to use and affordable. It wasn't just giant corporations, big universities, and government and military agencies anymore—smaller businesses and geeky middle-class early adopters could all get their own systems. It quickly became apparent that the true power of the personal computer was not personal at all, but social. Computers allowed people to tap into remote servers and connect with other computers, communicating and sharing information with people hundreds and thousands of miles away. Hundreds of thousands of people brought their computers home, plugged in their modems, and connected to a weird and early form of the Internet.

A few select companies had been providing ARPANET-like access to large corporations since the 1970s. But, in the late 1980s, all sorts of dial-up and networking services popped up across the country. There were big firms like CompuServe, Prodigy, and America Online as well as hundreds of smaller outfits. Some, no more than dial-up messaging boards, were run as hobbies on servers set up in basements and garages. Others were small businesses that served up a series of features: forums, chat rooms, email, rudimentary computer games, and news.[64] All of them were text-based and simple, a shadow of the real Internet that would emerge later, but they were extremely popular. Even Stewart Brand got onboard. He cofounded an early message board called The Well, which provided a forum and online meeting place for his vast network of hippie business associates, artists, writers, and journalists. The Well became popular very quickly, turning into a social hub for the up-and-coming "digirati"—Bay Area opinion makers, entrepreneurs, authors, hackers, and journalists who came to the fore in the 1990s to shape digital culture.

This was not the globally connected Internet we know today. Services like The Well and America Online were not connected to one another and allowed communication only between members of the same service. Effectively, they were siloed, at least for a time. Everyone in the industry understood that this was going to be a huge and extremely profitable industry, and that some kind of national network would connect it all. "It was no secret that whatever the network was then, it was going to become a big commercial success at some point. Nobody ever doubted that," Wolff told me in an interview.[65]

Indeed, NSFNET contractors began fighting for control of this untapped and growing market as soon as Stephen Wolff gave them the green light to privatize their operations—that's what the fight between providers like PSINET and ANS was all about. They were licking their chops, happy that the government bankrolled the network and even happier that it was about to get out of the business. There was a lot of money to be made. Indeed, by the end of the 1990s, Schrader's humble PSINET had customers in twenty-eight countries and was worth $3 billion on the NASDAQ.[66]

I asked Stephen Wolff about the stealth privatization of the Internet, wanting to know how it was possible that a decision of such magnitude was carried out with no input from the public or discussions about what it would entail. It was shocking to me that one person, or even a group of people, would have that much power.

Aside from interindustry wrangling, there was no real opposition to Stephen Wolff's plan to privatize the Internet—not from NFSNET insiders, not from Congress, and certainly not from the private sector.[67] "I had people working for me, and we all agreed this was the way to go," Wolff said. "There wasn't any conflict there."[68] In fact, the opposite was true. Whether inside or outside the NSF, it seemed everyone supported this plan.

Cable and phone companies pushed for privatization, as did Democrats and Republicans in Congress.[69] "There was little public debate or opposition to the privatization of the NSFNET," write Jay Kesan and Rajiv Shah in their detailed dissection of the Internet privatization process, "Fool Us Once Shame on You—Fool Us Twice Shame on Us." "By the early 1990s, telecommunications policy for both political parties was based upon notions of deregulation and competition. At numerous junctures before the privatization of the NSFNET, politicians and telecommunication executives made it clear that the private sector would own and operate the Internet."[70]

Senator Daniel Inouye, a Democrat from Hawaii, was one of the few elected officials in Washington who objected to this wholesale privatization. He wanted to soften the push for privatization with a proposal that would reserve 20 percent of future Internet capacity for noncommercial use by nonprofits, local community groups, and other public-benefit groups.[71] His reasoning was that because the federal government had funded the creation of this network, it should be able to reserve a small part for the public. But his modest proposal was no match for the industry lobbying and the privatization fervor of his colleagues in the Congress.

In 1995, the National Science Foundation officially retired the NSF-NET, handing control of the Internet to a handful of private network providers that it had created less than a decade earlier. There was no vote in Congress on the issue.[72] There was no public referendum or discussion. It happened by bureaucratic decree, and Stephen Wolff's government-funded privatized design of the network made the privatization seem seamless and natural.

A year later, President Bill Clinton signed the Telecommunications Act of 1996, a law that deregulated the telecommunications industry, allowing for the first time since the New Deal nearly unlimited corporate cross-ownership of the media: cable companies, radio stations, film studios, newspapers, phone companies, television broadcasters, and, of course, Internet service providers.[73] The law triggered massive consolidation, culminating in just a handful of vertically integrated companies owning the bulk of the American media market. "This law is truly revolutionary legislation that will bring the future to our doorstep," President Clinton declared when he signed the act.

A handful of powerful telecommunications companies absorbed most of the privatized NSFNET providers that had been set up with funds from the National Science Foundation a decade earlier. San Francisco Bay Area's regional provider became part of Verizon. Southern California's, which was part-owned by the military contractor General Atomics, was absorbed by AT&T. New York's became part of Cogent Communications, one of the largest backbone companies in the world. The backbone went to Time-Warner. And MCI, which had run the backbone along with IBM, merged with

WorldCom, combining two of the biggest Internet service providers in the world.[74]

All these mergers represented the corporate centralization of a powerful new telecommunications system that had been created by the military and ushered into commercial life by the National Science Foundation.[75] To put it another way, the Internet was born.[76]

Amid all this consolidation, a new tech publication appeared on the scene, one that grafted the utopian ideals of Stewart Brand's cybernetic communes to the free-market fervor of the 1990s. It helped sell this emerging privatized Internet as a true countercultural political revolution: it called itself *Wired*.

Whole Earth 2.0

Louis Rossetto, a lanky preppy with a Patrick Swayze haircut, started *Wired* in 1993. Rossetto grew up in Long Island in a conservative Catholic family. His father, Louis Rossetto Sr., was an executive at a printing company and had worked in missile development and weapons production during World War II.[77] The younger Rossetto enrolled at Columbia University in the late 1960s and was there during the student protests against the Vietnam War and ARPA's militarization of academic research.[78] He watched as his fellow students occupied buildings and clashed violently with police, but he didn't share their zeal.[79] Rossetto was on the opposite side of the barricades. He was against the left-wing antiwar politics that dominated New York's radical student circles. He was president of Columbia's College Republicans and a diehard Richard Nixon supporter.

All the political activity on campus and the increasingly violent nature of the protests only made him move further to the right: to Ayn Rand, libertarian anarchism, and the ideas of nineteenth-century antigovernment fundamentalists and Social Darwinists. He coauthored an essay in the *New York Times Magazine* that explained the philosophy of libertarianism and criticized the New Left's focus on wealth redistribution and democratic reforms. To him, this kind of expansive government was the enemy.[80] Among his heroes were Ayn Rand and Karl Hess III, former speechwriter for Senator Barry M. Goldwater who rebranded himself as a radical libertarian and saw computer technology as the ultimate antigovernment weapon: "Instead of learning how to make bombs, revolutionaries should master computer programming," he told a journalist in 1970.[81]

Rossetto did not heed Hess's advice. Instead, he enrolled in a business program at Columbia, graduated, dreamed of becoming a novelist, and then spent the next decade drifting around the world. For a man with right-wing libertarian tendencies, Rossetto sure had a penchant for showing up in places with left-wing insurgencies: he was in Sri Lanka for the Tamil rebellion and appeared in Peru just in time for the Maoist Shining Path insurgency. He also managed to hang out with mujahedeen in Afghanistan and filed glowing reports in the *Christian Science Monitor* on their fight against the Soviet Union with American-made weapons.[82] Rossetto traveled to the war zone by hitching a ride in a pickup with jihadi fighters.[83]

Amid all this, he found a job writing editorials for a small investment firm in Paris; met his future partner Jane Metcalfe, who hailed from an old family in Louisville, Kentucky; and launched an early tech magazine called *Electric Word* that was funded by a Dutch translation software company.[84] The magazine went out of business, but during his time there Rossetto got in touch with Stewart Brand and his crew of Bay Area tech boosters. Contact with this influential subculture made him realize that the world lacked a solid technology lifestyle magazine. He was intent on bringing one to life.

In 1991, Rossetto and Metcalfe moved to New York to start up the magazine, but all their stateside business and investor leads fizzled. For some reason, they couldn't drum up excitement. The computer and networking industries were on fire in the Bay Area, yet no one wanted to back their project. No one, that is, except one man: Nicholas Negroponte, a wealthy engineer and businessman who had spent more than two decades working for ARPA.

Negroponte came from an affluent, highly connected family. His father was a Greek shipping magnate. His older brother, John

Negroponte, was a career diplomat and Reagan administration official who had just finished a stint as the highly controversial ambassador to Honduras, where he was accused of playing a central role in a covert CIA-backed counterinsurgency campaign against the left-wing Sandinista government in neighboring Nicaragua.[85]

Nicholas Negroponte, like his older brother, was also connected to America's military-intelligence apparatus, but from a slightly different angle. He was a longtime ARPA contractor and had worked on a variety of military computer initiatives at MIT.[86] He had been a prominent member of the ARPANET Cambridge Project. He also ran his own ARPA-funded research outfit at MIT called the Machine Architecture Group (MAG).[87]

MAG did all kinds of research for the military. It worked on video conferencing technology that would enable the president and his top generals, scattered across the country in underground bunkers, to interact with each other in a natural manner in the event of a nuclear war.[88] It developed an interactive "video map" of Aspen, Colorado, an experimental virtual reality environment that could be used to practice military raids.[89] Perhaps MAG's creepiest experiment involved creating a robotic maze populated by gerbils. The project, called SEEK, was a giant cage filled with light blocks that the animals would bump into and shift as they moved through the environment. A computer watched the scene and deployed a robotic arm to reorganize the shifted blocks and place them into spots it "thought" the animals wanted them to be in. The idea was to create a computer-mediated dynamic environment—a "cybernetic world model"—that changed according to the demands and wishes of the gerbils.[90]

In 1985, Negroponte pivoted Machine Architecture Group into something cooler and more in line with the personal computer revolution: the MIT Media Lab, a hub that connected business, military contracting, and university research. He aggressively pursued corporate sponsorship, trying to find ways to commercialize and cash in on the development of the computer, networking, and graphics technology that he had been developing for ARPA. For a hefty annual membership fee, sponsors gained access to all the technology developed at the Media Lab without having to pay licensing fees. It was a runaway success. Just two years after opening its doors, the Media Lab racked up a huge list of corporate sponsors. Every major American newspaper and television network was part of the club, as were major automobile and computer companies, including General Motors, IBM, Apple, Sony, Warner Brothers, and HBO.[91] ARPA, which by that time had rebranded as DARPA, was a major sponsor as well.[92]

The MIT Media Lab was a big sensation at the time—so much so that Stewart Brand practically begged Negroponte for a chance to hang out there. In 1986, he was given an opportunity to spend a year at the Media Lab as a "visiting scientist." Later, he published a book about Negroponte and the cutting-edge technology his lab ushered into the world. It reads like marketing copy, giddy for a world of computer gadgets, virtual reality, artificial intelligence, and globe-encompassing computer networks. Brand described Negroponte as a "visionary" singularly driven to "invent the future," and he helped cement Negroponte's status as a rebellious High Tech Priest, who straddled the worlds of big corporations and big governments but transcended them both.

In the early 1990s, when Rossetto and Metcalfe were desperate for investors for their tech lifestyle magazine, Negroponte was one of the most respected and sought-after computer visionaries in the world. So, in 1992, armed with a mockup issue of *Wired* and a business plan, Rossetto and Metcalfe cornered him at the $1,000-a-head Technology, Entertainment, and Design Conference—today known as TED—in Monterey, California. They made their pitch, and to their surprise, Negroponte was impressed and agreed to help them get funding. He lined up meetings with Ted Turner and Rupert Murdoch, but neither expressed much interest. In the end, Negroponte decided to back the project on his own. He provided $75,000 of seed capital in return for a 10 percent stake. It was a paltry amount for a huge chunk of the business, but Rossetto and Metcalfe agreed. They smartly saw the opportunity: Nicholas Negroponte was a huge name with deep connections to the highest echelons of business, academia, and government. They bet that Negroponte would help prime the investment pump, with his money and involvement brining in other big players who would be willing to invest far greater sums in *Wired*. They were right. After he came on board, investment money flowed in like water.

To help him craft the new magazine, Rossetto hired Stewart Brand's old apprentice as *Wired*'s founding executive editor: Kevin Kelly. Pudgy, with an Amish-style beard, Kelly had worked for Stewart Brand in the late 1980s, just as the aging counterculture promoter was beginning to push his publishing business away from communes and into the booming personal computer industry. Kelly was an energetic and eager acolyte, a man ripe for a righteous mission.

The son of a *Time* magazine executive, Kelly spent most of the 1970s backpacking around the world. In 1979, while he was traveling through Israel, he had a divine vision. By his own account, he was locked out of his hotel and was forced to wander around Jerusalem at night. He fell asleep on a stone slab inside the Church of the Holy Sepulcher and upon waking had a religious vision in which he realized that Jesus was the son of God and had come back from the dead as humanity's savior. "In the end, it comes down to a decision that one makes. You go down one road and within that road, everything makes complete sense," Kelly later said of his conversion experience. "I think that is sort of what I did. It took going to Jerusalem on Easter morning out to the empty tombs to really trigger an acceptance of this alternative view. Once I accepted it, there is a logic, comfort, leverage that I have because of that view."[93]

Leverage is a good word for Kelly's sudden religious inspiration. His faith in God matched his faith in the power of technological progress, which he saw as a part of God's divine plan for the world. Over the years, he developed the belief that the growth of the Internet, the gadgetization and computerization of everything around us, the ultimate melding of flesh and computers, and the uploading of human beings into a virtual computer world were all part of a process that would merge people with God and allow us to become gods as well, creating and ruling over our own digital and robotic worlds just like our maker. "I had this vision of the unbounded God binding himself to his creation. When we make these virtual worlds in the future—worlds whose virtual beings will have autonomy to commit evil, murder, hurt, and destroy options—it's not unthinkable that the game creator would go in to try to fix the world from the inside. That's the story of Jesus' redemption to me. We have an unbounded God who enters this world in the same way that you would go into virtual reality and bind yourself to a limited being and try to redeem the actions of the other beings since they are your creations," Kelly explained in an interview with *Christianity Today.*

At *Wired,* Kelly injected this theology into every part of the magazine, infusing the text with an unquestioning belief in the ultimate goodness and rightness of markets and decentralized computer technology, no matter how it was used.

The first issue of *Wired* hit newsstands in January 1993. It was printed on glossy paper in neon inks and featured jarring layouts that deliberately copied the chaotic DIY zine aesthetic used by Stewart Brand's *Whole Earth Catalog.* Just like *Whole Earth, Wired* positioned itself as a publication for and by a new and radical digital counterculture that lived on the cutting edge of a new networked world. It was also a guide for outsiders who wanted to be a part of this exciting future, teaching readers how to talk and think about the technology revolution.[94] "There are a lot of magazines about technology," Rossetto explains in the magazine's inaugural issue. "*Wired* is not one of them. *Wired* is about the most powerful people on the planet today—the Digital Generation. These are the people who not only foresaw how the merger of computers, telecommunications and the media is transforming life at the cusp of the new millennium, they are making it happen."[95]

Wired was an immediate financial and critical success. It had thirty thousand subscribers by the end of its first year. In its second year of publication, it snagged a prestigious National Magazine Award and racked up two hundred thousand subscribers. It launched a television subsidiary and a search engine called HotBot. By 1996, Louis Rossetto was ready to cash in on the boom and take the company public. He recruited Goldman Sachs to make it happen, which gave *Wired* an estimated value of $450 million. The magazine was the face of the dot-com boom and an evangelist for the New Economy, a revolutionary moment in history in which technological progress was supposed to rewrite all the rules and make everything that had come before irrelevant and outdated.

America's computer industry press dated to the 1960s. It wasn't flashy or hip, but it covered the emerging computer and networking business very well—it did not shy away from critical reporting. Publications like *ComputerWorld* were at the forefront of covering the privacy debate and the danger of centralized computer databases in the 1970s and provided in-depth coverage of the NSFNET privatization scandals of the 1990s. *Wired* was different. Just like *Whole Earth*, *Wired* was not fully a journalistic enterprise; nor was it an industry publication.[96] It seemed more a networking hub and marketing vehicle for the industry, a booster intended to create a brand around the cult of technology and the people who made and sold it, and then repackage it for the mainstream culture. It was continuing a tradition that Stewart Brand had started, overlaying an increasingly powerful computer industry with images of the counterculture to give it a hip and grassroots revolutionary edge.

This wasn't just posturing. In those first few years, the energy and evangelism soaked every neon-colored page of *Wired*. The magazine covered cutting-edge Pentagon virtual reality battlefield technology.[97] It profiled cryptographers and fringe entrepreneurs rebelling against the federal government. It reported on a new class of computer capitalists building a new tech world among the ruins of the Soviet Union. It cheered the dot-com boom and the red-hot stock market, arguing that this was not a speculative bubble but a new phase in civilization when technological advances meant that the stock market would never crash again.[98] It reviewed books and films, showcased the latest computer gadgets, featured interviews with musicians like Brian Eno, and commissioned sci-fi authors like William Gibson to do investigative reporting. And, of course, Stewart Brand frequently graced the magazine's pages, starting with the inaugural issue. In *Wired*'s world, computers and the Internet were changing everything. Governments, armies, public ownership of resources, traditional left-right alignment of political parties, fiat money—all these were relics of the past. Computer networking technology was sweeping it all away and creating a new world in its place.

Wired's impact was not just cultural but also political. The magazine's embrace of a privatized digital world made it a natural ally of the powerful business interests pushing to deregulate and privatize American telecommunications infrastructure.

Among the pantheon of techno-heroes promoted in the magazine's pages were right-wing politicians and pundits, telecom tycoons, and corporate lobbyists who swirled around Washington to whip up excitement and push for a privatized, corporate-dominated Internet and telecommunications infrastructure. Republican congressman Newt Gingrich and Ronald Reagan's economics guru George Gilder graced the magazine's cover, their push for a privatized telecommunication system profiled—and their retrograde views on women's rights, abortion, and civil rights played down and ultimately ignored.[99] John Malone, the billionaire cable monopolist at the head of TCI and one of the largest landowners in the United States, made the cut as well. *Wired* put him on the cover as a punk counterculture rebel for his fight against the Federal Communications Commission, which was putting the brakes on his cable company's multi-billion-dollar merger with Bell Atlantic, a telephone giant. He is pictured walking down an empty rural highway with a dog by his side, wearing a tattered leather jacket and holding a shotgun. The reference is clear: he was Mel Gibson of *Road Warrior*, fighting to protect his town from being overrun by a savage band of misfits, which, to extend the metaphor, was the FCC regulators. The reason this billionaire was so cool? He had the guts to say that he'd shoot the head of the FCC if the man didn't approve his merger fast enough.[100]

Wired's promotion of cutthroat telecom businessmen and Republican politicians and players isn't so surprising. Louis Rossetto was, after all, a Republican-turned-libertarian who believed in the primacy of business and the free market. There was no ideological disagreement here.

One group that frequented *Wired*'s pages, and one that would later come to mainstream prominence, was the Electronic Frontier Foundation (EFF).[101] Founded in San Francisco in 1990 by three millionaires who hung out on Stewart Brand's The Well messaging board, EFF got its start lobbying for the budding Internet service provider industry.[102] In 1993, EFF cofounder Mitch Kapor wrote an article for *Wired* that laid out his and EFF's position on the future Internet: "Private, not public . . . life in cyberspace seems to be shaping up exactly like Thomas Jefferson would have wanted: founded on the primacy of individual liberty and a commitment to pluralism, diversity, and community."[103]

Wired backed up EFF's privatized vision, giving the organization space in the magazine to expound its views, while providing fawning coverage of the group's activities. It compared the lobbying work the EFF was doing on behalf of its powerful telecom donors to the authority-bucking counterculture scene of the 1960s Bay Area. "In some ways, they are the Merry Pranksters, those apostles of LSD, who tripped through the 1960s in a psychedelic bus named Furthur, led by novelist Ken Kesey and chronicled by Tom Wolfe in *The Electric Kool-Aid Acid Test*," wrote *Wired* journalist Joshua Quittner in a profile of the EFF's move to Washington, DC.[104] "Older and wiser now, they're on the road again, without the bus and the acid, but dispensing many similar-sounding bromides: Turn on, jack in, get connected. Feed your head with the roar of bits pulsing across the cosmos, and learn something about who you are."

Writing about corporate lobbyists working on behalf of telecoms to deregulate the Internet as if they were rebels and acid heads? It might seem cynical, even gauche. But *Wired* was serious and genuine, and it somehow fit, and people believed it. Because in the world *Wired* constructed for its readers, anything tied to the Internet was different and radical. It made sense. *Wired* and the EFF were extensions of the same larger business-counterculture-New-Right network and ideology that emerged out of Stewart Brand's *Whole Earth*. That's where *Wired*'s real cultural power lay: using cybernetic ideals of the counterculture to sell corporate politics as a revolutionary act.

Wired magazine was just the hippest, youngest outlet representing a bigger cultural and political trend in American society. In the 1990s, it seemed like wherever you looked—the *Wall Street Journal, Forbes,* the *New York Times*—pundits, journalists, economists, and politicians predicted an era of abundance where just about everything was going to change.[105] Old rules—scarcity, labor, wealth and poverty, political power—no longer applied. Computers and networking technology were ushering in the Information Age, where the human race would be freed at last, freed from overbearing governments and borders, freed even from its very identity.[106]

In 1996, the same year that the Telecommunications Act was passed, Louis Rossetto made a bold prediction: the Internet was going to change everything. It was even going to make the military obsolete. "I mean, everything—if you have a bunch of preconceived ideas about how the world works, you better reconsider them, because change is instantaneous out there," he said.[107] "And you don't need, you know, lumbering armies in a global village, you need maybe a police force at the most and you need good will on the part of the inhabitants, but otherwise you don't need these kinds of structures that have already been built."

Back in 1972, Stewart Brand tried to convince *Rolling Stone* readers that the young Pentagon contractors holed up in a Stanford lab, playing video games and building powerful computer tools for ARPA, were not really working in the service of war. They were hacking the system, using military computer technology to end the military. "Spacewar serves Earthpeace," he wrote back then. "So does any funky playing with computers, any computer-pursuit of your own peculiar goals, and especially any use of computers to offset other computers." Brand saw computers as a path toward a utopian world order where the individual wielded the ultimate power. Everything that came before—militaries, governments, big oppressive corporations—would melt away and an egalitarian system would spontaneously emerge. "When computers become available to everybody, the hackers take over: We are all Computer Bums, all more empow-ered as individuals and as cooperators."[108]

Twenty-four years later, Rossetto channeled the same sentiment, promoting personal computers and the Internet as tools that would radically empower the individual and wink armies out of existence. It was a wide-eyed and, perhaps, self-serving view for a man whose fame and fortune rested on the backing of Nicholas Negroponte, a career military contractor whose MIT Media Lab received funding from DARPA even as Rossetto spoke those words.

Not surprisingly, the future hasn't quite worked out according to Rossetto's dream. The village went global, true. But the lumbering armies of the past did not go away; indeed, as time showed, computer networks and the Internet only expanded the power of American mil-itary and intelligence agencies, making them global and omnipresent.

Chapter 5

Surveillance Inc.

The perfect search engine would be like the mind of God.

—Sergey Brin, in "What's Next for Google"

Everyone in America remembers where they were on the morning of September 11, 2001, when two airplanes brought down the World Trade Center.

I was in the middle of moving my belongings to a room on the south side of the University of California, Berkeley, campus, where I'd just transferred from a community college in San Mateo. I didn't have a television or a computer, and smartphones didn't exist. To get the news, I watched CNN all day with a friend in a grimy pizza joint off Telegraph Avenue, nibbling cold slices, drinking beer, and generally feeling confused and helpless.

Google cofounder Sergey Brin also remembers where he was on 9/11. But unlike most of us, he had the power to do something. Something of consequence.

That morning, Brin rushed into Google's headquarters on Bayshore Avenue in Mountain View. He quietly convened a small group of his most trusted engineers and managers and charged them with a top-secret assignment: mine Google's search logs for anything that might help uncover the identity of the people involved in that morning's attack.

"Google is big enough at this point that it's entirely possible the terrorists used it to help plan their attack," Brin told the antiterror data-mining posse gathered around him. "We can try to identify them based on intersecting sets of search queries conducted during the period prior to the hijackings." To get them started, he threw together a list of possible search terms, such as "Boeing," "fuel capacity," "aviation school."[1] If they discovered several terror-related keywords coming from the same computer, Brin instructed them to try to reverse-engineer the search to reveal the user's identity and possibly stop the next attack.

The plan had a good chance of success.

Three years had passed since Brin and his partner Larry Page used $25 million in venture capital to spin their Stanford graduate project into a lucrative search company. Google wasn't yet the ubiquitous presence it is today, nor had its name become a synonym for "search" yet. In fact, it was barely making any money. But Google was fast on its way to becoming the world's most popular search engine, and it sat atop a gold mine of behavioral data. It processed 150 million searches every day.[2] Each of those records contained a search query, the location of its origin, the date and time it was entered, the type of computer that was used, and the search result link the user ultimately clicked. All of this was tied to a tracking "cookie" file that Google placed on every computer that used its services.

Individually, these search queries were of limited value. But collectively, when mined for patterns of behavior over extended periods of time, they could paint a rich biographical portrait, including details about a person's interests, work, relationships, hobbies, secrets, idiosyncrasies, sexual preferences, medical ailments, and political and religious views. The more a person typed into Google's search box, the more refined the picture that emerged. Multiply this by hundreds of millions of people around the world, each using the site all day, and you start to get a sense of the unfathomable stores of data at Google's disposal.

The richness of the information in Google's search logs amazed and enchanted the company's data-obsessed engineers. It was like a continuous poll of public interests and preferences, a rolling picture of what people worried about, lusted after, and what kind of flu was spreading in their communities. "Google could be a broad sensor of human behavior," was how one Google employee described it.[3]

The data could be extremely specific, like a brain tap, allowing Google to profile individuals in unprecedented detail. People treated the search box as an impartial oracle that accepted questions, spat out answers, and moved on. Few realized it recorded everything typed into it, from details about relationship troubles to—Brin hoped— plans regarding future terror attacks.

The crack team of terrorist hunters Brin assembled that morning knew all about the type of information the search logs contained; many of them had spent the past three years building what would soon become a multi-billion-dollar targeted advertising business on top of it. So they went looking for suspects.

"In a first run, the logs team found about a hundred thousand queries a day that matched some of his criteria," recalled Douglas Edwards, Google's first marketing director, in his memoir *I'm Feeling Lucky: The Confessions of Google Employee Number 59*. He was there for the hunt, and he remembered how a deeper analysis of the logs proved disappointing. "The search of our logs for the 9/11 terrorists turned up nothing of interest. The closest we came was a cookie that had searched for both 'world trade center' and 'Egypt air hijack.' If the terrorists *had* used Google to plan their attack, they had done so in a way that we couldn't discover."[4]

It's never been clear whether Brin was searching the logs purely on his own initiative or whether it was an off-the-books request from the FBI or another law enforcement agency. But his data-mining effort preceded by more than a month President George W. Bush's signing of the Patriot Act, which would give the National Security Agency broad authority to extract and mine search-log data in a very similar way.

"This new law that I sign today will allow surveillance of all communications used by terrorists, including emails, the Internet and cellphones. As of today, we'll be able to better meet the technological challenges posed by this proliferation of communications technology," President Bush said on October 26, 2001, the day he signed the act into law. "The American people need to know that we're collecting a lot of information and we're spending a great deal of time trying to gather as much intelligence as we possibly can, to chase down every lead, to run down every hint so that we can keep America safe. And it's happening."[5]

On one level, Brin's quest to find terrorists was understandable. It was a terrifying time. America was gripped by a fear that more terrorist attacks were imminent. But given the US government's hunger for information—any information—on potential terrorists and their accomplices, the effort had a disturbing dimension. Right after 9/11, the CIA grabbed scores of suspected Al-Qaeda operatives in Afghanistan and Pakistan and dumped them in Guantanamo Bay, in many cases acting on second-hand information for which they'd paid million-dollar bounties. In the end, 731 of the 780 detainees, more than 90 percent, were released without being charged.[6] A series of searches like "Boeing," "fuel capacity," "aviation school," and "death to America," might sound incriminating, but they were hardly proof of complicity in terrorist acts. If a teenager in Islamabad had Googled those terms, and the company had turned that information over to the government, it's possible he could have found himself black-bagged in the middle of the night and shipped to Guantanamo.

But was Brin's vigilante effort effective? What were the net results?

Not really, and not much. To Douglas Edwards, who related this story in his memoir, the episode served as a cautionary tale. He had been with the company almost from the beginning, but only on September 11 did he finally begin to comprehend how much power Google—and, by extension, the rest of Silicon Valley—had locked in its files. "There was no way to avoid the fact that we were trying to sift out specific users on the basis of their searches. If we found them, we would try to determine their personal information from the data about them in our logs," wrote Edwards. "We had people's most intimate thoughts in our log files and, soon enough, people would realize it."[7]

first started using Google in 2001, around the time Sergey Brin started hunting for terrorists. For me, as for a lot of people who came of age in the early 2000s, Google was the first Internet company I really trusted. It did not demand money. It did not bombard you with obnoxious ads. It had a clean, white design, centering a simple search box against a blank background. It worked like nothing else on the Internet, helping you navigate through a chaotic and wondrous new world. It put whole libraries at your fingertips, allowed you to translate foreign languages on the fly, let you collaborate in real time with people on the other side of the planet. And you got all of it for free. It seemed to defy the laws of economics.

Even as it expanded into a transnational multi-billion-dollar corporation, Google managed to retain its geekily innocent "Don't Be Evil" image. It convinced its users that everything it did was driven by a desire to help humanity. That's the story you'll find in just about every popular book on Google: a gee-whiz tale about two brilliant nerds from Stanford who turned a college project into an epoch-defining New Economy dynamo, a company that embodied every utopian promise of the networked society: empowerment, knowledge, democracy. For a while, it felt true. Maybe this really was the beginning of a new, highly networked world order, where the old structures—militaries, corporations, governments—were helpless before the leveling power of the Internet. As *Wired*'s Louis Rossetto wrote in 1995, "Everything we know will be different. Not just a change from L.B.J. to Nixon, but whether there will be a President at all."[8]

Back then, anybody suggesting Google might be the herald of a new kind of dystopia, rather than a techno-utopia, would have been laughed out of the room. It was all but unthinkable.

Digital Library

Lawrence Page was a socially awkward child, born and raised around computers. In 1978, when he was five, his father, Carl, spent a year working as a researcher at NASA's Ames Research Center in

Mountain View, California. The center was an ARPANET site that Google would lease years later as it expanded its corporate campus.[9] Page's mother, Gloria, taught computer programming at Michigan State University. His older brother, Carl Page Jr., was a pioneering Internet entrepreneur who founded an early message board company later purchased by Yahoo! for nearly half a billion dollars.

Page grew up programming.[10] When he was twelve, he read a biography of Nikola Tesla, the brilliant Serbian American inventor who had developed everything from the electric motor, radio, and fluorescent lights to alternating current, all before dying in poverty, alone and out of his mind, while writing letters to a pigeon that lived on his windowsill.[11] Page devoured the book, and Tesla has remained an enduring inspiration. Not just Tesla's inventions obsessed Page but also his repeated failure to monetize his ideas. "He had all these problems commercializing his work. It's a very sad story. I realized Tesla was the greatest inventor, but he didn't accomplish as much as he should have," Page once told journalist John Battelle. "I realized I wanted to invent things, but I also wanted to change the world. I wanted to get them out there, get them into people's hands so they can use them, because that's what really matters."[12]

Wealth, fame, making a mark on the world—these were the things that the young Page fantasized about. Stanford University, and a research program funded by the Defense Advanced Research Projects Agency (previously known as ARPA), would allow him to achieve his dreams.[13]

Stanford sits on the edge of the San Francisco Bay, thirty-five miles south of the city. It was founded by Leland Stanford, a local railroad tycoon elected as the state's governor, then as a senator.[14] When the university opened in 1891, New York's *Mail and Express* mocked the project, writing, "the need for another university in California is about as great as that of an asylum for decayed sea captains in Switzerland."[15] But the institution and the surrounding area flourished in tandem. In the early twentieth century, the Bay Area developed a thriving radio and electronics industry, emerging as the center of vacuum-tube manufacturing. During World War II, the area boomed again, driven by the need for radio technology and advanced vacuum-tube design to support the military's radar technology. After the war, Stanford University became the West Coast's answer to the Massachusetts Institute of Technology, the elite engineering university closely linked to the US military-industrial complex.[16] The area surrounding the campus was the epicenter of computer and microprocessor development.

William Shockley was an MIT chemist and notorious eugenicist who made his name as part of the Bell Labs team that invented the solid-state transistor. In 1956, he returned to his hometown of Palo Alto to start Shockley Semiconductor inside the university's Stanford Industrial Park.[17] His company spawned several other microchip companies, including Intel, and gave Silicon Valley its name. Hewlett-Packard, Eastman Kodak, General Electric, Xerox PARC, and Lockheed Martin also set up shop inside Stanford's Industrial Park around the same time. There was so much military work going on in Silicon Valley that, throughout the 1960s, Lockheed was the biggest employer in the Bay Area.

ARPA had a huge presence on campus, too. The Stanford Research Institute did counterinsurgency and chemical warfare work for the agency as part of William Godel's Project Agile. It also housed the Augmentation Research Center, an ARPANET site run by the acid-dropping Douglas Engelbart. Indeed, the ARPANET was part-born at Stanford.[18]

Into the 1990s, Stanford University hadn't changed all that much. It was still home to cutting-edge computer and networking research and still awash in military cash and cybernetic utopianism. Perhaps the biggest change occurred in the suburbs surrounding the university—Mountain View, Cupertino, San Jose—which became thick with investors and Internet start-ups: eBay, Yahoo!, and Netscape. Stanford was the epicenter of the Bay Area dot-com boom when a young Larry Page parachuted right into the vortex.

Page started the computer science PhD program at Stanford in the autumn of 1995. He was in his element and immediately started scratching around for a research topic worthy of a dissertation. He toyed with various ideas, including a self-driving car, which Google would later get into in a heavy way. Eventually, he settled on Internet search.[19]

In the mid-1990s, the Internet was growing exponentially. The landscape was chaotic: a jumble of random websites, personal webpages, university sites, news sites, and corporate properties. Pages were popping up all over the place. But there was no good central or authoritative directory that could help people navigate to where they wanted to go or find a particular song, article, or webpage. Search engines and directory portals like Yahoo!, AltaVista, and Excite were crude and sometimes had to be curated by hand. Search algorithms were extremely primitive, matching searches word for word without the ability to find the most relevant results. Despite their primitive technology and awful search results, these early search sites attracted huge amounts of traffic and investment. The young programmers who started them were rich beyond belief.

In the parlance of Silicon Valley, it was a market ripe for disruption. Finding a way to improve search results not only was intellectually challenging but also could prove to be extremely lucrative.

With Nikola Tesla's ghost hanging over him, Page tackled the issue with his laser-guided brain. Page's tinkering was encouraged by his graduate adviser, Terry Winograd, a pioneer in linguistic artificial intelligence who had done work in the 1970s at MIT's Artificial Intelligence Lab, a part of the bigger ARPANET project. In the 1990s, Winograd was in charge of the Stanford Digital Libraries project, one component of the multi-million-dollar Digital Library Initiative sponsored by seven civilian, military, and law enforcement federal agencies, including NASA, DARPA, the FBI, and the National Science Foundation.[20]

The Internet had grown into a vast and labyrinthine ecosystem spanning every type of computer network and data type imaginable: documents, databases, photographs, sound recordings, text, executable programs, videos, and maps.[21] The purpose of the Digital Library Initiative was to find a way to organize and index this digital mess.

Though the project had a broad civilian mandate, it was also linked to the needs of intelligence and law enforcement agencies. More and more, life was taking place online. People were leaving behind trails of digital information: diaries, blogs, forums, personal photographs, videos. Intelligence and law enforcement agencies wanted a better way of accessing this valuable asset.

It made sense. Back in the 1960s, when the military was dealing with an avalanche of data and needed new tools to digest and analyze the information, ARPA was tasked with finding a solution. Three decades later, the Digital Library Initiative had evolved into an extension of the same project, driven by the same needs. And just like old times, DARPA played a role.[22] Indeed, in 1994, just one year before Page had arrived at Stanford, DARPA's funding of the Digital Library Initiative at Carnegie Mellon University produced a notable success: Lycos, a search engine named after Lycosidae, the scientific name for the wolf spider family.[23]

Larry Page's interest in search aligned perfectly with the goals of the Digital Library Initiative, and his research was carried out under its umbrella.[24] When he finally published his first research paper in 1998, it bore the familiar disclosure: "funded by DARPA." The agency that had created the Internet remained a central player.

Larry Page met Sergey Brin on his first day at Stanford, at graduate orientation. The two were at once similar and polar opposites. They fast became friends.

Page was withdrawn and quiet; some people thought maybe he was a bit autistic. He spoke with a strange lisp that some people mistook for an Eastern European accent.[25] Brin was the opposite. He was social and talkative, and into sports. When fellow students recall his time at Stanford, they remember Brin rollerblading through the halls and constantly dropping by the offices of his professors to chew the fat. Unlike Page, Brin was an actual Eastern European. One overarching activity united the two future billionaires: their early experimentation with computers and the Internet.

Sergey Brin's family had emigrated from Moscow to the United States in the 1970s and very successfully integrated into the engineering-academic world. His mother, Eugenia, was a NASA scientist. His father, Michael, was a tenured mathematics professor at the University of Maryland.

Brin was a math prodigy. When he was nine, he discovered the early Internet and spent his time hanging out in chatrooms and playing multiuser dungeon games, or MUDs.[26] He spent hours immersed in this new communication technology, souring on it when he realized that it was full of people just like him, "ten-year-old boys trying to talk about sex."[27]

Brin finished high school in 1990, a year early, and enrolled at the University of Maryland with a dual major in math and computer science. He graduated with honors in 1993 and moved to Palo Alto to continue his studies at Stanford under a National Science Foundation Graduate Research Fellowship.[28] At Stanford, he became interested in data mining: building computer algorithms that could predict what people would do on the basis of their past actions. What would they buy? What movies would they like?[29] He even founded a student group called MIDAS: "Mining Data at Stanford." In later years, behavioral data mining would prove to be Google's Midas touch. But that was well into the future. As Brin grew bored with the narrow focus of his data-mining research, he decided to join a new project with his buddy, Larry Page. "I talked to a lot of research groups, and this was the most exciting project, both because it tackled the Web, which represents human knowledge, and because I liked Larry," Brin recalled in an interview.[30]

The core problem of search was relevance. Some web pages were more important and authoritative than others, but the first search engines couldn't tell the difference. The key, Page understood, was to find a way to incorporate a ranking system into the search results. It was a simple but powerful idea, cribbed from the world of academia, where the importance of a research paper was measured by how many times it had been cited by other research papers. A paper cited a thousand times was assumed to be more important than a paper cited only ten times. Because of its hyperlinked design—with every webpage linking to other pages—the Internet was essentially one giant citation machine. This was Page's breakthrough. He called the resultant experimental project "PageRank" and with Brin's help began lashing the thing together.

They first coded a bot to crawl the entire Internet, scrape its contents, and save it all on their server at Stanford. They then refined and massaged the PageRank algorithm to produce relevant results. Because different links carried different values—a link from a newspaper like the *New York Times* was much more authoritative than a link from someone's personal homepage—they tweaked their calculations so that pages were scored by the number of links as well as the scores of those links themselves. In the end, the rank of any given webpage would be the sum total of all the links and their values that pointed to it. Once the values of a few initial webpages entered the PageRank algorithm, new rankings propagated recursively through the whole web. "We converted the entire web into a big equation with several hundred million variables, which are the page ranks of all the web pages," Brin explained not long after launching Google.[31] It was a dynamic mathematical model of the Internet. If one value changed, then the whole thing would be recomputed.[32]

They folded it into an experimental search engine they called "BackRub" and put it up on Stanford's internal network. The Back-Rub logo was creepy: it featured a black-and-white photo of a hand attached to a hairy arm rubbing a nude back. But it didn't matter. As word spread, students started using it—and they were amazed. This student project was better than any commercial search engine available at the time, such as Excite or AltaVista. The dominant search companies were valued in the billions but did not understand their own business. "They were looking only at text and not considering this other signal," Page said.[33]

The search engine, which the pair quickly renamed Google, became so popular it overwhelmed the bandwidth of Stanford's network connection. Brin and Page realized they'd hit on something very special. Google was much bigger than a research project.

Even at that early stage, they understood that Google's search algorithm wasn't just abstract mathematics. It catalogued and analyzed webpages, read their contents, looked at outgoing links, and ranked pages by importance and relevance. Because webpages were written and built by people, the two Google creators understood that their indexing system essentially depended on a kind of surveillance of the public Internet. "The process might seem completely automated, but in terms of how much human input goes into the final product, there are millions of people who spend time designing their webpages, determining who to link to and how, and that human element goes into it," Brin said.[34]

But there was more.

Brin was deeply fascinated by the art and science of extracting information from people's behavior in order to predict their future actions. Cataloguing the contents of the Internet was just the first step. The next was understanding the *intent* of the person doing the searching. Was it a teenager? A computer scientist? Male, female, or transgender? Where did they live? Where did they shop? If they searched for "cubs," were they nature lovers or baseball fans? When they typed "buy underwear" were they interested in lacy thongs or boxer shorts? The more Google knew about someone, the better its search results would be.

As Page and Brin worked on perfecting Google's relevance algorithm, they began to think about customizing search results to a person's interests and habits. Some of their initial ideas were rudimentary, including scanning a person's browser bookmarks or ingesting the contents of their academic homepage, which usually listed personal interests as well as an academic and professional history. "These search engines could save users a great deal of trouble by efficiently guessing a large part of their interests," the two wrote in the original 1998 paper that described Google's search methods.[35]

This short sentence would define the future company. Collecting data and profiling users became an obsession for them both. It would make them rich beyond belief and transform Google from a mere search engine into a sprawling global platform designed to capture as much information as possible about the people who came into contact with it.

The Brain Tap

In 1998, Larry Page and Sergey Brin moved into the garage of a house owned by Susan Wojcicki, the sister of Brin's future wife, Anne Wojcicki. They had an initial $100,000 check from Andy Bechtolsheim, the cofounder of Sun Microsystems, a powerful computer company that itself had come out of an ARPA-funded 1970s computer research program at Stanford University.[36] The initial small investment was followed by a $25 million tranche from two powerful venture capital outfits, Sequoia Capital and Kleiner Perkins.[37]

Brin and Page couldn't be happier. Flush with cash, the two young entrepreneurs hired a couple of their Stanford Digital Library Initiative colleagues and plowed their energy into improving Google's still-rudimentary search engine.

All the early search engine companies, from Lycos to Yahoo!, AltaVista to AOL, realized that they were sitting on something new and magical. "People came to our servers and they'd leave tracks. We could see every day exactly what people thought was important on the Internet," Tim Koogle, Yahoo's first CEO, said.[38] "The Net is all about connection. . . . We sat in the middle, connecting people." Yahoo! tried leveraging the data to gain insight into consumer demand, but its engineers barely scratched the surface of the valuable data they were amassing. Google's search logs were no different. What separated the company from the pack was the sophistication and aggressiveness Page and Brin brought to mining and monetizing the data trail.

Initially, Google's team focused on mining user behavior to improve the search engine to better guess user intent. "If people type something and then go and change their query, you could tell they aren't happy. If they go to the next page of results, it's a sign they're not happy. You can use those signs that someone's not happy with what we gave them to go back and study those cases and find places to improve search," explained one Google engineer.[39] Studying the logs for patterns, Google engineers turned user behavior into a system of crowdsourced free labor. It acted like a feedback loop that taught the search engine to be "smarter." An auto-suggest spell-checker feature allowed Google to recognize minor but important quirks in the way people used language in order to guess the meaning of what people typed rather than just matching text to text. "Today, if you type 'Gandhi bio,' we know that 'bio' means 'biography.' And if you type 'bio warfare,' it means 'biological,'" another Google engineer explained.

Steven Levy, a veteran tech journalist whose early career included a stint at Stewart Brand's *Whole Earth Software Catalog* in the 1980s, gained unprecedented insider access to write the history of Google. The result was *In the Plex: How Google Thinks, Works, and Shapes Our Lives,* a hagiographic but highly informative story of Google's rise to dominance. The book demonstrates that Page and Brin understood early on that Google's success depended on grabbing and maintaining proprietary control over the behavioral data they captured through their services. This was the company's biggest asset. "Over the years, Google would make the data in its logs the key to evolving its search engine," wrote Levy. "It would also use those data on virtually every other product the company would develop. It would not only take note of user behavior in its released products but measure such behavior in countless experiments to test out new ideas and various improvements. The more Google's system learned, the more new signals could be built into the search engine to better determine relevance."[40]

Improving Google's usability and relevance helped make it the most popular search engine on the Internet. By the end of 1999, the company was averaging seven million searches daily, a roughly 70,000 percent increase from the previous year.[41] Now that Google dominated the market, it was time to make money. It didn't take long for the company to figure out how.

In 2000, right after moving to its new expanded office at 2400 Bayshore in Mountain View, right next to the Ames NASA Center and a short drive from the Stanford campus, Page and Brin launched Google's first money-maker. It was called AdWords, a targeted advertising system that let Google display ads based on the content of a search query. It was simple but effective: an advertiser selected key-words, and if those keywords appeared in a search string, Google would display the ad alongside search results and would only be paid if a user clicked the link.

Google's search logs were vital to AdWords. The company fig-ured out that the better it knew the intention and interests of users when they hit the search button, the more effectively the company could pair users with a relevant advertiser, thus increasing the chance users would click ad links. AdWords was initially rudimentary, matching keyword to keyword. It couldn't always guess a person's interests with accuracy, but it was close. With time, Google got bet-ter at hitting the target, resulting in more relevant ads, more clicks, and more profits for Google. Multiplied by hundreds of millions of searches a day, even a tiny increase in the probability that a searcher would click an advertising link dramatically boosted company rev-enue. Over the coming years, Google became hungry for more and more data to refine the efficacy of the ad program. "The logs were money—we billed advertisers on the basis of the data they contained," explained Douglas Edwards.[42]

Indeed, money began raining from the sky. In 2001, Goo-gle hired Sheryl Sandberg, a former chief of staff for President Bill Clinton's Treasury secretary Larry Summers. She was tasked with developing and running the advertising business side of things, and she succeeded beyond anyone's expectations. With a targeted system based on user behavior, advertising revenue shot up from $70 million in 2001 to $3.14 billion in 2004, the bulk of it resulting from simply showing the right ad at the right time to the right eyeballs.[43] It was like a new form of alchemy: Google was turning useless scraps of data into mountains of gold.[44]

Barbecued Girl Meat

As Google engineers wrung personal information from their grow-ing millions of users, executives worried the smallest disclosure regarding the operation could trigger a fatal public relations disaster. Page especially realized Google could potentially lose users if people understood the ways the company used their search streams.[45] Guarding this secret became bedrock corporate policy.[46]

Page was incredibly paranoid about disclosing any hint of information. At his insistence, the company's privacy policy was kept vague and brief, recalled Douglas Edwards in *I'm Feeling Lucky*. "Larry's refusal to engage the privacy discussion with the public always frustrated me. I remained convinced we could start with basic information and build an information center that would be clear and forthright about the tradeoffs users made when they entered their queries on Google or any other search engine," he wrote. "Those who truly cared would see we were being transparent. Even if they didn't like our policies on data collection or retention, they would know what they were. If they went elsewhere to search, they would be taking a chance that our competitors' practices were far worse than ours."[47]

Page didn't see things this way.

The founder wanted total secrecy. His paranoia reached such a pitch that he began to worry about a scrolling ticker screen in Google's Mountain View office lobby that displayed random Google searches from around the world in real time. "Journalists who came to Google stood in the lobby mesmerized by this peek into the global gestalt and later waxed poetical about the international impact of Google and the deepening role search plays in all our lives. Visitors were so entranced that they stared up at the display as they signed in for their temporary badges, not bothering to read the restrictive non-disclosure agreements they were agreeing to," wrote Edwards. "Larry never cared for the scrolling queries screen. He constantly monitored the currents of public paranoia around information seepage, and the scrolling queries set off his alarm." Page believed that the rolling marquee gave visitors too much insight into what his company was really doing.

Ironically, a struggling Internet has-been provided the public with a rare and inadvertent glimpse at the kind of intimate data search engines had been storing in their search logs. In August 2006, AOL, the giant prehistoric network provider, released into the public domain a few gigabytes worth of anonymized search logs: 20 million search queries made by 657,000 of its customers over a three-month period. The search results had been powered by Google, which owned 5 percent of AOL and ran the company's search engine.[48]

Page saw these logs as a lucrative but volatile asset, one that threatened the company's core business if made public. An AOL research team thought differently: they released the batch of logs as a good deed in the name of furthering social research. As far as the public was concerned, it was a good deed. But for AOL, and by extension Google, the logs were a public relations fiasco, shining light on the massive and systemic privacy intrusion upon which the search economy was based.

Responding to the uproar, AOL claimed its engineers had anonymized the logs by replacing personally identifying user account information with randomized numbers. But journalists quickly discovered that user identities could easily be reverse-engineered with just a half dozen searches. One such user—known in the logs as "4417749"—was easily unmasked by a pair of enterprising *New York Times* reporters as a grandmotherly senior in rural Georgia:

> No. 4417749 conducted hundreds of searches over a three-month period on topics ranging from "numb fingers" to "60 single men" to "dog that urinates on everything." And search by search, click by click, the identity of AOL user No. 4417749 became easier to discern. There are queries for "landscapers in Lilburn, Ga," several people with the last name Arnold and "homes sold in shadow lake subdivision gwinnett county georgia." It did not take much investigating to follow that data trail to Thelma Arnold, a 62-year-old widow who lives in Lilburn, Ga., frequently researches her friends' medical ailments and loves her three dogs.[49]

The AOL log data revealed something else. Many of the search queries were extremely private, humiliating, disturbing, and possibly incriminating. Interspersed with searches on mundane topics like restaurants, television programs, and digital camera reviews were searches for medical ailments and advice on what to do "the morning after being raped" and, in some cases, queries that seemed to show unstable individuals on the verge of doing something violent and dangerous. To fully grasp the personal nature of the now-public searches, here is a sample of the raw logs:

> User 2281868
> "how destroy demons that live in apt above"
> "is hip hop and rap music a form of satanism"
> "are niggers satan or demons or gremlins"
> "animal sex"
> "do niggers have x-ray vision"
> User 6416389
> "girls fattened for butchering"
> "cooked tender flesh of girls"
> "cutting steaks from buttocks of girls"
> "girls strangled and eaten"
> "girls cut up into steaks"
> User 1879967
> "i eat my ejaculate and how long can it stay fresh"
> "livingontheedge"
> "i use my cum as an after shave"
> "is it unhealthy to store up seman or cum in a glass and drink
>   it in a week"
> "i put cum on face as scent to atract girtls"

I looked through the logs, and one search stream caught my attention. It belonged to user 5342598 and featured multiple queries about an unsolved murder of a woman in San Jose, followed by searches for resources that could help a person determine whether they were a serial killer. Here's a sample of the stream:

> User 5342598
> "unsolved murders in san jose"
> "tara marowski"

"unsolved murder of tar a marowski"
"tara marowski found dead in car"
"tara found dead in car"
"unsolved mysteries tara marowski"
"san jose police departments cold cases"
"psychological test given to prisoners"
"test to see if you are a serial killer"

Did this person murder someone? Was this a serial killer? Was the other searcher a cannibal? Did the other user really believe the neighbors were demons? Or were these people just searching for weird things on the Internet? It is impossible to say. As for the murder searches, they were a matter for law enforcement to figure out, and indeed search logs have become an increasingly important component of criminal investigations.

One thing was certain in the wake of the AOL release: search logs provided an unadulterated look into the details of people's inner lives, with all the strangeness, embarrassing quirks, and personal anguish those details divulged. And Google owned it all.

You Have Spy Mail

It's April 2004 and Google is in crisis mode. Sergey Brin and Larry Page set up a war room and bring top executives from across the company together to deal with a dangerous development. They aren't hunting for terrorists this time, but repelling an attack in progress.

About a month earlier, Google had started to roll out the beta version of Gmail, its email service. It was a big deal for the young company, representing its first product offering beyond search. At the beginning, everything was going smoothly. Then events quickly spiraled out of control.

Gmail aimed to poach users from established email providers such as Microsoft and Yahoo. To do that, Google shocked everyone by offering one gigabyte of free storage space with every account—an incredible amount of space at the time, considering Microsoft's Hotmail offered just two megabytes of free storage. Naturally, people rushed to sign up. Some were so eager to get their accounts that Gmail's prepublic release invites were fetching up to $200 on eBay.[50] "One gigabyte changes everything. You no longer live in terror that somebody will send you a photo, thereby exceeding your two-megabyte limit and making all subsequent messages bounce back to their senders," wrote *New York Times* tech columnist David Pogue. "In fact, Google argues that with so much storage, you should get out of the habit of deleting messages."[51]

The Google service seemed too good to be true, once again upending the laws of economics. Why would a company give away something so valuable? It felt like charity. An example of Internet magic at work. Turned out there was a huge upside for Google.

The search box was a powerful thing. It allowed Google to peer into people's lives, habits, and interests. But it only worked as long as users stayed on Google's site. As soon as they clicked a link, they were gone, and their browsing stream vanished. What did people do after they left Google.com? What websites did they visit? How often? When? What were those websites about? To these questions, Google's search logs offered dead silence. That's where Gmail came in.

Once users logged their Internet browser in to their email account, Google was able to track their every movement on the Internet, even if they used multiple devices. People could even use a rival search engine, and Google could keep a bead on them. Gmail gave Google something else as well.[52]

In return for the "free" gigabyte of email storage, users gave the company permission to read and analyze all their email in the same way that the company analyzed their search streams and to display targeted ads based on content. They also gave Google permission to tie their search history and browsing habits to their email address.

In this sense, Gmail opened up a whole new dimension of behavior tracking and profiling: it captured personal and business correspondence, private documents, postcards, vacation photos, love letters, shopping receipts, bills, medical records, bank statements, school records, and anything else people routinely sent and received by email. Google argued that Gmail would benefit users, allowing the company to show them relevant ads rather than inundate them with spam.

Not everyone saw it this way.

Less than a week after Gmail's public launch, thirty-one privacy and civil liberties organizations, led by the World Privacy Forum, published an open letter addressed to Sergey Brin and Larry Page asking them to immediately suspend the email service. "Google has proposed scanning the text of all incoming emails for ad placement. The scanning of confidential email violates the implicit trust of an email service provider," the organizations wrote. "Google could—tomorrow—by choice or by court order, employ its scanning system for law enforcement purposes. We note that in one recent case, the Federal Bureau of Investigation obtained a court order compelling an automobile navigation service to convert its system into a tool for monitoring in-car conversations. How long will it be until law enforcement compels Google into a similar situation?"[53]

The press, which until then had nary a negative thing to say about Google, turned critical. The company got bruised by journalists for its "creepy" scanning of emails. One reporter for Canada's *Maclean's* magazine recounted her experience with using Gmail's targeted ad system: "I discovered recently just how relevant when I wrote an email to a friend using my Gmail account. My note mentioned a pregnant woman whose husband had an affair. The Google ads didn't push baby gear and parenting books. Rather, Gmail understood that 'pregnant' in this case wasn't a good thing because it was coupled with the word 'affair.' So it offered the services of a private investigator and a marriage therapist."[54]

Showing ads for spy services to betrayed mothers? It wasn't a good look for a company that still draped itself in a progressive "Don't Be Evil" image.

True to Larry Page's paranoia about letting the privacy "toothpaste out of the tube," Google stayed tightlipped about the inner workings of its email scanning program in the face of criticism. But a series of profiling and targeted advertising technology patents filed by the company that year offered a glimpse into how Gmail fit into Google's multiplatform tracking and profiling system.[55] They revealed that all email communication was subject to analysis and parsed for meaning; names were matched to real identities and addresses using third-party databases as well as contact information stored in a user's Gmail address book; demographic and psychographic data, including social class, personality type, age, sex, personal income, and marital status were extracted; email attachments were scraped for information; even a person's US residency status was established. All of this was then cross-referenced and combined with data collected through Google's search and browsing logs, as well as third-party data providers, and added to a user profile. The patents made it clear that this profiling wasn't restricted to registered Gmail users but applied to anyone who sent email to a Gmail account.

Taken together, these technical documents revealed that the company was developing a platform that attempted to track and profile everyone who came in touch with a Google product. It was, in essence, an elaborate system of private surveillance.

There was another quality to it. The language in the patent filings—descriptions of using "psychographic information," "personality characteristics," and "education levels" to profile and predict people's interests—bore eerie resemblance to the early data-driven counterinsurgency initiatives funded by ARPA in the 1960s and 1970s. Back then, the agency had experimented with mapping the value systems and social relationships of rebellious tribes and political groups, in the hope of isolating the factors that made them revolt and, ultimately, use that information to build predictive models to stop insurgencies before they happened. The aborted Project Camelot was one example. Another was J. C. R. Licklider and Ithiel de Sola Pool's 1969 ARPA Cambridge Project, which aimed to develop a suite of computer tools that would allow military researchers to build predictive models using complex data, including factors such as "political participation of various countries," "membership in associations," "youth movements," and "peasant attitudes and behavior."

The Cambridge Project had been an early attempt at the underlying technology that made prediction and analysis possible. Naturally, Google's predictive system, which arrived thirty years later, was
more advanced and sophisticated than ARPA's crude first-generation
database tools. But it was also very similar. The company wanted to
ingest search, browsing history, and email data to build predictive
profiles capable of guessing the future interests and behavior of its
users. There was only one difference: instead of preventing political
insurgencies, Google wanted the data to sell people products and services with targeted ads. One was military, the other commercial. But
at their core, both systems were dedicated to profiling and prediction.
The type of data plugged into them was irrelevant.

UC Berkeley law professor Chris Hoofnagle, an expert on information privacy law, argued before the California Senate that the difference between military and commercial profiling was illusory. He
compared Google's email scanning to the surveillance and prediction
project at DARPA's then-active Total Information Awareness (TIA)
program, a predictive policing technology that was initially funded
by DARPA and handed to the National Security Agency after the
September 11 terrorist attacks.[56]

A year after Google launched Gmail, Hoofnagle testified at
hearings on email and privacy held by California's Senate Judiciary
Committee. "The prospect that a computer could, en masse, view
transactional and content data and draw conclusions was the plan of
John Poindexter's Total Information Awareness," he said, referring
to President Ronald Reagan's national security adviser who, under
President George W. Bush, was put in charge of helping DARPA
fight terrorism.[57] "TIA proposed to look at a wide array of personal
information and make inferences for the prevention of terrorism or
general crime. Congress rejected Poindexter's plan. Google's content
extraction is different than TIA in that it is designed to pitch advertising rather than catch criminals." To Hoofnagle, Google's data
mining wasn't just technically similar to what the government was
doing; it was a privatized version of the same thing. He predicted
that the information collected by Gmail would eventually be tapped

by the US government. It was a no-brainer. "Allowing the extraction of this content from e-mail messages is likely to have profound consequences for privacy. First, if companies can view private messages to pitch advertising, it is a matter of time before law enforcement will seek access to detect criminal conspiracies. All too often in Washington, one hears policy wonks asking, 'if credit card companies can analyze your data to sell your cereal, why can't the FBI mine your data for terrorism?'"[58]

The language of the patents underscored Hoofnagle's criticism that there was little difference between commercial and military technology. It also brought the conversation back to the fears of the 1970s, when computer and networking technology was first becoming commonplace. Back then, there was widespread understanding that computers were machines built for spying: gathering data about users for processing and analysis. It didn't matter if it was stock market data, weather, traffic conditions, or a person's purchasing history.[59]

To the Electronic Privacy Information Center, Gmail posed both ethical and legal challenges.[60] The organization believed Google's interception of private digital communication to be a potential violation of California's wiretapping laws. The organization called on the state's attorney general to investigate the company.

Google's first political challenge came from an unlikely source: California state senator Liz Figueroa, whose district spanned a huge swath of Silicon Valley and included Google HQ in Mountain View. Disturbed by Google's email scanning, the senator introduced legislation to prohibit email providers from collecting personally identifying information unless they received explicit consent from all parties in an email conversation. Her office described it as a pioneering privacy law for the Internet age: "First-in-the-nation legislation would require Google to obtain the consent of every individual before their e-mail messages are scanned for targeted advertising purposes.

"Telling people that their most intimate and private e-mail thoughts to doctors, friends, lovers, and family members are just another direct marketing commodity isn't the way to promote e-commerce," Senator Figueroa explained, when she announced the bill on April 21, 2004. "At minimum, before someone's most intimate and private thoughts are converted into a direct marketing opportunity for Google, Google should get everyone's informed consent."[61]

The proposed law sent Page and Brin into a panic. Just as the two were preparing to take the company public, they faced legislation that threatened their business model. Getting people's consent—telling them upfront about the invasive way Google tracked them and their every move—was Page's nightmare scenario of a public disclosure of the company's data collection practices; it could trigger a public relations disaster and worse.

Google executives set up a war room to deal with the growing avalanche of criticism. Brin commanded the effort.[62] He was furious at Google's critics: they were ignorant; they did not understand the technology; they had no clue about *anything*. "Bastards, bastards!" he yelled.[63] Page made personal calls to sympathetic tech journalists, explaining that there was no privacy problem and that Google didn't really spy on users. He also organized a face-to-face meeting with Senator Figueroa and her chief of staff.[64]

"We walk into this room, and it's myself and two of my staff—my chief of staff and one of my attorneys. And across from us was Larry, Sergey, and their attorney," recounted the senator. Brin immediately launched into a lengthy explanation of the company's privacy policies, arguing that Figueroa's criticisms were baseless.

"Senator, how would you feel if a robot went into your home and read your diary and read your financial records, read your love letters, read everything, but before leaving the house, it imploded? That's not violating privacy."

"Of course it is," she replied.

But Sergey persisted: "No, it isn't. Nothing's kept. Nobody knows about it."

"That robot has read everything. Does that robot know if I'm sad or if I'm feeling fear, or what's happening?" she answered, still defiant and unwilling to bend.

Brin looked directly at her and answered cryptically: "Oh, no. That robot knows a lot more than that."

When Brin's attempt to talk the senator down didn't work, the company brought in a team of high-powered lobbyists and PR people to massage the message and restore Google's righteous image. Leading the pack was Andrew McLaughlin, Google's smooth and smiley chief public relations strategist who would later serve as President Barack Obama's deputy chief technology officer. He knew exactly how to neutralize Senator Liz Figueroa: Al Gore. "I mobilized the Big Al," he later bragged.[65]

After losing the 2000 presidential election to George Bush, Vice President Gore pivoted to a lucrative career as a tech venture capitalist. As part of that pivot, he accepted Google's offer to be a "virtual board member," meaning that from time to time he used his power and connections to resolve Google's political problems. Now, at McLaughlin's request, Gore summoned the prickly senator to his suites at the Ritz-Carlton in downtown San Francisco. There he gave her a stern talking to, lecturing her about algorithms and robotic analysis. "He was incredible," recounted McLaughlin. "He stood up and was drawing charts and did this long analogy to the throw weight of the ICBM, the Minuteman missile."[66]

Whatever he did in that room, it worked. Senator Figueroa dropped her opposition, and the first legal challenge to Google's surveillance business model faded. And at least one journalist rejoiced: "The only population likely not to be delighted by Gmail are those still uncomfortable with those computer-generated ads. Those people are free to ignore or even bad-mouth Gmail, but they shouldn't try to stop Google from offering Gmail to the rest of us," declared *New York Times* technology journalist David Pogue in May. "We know a good thing when we see it."[67]

A few months later, on August 19, 2004, Google went public. When the bell rang that afternoon to close NASDAQ trading, Google was worth $23 billion.[68] Sergey Brin and Larry Page attained oligarch status in the space of a single workday, while hundreds of their employees became instant multimillionaires, including the company cook.

But concerns about Google's business model would continue to haunt the company. Time proved Hoofnagle right. There wasn't very much difference between Google's approach and the surveillance technology deployed by the NSA, CIA, and Pentagon. Indeed, sometimes they were identical.

Minority Report

October 6, 2014. I'm at the office of UCLA professor Jeffrey Brantingham. It's warm and sunny, and students lounge on the grass outside his windows. Inside, the two of us lean over his computer screen, inspecting an interactive crime map. He zooms in on Venice Beach.

"This used to be the heroin capital of LA. A lot of heroin trafficking going on here. You can see how it changes," he says, toggling between day and night crime patterns for West Los Angeles. "Then, if you look farther afield in Pacific, you say what's going on with some of these other places? Like in here. This is Playa Vista. Up here, Palms."[69]

Brantingham, willowy and soft-spoken with a short gray beard and spiky gelled hair, is a professor of anthropology. He is also a co-founder of PredPol Inc., a hot new predictive policing start-up that came out of counterinsurgency research funded by the Pentagon to predict and prevent attacks on American soldiers in Iraq.[70] In 2012, the researchers worked with the Los Angeles Police Department to apply their algorithmic modeling to predicting crime. Thus, PredPol was born.

The company's name evokes Philip K. Dick's *Minority Report*, but the company itself boasts a spectacular success rate: cutting crime by up to 25 percent in at least one city that deployed it.[71] It works by ingesting decades of crime data, combining them with data about the local environment—factors such as the location of liquor stores, schools, highway on-ramps—and then running all the variables through a proprietary algorithm that generates hotspots where criminals are most likely to strike next.

"It was adapted and modified from something that was predicting earthquakes," Brantingham explains over coffee. "If you think about L.A. and earthquakes, for any given earthquake that happens, you can actually assign where that comes from in a causal sense quite well. After an earthquake happens on one of these faults, you get aftershocks, which occur nearby to where the main shock was and close in time.

"Crime is exactly the same," he continues. "Our environment has lots of built features that are crime generators that are not going anywhere. A great example is a high school. High schools are not going anywhere for the most part. It is a built feature of the environment. And what do high schools have? Lots of young men aged fifteen to seventeen or fifteen to eighteen, and no matter where you go on the planet, young men ages fifteen to seventeen get into trouble. They do. It will always be that way, because of testosterone or girls or whatever it is. It's our primate heritage."

I scratch my head, nodding in agreement. It still doesn't make much sense to me. Surely, one has to account for the fact that humans have free will. Surely, they would resist being treated like giant slabs of floating lava rock violently rubbing against one another? Weren't there deeper social and political causes of crime beyond simple infrastructure—things like poverty and drug addiction? On the topic of high schools and kids being kids, shouldn't there be other ways of dealing with teenage troublemakers than criminalization and concentrated policing?

Brantingham counters that PredPol isn't trying to fix society, just help cops prevent crime. "PredPol is not about fighting the root causes of crime," he says. "PredPol is all about getting that officer the tool to make it harder for that crime to occur, and not about saying we don't need to fix meth addiction. We do need to fix meth addiction." In short: someone else has to do the hard work of improving society by dealing with root social and economic causes of crime. PredPol is simply in the business of helping cops more efficiently contain the mess that exists today.

In 2014, PredPol was one of many companies competing for a fledgling but rapidly expanding market in predictive policing technologies.[72] Big, established companies like IBM, LexisNexis, and

Palantir all offered predictive crime products.[73] PredPol, though small, has raked in contracts with police departments across the country: Los Angeles; Orange County in central Florida; Reading, Pennsylvania; Tacoma, Washington. Local newspapers and television stations loved PredPol's story: the high-tech miracle cure cash-strapped police departments had been waiting for. It enabled law enforcement officers to reduce crime at low cost. With a price tag of $25,000 to $250,000 a year, depending on a city's population, PredPol seemed like a bargain.

Predictive policing was young, but already it was criticized by activists and social scientists who saw it as a rebranding of the age-old tactic of racial and economic profiling spiffed up with an objective, data-driven sheen.[74] Wealthy areas and individuals never seemed to be targeted for predictive policing, nor did the technique focus on white-collar criminals. Journalists and criminologists blasted PredPol, in particular for making claims that it simply could not back up.[75]

Despite these knocks, PredPol had supporters and backers in Silicon Valley. Its board of directors and advisory board included serious heavy hitters: executives from Google, Facebook, Amazon, and eBay, as well as a former managing director of In-Q-Tel, the CIA venture capital outfit operating in Silicon Valley.[76]

Back in his office, Brantingham offers little about the company's ties to these Internet giants. Another PredPol executive informed me that, behind the scenes, Google was one of PredPol's biggest boosters and collaborators. "Google actually came to us," Donnie Fowler, PredPol's director of business development, told me by phone.[77] "This is not the case of a little, tiny company going to a big behemoth like Google and saying that the only way we'll survive is if we piggyback on you. It is a very mutually beneficial relationship."

He bragged that, unlike other companies, PredPol did more than simply license Google's technology to render the mapping system embedded in its product, but also worked with Google to develop customized functionality, including "building additional bells and whistles and even additional tools for law enforcement." He was straightforward about why Google was so proactive about working with his company. "Their last frontier is to sell their technology to governments. They've done consumers. They've done business." And PredPol was a perfect sales prop—a powerful example of police departments leveraging Google technology to keep people safe. "One of those Google guys told me: 'You complete us,'" Fowler said with an air of satisfaction.

Cops? Government contractors? Data-driven counterinsurgency technology? Crime prediction powered by a ubiquitous Internet platform? Was he talking about Google? Or was it one of those Cold War cybernetic counterinsurgency systems the Pentagon dreamed about for so long? Was there a difference?

I shake Brantingham's hand and leave his office. As I walk across UCLA's campus to my car, I think about our conversation. Based on what I have already found investigating Silicon Valley's private surveillance business, I am not that surprised to learn that Google is in bed with a crime prediction start-up spun off from counterinsurgency research.

The Internet has come a long way since Larry Page and Sergey Brin converted Google from a Stanford PhD project to a multi-billion-dollar company. But in a lot of ways it hasn't changed much from its ARPANET days. It's just gotten more powerful.

Development on the consumer front was the most dramatic. The commercial Internet we know today formed in the early 1990s, when the National Science Foundation privatized the NSFNET. Within the space of two decades, the network grew from a simple data and telecommunications medium into a vast global internetwork of computers, smartphones, apps, fiber-optic cables, cellular networks, and warehouse data centers so large they could fit entire Manhattan neighborhoods inside them. Today, the Internet surrounds us. It mediates modern life. We read books and newspapers on the Internet; bank, shop, and play video games on the Internet. We talk on the phone, attend college, find jobs, flirt, work, listen to music and watch movies, make dentist appointments, and get psychological counseling on the

Internet. Air conditioners, phones, watches, pet food dispensers, baby monitors, cars, refrigerators, televisions, light bulbs—they all connect to the Internet, too. The world's poorest places may lack plumbing and electricity, but they, sure enough, have access to the Internet.

The Internet is like a giant, unseen blob that engulfs the modern world. There is no escape, and, as Page and Brin so astutely understood when they launched Google, everything that people do online leaves a trail of data. If saved and used correctly, these traces make up a gold mine of information full of insights into people on a personal level as well as a valuable read on macro cultural, economic, and political trends.

Google was the first Internet company to fully leverage this insight and build a business on the data people leave behind. But it wasn't alone for long. Something in technology pushed other companies in the same direction. It happened just about everywhere, from the smallest app to the most sprawling platform.

Netflix monitored the films people watched to suggest other films but also to guide the licensing of content and the production of new shows.[78] Angry Birds, the game out of Finland that went viral, grabbed data from people's smartphones to build profiles, with data points like age, gender, household income, marital status, sexual orientation, ethnicity, and even political alignment, and to transmit them to third-party targeted advertising companies.[79] Executives at Pandora, the music streaming service, built a new revenue stream by profiling their seventy-three million listeners, grabbing their political beliefs, ethnicity, income, and even parenting status, then selling the info to advertisers and political campaigns.[80] Apple mined data on people's devices—photos, emails, text messages, and locations—to help organize information and anticipate users' needs. In its promotional materials, it touted this as a kind of digital personal assistant that could "make proactive suggestions for where you're likely to go."

Pierre Omidyar's eBay, the world's biggest online auction site, deployed specialized software that monitored user data and matched them with information available online to unmask fraudulent sellers.[81] Jeff Bezos dreamed of building his online retailer Amazon into the "everything store," a global sales platform that would anticipate users' every need and desire and deliver products without being asked.[82] To do that, Amazon deployed a system for monitoring and profiling. It recorded people's shopping habits, their movie preferences, the books they were interested in, how fast they read books on their Kindles, and the highlights and margin notes they made. It also monitored its warehouse workers, tracking their movements and timing their performance.[83] Amazon requires incredible processing power to run such a massive data business, a need that spawned a lucrative side business of renting out space on its massive servers to other companies. Today, the company is not just the world's biggest retailer but also the world's biggest Internet hosting company, bringing in $10 billion a year from storing other firms' data.[84]

Facebook, which started out as a "hot or not" rating game at Harvard, grew into a global social media platform powered by a Google-like targeted advertising model. The company gobbled up everything its users did: posts, texts, photos, videos, likes and dislikes, friend requests accepted and rejected, family connections, marriages, divorces, locations, political views, and even deleted posts that had never been published. All of it was fed into Facebook's secret profiling algorithm that turned the details of private lives into private commodities. The company's ability to link people's opinions, interests, and group and community affiliations made it a favorite of advertising and marketing firms of all kinds.

Political campaigns in particular loved the direct access Facebook offered. Instead of blanketing airwaves with a single political ad, they could use detailed behavioral profiles to micro-target their messaging, showing ads that appealed specifically to individuals and the issues they held dear. Facebook even allowed campaigns to upload lists of potential voters and supporters directly into the company's data system, and then use those people's social networks to extrapolate other people who might be supportive of a candidate.[85] It was a powerful and profitable tool. A decade after Mark Zuckerberg transfigured the company from a Harvard project, 1.28 billion people worldwide used the platform daily, and Facebook minted $62 in revenue for every one of its users in America.[86]

Uber, the Internet taxi company, deployed data to evade government regulation and oversight in support of its aggressive expansion into cities where it operated illegally. To do this, the company developed a special tool that analyzed user credit card information, phone numbers, locations and movements, and the way that users used the app to identify whether or not they were police officers or government officials who might be hailing an Uber only to ticket drivers or impound their cars. If the profile was a match, these users were silently blacklisted from the app.[87]

Uber, Amazon, Facebook, eBay, Tinder, Apple, Lyft, FourSquare, Airbnb, Spotify, Instagram, Twitter, Angry Birds. If you zoom out and look at the bigger picture, you can see that, taken together, these companies have turned our computers and phones into bugs that are plugged in to a vast corporate-owned surveillance network. Where we go, what we do, what we talk about, who we talk to, and who we see—everything is recorded and, at some point, leveraged for value. Google, Apple, and Facebook know when a woman visits an abortion clinic, even if she tells no one else: the GPS coordinates on the phone don't lie. One-night stands and extramarital affairs are a cinch to figure out: two smartphones that never met before suddenly cross paths in a bar and then make their way to an apartment across town, stay together overnight, and part in the morning. They know us intimately, even the things that we hide from those closest to us. And, as Uber's Greyball program so clearly shows, no one escapes—not even the police.

In our modern Internet ecosystem, this kind of private surveillance is the norm. It is as unnoticed and unremarkable as the air we breathe. But even in this advanced data-hungry environment, in terms of sheer scope and ubiquity, Google reigns supreme.

As the Internet expanded, Google grew along with it. Flush with cash, Google went on a dizzying shopping spree. It bought companies and start-ups, absorbing them into its burgeoning platform. It went beyond search and email, broadened into word processing, databases, blogging, social media networks, cloud hosting, mobile platforms, browsers, navigation aids, cloud-based laptops, and a whole range of office and productivity applications. It could be hard to keep track of them all: Gmail, Google Docs, Google Drive, Google Maps, Android, Google Play, Google Cloud, YouTube, Google Translate, Google Hangouts, Google Chrome, Google+, Google Sites, Google Developer, Google Voice, Google Analytics, Android TV. It blasted beyond pure Internet services and delved into fiber-optic telecommunication systems, tablets, laptops, home security cameras, self-driving cars, shopping delivery, robots, electric power plants, life extension technology, cyber security, and biotech. The company even launched a powerful in-house investment bank that now rivals Wall Street companies, investing money in everything from Uber to obscure agricultural crop monitoring start-ups, ambitious human DNA sequencing companies like 23andME, and a secretive life extension research center called Calico.[88]

No matter what service it deployed or what market it entered, surveillance and prediction were cooked into the business. The data flowing through Google's system are staggering. By the end of 2016, Google's Android was installed on 82 percent of all new smartphones sold around the world, with over 1.5 billion Android users globally.[89] At the same time, Google handled billions of searches and YouTube plays daily and had a billion active Gmail users, which meant it had access to most of the world's emails.[90] Some analysts estimate that 25 percent of all Internet traffic in North America goes through Google servers.[91] The company isn't just connected to the Internet, it *is* the Internet.

Google has pioneered a whole new type of business transaction. Instead of paying for Google's services with money, people pay with their data. And the services it offers to consumers are just the lures— used to grab people's data and dominate their attention, attention that is contracted out to advertisers. Google has used data to grow its empire. By 2017, it had $90 billion in revenues and $20 billion in profits, with seventy-two thousand full-time employees working out of seventy offices in more than forty countries.[92] It had a market capitalization of $593 billion, making it the second-most-valuable public company in the world—second only to Apple, another Silicon Valley giant.[93]

Meanwhile, other Internet companies depend on Google for survival. Snapchat, Twitter, Facebook, Lyft, and Uber—all have built multi-billion-dollar businesses on top of Google's ubiquitous mobile operating system. As the gatekeeper, Google benefits from their success as well. The more people use their mobile devices, the more data it gets on them.

What does Google know? What can it guess? Well, it seems just about everything. "One of the things that eventually happens . . . is that we don't need you to type at all," Eric Schmidt, Google's CEO, said in a moment of candor in 2010. "Because we know where you are. We know where you've been. We can more or less guess what you're thinking about."[94] He later added, "One day we had a conversation where we figured we could just try to predict the stock market. And then we decided it was illegal. So we stopped doing that."

It is a scary thought, considering Google is no longer a cute start-up but a powerful global corporation with its own political agenda and a mission to maximize profits for shareholders. Imagine if Philip Morris, Goldman Sachs, or a military contractor like Lockheed Martin had this kind of access.

Google Government

Not long after Sergey Brin and Larry Page incorporated Google, they began to see their mission in bigger terms. They weren't just building a search engine or a targeted advertising business. They were organizing the world's information to make it accessible and useful for everyone. It was a vision that also encompassed the Pentagon.

Even as Google grew to dominate the consumer Internet, a second side of the company emerged, one that rarely got much notice: Google the government contractor. As it turns out, the same platforms and services that Google deploys to monitor people's lives and grab their data could be put to use running huge swaths of the US government, including the military, spy agencies, police departments, and schools. The key to this transformation was a small start-up now known as Google Earth.

In 2003, a San Francisco company called Keyhole Incorporated was on the ropes. Named like the CIA's secret 1960s "Keyhole" spy satellite program, the company had been launched two years earlier as a spinoff from a video game outfit. Its CEO, John Hanke, hailed from Texas and had worked for a time in the US Embassy in Myanmar. He told journalists that the inspiration for his company came from Neal Stephenson's *Snow Crash*, a cult sci-fi novel in which the hero taps into a program created by the "Central Intelligence Corporation" called Planet Earth, a virtual reality construct designed to "keep track of every bit of spatial information that it owns—all the maps, weather data, architectural plans, and satellite surveillance stuff."[95]

Life would imitate art.[96]

Keyhole derived from video game technology but deployed it in the real world, creating a program that stitched satellite images and aerial photographs into seamless three-dimensional computer models of the earth that could be explored as if they were in a virtual reality game world. It was a groundbreaking product that allowed anyone with an Internet connection to virtually fly over anywhere in the world. The only problem was Keyhole's timing; it was a bit off. It launched just as the dot-com bubble blew up in Silicon Valley's face. Funding dried up, and Keyhole found itself struggling to survive.[97] Luckily, the company was saved just in time by the very entity that inspired it: the Central Intelligence Agency.

In 1999, at the peak of the dot-com boom, the CIA had launched In-Q-Tel, a Silicon Valley venture capital fund whose mission was to invest in start-ups that aligned with the agency's intelligence needs.[98] Keyhole seemed a perfect fit.[99]

The CIA poured an unknown amount of money into Keyhole; the exact number remains classified. The investment was finalized in early 2003, and it was made in partnership with the National Geospatial-Intelligence Agency, a major intelligence organization with 14,500 employees and a $5 billion budget whose job was to deliver satellite intelligence to the CIA and the Pentagon. Known by its alphabet-soup acronym "NGA," the spy agency's motto was: "Know the Earth . . . Show the Way . . . Understand the World."[100]

The CIA and NGA were not just investors; they were also clients, and they involved themselves in customizing Keyhole's virtual map product to meet their own needs.[101] Months after In-Q-Tel's investment, Keyhole software was already integrated into operational service and deployed to support American troops during Operation Iraqi Freedom, the shock-and-awe campaign to overthrow Saddam Hussein.[102] Intelligence officials were impressed with the "video game-like" simplicity of its virtual maps. They also appreciated the ability to layer visual information over other intelligence.[103] The possibilities were limited only by what contextual data could be fed and grafted onto a map: troop movements, weapons caches, real-time weather and ocean conditions, intercepted emails and phone call intel, cell phone locations. Keyhole gave an intelligence analyst, a commander in the field, or an air force pilot up in the air the kind of capability that we now take for granted: using digital mapping services on our computers and mobile phones to look up restaurants, cafes, museums, traffic conditions, and subway routes. "We could do these mashups and expose existing legacy data sources in a matter of hours, rather than weeks, months, or years," an NGA official gushed a few years later.[104]

Military commanders weren't the only ones who liked Keyhole. So did Sergey Brin. He liked it so much he insisted on personally demo-ing the app for Google executives. In an account published in *Wired,* he barged in on a company meeting, punched in the address of every person present, and used the program to virtually fly over their homes.[105]

In 2004, the same year Google went public, Brin and Page bought the company outright, CIA investors and all.[106] They then absorbed the company into Google's growing Internet applications platform. Keyhole was reborn as Google Earth.

The purchase of Keyhole was a major milestone for Google, marking the moment the company stopped being a purely consumer-facing Internet company and began integrating with the US government. When Google bought Keyhole, it also acquired an In-Q-Tel executive named Rob Painter, who came with deep connections to the world of intelligence and military contracting, including US Special Operations, the CIA, and major defense firms like

Raytheon, Northrop Grumman, and Lockheed Martin.[107] At Google, Painter was planted in a new dedicated sales and lobbying division called Google Federal, located in Reston, Virginia, a short drive from the CIA's headquarters in Langley. His job at Google was to help the company grab a slice of the lucrative military-intelligence contracting market. Or, as Painter described in contractor-bureaucratese, "evangelizing and implementing Google Enterprise solutions for a host of users across the Intelligence and Defense Communities."

Google had closed a few previous deals with intelligence agencies. In 2003, it scored a $2.1 million contract to outfit the NSA with a customized search solution that could scan and recognize millions of documents in twenty-four languages, including on-call tech support in case anything went wrong. In 2004, as it was dealing with the fallout over Gmail email scanning, Google landed a search contract with the CIA. The value of the deal isn't known, but the CIA did ask Google's permission to customize the CIA's internal Google search page by placing the CIA's seal in one of the Google Os. "I told our sales rep to give them the okay if they promised not to tell anyone. I didn't want it spooking privacy advocates," Douglas Edwards wrote in *I'm Feeling Lucky*.[108] Deals like these picked up pace and increased in scope after Google's Keyhole acquisition.

In 2006, Painter's Google Federal went on a hiring spree, snapping up managers and salespeople from the army, air force, CIA, Raytheon, and Lockheed Martin.[109] It beefed up its lobbying muscle and assembled a team of Democratic and Republican operatives. Google even grabbed ARPA's old show pony: Vint Cerf, who, as Google's vice president and chief Internet evangelist, served as a symbolic bridge between Google and the military.

While Google's public relations team did its best to keep the company wrapped in a false aura of geeky altruism, company executives pursued an aggressive strategy to become the Lockheed Martin of the Internet Age.[110] "We're functionally more than tripling the team each year," Painter said in 2008.[111] It was true. With insiders plying their trade, Google's expansion into the world of military and intelligence contracting took off.

In 2007, it partnered with Lockheed Martin to design a visual intelligence system for the NGA that displayed US military bases in Iraq and marked out Sunni and Shiite neighborhoods in Baghdad—important information for a region that had experienced a bloody sectarian insurgency and ethnic cleansing campaign between the two groups.[112] In 2008, Google won a contract to run the servers and search technology that powered the CIA's Intellipedia, an intelligence database modeled after Wikipedia that was collaboratively edited by the NSA, CIA, FBI, and other federal agencies.[113] Not long after that, Google contracted with the US Army to equip fifty thousand soldiers with a customized suite of mobile Google services.[114]

In 2010, as a sign of just how deeply Google had integrated with US intelligence agencies, it won a no-bid exclusive $27 million contract to provide the NGA with "geospatial visualization services," effectively making the Internet giant the "eyes" of America's defense and intelligence apparatus. Competitors criticized the NGA for not opening the contract to the customary bidding process, but the agency defended its decision, saying it had no choice: it had spent years working with Google on secret and top-secret programs to build Google Earth technology according to its needs and could not go with any other company.[115]

Google has been tightlipped about the details and scope of its contracting business. It does not list this revenue in a separate column in quarterly earnings reports to investors, nor does it provide the sum to reporters. But an analysis of the federal contracting database maintained by the US government, combined with information gleaned from Freedom of Information Act requests and published periodic reports on the company's military work, reveals that Google has been doing brisk business selling Google Search, Google Earth, and Google Enterprise (now known as G Suite) products to just about every major military and intelligence agency: navy, army, air force, Coast Guard, DARPA, NSA, FBI, DEA, CIA, NGA, and the State Department.[116] Sometimes Google sells directly to the government, but it also works with established contractors like Lockheed Martin, Raytheon, Northrop Grumman, and SAIC (Science Applications International Corporation), a California-based intelligence mega-contractor that has so many former NSA employees working for it that it is known in the business as "NSA West."[117]

Google's entry into this market makes sense. By the time Google Federal went online in 2006, the Pentagon was spending the bulk of its budget on private contractors. That year, of the $60 billion US intelligence budget, 70 percent, or $42 billion, went to corporations. That means that, although the government pays the bill, the actual work is done by Lockheed Martin, Raytheon, Boeing, Bechtel, Booz Allen Hamilton, and other powerful contractors.[118] And this isn't just in the defense sector. By 2017, the federal government was spending $90 billion a year on information technology.[119] It's a huge market—one in which Google seeks to maintain a strong presence. And its success has been all but guaranteed. Its products are the best in the business.[120]

A sign of how vital Google has become to the US government: in 2010, following a disastrous intrusion into its system by what the company believes was a group of Chinese government hackers, Google entered into a secretive agreement with the National Security Agency.[121] "According to officials who were privy to the details of Google's arrangements with the NSA, the company agreed to provide information about traffic on its networks in exchange for intelligence from the NSA about what it knew of foreign hackers," wrote defense reporter Shane Harris in *@War*, a history of warfare. "It was a quid pro quo, information for information. And from the NSA's perspective, information in exchange for protection."[122]

This made perfect sense. Google servers supplied critical services to the Pentagon, the CIA, and the State Department, just to name a few. It was part of the military family and essential to American society. It needed to be protected, too.

Google didn't just work with intelligence and military agencies but also sought to penetrate every level of society, including civilian federal agencies, cities, states, local police departments, emergency responders, hospitals, public schools, and all sorts of companies and nonprofits. In 2011, the National Oceanic and Atmospheric

Administration, the federal agency that researches weather and the environment, switched over to Google.[123] In 2014, the city of Boston deployed Google to run the information infrastructure for its eighty thousand employees—from police officers to teachers—and even migrated its old emails to the Google cloud.[124] The Forest Service and the Federal Highway Administration use Google Earth and Gmail. In 2016, New York City tapped Google to install and run free Wi-Fi stations across the city.[125] California, Nevada, and Iowa, meanwhile, depend on Google for cloud computing platforms that predict and catch welfare fraud.[126] Meanwhile, Google mediates the education of more than half of America's public school students.[127]

"What we really do is allow you to aggregate, collaborate and enable," explained Scott Ciabattari, a Google Federal sales rep, during a 2013 government contracting conference in Laramie, Wyoming. He was pitching a room full of civil servants, telling them that Google was all about getting them—intelligence analysts, commanders, government managers, and police officers—access to the right information at the right time.[128] He ran through a few examples: tracking flu outbreaks, monitoring floods and wildfires, safely serving criminal warrants, integrating surveillance cameras and face recognition systems, and even helping police officers respond to school shootings. "We are starting to see, unfortunately, with some of the incidents that happen with schools, the ability to do a floor plan," he said. "We are getting this request more and more. 'Can you help us publish all the floorplans for our school district. If there is a shooting disaster, God forbid, we want to know where things are.' Having that ability on a smart phone. Being able to see that information quickly at the right time saves lives." A few months after this presentation, Ciabattari met with Oakland officials to discuss how Google could help the California city build its police surveillance center.

This mixing of military, police, government, public education, business, and consumer-facing systems—all funneled through Google—continues to raise alarms. Lawyers fret over whether Gmail violates attorney-client privilege.[129] Parents wonder what Google does with the information it collects on their kids at school. What does

Google do with the data that flow through its system? Is all of it fed into Google's big corporate surveillance pot? What are Google's limits and restrictions? Are there any? In response to these questions, Google offers only vague and conflicting answers.[130]

Of course, this concern isn't restricted to Google alone. Under the hood of most other Internet companies we use every day are vast systems of private surveillance that, in one way or another, work with and empower the state.

eBay built up an internal police division headed by veterans of the Drug Enforcement Agency and the Department of Justice. It is staffed by over a thousand private investigators, who work closely with intelligence and law enforcement agencies in every country where it operates.[131] The company runs seminars and training sessions and offers travel junkets to cops around the world.[132] eBay is proud of its relationship with law enforcement and boasts that its efforts have led to the arrests of three thousand people around the world—roughly three per day since the division started.[133]

Amazon runs cloud computing and storage services for the CIA.[134] The initial contract, signed in 2013, was worth $600 million and was later expanded to include the NSA and a dozen other US intelligence agencies.[135] Amazon founder Jeff Bezos used his wealth to launch Blue Origin, a missile company that partners with Lockheed Martin and Boeing.[136] Blue Origin is a direct competitor of SpaceX, a space company started by another Internet mogul: PayPal cofounder Elon Musk. Meanwhile, another PayPal founder, Peter Thiel, spun off PayPal's sophisticated fraud-detection algorithm into Palantir Technologies, a major military contractor that provides sophisticated data-mining services for the NSA and CIA.[137]

Facebook, too, is cozy with the military. It poached former DARPA head Regina Dugan to run its secretive "Building 8" research division, which is involved in everything from artificial intelligence to drone-based wireless Internet networks. Facebook is betting big on virtual reality as the user interface of the future. The Pentagon is, too. According to reports, Facebook's Oculus virtual reality headset has already been integrated into DARPA's Plan X, a $110 million project to build an immersive, fully virtual reality environment to fight cyberwars.[138] It sounds like something straight out of William Gibson's *Neuromancer*, and it seems to work, too. In 2016, DARPA announced that Plan X would be transitioned to operational use by the Pentagon's Cyber Command within a year.[139]

On a higher level, there is no real difference between Google's relationship with the US government and that of these other Internet companies. It is just a matter of degree. The sheer breadth and scope of Google's technology make it a perfect stand-in for the rest of the commercial Internet ecosystem.

Indeed, Google's size and ambition make it more than a simple contractor. It is frequently an equal partner that works side by side with government agencies, using its resources and commercial dominance to bring companies with heavy military funding to market. In 2008, it launched a private spy satellite called *GeoEye-1* in partnership with the National Geospatial-Intelligence Agency.[140] It bought Boston Dynamics, a DARPA-seeded robotics company that made experimental robotic pack mules for the military, only to sell it off after the Pentagon determined it would not be putting these robots into active use.[141] It has invested $100 million in CrowdStrike, a major military and intelligence cyber defense contractor that, among other things, led the investigation into the alleged 2016 Russian government hacks of the Democratic National Committee.[142] And it also runs JigSaw, a hybrid think tank–technology incubator aimed at leveraging Internet technology to solve thorny foreign policy problems, everything from terrorism to censorship and cyberwarfare.[143]

Founded in 2010 by Eric Schmidt and Jared Cohen, a twenty-nine-year-old State Department whiz kid who served under both President George W. Bush and President Barack Obama, JigSaw has launched multiple projects with foreign policy and national security implications.[144] It ran polling for the US government to help war-torn Somalia draft a new constitution, developed tools to track global arms sales, and worked with a start-up funded by the State Department to help people in Iran and China route around Internet censorship.[145] It also built a platform to combat online terrorist recruitment and radicalization, which worked by identifying Google users interested in Islamic extremist topics and diverting them to State Department webpages and videos developed to dissuade people from taking that path.[146] Google calls this the "Redirect Method," a part of Cohen's larger idea of using Internet platforms to wage "digital counterinsurgency."[147] And, in 2012, as the civil war in Syria intensified and American support for rebel forces there increased, JigSaw brainstormed ways it could help push Bashar al-Assad from power. Among them: a tool that visually maps high-level defections from Assad's government, which Cohen wanted to beam into Syria as propaganda to give "confidence to the opposition." "I've attached a few visuals that show what the tool will look like," Cohen wrote to several top aides of Hillary Clinton, who was then secretary of state. "Please keep this very close hold and let me know if there is anything else you think we need to account for or think about before we launch."[148] As leaked emails show, Secretary Clinton was intrigued, telling her aides to print out Cohen's mockup of the application so she could look at it herself.[149]

JigSaw seemed to blur the line between public and corporate diplomacy, and at least one former State Department official accused it of fomenting regime change in the Middle East.[150] "Google is getting [White House] and State Dept. support & air cover. In reality, they are doing things the CIA cannot do," wrote Fred Burton, a Stratfor executive and former intelligence agent of the Diplomatic Security Service, the armed security branch of the State Department.[151]

But Google rejected the claims of its critics. "We're not engaged in regime change," Eric Schmidt told *Wired*.[152] "We don't do that stuff. But if it turns out that empowering citizens with smartphones and information causes changes in their country . . . you know, that's probably a good thing, don't you think?"

Mediating Everything and Everyone

JigSaw's work with the State Department has raised eyebrows, but its function is a mere taste of the future if Google gets its way.

As the company makes new deals with the NSA and continues its merger with the US security apparatus, its founders see it playing an even greater role in global society.

"The societal goal is our primary goal. We've always tried to say that with Google. Some of the most fundamental questions which people are not thinking about, there's the question of how do we organize people, how do we motivate people. It's a really interesting problem, how do we organize our democracies?" ruminated Larry Page during a rare interview in 2014 with the *Financial Times*. He looked a hundred years into the future and saw Google at the center of progress. "We could probably solve a lot of the issues we have as humans."[153]

Spend time listening to and reading the words of Google executives, and you quickly realize they see no hard line separating government and Google. They look into the future and see Internet companies morphing into operating systems for society. To them, the world is too big, and moves too quickly, for traditional governments to keep up.[154] The world needs the help of Google to lead the way, to provide ideas, investment, and technical knowledge. And, anyway, there is no stopping the spread of technology.[155] Transportation, entertainment, power plants and power grids, police departments, jobs, public transportation, health care, agriculture, housing, elections and political systems, war, and even space exploration—it is all plugged into the Internet, and companies like Google can't help but be at the center. There is no escape.

Some people at Google talk about building a new city from the "Internet up," using Google's data architecture as the foundation, unencumbered by government regulations that restrict innovation and progress.[156] This brave new world, wired thick with Google biosensors and blinking with nonstop data flows, is really just the old cyber-libertarian dream world as first seen in the *Whole Earth Catalog* and Richard Brautigan's utopian poetry, a world where "mammals and computers / live together in mutually / programming harmony . . . a cybernetic forest . . . where deer stroll peacefully / past computers . . . and all watched over by machines of loving grace." Except in

Google's version of this future, the machines of loving grace aren't a benevolent abstraction but a powerful global corporation.[157]

The parallel does not inspire confidence. Back in the 1960s, many of Brand's New Communalists built microcommunities based on cybernetic ideas, believing that flat hierarchies, social transparency, and radical interconnectedness between individuals would abolish exploitation, hierarchy, and power. In the end, the attempt to replace politics with technology was the fatal flaw: without organized protection for the weak, these would-be utopias devolved into cults controlled by charismatic and dominant leaders who ruled their fiefdoms through bullying and intimidation. "There was constantly a background of fear in the house—like a virus running in the background. Like spyware. You know it's there, but you don't know how to get rid of it," recalled a member of a New Mexico commune that had descended into a nightmare world of sexual abuse and exploitation.

Spyware running in the background.

It is a curious choice of words to explain what it felt like to live in a 1970s cybernetic utopia gone bad. It is also an accurate description of the world Google and the Internet have made today.

Chapter 6

Edward Snowden's Arms Race

A specter is haunting the modern world, the specter of crypto anarchy.

—Timothy C. May, *The Crypto Anarchist Manifesto*, 1988

I n June 2013, headlines flashed across the world: an employee of the National Security Agency had fled the country with a huge cache of top-secret documents and was blowing the whistle on America's global surveillance apparatus. At first the identity of this NSA leaker remained shrouded in mystery. Journalists descended on Hong Kong, scouring hotel lobbies desperately hunting for leads. Finally, a photograph emerged: a thin, pale young man with disheveled hair, wire-rim glasses, and a gray shirt open at the collar sitting on a hotel room sofa—calm but looking like he hadn't slept for days.

His name was Edward Snowden—"Ed," as he wanted people to call him. He was twenty-nine years old. His résumé was a veritable treasure trove of spook world subcontracting: Central Intelligence Agency, US Defense Intelligence Agency, and, most recently, Booz Allen Hamilton, a defense contractor that ran digital surveillance operations for the National Security Agency.[1]

Sitting in his room at the five-star Hotel Mira in Hong Kong, Snowden told journalists from the *Guardian* that watching the global surveillance system operated by NSA had forced his hand and compelled him to become a whistleblower. "The NSA has built an infrastructure that allows it to intercept almost everything," he said in a calm, measured voice during a videotaped interview that first introduced the leaker and his motives to the world. "I don't want to live in a society that does these sorts of things. . . . I do not want to live in a world where everything I do and say is recorded. That is not something I am willing to support or live under."[2]

Over the next few months, a small group of journalists reviewed and reported on the documents Snowden had taken from the NSA. The material backed up his claims, no doubt about it. The US government was running a vast Internet surveillance program, hacking mobile phones, splicing into undersea fiber-optic cables, subverting encryption protocols, and tapping just about every major Silicon Valley platform and company—Facebook, Google, Apple, Amazon. Even mobile games like Angry Birds didn't escape the spy agency's notice. Nothing seemed to be off limits.

The revelations triggered a scandal of global proportions. Privacy, surveillance, and data gathering on the Internet were no longer considered fringe matters relegated mostly to the margins but important subjects that won Pulitzers and deserved front-page treatment in the *New York Times, Wall Street Journal,* and *Washington Post.* And Snowden himself, on the run from the US government, became the stuff of legend, his story immortalized on the big screen: an Academy Award–winning documentary and a Hollywood film directed by Oliver Stone, his role played by Joseph Gordon-Levitt.

Following Snowden's disclosures, people were suddenly appalled and outraged that the US government would use the Internet for surveillance. But given the Internet's counterinsurgency origins, its role in spying on Americans going back to the 1970s, and the close ties between the Pentagon and such companies as Google, Facebook, and Amazon, this news should not have come as a surprise. That it *did* shock so many is a testament to the fact that the military history of the Internet had been flushed from society's collective memory.

The truth is that the Internet came out of a Pentagon project to develop modern communication and information systems that would allow the United States to get the drop on its enemies, both at home and abroad. That effort was a success, exceeding all expectations. So, of course, the US government leveraged the technology it had created, and keeps leveraging it to the max. How could it not?

Plug 'n Play

Governments have been spying on telecommunications systems for as long as they've been around, going back to the days of the telegraph and the early phone systems. In the nineteenth century, President Abraham Lincoln gave his secretary of war, Edwin Stanton, broad powers over the country's telegraph network, allowing him to spy on communications and to control the spread of unwanted information during the Civil War. In the early twentieth century, the Federal Bureau of Investigation tapped phone systems with impunity, spying on bootleggers, labor activists, civil rights leaders, and anyone J. Edgar Hoover considered a subversive and a threat to America. In the twenty-first century, the Internet opened up whole new vistas and possibilities.[3]

The ARPANET was first used to spy on Americans in 1972, when it was employed to transfer surveillance files on antiwar protesters and civil rights leaders that the US Army had collected. Back then, the network was just a tool to let the Pentagon quickly and easily share data with other agencies.[4] To actually spy on people, the army first had to gather the information. That meant sending agents into the world to watch people, interview neighbors, bug phones, and spend nights staking out targets. It was a laborious process and, at one point, the army had set up its own fake news outfit so that agents could film and interview antiwar protesters more easily. The modern Internet changed the need for all these elaborate schemes.

Email, shopping, photo and video sharing, dating, social media, smartphones—the world doesn't just communicate via the Internet, it lives on the Internet. And all of this living leaves a trail. If the platforms run by Google, Facebook, and Apple could be used to spy on users in order to serve them targeted ads, pinpoint movie preferences, customize news feeds, or guess where people will go for dinner, why couldn't they also be used to fight terrorism, prevent crime, and keep the world safe? The answer is: Of course they can.

By the time Edward Snowden appeared on the scene, police departments from San Francisco to Miami were using social media platforms to infiltrate and watch political groups and monitor protests. Investigators created fake accounts and ingratiated themselves into their mark's social network, then filed warrants to access private messages and other underlying data not available publicly. Some, like the New York Police Department, launched specialized divisions that used social media as a central investigative tool. Detectives could spend years monitoring suspects' Internet activity, compiling posts from YouTube, Facebook, and Twitter, mapping social relationships, deciphering slang, tracking movements, and then correlating them with possible crimes.[5] Others, like the state of Maryland, built custom solutions that included facial recognition software so that police officers could identify people photographed at protests by matching the images scraped off Instagram and Facebook to those in the state's driver's license database.[6] A publishing industry that taught cops how to conduct investigations using the Internet flourished, with training manual titles like *The Poor Cops Wiretap: Turning a Cell Phone into a Surveillance Tool Using Free Applications* and *Google Timeline: Location Investigations Involving Android Devices;* it was a popular genre.[7]

Naturally, federal intelligence agencies were pioneers in this space.[8] The Central Intelligence Agency was a big and early fan of what it called "open source intelligence"—information that it could grab from the public Web: videos, personal blogs, photos, and posts on platforms like YouTube, Twitter, Facebook, Instagram, and Google+.[9] In 2005, the agency partnered with the Office of the Director of National Intelligence to launch the Open Source Center, dedicated to building open-source collection tools and sharing them with other federal intelligence agencies.[10] Through its In-Q-Tel venture capital fund, the CIA invested in all sorts of companies that mined the Internet for open-source intelligence.[11] It invested in Dataminr, which bought access to Twitter data and analyzed people's tweets to spot potential threats.[12] It backed "a social media intelligence" company called PATHAR that monitored Facebook, Instagram, and Twitter accounts for signs of Islamic radicalization. And it supported a popular product called Geofeedia, which allowed its clients to display social media posts from Facebook, YouTube, Twitter, and Instagram from specific geographic locations, down to the size of a city block. Users could watch in real time or wind the clock back to earlier times.[13] In 2016, Geofeedia had five hundred police departments as clients and touted its ability to monitor "overt threats": unions, protests, rioting, and activist groups.[14] All these CIA-backed companies paid Facebook, Google, and Twitter for special access to social media data—adding another lucrative revenue stream to Silicon Valley.[15]

Surveillance is just a starting point. Harking back to the original Cold War dream of building predictive systems, military and intelligence officials saw platforms like Facebook, Twitter, and Google as more than just information tools that could be scoured for information on individual crimes or individual events. They could be the eyes and ears of a vast interconnected early warning system predicting human behavior—and ultimately change the course of the future.

By the time Edward Snowden blew the whistle on the NSA in the summer of 2013, at least a dozen publicly disclosed US government programs were leveraging open source intelligence to predict the future. The US Air Force had a "Social Radar" initiative to tap intelligence coming in from the Internet, a system explicitly patterned after the early warning radar systems used to track enemy airplanes.[16] The Intelligence Advanced Research Project Agency, run by the Office of the Director of National Intelligence, had multiple "anticipatory intelligence" research programs involving everything from mining

YouTube videos for terrorist threats to predicting instability by scanning Twitter feeds and blogs and monitoring the Internet to predict future cyberattacks.[17] DARPA ran a human radar project as well: the World-Wide Integrated Crisis Early Warning System, or ICEWS, which is pronounced as "IQs." Started in 2007 and built by Lockheed Martin, the system ultimately grew into a full-fledged operational military prediction machine that had modules ingesting all sorts of open source network data—news wires, blogs, social media and Facebook posts, various Internet chatter, and "other sources of information"—and routing it through "sentiment analysis" in an attempt to predict military conflicts, insurgencies, civil wars, coups, and revolutions.[18] DARPA's ICEWS proved to be a success. Its core technology was spun off into a classified, operational version of the same system called ISPAN and absorbed into the US Strategic Command.[19]

The dream of building a global computer system that could watch the world and predict the future—it had a long and storied history in military circles. And, as the documents released by Snowden showed, the NSA played a central role in building the interception and analysis tools that would bring that dream to reality.[20]

The National Security Agency was established by a classified executive order signed by President Harry Truman in 1952. A highly secretive body whose very existence remained hushed for years after it was created, the agency had a dual mandate. One was offensive: to collect electronic communication and signals intelligence abroad, which meant grabbing radio and satellite transmissions, tapping telephone wires, and breaking the encryption used by foreign governments. The other was defensive: to prevent the penetration of critical US government communication systems by foreign powers. In the mid-1970s, when the existence of the NSA first came to public attention in a series of congressional hearings, the agency employed 120,000 people and had 2,000 overseas listening posts with giant antennas set up around the world listening to every pin drop and mouse scratch that came out of the Soviet Union.[21]

The NSA was involved with the Internet from the network's very beginnings as an ARPA research project. Starting in the early 1970s, it maintained a node on the early ARPANET and was directly implicated in using the network to transfer surveillance files on anti-war protesters and civil rights leaders that the US Army had illegally compiled.[22] In 1972, the NSA hired ARPA contractor Bolt, Beranek and Newman, where J. C. R. Licklider had served as vice president, to build an upgraded ARPANET version of its COINS intelligence network that eventually plugged in to the ARPANET, CIA, State Department, and Defense Intelligence Agency.[23] At the same time, it funded work on other classified ARPANET projects that would over the decades evolve into operational classified network systems, including the one that the NSA uses today: the NSANET.[24]

In the 2000s, as the Internet grew into a commercial telecommunications network, the NSA's signals intelligence mission expanded as well. By the time Edward Snowden transferred to his last and final NSA contracting job at Booz Allen Hamilton in Hawaii in 2013, the agency had a bead on just about everything that flowed over the Internet. True to its spy nature, NSA played a dual role. On the one hand, it worked with companies like Google and Amazon, buying their services and helping defend them from foreign hacks and cyberattacks. And on the other hand, the agency hacked these companies behind their back—punching holes and placing bugs in every device that it could penetrate. It was just doing its job.

Snowden's leaks revealed that the NSA had spy implants embedded in Internet exchange points where the backbones connecting countries met. It ran an elite hacker Tailored Access Operations unit that provided customized penetration solutions when the agency's general surveillance tools could not get the job done. It ran programs targeting every major personal computer platform: Microsoft Windows, Apple iOS, and Google Android, allowing spies to extract anything and everything those devices had.[25] In partnership with the United Kingdom's Government Communications Headquarters spy agency, the NSA launched a program called MUSCULAR that secretly spliced into the internal fiber-optic cable networks connecting one Silicon Valley data center to another, allowing the agency to get a "full take" of internal company data. Yahoo! was a target; so was Google—meaning the agency vacuumed up everything that Google had, including the profiles and dossiers the company kept on all its users. NSA documents gushed about the agency's ability to provide "a retrospective look at target activity," meaning all the emails and messages targets sent, all the places they went with an Android phone in their pocket.[26]

Perhaps the most scandalous NSA program revealed by Snowden's disclosures is called PRISM, which involves a sophisticated on-demand data tap housed within the datacenters of the biggest and most respected names in Silicon Valley: Google, Apple, Facebook, Yahoo!, and Microsoft. These devices allow the NSA to siphon off whatever the agency requires, including emails, attachments, chats, address books, files, photographs, audio files, search activity, and mobile phone location history.[27] According to the *Washington Post*, these companies knew about PRISM and helped the NSA build the special access to their network systems that PRISM requires, all without raising public alarm or notifying their users. "The engineering problems are so immense, in systems of such complexity and frequent change, that the FBI and NSA would be hard pressed to build in back doors without active help from each company."[28]

The *Washington Post* revealed that PRISM is administered for the NSA by the FBI's secretive Data Intercept Technology Unit, which also handles wiretaps on the Internet and telephone traffic flowing through major telecommunications companies like AT&T, Sprint, and Verizon. PRISM resembles traditional taps that the FBI maintained throughout the domestic telecommunications system. It works like this: using a specialized interface, an NSA analyst creates a data request, called a "tasking," for a specific user of a partnering company. "A tasking for Google, Yahoo, Microsoft, Apple and other providers is routed to equipment ["interception units"] installed at each company. This equipment, maintained by the FBI, passes the NSA request to a private company's system."[29] The tasking creates a digital wiretap that then forwards intelligence to the NSA in real time, all without any input from the company itself.[30] Analysts could even opt-in for alerts for when a particular target logs in to an account.[31] "Depending on the company, a tasking may return e-mails, attachments, address books, calendars, files stored in the cloud, text or audio or video chats and 'metadata' that identify the locations, devices used and other information about a target."[32]

The program, which began in 2007 under President George W. Bush and which was expanded under President Barack Obama, became a gold mine for American spies. Microsoft was the first to join in 2007. Yahoo! came online a year later, and Facebook and Google plugged in to PRISM in 2009. Skype and AOL both joined in 2011. Apple, the laggard of the bunch, joined the surveillance system in 2012.[33] Intelligence officials described PRISM as a key feeder system for foreign intelligence.[34] In 2013, PRISM was used to spy on over a hundred thousand people—"targets," in the parlance of the NSA. James R. Clapper, director of National Intelligence, described the products of PRISM as "among the most important and valuable foreign intelligence information we collect."[35]

The NSA documents, as revealed by the *Washington Post,* offered only a glimpse into the PRISM program but enough to show that the NSA had turned Silicon Valley's globe-spanning platforms into a de facto intelligence collection apparatus. All with the help of the industry itself. PRISM even featured an easy-to-use interface, with text alerts, no less.

These were damning revelations. And, for Silicon Valley, they carried an edge of danger.

A Threat Emerges

From their inception, Internet companies banked heavily on the utopian promise of a networked world. Even as they pursued contracts with the military and their founders joined the ranks of the richest people on the planet, they wanted the world to see them not just as the same old plutocrats out to maximize shareholder value and their own power but also as progressive agents leading the way into a bright techno-utopia. For a long time, they succeeded. Despite the slow dribble of news stories about Silicon Valley inking deals with the CIA and NSA, the industry was somehow able to convince the world that it was different, that it somehow stood in opposition to traditional power.

Then Edward Snowden screwed everything up.

Public disclosure of the NSA's PRISM program gave a glimpse into the symbiotic relationship between Silicon Valley and the US government and threatened to upend the industry's carefully cultivated image. This wasn't rumor or speculation but came from primary documents lifted from the depths of the most powerful spy agency in the world. They provided the first tangible evidence that the biggest and most respected Internet companies had worked in secret to funnel data on hundreds of thousands of users to the NSA, revealing by extension the vast amounts of personal data that these companies collected on their users—data that they owned and could use in any way they wanted.

You didn't have to be a tech expert to see that the government surveillance on the Internet simply could not exist without the private infrastructure and consumer services provided by Silicon Valley. Companies like Google, Facebook, Yahoo!, eBay, and Apple did all the heavy lifting: they built the platforms that drew in billions of users and collected a boggling amount of data about them. All that the NSA had to do to get at the data was connect a few wires, which the agency did with full cooperation and total discretion from the companies themselves.

In the months after Snowden went public, Silicon Valley and surveillance were suddenly front and center and intertwined. Arguments about the need to pass new laws that restricted data collection on the Internet by private companies joined calls to rein in the NSA's surveillance program. Everyone now knew that Google and Facebook were gobbling up every piece of data on us that they could get their hands on. A groundswell emerged around the idea that this had gone on for far too long. New controls and limits on data collection had to be put in place.

"Google may possess more information about more people than any entity in the history of the world. Its business model and its ability to execute it demonstrate that it will continue to collect personal information about the public at a galloping pace," warned the influential watchdog Public Citizen in a report that made headlines around the world. "The amount of information and influence that Google has amassed is now threatening to gain such a stranglehold on experts, regulators and lawmakers that it could leave the public powerless to act if it should decide that the company has become too pervasive, too omniscient and too powerful."[36]

The Internet companies responded with proclamations of innocence, denying any role in NSA's PRISM program. "Facebook is not and has never been part of any program to give the US or any other government direct access to our servers. We have never received a blanket request or court order from any government agency asking for information or metadata in bulk, like the one Verizon reportedly received. And if we did, we would fight it aggressively. We hadn't even heard of PRISM before yesterday," Mark Zuckerberg wrote in a Facebook post. He blamed the government and positioned Facebook as a victim. "I've called President Obama to express my frustration over the damage the government is creating for all of our future. Unfortunately, it seems like it will take a very long time for true full reform." Apple, Microsoft, Google, and Yahoo! all reacted in much the same way, denying the allegations and painting themselves as the victims of government overreach. "It's tremendously disappointing that the government sort of secretly did all this stuff and didn't tell us. We can't have a democracy if we're having to protect you and our users from the government," Larry Page told Charlie Rose in an interview on CBS.[37]

But their excuses rang hollow. "Despite the tech companies' assertions that they provide information on their customers only when required under law—and not knowingly through a back door—the perception that they enabled the spying program has lingered," reported the *New York Times* in 2014.[38]

For a moment after Snowden's leaks, Silicon Valley entered a state of paralyzed shock, frozen with fear over how to handle the scandal. It was an astounding time in history. You could almost hear the giant wheels of the Silicon Valley public relations machine grind to a halt. While analysts predicted multi-billion-dollar losses to the industry as a result of Snowden's revelations, an army of friendly bloggers, academics, think tanks, Astroturf groups, lobbyists, and journalists sat at their keyboards, staring at their hands, waiting with bated breath for a backlash.[39]

Edward Snowden terrified the industry.

Catapulted to the status of a cult hero, he now wielded massive influence. He could easily focus on Silicon Valley's private surveillance apparatus and explain that it was an integral part of the bigger surveillance machine operated by the NSA—that it was one of the two parts of the same system. With just a few words, he had the power to start a real political movement and galvanize people to push for real and meaningful privacy laws. In that moment, he had all the power. He was Larry Page's nightmare, the embodiment of why Google had to warn its investors that privacy laws posed an existential threat to its business: "Privacy concerns relating to elements of our technology could damage our reputation and deter current and potential users from using our products and services."[40]

But Silicon Valley was lucky. Snowden, a lifelong libertarian, had other ideas.

Lock and Load

Edward Joseph Snowden was born into a conservative family on June 21, 1983, in Elizabeth City, North Carolina. His father was a Coast Guard officer. His mother was a court administrator. He moved to Maryland in his teens and dropped out of high school in his sophomore year. It was then that he began to deepen a childhood interest in computers. He hung out on the web forum of Ars Technica, a technology news site with an active forum for likeminded geeks. There he came out as a right-wing libertarian: he hated the

New Deal, wanted to shrink the government to the size of a peanut, and believed the state had no right to control the money supply. He preferred the gold standard. He mocked old people for needing old-age pensions. "Somehow, our society managed to make it hundreds of years without social security just fine," he wrote on the forum. "Magically the world changed after the new deal, and old people became made of glass." He called people who defended America's Social Security system "fucking retards."[41]

In 2004, a year after the United States invaded Iraq, Snowden enlisted in the Army Special Forces program. He listed his religion as "Buddhist." Describing his decision to join the army, he said he felt an "obligation as a human being to help free people from oppression" and that he believed that the Special Forces were a noble bunch. "They are inserted behind enemy lines. It is a squad that has a number of different specialties. And they teach and enable the local population to resist or to support US forces in a way that allows the local population a chance to determine their own destiny."[42] Snowden never made it to Iraq (which always seemed a strange mission for a libertarian). He broke both legs in an exercise and failed to complete basic training. His life took a different turn.

He found work as a security guard at the NSA's Center for Advanced Study of Language at the University of Maryland. He moved quickly up the career ladder. In 2006, the CIA hired him as an information technology security specialist, a job that gave him top-secret security clearance and sent him to Geneva under State Department cover. This was no simple IT assignment. He was now a CIA field officer living in Europe. "I don't have a degree of ANY type. I don't even have a high school diploma," he anonymously bragged to his online friends at Ars Technica. An acquaintance of Snowden from his CIA days in Geneva described him as an "IT genius" as well as an accomplished martial arts fighter. His father boasted that his son possessed a genius-level IQ of 145.

In a note attached to his leaks, Snowden gave journalists a breakdown of his work experience:[43]

Edward Joseph Snowden, SSN: ****
CIA Alias "*****"
Agency Identification Number: *****
Former Senior Advisor | United States National Security
    Agency, under corporate cover
Former Field Officer | United States Central Intelligence
    Agency, under diplomatic cover
Former Lecturer | United States Defense Intelligence
    Agency, under corporate cover

Despite his work as an intelligence operative at the exact moment the CIA was expanding its global surveillance and drone assassination programs, it seemed Snowden somehow remained unaware that spying was taking place all over the Internet. As he recounted his story, it was only in 2009, after taking his first private contractor job, working for Dell at an NSA facility in Japan, that it really hit him. "I watched as Obama advanced the very policies that I thought would be reined in," he said. The US government was running a global surveillance operation. The world needed to know, and he began to see himself as the man to tell it.[44] "You can't wait around for someone else to act. I had been looking for leaders, but I realized that leadership is about being the first to act."[45]

He began to prepare. In 2012, he relocated to another NSA assignment for Dell, this time in Hawaii. There, working for the NSA's information-sharing office out of an underground bunker once used as a storage facility, Snowden began collecting the documents he would use to expose America's surveillance apparatus. He even applied for a transfer to a different NSA division—this one under contractor Booz Allen Hamilton—because it would give him access to a set of documents on US cyberwar operations that he thought the American people should see.[46] "My position with Booz Allen Hamilton granted me access to lists of machines all over the world the NSA hacked. That is why I accepted that position about three months ago," he told the *South China Morning Post* from his hideout in Hong Kong.[47]

Snowden explained his motive in simple moral terms. It was something that many could relate to, and he soon emerged as a global cult icon who cut through left and right political divides. To Michael Moore, he was the "hero of the year." To Glenn Beck, he was a patriotic leaker—courageous and not afraid to accept the consequences.[48] Even fellow NSA whistle-blowers were impressed. "I've never run across anyone quite like Snowden. He is a uniquely postmodern breed of whistle-blower," wrote James Bamford.[49] But for all the praise he received, this modern-day Daniel Ellsberg cut a peculiar political profile.

Edward Snowden eventually escaped to Russia, the only country that could guarantee his safety from the long arm of the United States. There, while living under state protection at an undisclosed location in Moscow, he swept Silicon Valley's role in Internet surveillance under the rug. Asked about it by *Washington Post* reporter Barton Gellman, who had first reported on the NSA's PRISM program, Snowden shrugged off the danger posed by companies like Google and Facebook. The reason? Because private companies do not have the power to arrest, jail, or kill people. "Twitter doesn't put warheads on foreheads," he joked.[50]

For someone who spent years cycling through the CIA and NSA, enjoying access to the deepest secrets of America's surveillance state, Snowden's views were curiously simple and naive. He seemed ignorant of the deep historical ties between technology companies and the US military. Indeed, he seemed ignorant about key aspects of the very documents he had lifted from the NSA, which showed just how integral data produced by consumer technology companies were to deadly government operations abroad. That included the CIA's global drone assassination program, which depended on the NSA tracking cellphones to Al-Qaeda operatives in Pakistan and Yemen, and then using that geolocation data to carry out missiles strikes.[51] Even General Michael Hayden, former director of the CIA and NSA, admitted that data taken from commercial technologies are used for strikes and hits. "We kill people based on metadata," he said during a debate at Johns Hopkins University.[52] In other words, Snowden's NSA documents proved the exact opposite of what Snowden was arguing. Wittingly or unwittingly, whether for good or ill, personal information generated by private companies—companies like Twitter, Google, and telecoms in Pakistan—did in fact *help* put warheads on foreheads.

Snowden's views on private surveillance were simplistic, but they seemed to be in line with his politics. He was a libertarian and believed the utopian promise of computer networks. He believed that the Internet was an inherently liberating technology that, if left alone, would evolve into a force of good in the world. The problem wasn't Silicon Valley; it was government power. To him, cynical intelligence agencies like the NSA had warped the utopian promise of the Internet, turning it into a dystopia where spies tracked our every move and recorded everything we said. He believed the government was the central problem and distrusted legislative or political solutions to curb surveillance, which would only involve the government even more. As it so happened, his line of thinking tracked perfectly with the antigovernment privacy initiatives that Internet companies like Google and Facebook had started pushing to deflect attention from their private surveillance practices.

"We need ways of engaging in private communications. We need mechanisms affording for private associations. And ultimately, we need ways to engage in private payment and shipping, which are the basis of trade," Snowden explained to Micah Lee in a posh Moscow hotel near Red Square. Lee was a former technologist with the EFF who, from his home in Berkeley, California, had worked in secret to help Snowden securely communicate with journalists and carry out his leaks. He'd trekked to Moscow to talk to Snowden face to face about what people could do to "reclaim their privacy."

"I think reform comes with many faces," Snowden told Lee. "That can be through technology, that can be through politics, that can be through voting, that can be through behavior. But technology is . . . perhaps the quickest and most promising means through which we can respond to the greatest violations of human rights in a manner that is not dependent on every single legislative body on the planet to reform itself at the same time, which is probably somewhat optimistic to hope for. We would be instead able to create systems . . . that enforce and guarantee the rights that are necessary to maintain a free and open society."[53]

To Snowden, the Internet was broken, but all was not lost. Laws, regulations, rules—in the long run none of these would do any good. The only truly permanent solution was technology.

What kind of technology? The Tor Project.

End of Government

In 2011, a mysterious store appeared on the Internet. Called Silk Road, it was an online store like any other, complete with customer reviews and a merchant rating system. But there was also something unique about this marketplace: it sold illegal drugs and was only accessible through a network called Tor, a novel Internet system that supposedly made the store and its users impervious to the law by moving all transactions onto a parallel anonymous network that sat atop the real Internet. Tor is what's now known as the "dark web."

"Making small talk with your pot dealer sucks. Buying cocaine can get you shot. What if you could buy and sell drugs online like books or light bulbs? Now you can: Welcome to Silk Road," wrote Adrian Chen, the reporter who broke the story for Gawker. "Through a combination of anonymity technology and a sophisticated user-feedback system, Silk Road makes buying and selling illegal drugs as easy as buying used electronics—and seemingly as safe. It's Amazon—if Amazon sold mind-altering chemicals."[54]

Built and operated by a mysterious figure who went by the name of Dread Pirate Roberts, Silk Road had two components that allowed it to operate in total anonymity. One, all purchases were processed using a new digital crypto-currency called Bitcoin, which was created by the mysterious pseudonymous cryptographer Satoshi Nakamoto.

Two, to use Silk Road, both buyers and sellers first had to download a program called Tor and use a specialized browser to access a specialized store URL—http://silkroad6ownowfk.onion—that took them off the Internet and into the Tor cloud, a.k.a. the dark web.

Tor was a cutting-edge anonymity tool made by Tor Project, a nonprofit set up in 2004 by a plump and ponytailed cryptographer named Roger Dingledine, who at the time ran it out of a cluttered office above a YMCA in Cambridge, Massachusetts. It had about a $2 million annual budget, a half dozen full-time employees, and a small group of dedicated volunteer coders around the world who helped develop, test, and release its product: a free cloaking app that worked on the basis of a technique called "onion routing." Users downloaded and launched a specialized Tor Internet browser that redirected their traffic onto a parallel volunteer peer-to-peer network, bouncing it around randomly before sending it off to its final destination. This trick disconnected the origin and destination of a person's Internet browsing stream and theoretically made it impossible for cops, spies, hackers, or anyone else monitoring Internet traffic to observe where users were coming from and where they were going. In lay terms, onion routing is like a street hustler playing a shell game with network traffic: people can see it go under one of the shells, but they never know where it ends up. Tor powered the bulk of the dark web. Tor pretty much *was* the dark web.

Thanks to Tor, Silk Road ran without a hitch. It developed a mass following and built a booming drug dealer community, like eBay did for amateur collectors. Former small-time drug dealers moved their operations online and expanded their client bases, which were no longer limited to personal connections and neighborhoods. Meanwhile, cops logged into Silk Road through Tor like anyone else and clicked through offerings of PCP, LSD, MDMA, cocaine, crystal meth, and ketamine and read customer reviews, but they didn't have a clue about the real-world identity of the people selling and buying the drugs; nor could they know where to serve their arrest warrants or which datacenters to raid. Everyone was anonymous and was trading anonymous cash. And Silk Road itself ran as a Tor "hidden service," which meant that it could be hosted in San Francisco or across the globe in Moscow. The only thing not anonymous was that the drugs had to be shipped, so drug sellers developed routines where they would drive for hours to neighboring cities to ship the goods; they never shipped from one location two times in a row. The FBI and Drug Enforcement Agency watched as kids bought and sold drugs in plain sight, while the Dread Pirate Roberts raked in an estimated $32 million a year in commissions, but they couldn't do anything to stop it.[55] Thanks to Tor, everyone was anonymous and safe. That's how powerful the technology was supposed to be. It seemed like magic.

Tor was the realization of a dream decades in the making.

Since the early 1990s, an influential group of programmers and hackers calling themselves "cypherpunks" had pursued a radical political idea. They believed that powerful encryption and anonymity technology, combined with untraceable digital currencies, would bring a revolution that swept away government power and established a decentralized global world order based on free markets and voluntary association.[56] "The State will of course try to slow or halt the spread of this technology, citing national security concerns, use of the technology by drug dealers and tax evaders, and fears of societal disintegration. Many of these concerns will be valid; crypto anarchy will allow national secrets to be traded freely and will allow illicit and stolen materials to be traded. An anonymous computerized market will even make possible abhorrent markets for assassinations and extortion," predicted Timothy May, a bearded, pioneering engineer at Intel and one of the key founders of the cypherpunk movement, back in 1992. May proselytized his ideas with a messianic zeal. By 1994, he was predicting that a global cryptorevolution was just around the corner and that it would create a new world free of governments and centralized control. "A phase change is coming," he wrote, echoing the prediction that Louis Rossetto was making at the same time in the pages of *Wired* magazine, which itself was a promoter of the cypherpunk movement and his ideas.[57]

The cypherpunk vision of the future was an inverted version of the military's cybernetic dream pursued by the Pentagon and Silicon

Valley: instead of leveraging global computer systems to make the world transparent and predictable, cypherpunks wanted to use computers and cryptography to make the world opaque and untrackable. It was a counterforce, a cybernetic weapon of individual privacy and freedom against a cybernetic weapon of government surveillance and control.

Tor offered a realization of this cypher-cybernetic dream: total anonymity on the Internet. Starting in the mid-2000s, Tor developed a cult following among a small but influential group of techno-libertarians, hackers, and cypherpunks who saw it as a magic cloak that could render the government—cops, militaries, tax collectors, regulators, and spies—powerless.

The mysterious creator of the Silk Road, the Dread Pirate Roberts, adhered to the cypherpunk ideology. He believed in the liberatory promise of Tor and cryptography. In his public statements, Dread Pirate Roberts came off as a typical libertarian, not much different from Edward Snowden. He followed Austrian Economics, argued against environmental regulations and child labor laws, praised sweatshops, and mocked the need for minimum wage: "How about someone whose labor is worth less than minimum wage?" As for Silk Road, it was much more than a business. From his hideout somewhere in the dark web, Dread Pirate Roberts saw it as a revolutionary act straight out of an Ayn Rand novel. Government was the ultimate political evil—a parasite, a form of slavery. Tor was the weapon that let a little guy like him fight back. Silk Road was just the beginning. He wanted to use Tor and other crypto tools to scale up the experiment to encompass all parts of life, not just drug purchases.

"What if one day we had enough power to maintain a physical presence on the globe, where we shunned the parasites and upheld the rule of law, where the right to privacy and property was unquestioned and enshrined in the very structure of society. Where police are our servants and protectors beholden to their customers, the people. Where our leaders earn their power and responsibility in the harsh and unforgiving furnace of the free market and not from behind a gun, where the opportunities to create and enjoy wealth are as boundless as one's imagination," he wrote to users of Silk Road on the site's messaging board. "Once you've seen what's possible, how can you do otherwise? How can you plug yourself into the tax eating, life sucking, violent, sadistic, war mongering, oppressive machine ever again? How can you kneel when you've felt the power of your own legs? Felt them stretch and flex as you learn to walk and think as a free person? I would rather live my life in rags now than in golden chains. And now we can have both! Now it is profitable to throw off one's chains, with amazing crypto technology reducing the risk of doing so dramatically. How many niches have yet to be filled in the world of anonymous online markets? The opportunity to prosper and take part in a revolution of epic proportions is at our fingertips!"[58]

And why not? If Silk Road could withstand the power of the American government, anything seemed possible.

More practically, the Dread Pirate Roberts proved that you could use Tor to run a massively illegal business on the Internet and keep law enforcement at bay, while raking in millions. His success spawned a mass of copycats—dark web entrepreneurs who set up online stores in Silk Road's image, allowing people to anonymously buy whatever they wanted: weed, marijuana, ecstasy, cocaine, meth, guns, grenades, and even assassinations.[59] Some of the sites were possibly a racket, meant to bilk people of their Bitcoins, but others appeared dead serious. Tor's dark web became a haven for child abuse pornography, allowing forums and markets where such material was swapped and sold to exist beyond the reach of law enforcement. It also housed websites operated by terrorist cells, including recruitment platforms run by the Islamic State of Iraq and the Levant.[60]

Tor's ease of use and bullet-proof anonymity didn't just empower the seedy side of the Internet. Journalists and political activists used it to avoid government surveillance and repression in countries like China and Iran. Leakers and whistle-blowers used the network, too. That's where Edward Snowden came into the story: Tor's ability to hide people from the prying eyes of the NSA was a key factor in his leaks; he couldn't have carried them out successfully without it.

Snowden ♥ Tor

Edward Snowden was a huge fan of the Tor Project. He, like the Dread Pirate Roberts, believed in the power of cryptography to liberate the Internet from government control. In Hawaii, when he had worked as an NSA contractor at Dell and the Silk Road was booming, he controlled one of the most powerful nodes on the Tor network, running a physical server that helped mix and anonymize traffic. He also took it upon himself to educate people in Hawaii about how to use the Tor network to hide from the government.

In November 2012, while in the middle of exfiltrating documents, Snowden reached out to Runa Sandvik, a Tor employee, and asked for some Tor stickers to hand out to his buddies at work.[61] He did not tell her that his "work" was for the NSA. But in the course of their back-and-forth, he found out that Sandvik was planning to visit Hawaii for vacation, and she suggested they meet up there. In her capacity as a Tor ambassador, Sandvik offered to give a talk for locals about communication security and encryption. Snowden was enthusiastic about the idea, and they agreed to cohost a "crypto party," a kind of public teach-in about encryption tools. The event went down in early December 2012 at an art space in Honolulu, where Snowden and Sandvik taught about twenty people how to use Tor and encrypt their hard drives. Snowden personally hosted a session about how to set up and run a Tor server.[62]

Snowden hooking up with Tor employees, running Tor servers, and hosting Tor training sessions—all while planning the biggest heist of NSA documents in history? It seemed to be a reckless step for someone as meticulous as he was. Why would he risk outing himself? To those in the privacy world, Snowden's desire to educate people about privacy, even in the face of personal danger, was a testament to his belief in the power of Tor and cryptography and his dedication to the cause. "That Snowden organized such an event himself while still an NSA contract worker speaks volumes about his motives," wrote *Wired* reporter Kevin Poulsen, who broke the story about Snowden's Tor server and crypto party.

But Snowden wasn't just a true believer. He was also an active user. After fleeing to Moscow, he explained that the Tor Project was vital to carrying out his mission. He had relied on Tor to cover his tracks and avoid detection while communicating with journalists, transferring documents, and planning his escape from Hawaii. He was such a fan that the first photographs of him in Hong Kong showed him sitting on his hotel bed, a black laptop with a giant green oval "Tor Project" sticker plastered on its cover perched on his lap. "I think Tor is the most important privacy-enhancing technology project being used today. I use Tor personally all the time," he said in an interview from Moscow.

As he settled into a life in Russian exile, he built up a lucrative speaking practice, making hundreds of thousands of dollars a year presenting remotely to universities, tech conferences, and investor groups.[63] In his speeches and keynote addresses, he gave voice to the old cypherpunk dream, holding up Tor as a powerful example of grassroots privacy technology that could defeat the corrupting power of government surveillance and restore what he saw as the original utopian promise of the Internet. He called on his fellow techies—computer programmers, cryptographers, and cybersecurity types of every stripe and rank—to build powerful anonymity and privacy tools in Tor's image.

In these talks, Snowden portrayed the Internet as a scary and violent place, a cyber-medieval landscape filled with roaming government bandits, hostile armies, and booby traps. It was a place where regular people were always at risk. The only islands of safety were the private datacenters controlled by private companies—Google, Apple, Facebook. These were the cyber-fortresses and walled cities that offered sanctuary to the masses. In this chaotic landscape, computer engineers and cryptographers played the role of selfless galloping knights and wizard-warriors whose job was to protect the weak folk of the Internet: the young, the old and infirm, families. It was their duty to ride out, weapons aloft, and convey people and their precious data safely from fortress to fortress, not letting any of the information fall into the hands of government spies. He called on them to start a people's privacy war, rallying them to go forth and liberate the Internet, to reclaim it from the governments of the world.

"The lesson of 2013 is not that the NSA is evil. It's that the path is dangerous. The network path is something that we need to help users get across safely. Our job as technologists, our job as engineers, our job as anybody who cares about the internet in any way, who has any kind of personal or commercial involvement is literally to armor the user, to protect the user and to make it that they can get from one end of the path to the other safely without interference," he told an auditorium filled with the world's foremost computer and network engineers at a 2015 meeting of the Internet Engineering Task Force in Prague.[64] He reaffirmed his view a year later at Fusion's 2016 Real Future Fair in Oakland, California. "If you want to build a better future, you're going to have to do it yourself. Politics will take us only so far and if history is any guide, they are the least reliable means of achieving the effective change. . . . They're not gonna jump up and protect your rights," he said. "Technology works differently than law. Technology knows no jurisdiction."

Snowden's disregard for political solutions and his total trust in the ability of technology to solve complex social problems wasn't surprising. He was simply reaffirming what he had told journalists back in 2013: "Let us speak no more of faith in man, but bind him down from mischief by chains of cryptography."[65]

Snowden's call to arms was taken up by people all over the world: Silicon Valley companies, privacy groups, corporate think tanks and lobbyists, political activists, and thousands of eager techies around the globe. Even Google's Sergey Brin posed for a selfie with the infamous leaker—or the video-equipped "telepresence" robot that Snowden used to speak at conferences for him.[66] Thanks to Snowden, the privacy movement was going mainstream, and the Tor Project was at the center of it all.

No matter where you turned in the privacy world, people were united in their admiration for Tor as a solution to surveillance on the Internet. This was true of powerful groups like the Electronic Frontier Foundation and the American Civil Liberties Union, Pulitzer

Prize–winning journalists, hackers, and whistle-blowers.[67] Google subsidized further development of Tor, as did eBay.[68] Facebook built support for Tor, allowing users to access the social network as if it were a dark web site, in the same exact way people accessed Silk Road. Within a short time, Facebook boasted that over a million people logged in to their accounts using Tor's cloaking system.[69] Many saw Tor in almost sacred terms: it was salvation, a real-world example of technology defeating government intrusion into people's private lives.

Daniel Ellsberg, the legendary whistle-blower who in 1971 leaked the Pentagon Papers, backed Tor as a powerful weapon of the people.[70] "The government now has capabilities the Stasi couldn't even imagine, the possibility for a total authoritarian control. To counter that is courage," he explained. "And that is what Tor facilitates. So I would say that the future, the future of democracy, and not only in this country, depends upon countering the abilities of this government and every other government in this world to know everything about our private lives while they keep secret everything about what they're doing officially."

Tor's underdog story grew in appeal. Before long, Hollywood celebrities joined in and helped promote the cause. "While law enforcement and the media have painted a picture that Tor and the darknet are nefarious tools for criminals, it is important to understand that they are largely used for good by government agencies, journalists and dissidents around the world," said Keanu Reeves, narrating a documentary called *Deep Web*, a film made by his old *Bill and Ted's Excellent Adventure* costar Alex Winter, which depicted Tor as resistant to government control.

But what about Tor's criminal underbelly? To many in the new privacy movement, none of it mattered. In fact, people celebrated Tor's dark side. Its ability to protect child pornographers from accountability only proved its effectiveness, demonstrating that the technology really was the powerful privacy tool Edward Snowden claimed it to be. Tor was the Internet's AK-47—a cheap, durable field weapon everyday people could use to overthrow America's surveillance state.

Tor was supposed to be so radical and so subversive that Tor employees constantly spoke of their harassment and intimidation at the hands of the US government. They lived a paranoid existence, some on the run, seeking refuge in foreign countries. For them, it wasn't just a job but a revolutionary life. One prominent Tor developer described his work as a valiant act on par with fighting with the anarchist revolutionaries who warred against Franco's Fascists.[71]

Tor was just the beginning. Soon other grassroots crypto organizations emerged, releasing encryption technology that promised to hide our digital lives from prying eyes. Open Whisper Systems, headed by a dreadlocked anarchist, developed a powerful crypto text and voice call app called Signal. A radical anarchist communication collective called RiseUp offered encrypted email services, while a group of techies banded together to create the ultimate encrypted operating system called Qubes; supposedly, even the NSA couldn't hack it. Others formed training groups and held spontaneous crypto parties to educate the masses on how to handle these powerful new privacy tools.[72]

Crypto culture even made its way into museums and art galleries.[73] The Whitney Museum of American Art held a "Surveillance Tech-In." Trevor Paglen, an award-winning visual artist, partnered with the Tor Project to set up cryptographic anonymity cubes in museums and art galleries in New York, London, and Berlin. "What would the infrastructure of the Internet look like if mass surveillance wasn't its business model?" Paglen asked in an interview with *Wired*. "My job as an artist is to learn how to see what the world looks like at this historical moment. But it's also to try to make things that help us see how the world could be different."[74]

Yes, suddenly, with crypto, the art world was part of the resistance.

As a reporter for *Pando*, a magazine based in San Francisco that covered the tech industry, I watched these developments with skepticism. Rebels arming themselves to the teeth and taking on the power of an evil government with nothing but their brains and their scrappy crypto tech? There was something off about this narrative. It was too clean. Too scripted. Too much like a cheap sci-fi plot, or maybe an Internet version of the old gunslinger National Rifle Association fantasy: if everyone was armed with a powerful (cryptographic) weapon, then there would be no government tyranny because people would be able to defend themselves and neutralize government force on their own. It was yet another version of a cyber-libertarian utopia: the idea that you could equalize power levels with nothing more than technology.

I knew reality was usually more complicated. And, sure enough, so was the Tor story.

Down the Rabbit Hole

The year was 2014. On a warm and sunny November morning, I woke up, brewed a cup of coffee, and sat down at my desk to watch a couple of surfers make their way down to Venice Beach. I had just returned from Ukraine, where I spent a month reporting on the slow-grinding civil war and brutal economic collapse that was tearing that country apart. I was jet-lagged and weary, my mind still fixed on the horrific images of war and destruction in my ancestral homeland. I looked forward to a bit of rest and quiet time. But then I checked my email.

All hell had broken loose on the Internet.

The threats and attacks had begun sometime overnight while I slept. By morning, they had reached a vicious and murderous pitch. There were calls for my death—by fire, by suffocation, by having my throat slit with razor blades. People I had never met called me a rapist, and alleged that I took delight in beating women and forcing them to have sex with me. I was accused of homophobia. Anonymous people filed bogus complaints with my editor. Allegations that I was a CIA agent poured in, as did claims that I worked with British intelligence. The fact that I had been born in the Soviet Union didn't do me any favors; naturally, I was accused of being an FSB spy and of working for Russia's successor to the KGB. I was informed that my name was added to a dark net assassination list—a site where people could place anonymous bids for my murder.[75] The roaming eye of the Internet hate machine had suddenly fixed on me.

Things got even weirder when the Anonymous movement joined the fray. The collective issued a fatwa against me and my colleagues, vowing not to stop until I was dead. "May an infinitude of venomous insects dwell in the fascist Yasha Levine's intestines," proclaimed the Anonymous Twitter account with 1.6 million followers.[76] It was a bizarre turn. Anonymous was a decentralized hacker and script kiddie movement best known for going after the Church of Scientology. Now they were going after me—painting a giant target on my back.

I paced my living room, nervously scanning the street outside my window. Reflexively, I lowered the blinds, wondering just how far this was going to go. For the first time, I began to fear for my family's safety. People knew where I lived. The apartment my wife, Evgenia, and I shared at the time was on the first floor, open to the street, with expansive windows on all sides, like a fishbowl. We contemplated staying at a friend's house on the other side of town for a few days until things cooled down.

I had been on the receiving end of vicious Internet harassment campaigns before; it comes with the territory of being an investigative journalist. But this one was different. It went beyond anything I had ever experienced. Not just the intensity and viciousness scared me but also the reason why it was happening.

My problems had begun when I started digging into the Tor Project. I investigated Tor's central role in the privacy movement after Edward Snowden presented the project as a panacea to surveillance on the Internet. I wasn't convinced, and it didn't take long to find a basis for my initial suspicions.

The first red flag was its Silicon Valley support. Privacy groups funded by companies like Google and Facebook, including the Electronic Frontier Foundation and Fight for the Future, were some of Tor's biggest and most dedicated backers.[77] Google had directly bankrolled its development, paying out generous grants to college students who worked at Tor during their summer vacations.[78] Why would an Internet company whose entire business rested on tracking people online promote and help develop a powerful privacy tool? Something didn't add up.

As I dug into the technical details of how Tor worked, I quickly realized that the Tor Project offers no protection against the private tracking and profiling Internet companies carry out. Tor works only if people are dedicated to maintaining a strict anonymous Internet routine: using only dummy email addresses and bogus accounts, carrying out all financial transactions in Bitcoin and other cryptocurrencies, and never mentioning their real name in emails or messages. For the vast majority of people on the Internet—those who use Gmail, interact with Facebook friends, and shop on Amazon—Tor does nothing. The moment you log into your personal account—whether on Google, Facebook, eBay, Apple, or Amazon—you reveal your identity. These companies know who you are. They know your name, your shipping address, your credit card information. They continue to scan your emails, map your social networks, and compile dossiers. Tor or not, once you enter your account name and password, Tor's anonymity technology becomes useless.

Tor's ineffectiveness against Silicon Valley surveillance made it an odd program for Snowden and other privacy activists to embrace. After all, Snowden's leaked documents revealed that anything Internet companies had, the NSA had as well. I was puzzled, but at least I understood why Tor had backing from Silicon Valley: it offered a false sense of privacy, while not posing a threat to the industry's underlying surveillance business model.

What wasn't clear, and what became apparent as I investigated Tor further, was why the US government supported it.

A big part of Tor's mystique and appeal was that it was supposedly a fiercely independent and radical organization—an enemy of the state. Its official story was that it was funded by a wide variety of sources, which gave it total freedom to do whatever it wanted. But as I analyzed the organization's financial documents, I found that the opposite was true. Tor had come out of a joint US Navy–DARPA military project in the early 2000s and continued to rely on a series

214 | Surveillance Valley

of federal contracts after it was spun off into a private nonprofit. This funding came from the Pentagon, the State Department, and at least one organization that derived from the CIA. These contracts added up to several million dollars a year and, most years, accounted for more than 90 percent of Tor's operating budget. Tor was a federal military contractor. It even had its own federal contracting number.

The deeper I went, the stranger it got. I learned that just about everyone involved in developing Tor was in some way tied up with the very state that they were supposed to be protecting people from. This included Tor's founder, Roger Dingledine, who spent a summer working at the NSA and who had brought Tor to life under a series of DARPA and US Navy contracts.[79] I even uncovered an old audio copy of a talk Dingledine gave in 2004, right as he was setting up Tor as an independent organization. "I contract for the United States Government to build anonymity technology for them and deploy it," he admitted at the time.[80]

I was confused. How could a tool at the center of a global privacy movement against government surveillance get funding from the very US government it was supposed to elude? Was it a ruse? A sham? A honey trap? Was I having paranoid delusions? Though mystified, I decided to try to make sense of it as best I could.

In the summer of 2014, I assembled all the verifiable financial records related to Tor, dug into the histories of the US government agencies that funded it, consulted privacy and encryption experts, and published several articles in *Pando Daily* exploring the conflicted ties between Tor and the government. They were straightforward and stuck to an old journalistic adage: when you're faced with a mystery, first thing you do is follow the money—see who benefits. I naively thought that background funding information on Tor would be welcomed by the privacy community, a paranoid group of people who are always on the hunt for bugs and security vulnerabilities. But I was wrong. Instead of welcoming my reporting on Tor's puzzling government support, the leading lights of the privacy community answered it with attacks.

Micah Lee, the former EFF technologist who helped Edward Snowden communicate securely with journalists and who now works at *The Intercept*, attacked me as a conspiracy theorist and accused me and my colleagues at *Pando* of being sexist bullies; he claimed that my reporting was motivated not by a desire to get at the truth but by a malicious impulse to harass a female Tor developer.[81] Although Lee conceded that my information about Tor's government funding was correct, he counterintuitively argued that it didn't matter. Why? Because Tor was open source and powered by math, which he claimed made it infallible. "[Of] course funders might try to influence the direction of the project and the research. In Tor's case this is mitigated by the fact that 100% of the scientific research and source code that Tor releases is open, that the crypto math is peer-reviewed and backed up by the laws of physics," he wrote. What Lee was saying, and what many others in the privacy community believed as well, was that it did not matter that Tor employees depended on the Pentagon for their paychecks. They were impervious to influence, careers, mortgages, car payments, personal relationships, food, and all the other "squishy" aspects of human existence that silently drive and affect people's choices. The reason was that Tor, like all encryption algorithms, was based on math and physics—which made it impervious to coercion.[82]

It was a baffling argument. Tor was not "a law of physics" but computer code written by a small group of human beings. It was software like any other, with holes and vulnerabilities that were constantly being discovered and patched. Encryption algorithms and computer systems might be based on abstract mathematical concepts, but translated into the real physical realm they become imperfect tools, constrained by human error and the computer platforms and networks they run on. After all, even the most sophisticated encryption systems are eventually cracked and broken. And neither Lee nor anyone else could answer the bigger question raised by my reporting: If Tor was such a danger to the US government, why would this same government continue to spend millions of dollars on the project's development, renewing the funding year after year? Imagine if, during World War II, the Allies funded the development of Nazi Germany's Enigma machine instead of mounting a massive effort to crack the code.

I never got a good answer from the privacy community, but what I did get was a lot of smears and threats.

Journalists, experts, and technologists from groups like the ACLU, EFF, Freedom of the Press Foundation, and *The Intercept* and employees of the Tor Project joined in to attack my reporting. Unlike Lee, most did not attempt to engage my reporting but employed a range of familiar PR smear tactics—tactics you usually see used by corporate flacks, not principled privacy activists. They took to social media, telling anyone who showed interest in my articles that they should ignore them instead.[83] Then, when that didn't work, they tried to discredit my reporting with ridicule, misdirection, and crude insults.

A respected ACLU privacy expert who now works as a congressional staffer, called me "a conspiracy theorist who sees black helicopters everywhere" and compared my reporting about Tor to the *Protocols of the Elders of Zion*.[84] As someone who escaped state-sponsored anti-Semitism in the Soviet Union, I found the comparison extremely offensive, especially coming from the ACLU. The *Protocols* were an anti-Semitic forgery disseminated by the Russian Tsar's secret police that unleashed waves of deadly pogroms against Jews across the Russian Empire in the early twentieth century.[85] Tor employees put forth a torrent of childish insults, calling me a "dumb Stalinist state-felcher" and a "fucktard's fucktard." They accused me of being funded by spies to undermine faith in cryptography. One of them claimed that I was a rapist, and hurled homophobic insults about the various ways in which I had supposedly performed sexual favors for a male colleague.[86]

In the way that these Internet hazing sessions go, the campaign evolved and spread. Strange people began threatening me and my colleagues on social media. Some accused me of having blood on my hands and of racking up an "activist body count"—that people were actually dying because my reporting undermined trust in Tor.[87]

The attacks widened to include regular readers and social media users, anyone who had the nerve to ask questions about Tor's funding sources. An employee of the Tor Project went so far as to dox an anonymous Twitter user, exposing his real identity and contacting his employer in the hopes of getting him fired from his job as a junior pharmacist.[88]

It was bizarre. I watched all this unfold in real time but had no idea how to respond. Even more disconcerting was that the attacks soon expanded to include libelous stories placed in reputable media outlets. The *Guardian* published a story by a freelancer accusing me of running an online sexual harassment and bullying campaign.[89] The *Los Angeles Review of Books*, generally a good journal of arts and culture, ran an essay by a freelancer alleging that my reporting was funded by the CIA.[90] Paul Carr, my editor at *Pando*, lodged official complaints and demanded to know how these reporters came to their conclusions. Both publications ultimately retracted their statements and printed corrections. An editor at the *Guardian* apologized and described the article as a "fuck up."[91] But the online attacks continued.

I was no stranger to intimidation and threats. But I knew that this campaign wasn't just meant to shut me up but was designed to shut down debate around the official Tor story. After the initial outbreak, I laid low and tried to understand why my reporting elicited such a vicious and weird reaction from the privacy community.

Military contractors hailed as privacy heroes? Edward Snowden promoting a Pentagon-funded tool as a solution to NSA surveillance? Google and Facebook backing privacy technology? And why were privacy activists so hostile to information that their most trusted app was funded by the military? It was a bizarro world. None of it quite made sense.

When the smears first started, I had thought they might have been driven by a petty defensive reflex. Many of those who attacked me either worked for Tor or were vocal supporters, recommending the tool to others as protection from government surveillance. They were supposed to be experts in the field; maybe my reporting on Tor's ongoing ties to the Pentagon caught them off-guard or made them feel stupid. After all, no one likes being made to look like a sucker.

Turns out, it wasn't that simple. As I pieced the story together, bit by bit, I realized there was something much deeper behind the attacks, something so spooky and startling that at first I didn't believe it.

Chapter 7

Internet Privacy, Funded by Spies

This so-called Internet Freedom, is in nature, freedom under US control.

—China's *Global Times* newspaper, 2010

December 2015. A few days after Christmas in Hamburg. The mercury hovers just above freezing. A gray fog hangs over the city.

In the town's historic core, several thousand people have gathered inside a modernist cube of steel and glass known as Congress Center. The attendees, mostly geeky men, are here for the thirty-second annual meeting of the Chaos Computer Club, better known as 32c3. The conference atmosphere is loud and cheery, a counterpoint to the head-down foot traffic and dreary weather outside the center's high glass walls.

32c3 is the Hacktivist Davos, an extravaganza put on by the oldest and most prestigious hacker collective in the world. Everyone who is anyone is here: cryptographers, Internet security experts, script kiddies, techno-libertarians, cypherpunks and cyberpunks, Bitcoin entrepreneurs, military contractors, open source enthusiasts, and privacy activists of all nationalities, genders, age groups, and intel classification levels. They descend on the event to network, code, dance to techno, smoke e-cigarettes, catch the latest crypto trends, and consume oceans of Club-Mate, Germany's official hacker beverage.

Look this way and see Ryan Lackey, cofounder of HavenCo, the world's first extralegal offshore hosting company, run out of an abandoned World War II cannon platform in the North Sea off England's coast. Look that way and find Sarah Harrison, WikiLeaks member and Julian Assange confidante who helped Edward Snowden escape arrest in Hong Kong and find safety in Moscow. She's laughing and having a good time. I wave as I pass her on an escalator. But not everyone here is so friendly. Indeed, my reputation as a Tor critic has preceded me. In the days leading up to the conference, social media had again lit up with threats.[1] There was talk of assault and of spiking my drink with Rohypnol if I had the nerve to show my face at the event.[2] Given my previous run-in with the privacy community, I can't say I expected a particularly warm reception.

The Tor Project occupies a hallowed place in the mythology and social galaxy of the Chaos Computer Club. Every year, Tor's annual presentation—"The State of the Onion"—is the most well-attended event in the program. An audience of several thousand packs a massive auditorium to watch Tor developers and celebrity supporters talk about their fights against Internet surveillance. Last year, the stage featured Laura Poitras, the Academy Award–winning director of the Edward Snowden documentary, *Citizen Four.* In her speech, she held up Tor as a powerful antidote to America's surveillance state. "When I was communicating with Snowden for several months before I met him in Hong Kong, we talked often about the Tor network, and it is something that actually he feels is vital for online privacy and to defeat surveillance. It is our only tool to be able to do that," she said to wild applause, Snowden's face projected onto a giant screen behind her.[3]

This year, the presentation is a bit more formal. Tor has just hired a new executive director, Shari Steele, the former head of the Electronic Frontier Foundation. She takes the stage to introduce herself to the privacy activists assembled in the hall and pledges her allegiance to Tor's core mission: to make the Internet safe from surveillance.

Up there, emceeing the event, stands Jacob Appelbaum, "Jake," as everyone calls him. He is the true star of the show, and he lavishes praise on the new director. "We found someone who will keep the Tor Project going long after all of us are dead and buried, hopefully not in shallow graves," he says to cheers and applause.[4]

I catch a glimpse of him walking the halls after the event. He's dressed in jeans and a black T-shirt, a tattoo peeking out from under one of the sleeves. His jet-black hair and thick-rimmed glasses frame a rectangular, fleshy face. He is a familiar sight to people at 32c3. Indeed, he carries himself like a celebrity, glad-handing attendees while his fans cluster nearby to listen to him boast of daring exploits against oppressive governments all around the world.

He ducks into an auditorium where a speaker is talking about human rights in Ecuador and immediately hijacks the discussion. "I am of the eliminate-the-state crypto world. I want to get rid of the state. The state is dangerous, you know," he says into a microphone. Then he cracks a devious grin, leading a few people in the audience to hoot and cheer. He transitions into a wild story that puts him at the center of a failed coup attempt hatched by Ecuador's secret police against their president, Rafael Correa. Naturally, Appelbaum is the hero of the tale. President Correa is widely respected in the international hacker community for granting Julian Assange political asylum and for giving him refuge at the Ecuadorian embassy in London. Like a modern Smedley Butler, Appelbaum explains how he refused to go along. He did not want to use his righteous hacker skills to take down a good, honest man, so he helped foil the plot and saved the president instead. "They asked me to build a mass surveillance system to tap the entire country of Ecuador," he said. "I told them to go fuck themselves, and I reported them to the presidency. I think you are proposing a coup. I have your names—you're fucked."

A few people on stage look embarrassed, not believing a word. But the audience laps it up. They love Jacob Appelbaum. Everyone at 32c3 loves Jacob Appelbaum.

Appelbaum is the most storied member of the Tor Project. After Edward Snowden and Julian Assange, he is arguably the most famous personality in the Internet privacy movement. He is also the most outrageous. For five years he's played the role of a self-facilitating media node and counterculture Ethan Hunt, a celebrity hacker who constantly changes his appearance, travels the world to speak at conferences and conduct teach-ins, and fights injustice and censorship wherever they rear their ugly government heads. Appelbaum wields cultural power and influence. While Assange was stuck in a London embassy and Snowden was stranded in Moscow, Appelbaum was the face of the antisurveillance movement. He spoke for its heroes. He was their friend and collaborator. Like them, he lived on the edge, an inspiration to countless people—hundreds, if not thousands became privacy activists because of him. You'd hear it over and over: "Jake's the reason I'm here."

But that year's Chaos Computer Club party represented the peak of his career. For years, rumors had spread inside the cliquish Internet privacy community about his history of sexual harassment, abuse, and bullying. Six months after the conference, the *New York Times* ran a story that brought these allegations to light, revealing a scandal that saw Appelbaum ejected from the Tor Project and that threatened to tear the organization apart from the inside.[5]

But all that was in the future. That evening in Hamburg, Appelbaum was still enjoying his fame and celebrity, feeling comfortable and secure. Yet he was carrying another dark secret. He was more than just a world-renowned Internet freedom fighter and confidant of Assange and Snowden. He was also an employee of a military contractor, earning $100,000 a year plus benefits working on one of the most disorienting government projects of the Internet Era: the weaponization of privacy.[6]

The Box

A few weeks after I glimpsed Jacob Appelbaum at 32c3, I arrived home in the United States to find a heavy brown box waiting for me on my doorstep. It was postmarked from the Broadcasting Board of Governors, a large federal agency that oversees America's foreign broadcasting operations and one of the Tor Project's main government funders.[7] The box contained several thousand pages of internal documents on the agency's dealings with Tor that I had obtained through the Freedom of Information Act. I had been impatiently waiting for months for it to arrive.

By then I had spent almost two years investigating the Tor Project. I knew that the organization had come out of Pentagon research. I also knew that even after it became a private nonprofit in 2004, it relied almost entirely on federal and Pentagon contracts. In the course of my reporting, representatives of Tor grudgingly conceded that they accepted government funding, but they remained adamant that they ran an independent organization that took orders from no one, especially not the dreaded federal government, which their anonymity tool was supposed to oppose.[8] They repeatedly stressed that they would never put backdoors in the Tor network and told stories of how the US government had tried but failed to get Tor to tap its own network.[9] They pointed to Tor's open source code; if I was really worried about a backdoor, I was free to inspect the code for myself.

The open source argument appeared to nullify concerns in the privacy community. But backdoors or not, my reporting kept butting up against the same question: If Tor was truly the heart of the modern privacy movement and a real threat to the surveillance power of agencies like the NSA, why would the federal government—including the Pentagon, the parent of the NSA—continue to fund the organization? Why would the Pentagon support a technology that subverted its own power? It did not make any sense.

The documents in the box waiting on my doorstep contained the answer. Combined with other information unearthed during my investigation, they showed that Tor, as well as the larger app-obsessed privacy movement that rallied around it after Snowden's NSA leaks, does not thwart the power of the US government. It enhances it.

The disclosures about Tor's inner workings I obtained from the Broadcasting Board of Governors—which was rebranded in mid-2018, and is now known as the United States Agency for Global

Media—have never been made public before now. The story they tell is vital to our understanding of the Internet; they reveal that American military and intelligence interests are so deeply embedded in the fabric of the network that they dominate the very encryption tools and privacy organizations that are supposed to stand in opposition to them. There is no escape.

Spies Need Anonymity

The story of how a military contractor wound up at the heart of the privacy movement starts in 1995 at the Naval Research Laboratory inside the Anacostia-Bolling military base on the Potomac in southeast Washington, DC.[10] There, Paul Syverson, an affable military mathematician with big hair and an interest in secure communication systems, set out to solve an unexpected problem brought on by the explosive success of the Internet.

Everything was being hooked up to the Internet: banks, phones, power plants, universities, military bases, corporations, and foreign governments, both hostile and friendly. In the 1990s, hackers, who some believed to be tied to Russia and China, were already using the Internet to probe America's defense network and steal secrets.[11] The United States was beginning to do the same to its adversaries: collecting intelligence, bugging and hacking targets, and intercepting communications. It was also using commercial Internet infrastructure for covert communication.

The problem was anonymity. The open nature of the Internet, where the origin of a traffic request and its destination were open to anyone monitoring the connection, made cloak-and-dagger work tricky business. Imagine a CIA agent in Lebanon under deep cover as a businessman trying to check his operative email. He couldn't just type "mail.cia.gov" into his web browser from his suite in the Beirut Hilton. Simple traffic analysis would immediately blow his cover. Nor could a US Army officer infiltrate an Al-Qaeda recruiting forum without revealing the army base's IP address. And what if the

NSA needed to hack a Russian diplomat's computer without leaving a trail that led right back to Fort Meade, Maryland? Forget about it. "As military grade communication devices increasingly depend on the public communications infrastructure, it is important to use that infrastructure in ways that are resistant to traffic analysis. It may also be useful to communicate anonymously, for example when gathering intelligence from public databases," Syverson and colleagues explained in the pages of an in-house magazine put out by his research lab.[12]

American spies and soldiers needed a way to use the Internet while hiding their tracks and cloaking their identity. It was a problem that researchers at the US Navy, which has historically been at the forefront of communications technology research and signals intelligence, were determined to solve.

Syverson assembled a small team of military mathematicians and computer systems researchers. They came up with a solution: called "the onion router" or Tor. It was a clever system: the navy set up a bunch of servers and linked them together in a parallel network that sat atop the normal Internet. All covert traffic was redirected through this parallel network; once inside it was bounced around and scrambled in such a way as to obfuscate where it was going and from where it came. It used the same principle as money laundering: shifting information packets from one shell Tor node to another until it is impossible to figure out where the data came from. With onion routing, the only thing an Internet provider—or anyone else watching a connection—saw was that the user connected to a computer running Tor. No indication of where the communications were actually going was apparent. And when the data popped out of the parallel network and back onto the public Internet on the other side, no one there could see where the information had come from either.

Syverson's team of Naval scientists worked on several iterations of this system. A few years later, they hired two fresh-faced programmers, Roger Dingledine and Nick Mathewson, from the Massachusetts Institute of Technology to help build a version of the router that could be used in the real world.[13]

Dingledine, who received his master's in electrical engineering and computer science and who was interested in cryptography and secure communications, had interned at the National Security Agency. Mathewson had similar interests and had developed a truly anonymous email system that hid a sender's identity and source. Mathewson and Dingledine had met as freshman at MIT and became fast friends, spending most of their days in their rooms reading *Lord of the Rings* and hacking away at stacks of computers. They, too, believed in the cypherpunk vision. "Network protocols are the unacknowledged legislators of cyberspace," Mathewson bragged to journalist Andy Greenberg. "We believed that if we were going to change the world, it would be through code." In college, the two saw themselves in romantic terms, hacker rebels taking on the system, using computer code to fight government authoritarianism. They were out there to fight The Man. But that did not stop them from going to work for the Pentagon after graduation. Like too many hacker rebels, they had a very limited conception of who "The Man" was and what it would mean in real political terms to fight "him."

In 2002, the pair went to work for the Naval Research Laboratory under a DARPA contract.[14] For two years, Dingledine and Mathewson worked with Syverson to upgrade the onion router network's underlying routing protocols, improve security, and run a small test network that allowed the military to experiment with onion routing in the field. One military team tested it for gathering open source intelligence, which required them to visit websites and interact with people online without giving away their identity. Another team used it to communicate while deployed on a mission in the Middle East.[15] By 2004, Tor, the resultant network, was finally ready for deployment.[16] Well, except for one little detail.

Everyone working on the project understood that a system that merely anonymized traffic was not enough—not if it was used exclusively by military and intelligence agencies. "The United States government can't simply run an anonymity system for everybody and then use it themselves only," Dingledine explained at a 2004 computer conference in Berlin. "Because then every time a connection came from it people would say, 'Oh, it's another CIA agent.' If those are the only people using the network."[17]

To truly hide spies and soldiers, Tor needed to distance itself from its Pentagon roots and include as many different users as possible. Activists, students, corporate researchers, soccer moms, journalists, drug dealers, hackers, child pornographers, agents of foreign intelligence services, terrorists. Tor was like a public square—the bigger and more diverse the group assembled there, the better spies could hide in the crowd.

In 2004, Dingledine struck out on his own, spinning the military onion routing project into a nonprofit corporation called the Tor Project and, while still funded by DARPA and the navy, began scratching around for private funding.[18] He got help from an unexpected ally: the Electronic Frontier Foundation (EFF), which gave Tor almost a quarter million dollars to keep it going while Dingledine looked for other private sponsors.[19] The EFF even hosted Tor's website. To download the app, users had to browse to tor.eff.org, where they'd see a reassuring message from the EFF: "Your traffic is safer when you use Tor."[20]

Announcing its support, the EFF sang Tor's praises. "The Tor project is a perfect fit for EFF, because one of our primary goals is to protect the privacy and anonymity of Internet users. Tor can help people exercise their First Amendment right to free, anonymous speech online," EFF's technology manager Chris Palmer explained in a 2004 press release, which curiously failed to mention that Tor was developed primarily for military and intelligence use and was still actively funded by the Pentagon.[21]

Why would the EFF, a Silicon Valley advocacy group that positioned itself as a staunch critic of government surveillance programs, help sell a military intelligence communications tool to unsuspecting Internet users? Well, it wasn't as strange as it seems.

EFF was only a decade old at the time, but it already had developed a history of working with law enforcement agencies and aiding the military. In 1994, EFF worked with the FBI to pass the Communications Assistance for Law Enforcement Act, which required all telecommunications companies to build their equipment so that it could be wiretapped by the FBI.[22] In 1999, EFF worked to support NATO's bombing campaign in Kosovo with something called the "Kosovo Privacy Project," which aimed to keep the region's Internet access open during military action.[23] Selling a Pentagon intelligence project as a grassroots privacy tool—it didn't seem all that wild. Indeed, in 2002, a few years before it funded Tor, EFF cofounder Perry Barlow casually admitted that he had been consulting for intelligence agencies for a decade.[24] It seemed that the worlds of soldiers, spies, and privacy weren't as far apart as they appeared.

EFF's support for Tor was a big deal. The organization commanded respect in Silicon Valley and was widely seen as the ACLU of the Internet Age. The fact that it backed Tor meant that no hard questions would be asked about the anonymity tool's military origins as it transitioned to the civilian world. And that's exactly what happened.[25]

Freedom Isn't Free

It was Wednesday morning, February 8, 2006, when Roger Dingledine got the email he had been badly waiting for. The Broadcasting Board of Governors had finally agreed to back the Tor Project.

"OK—we want to move forward on this, Roger. We would like to offer some funding," wrote Ken Berman, director of the Broadcasting Board of Governors' Internet Technology unit. "For this first effort, we were going to offer $80,000 to you, with more possibly depending on how things evolve. Give us the particulars for how to establish a contractual relationship with you, name business contact information."[26]

It had been two years since Dingledine had made Tor independent, and his time in the wild world of private donors and civilian nonprofits hadn't been very successful.[27] Other than the initial funding from the Electronic Frontier Foundation, Dingledine didn't raise money from the private sector, at least not enough to fund the operation.

The Broadcasting Board of Governors, or BBG, seemed to offer a compromise. A large federal agency with close ties to the State Department, the BBG ran America's foreign broadcasting operations: Voice of America, Radio Free Europe/Radio Liberty, and Radio Free Asia. It was a government agency, so that wasn't ideal. But at least it had an altruistic-sounding mission: "to inform, engage and connect people around the world in support of freedom and democracy." Anyway, government or not, Dingledine didn't have much choice. Money was tight and this seemed to be the best he could line up. So he said yes.

It was a smart move. The initial $80,000 was just the beginning. Within a year, the agency increased Tor's contract to a quarter million dollars and then bumped it up again to almost a million just a few years later. The relationship also led to major contracts with other federal agencies, boosting Tor's meager operating budget to several million dollars a year.[28]

Dingledine should have been celebrating, but something nagged at his conscience.

Immediately after signing the contract, he emailed Ken Berman, his contact at the BBG, to tell him he was worried about the optics of the deal.[29] Dingledine wanted to do everything he could to maintain Tor's independent image, but as head of a tax-exempt nonprofit that received funding from the federal government, he was required by law to publicly disclose his funding sources and publish financial audits. He knew that whether he liked it or not, Tor's relationship with the federal government would come out sooner or later. "We also need to think about a strategy for how to spin this move in terms of Tor's overall direction. I would guess that we don't want to loudly declare war on China, since this only harms our goals?" he wrote. "But we also don't want to hide the existence of funding from [the BBG], since 'they're getting paid off by the feds and they didn't tell anyone' sounds like a bad Slashdot title for a security project. Is it sufficient just to always talk about Iran, or is that not subtle enough?"[30]

In college Dingledine had dreamed of using technology to create a better world. Now he was suddenly talking about whether or not they should declare war on China and Iran and worrying about being labeled a federal agent? What was going on?

Berman emailed back, reassuring Dingledine that he and his agency were ready to do anything it took to protect Tor's independent image. "Roger—we will do any spin you want to do to help preserve the independence of TOR," he wrote. "We can't (nor should we) hide it for the reasons you have outlined below, but we also don't want to shout if from the rafters, either."

Berman was an old hand at this. He had spent years funding anticensorship technology at the agency, and he offered a simple solution. He recommended that Dingledine be transparent about Tor's government funding but also downplay the significance of this relationship and instead focus on the fact that it was all for a good cause: Tor helped guarantee free speech on the Internet. It was sage advice. Saying this would head off any potential criticism, and admitting that Tor got a bit of money from the US government would only serve as proof that Tor had nothing to hide. After all, what could be nefarious about the government funding freedom of speech on the Internet?

Others chimed in with advice, as well. One BBG contractor replied to the email thread to tell Dingledine not to worry. No one will care. There will be no backlash. He explained that, in his experience, if people knew about the BBG at all, they considered it totally harmless. "I think most people, especially the smart people who count, understand that government can be good or bad, and government offices, like puppies, should be encouraged when they do the right thing," he wrote.[31]

Despite their reassurances, Dingledine was right to be concerned.

To be truly effective, Tor couldn't be perceived as a government system. That meant he needed to put as much distance as possible between Tor and the military intelligence structures that created it. But with funding from the BBG, Dingledine brought Tor right back into the heart of the beast. The BBG might have had a bland name and professed a noble mission to inform the world and spread democracy (today it has a more elaborate and perhaps even more misleadingly bland name, now that it is known as the United States Agency for Global Media). In truth, the organization was an outgrowth of the Central Intelligence Agency.

Covert Operations

The story of the United States Agency for Global Media—until recently the Broadcasting Board of Governors—begins in Eastern Europe in 1948.

World War II was over, but the United States was already busy gearing up for battle with its main ideological enemy, the Soviet Union. Many generals believed that nuclear war was imminent and that the final confrontation between capitalism and communism was at hand. They drew up elaborate plans for nuclear conquest. America would take out major Soviet cities with nukes and send anticommunist commandos who had been recruited from local populations to take charge and set up provisional governments. The Central Intelligence Agency, along with clandestine military services, trained Eastern Europeans, many of whom had been Nazi collaborators, for the fateful day when they would be parachuted into their homelands to take charge.[32]

Though the more hawkish US generals seemed eager for nuclear conflict, many believed that open war with the Soviet Union was too dangerous and cooler heads prevailed. They counseled instead for a more measured approach. George Kennan—the architect of the post–World War II policy of "containment"—pushed for expanding the role of covert programs to fight the Soviet Union. The plan was to use sabotage, assassinations, propaganda, and covert financing of political parties and movements to halt the spread of communism in postwar Europe, and then to use these same covert tools to defeat the Soviet Union itself. Kennan believed that closed authoritarian societies were inherently unstable in comparison with open democratic ones like the United States. To him, traditional war with the Soviet Union was not necessary. Given enough external pressure, he believed, the country would eventually collapse from the weight of its own "internal contradictions."[33]

In 1948, George Kennan helped craft National Security Council Directive 10/2, which officially authorized the CIA—with consultation and oversight from the State Department—to engage in "covert operations" against the communist influence, including everything from economic warfare to sabotage, subversion, and support for armed guerrillas. The directive gave the CIA carte blanche to do whatever was required to fight communism wherever it reared its head.[34] Naturally, propaganda emerged as a key part of the agency's covert operations arsenal. The CIA established and funded radio stations, newspapers, magazines, historical societies, émigré research institutes, and cultural programs all over Europe.[35] "These were very broad programs designed to influence world public opinion at virtually every level, from illiterate peasants in the fields to the most sophisticated scholars in prestigious universities," wrote historian Christopher Simpson in *Blowback*, a book about the CIA's use of Nazis and collaborators after World War II. "They drew on a wide range of resources: labor unions, advertising agencies, college professors, journalists, and student leaders."[36]

In Munich, the CIA set up Radio Free Europe and Radio Liberation From Bolshevism (later renamed Radio Liberty), which beamed propaganda in several languages via powerful antennas in Spain into the Soviet Union and Soviet satellite states of Eastern Europe. These stations had a combined annual CIA budget of $35 million—an enormous sum in the 1950s—but the agency's involvement was hidden by running everything through private front groups.[37] They broadcast a range of materials, from straight news and cultural programming to purposeful disinformation and smears aimed at spreading panic and delegitimizing the Soviet government. In some cases, the stations, especially those targeting Ukraine, Germany, and the Baltic States, were staffed by known Nazi collaborators and broadcast anti-Semitic propaganda.[38] Although slanted and politicized, these stations provided the only source of unsanctioned outside information to the people of the Soviet bloc. They became highly effective at communicating American ideals and influencing cultural and intellectual trends.

These projects were not restricted to Europe. As America's fight against communism shifted and spread around the world, new destabilization and propaganda initiatives were added. The People's Republic of China was targeted in 1951, when the agency launched

Radio Free Asia, which broadcast into mainland China from an office in San Francisco via a radio transmitter in Manila.[39] In the 1960s, the CIA launched projects targeting leftist movements in Central and South America. Broadcasts targeting Vietnam and North Korea came online as well.[40]

In the words of the CIA, these stations were leading a fight for the "minds and loyalties" of people living in communist countries. The agency later boasted that these early "psychological warfare" radio projects were "one of the longest running and successful covert action campaigns ever mounted by the United States."[41] It was all part of a larger push that Princeton professor Stephen Kotkin refers to as a proactive sphere of cultural and economic influence. "It was a strategy, and that is how the Cold War was won."[42]

This anticommunist global radio network was exposed in a spectacular 1967 CBS program hosted by Mike Wallace, "In the Pay of the CIA."[43] Subsequent congressional investigations brought the agency's role under further scrutiny, but exposure did not stop the projects; it simply led to a management shakeup: Congress agreed to take over funding of this propaganda project and to run it out in the open.

Over the next several decades, these radio stations were shuffled, reorganized, and steadily expanded. By the early 2000s, they had grown into the Broadcasting Board of Governors, a federal agency apparatus that functioned like a holding company for rehabilitated CIA propaganda properties. Today it has been rebranded as the United States Agency for Global Media and is a big operation that broadcasts in sixty-one languages and blankets the globe: Cuba, China, Iraq, Lebanon, Libya, Morocco, Sudan, Iran, Afghanistan, Russia, Ukraine, Serbia, Azerbaijan, Belarus, Georgia, North Korea, Laos, and Vietnam.[44]

The bulk of the United States Agency for Global Media is no longer funded from the CIA's black budget, but the agency's original Cold War goal and purpose—subversion and psychological operations directed against countries deemed hostile to US interests—remain the same.[45] The only thing that did change about the United States Agency for Global Media is that today more and more of its broadcasts are taking place online.

The agency's relationship with the Tor Project started with China.

Internet Freedom

The CIA had been targeting the People's Republic of China with covert broadcasting since at least 1951, when the agency launched Radio Free Asia. Over the decades, the agency shut down and re-launched Radio Free Asia under different guises and, ultimately, handed it off to the Broadcasting Board of Governors.[46]

When the commercial Internet began to penetrate China in the early 2000s, BBG and Radio Free Asia channeled their efforts into web-based programming. But this expansion didn't go very smoothly. For years, China had been jamming Voice of America and Radio Free Asia programs by playing loud noises or looping Chinese opera music over the same frequencies with a more powerful radio signal, which bumped American broadcasts off the air.[47] When these broadcasts switched to the Internet, Chinese censors hit back, blocking access to BBG websites as well as sporadically cutting access to private Internet services like Google.[48] There was nothing surprising about this. Chinese officials saw the Internet as just another communication medium being used by America to undermine their government. Jamming this kind of activity was standard practice in China long before the Internet arrived.[49]

Expected or not, the US government did not let the matter drop. Attempts by China to control its own domestic Internet space and block access to material and information were seen as belligerent acts—something like a modern trade embargo that limited US businesses' and government agencies' ability to operate freely. Under President George W. Bush, American foreign policy planners formulated policies that would become known over the next decade as "Internet Freedom."[50] While couched in lofty language about fighting censorship, promoting democracy, and safeguarding "freedom of expression," these policies were rooted in big power politics: the fight to open markets to American companies and expand America's dominance in the age of the Internet.[51] Internet Freedom was enthusiastically backed by American businesses, especially budding Internet giants like Yahoo!, Amazon, eBay, Google, and later Facebook and Twitter. They saw foreign control of the Internet, first in China but also in Iran and later Vietnam, Russia, and Myanmar, as an illegitimate check on their ability to expand into new global markets, and ultimately as a threat to their businesses.

Internet Freedom required a new set of "soft-power" weapons: digital crowbars that could be used to wrench holes in a country's telecommunications infrastructure. In the early 2000s, the US government began funding projects that would allow people inside China to tunnel through their country's government firewall.[52] The BBG's Internet Anti-Censorship Division led the pack, sinking millions into all sorts of early "censorship circumvention" technologies. It backed SafeWeb, an Internet proxy funded by the CIA's venture capital firm In-Q-Tel. It also funded several small outfits run by practitioners of Falun Gong, a controversial Chinese anticommunist cult banned in China whose leader believes that humans are being corrupted by aliens from other dimensions and that people of mixed blood are subhumans and unfit for salvation.[53]

The Chinese government saw these anticensorship tools as weapons in an upgraded version of an old war. "The Internet has become a new battlefield between China and the U.S." declared a 2010 editorial of the Xinhua News Agency, China's official press agency. "The U.S. State Department is collaborating with Google, Twitter and other IT giants to jointly launch software that 'will enable everyone to use the Internet freely,' using a kind of U.S. government provided antiblocking software, in an attempt to spread ideology and values in line with the United States' demands."[54]

China saw Internet Freedom as a threat, an illegitimate attempt to undermine the country's sovereignty through "network warfare," and began building a sophisticated system of Internet censorship and control, which grew into the infamous Great Firewall of China. Iran soon followed in China's footsteps.

It was the start of a censorship arms race. But there was a problem: the early anticensorship tools backed by the BBG didn't work very well. They had few users and were easily blocked. If Internet Freedom was going to triumph, America needed bigger and stronger weapons. Luckily, the US Navy had just developed a powerful anonymity technology to hide its spies, a technology that could easily be adapted to America's Internet Freedom war.

Russia Deployment Plan

When Tor joined the Broadcasting Board of Governors (now USAGM) in early 2006, Roger Dingledine was aware of America's escalating Internet Freedom conflict and accepted Tor's role as a weapon in this fight. China and Iran were throwing up ever more sophisticated censorship techniques to block US programming, and Dingledine talked up Tor's ability to meet this challenge. "We already have tens of thousands of users in Iran and China and similar countries, but once we get more popular, we're going to need to be prepared to start the arms race," he wrote to the BBG in 2006, laying out a plan to progressively add features to the Tor network that would make it harder and harder to block.[55]

The Tor Project was the BBG's most sophisticated Internet Freedom weapon, and the agency pushed Dingledine to reach out to foreign political activists and get them to use the tool. But as Dingledine quickly discovered, his organization's ties to the US government aroused suspicion and hampered his ability to attract users.

One of those lessons came in 2008. Early that year, the BBG instructed Dingledine to carry out what he dubbed the "Russian Deployment Plan," which involved adding a Russian language option to Tor's interface and working to train Russian activists in how to properly use the service.[56]

In February 2008, weeks before Russia's presidential elections, Dingledine sent an email request to a Russian privacy activist named Vlad. "One of our funders . . . [the Broadcasting Board of Governors] wants us to start reaching out to real users who might need these tools at some point," Dingledine explained. "So we settled on Russia, which is increasingly on their radar as a country that may have a serious censorship problem in the next few years. . . . So: please don't advertise this anywhere yet. But if you'd like to be involved in some way, or you have advice, please do let me know."[57]

Vlad was glad to hear from Dingledine. He knew about Tor and was a fan of the technology, but he had doubts about the plan. He explained that censorship was not currently an issue in Russia. "The main problem in Russia at this time is not a government censorship (in the sense of the Great Firewall of China or some Arab states), but a self-censorship of many websites, especially of regional organizations. Unfortunately, this is not what Tor can entirely solve by itself," he replied. In other words: Why fix a problem that did not exist?

But a bigger question hung over Dingledine's request, one concerning Tor's ties to the US government. Vlad explained that he and others in Russia's privacy community were concerned about what he described as Tor's "dependence on 'Uncle Sam's' money" and that "some sponsors of the Tor Project are associated with the US State Department." He continued: "I understand this is an ambiguous and quite vague question, but do such sponsorship brings up any unusual issues to the Tor Project and Tor development process?"

Given the deteriorating political relations between Russia and the United States, the subtext of the question was obvious: How close was Tor to the US government? And, in this strained geopolitical climate, will these ties cause problems for Russian activists like him back home? These were honest questions, and relevant ones. The emails I obtained through the Freedom of Information Act do not show whether Dingledine ever replied. How could he? What would he say?

The Tor Project had positioned itself as an "independent nonprofit," but when Dingledine reached out to Vlad in early 2008, it was operating as a de facto arm of the US government.

The correspondence left little room for doubt. The Tor Project was not a radical indie organization fighting The Man. For all intents and purposes, it *was* The Man. Or, at least, The Man's right hand. Intermixed with updates on new hires, status reports, chatty suggestions for hikes and vacation spots, and the usual office banter, internal correspondence reveals Tor's close collaboration with the BBG and multiple other wings of the US government, in particular those that dealt with foreign policy and soft-power projection. Messages describe meetings, trainings, and conferences with the NSA, CIA, FBI, and State Department.[58] There are strategy sessions and discussions about the need to influence news coverage and control bad press.[59] The correspondence also shows Tor employees taking orders from their handlers in the federal government, including plans to deploy their anonymity tool in countries deemed hostile to US interests: China, Iran, Vietnam, and, of course, Russia. Despite Tor's public insistence it would never put in any backdoors that gave the US government secret privileged access to Tor's network, the correspondence shows that in at least one instance in 2007, Tor revealed a security vulnerability to its federal backer before alerting the public, potentially giving the government an opportunity to exploit the weakness to unmask Tor users before it was fixed.[60]

The funding record tells the story even more precisely. Aside from Google paying a handful of college students to work at Tor via the company's Summer of Code program, Tor was subsisting almost exclusively on government contracts. By 2008, that included contracts with DARPA, the navy, the BBG, and the State Department as well as Stanford Research Institute's Cyber-Threat Analytics program.[61] Run by the US Army, this initiative had come out of the NSA's Advanced Research and Development Activity division—a "sort of national laboratory for eavesdropping and other spycraft" is how James Bamford describes it in *The Shadow Factory*.[62] And a few months after reaching out to Vlad, Dingledine was in the middle of closing another $600,000 contract with the State Department,[63] this time from its Democracy, Human Rights, and Labor division, which had been created during President Bill Clinton's first term and which was tasked with doling out grants for "democracy assistance."[64]

What would someone like Vlad think of all this? Obviously, nothing good. And that was an issue.

The Tor Project needed users to trust its technology and show enthusiasm. Credibility was key. But Dingledine's outreach to Russian privacy activists was a rude reminder that Tor couldn't shake its government affiliation and all the negative connotations that came with it. It was a problem that Dingledine had guessed would haunt Tor when he accepted BBG's first contract back in 2006.

Clearly, Tor needed to do something to change public perception, something that could help distance Tor from its government sponsors once and for all. As luck would have it, Dingledine found the perfect man for the job: a young, ambitious Tor developer who could help rebrand the Tor Project as a group of rebels that made Uncle Sam tremble in his jackboots.

A Hero Is Born

Jacob Appelbaum was born in 1983 on April Fools' Day. He grew up in Santa Rosa, a city just north of San Francisco, in a bohemian family. He liked to talk up his rough upbringing: a schizophrenic mother, a musician-turned-junkie dad, and a domestic situation that got so bad he had to fish used needles out of the couch as a kid. But he was also a smart middle-class Jewish kid with a knack for programming and hacking. He attended Santa Rosa Junior College and took classes in computer science.[65] He dressed in goth black and dabbled in steampunk photography, taking retro-futuristic pictures of young women decked out in Victorian-era dresses in front of steam engines and locomotives. Politically, he identified as a libertarian.

Like most young libertarians, he was enchanted by Ayn Rand's *The Fountainhead*, which he described as one of his favorite books. "I took up this book while I was traveling around Europe last year. Most of my super left wing friends really dislike Ayn Rand for some reason or another. I cannot even begin to fathom why, but hey, to each their own," he wrote in his blog diary. "While reading The Fountainhead I felt like I was reading a story about people that I knew in my everyday life. The characters were simple. The story was simple. What I found compelling was the moral behind the story. I suppose it may be summed up in one line . . . *Those that seek to gather you together for selfless actions, wish to enslave you for their own gain.*"[66]

He moved to San Francisco and worked low-level computer jobs with an emphasis in network management, but he chafed at regular tech jobs and pined for something meaningful.[67] He took time off to volunteer in New Orleans after Hurricane Katrina and somehow wound up in Iraq hanging out with a military contractor buddy who was installing satellite service in the war-torn country. He returned to the Bay Area more determined than ever to live an exciting life. "Life is too short to waste it on jobs that I do not enjoy," he said in a 2005 interview.[68] One day he'd join a porn start-up company, dress in black, dye his hair red, and pose with a power tool dildo for *Wired* magazine.[69] The next day he'd travel halfway around the world to use his skills for the greater good. "I'm a freelance hacker. I work helping groups that I feel really need my help. They come to me and ask me for my services," he said. "More often than not, I'm simply setting up their networks and systems around the world. It depends on how I feel about the work they're doing. It has to be both an interesting job and for an interesting result."

Appelbaum also began to develop a bad reputation in the Bay Area hacker scene for his aggressive, unwanted sexual advances. San Francisco journalist Violet Blue recounted how he spent months trying to coerce and bully women into having sex with him, attempted to forcefully isolate his victims in rooms or stairwells at parties, and resorted to public shaming if his advances were rebuffed.[70] This pattern of behavior would trigger his downfall almost a decade later. But for now, his star was ascendant. And in 2008, Appelbaum finally got his dream job—a position that could expand with his giant ego and ambition.

In April of that year, Dingledine hired him as a full-time Tor contractor.[71] He had a starting salary of $96,000 plus benefits and was put to work making Tor more user-friendly. He was a good coder, but he didn't stay focused on the technical side for long. As Dingledine discovered, Appelbaum proved better and much more useful at something else: branding and public relations.

Tor employees were computer engineers, mathematicians, and encryption junkies. Most of them were introverts, and socially awkward. Even worse: some, like Roger Dingledine, had spent time at US intelligence agencies and proudly displayed this fact on their online CVs—a not-so-subtle sign of a lack of radicalness.[72] Appelbaum added a different element to the organization. He had flair, a taste for drama and hyperbole. He was full of tall tales and vanity, and he had a burning desire for the spotlight.

Within months of getting the job, he assumed the role of official Tor Project spokesman and began promoting Tor as a powerful weapon against government oppression.

While Dingledine focused on running the business, Jacob Appelbaum jet-setted to exotic locations around the world to evangelize and spread the word. He'd hit ten countries in a month and not bat an eye: Argentina, India, Poland, South Korea, Belgium, Switzerland, Canada, Tunisia, Brazil, and even Google's campus in Mountain View, California.[73] He gave talks at technology conferences and hacker events, pow-wowed with Silicon Valley executives, visited Hong Kong, trained foreign political activists in the Middle East, and showed former sex workers in Southeast Asia how to protect themselves online. He also met with Swedish law enforcement agencies, but that was done out of the public eye.[74]

Over the next several years, Dingledine's reports back to the BBG were filled with descriptions of Appelbaum's successful outreach. "Lots of Tor advocacy," wrote Dingledine. "Another box of Tor stickers applied to many many laptops. Lots of people were interested in Tor and many many people installed Tor on both laptops and servers. This advocacy resulted in at least two new high bandwidth nodes that he helped the administrators configure."[75] Internal documents show that the proposed budget for Dingledine and Appelbaum's global publicity program was $20,000 a year, which included a public relations strategy.[76] "Crafting a message that the media can understand is a critical piece of this," Dingledine explained in a 2008 proposal. "This isn't so much about getting good press about Tor as it is about preparing journalists so if they see bad press and consider spreading it further, they'll stop and think. . . ."[77]

Appelbaum was energetic and did his best to promote Tor among privacy activists, cryptographers, and, most important of all, the radical cypherpunk movement that dreamed of using encryption to take on the power of governments and liberate the world from centralized control. In 2010, he snagged the support of Julian Assange, a silver-haired hacker who wanted to free the world of secrets.

Tor Gets Radical

Jacob Appelbaum and Julian Assange had met in Berlin sometime in 2005, just as the mysterious Australian hacker was getting ready to set WikiLeaks in motion. Assange's idea for WikiLeaks was simple: government tyranny can only survive in an ecosystem of secrecy. Take away the ability of the powerful to keep secrets, and the whole facade will come crashing down around them. "We are going to fuck them all," wrote Assange giddily on a secret listserv, after announcing his goal of raising $5 million for the WikiLeaks effort. "We're going to crack the world open and let it flower into something new. If fleecing the CIA will assist us, then fleece we will."[78]

Appelbaum watched as Assange slowly erected WikiLeaks from nothing, building up a dedicated following by trawling hacker conferences for would-be leakers. The two became good friends, and Appelbaum would later brag to journalist Andy Greenberg that they were so close, they'd fuck chicks together. One New Year's morning the two woke up in an apartment in Berlin in one bed with two women. "That was how we rolled in 2010," he said.

Soon after that supposedly wild night, Appelbaum decided to attach himself to the WikiLeaks cause. He spent a few weeks with Assange and the original WikiLeaks crew in Iceland as they prepared their first major release and helped secure the site's anonymous submissions system using Tor's hidden service feature, which hid the physical location of WikiLeaks servers and in theory made them much less susceptible to surveillance and attack. From then on, the WikiLeaks site proudly advertised Tor: "secure, anonymous, distributed network for maximum security."

Appelbaum's timing couldn't have been better. Late that summer WikiLeaks caused an international sensation by publishing a huge cache of classified government documents stolen and leaked by Chelsea (née Bradley) Manning, a young US Army private who was stationed in Iraq. First came the war logs from Afghanistan, showing how the United States had systematically underreported civilian casualties and operated an elite assassination unit. Next came the Iraq War logs, providing irrefutable evidence that America had armed and trained death squads in a brutal counterinsurgency campaign against Iraq's Sunni minority, which helped fuel the Shia-Sunni sectarian war that led to hundreds of thousands of deaths and ethnic cleansing in parts of Baghdad.[79] Then came the US diplomatic cables, offering an unprecedented window into the inner workings of American diplomacy: regime change, backroom deals with dictators, corruption of foreign leaders brushed under the table in the name of stability.[80]

Assange was suddenly one of the most famous people in the world—a fearless radical taking on the awesome power of the United States. Appelbaum did his best to be Assange's right-hand man. He served as the organization's official American representative and bailed the founder of WikiLeaks out of tough spots when the heat from US authorities got too hot.[81] Appelbaum became so intertwined with WikiLeaks that apparently some staffers talked about him leading the organization if something were to happen to Assange.[82] But Assange kept firm control of WikiLeaks, even after he was forced to go into hiding at the Ecuadorian embassy in London to escape extradition back to Sweden to face an investigation of rape allegations.

It's not clear whether Assange knew that Appelbaum's salary was being paid by the same government he was trying to destroy. What is clear is that Assange gave Appelbaum and Tor wide credit for helping WikiLeaks. "Jake has been a tireless promoter behind the scenes of our cause," he told a reporter. "Tor's importance to WikiLeaks cannot be understated."[83]

With those words, Appelbaum and the Tor Project became central heroes in the WikiLeaks saga, right behind Assange. Appelbaum leveraged his new rebel status for all it was worth. He regaled reporters with wild stories of how his association with WikiLeaks made him a wanted man. He talked about being pursued, interrogated, and threatened by shadowy government forces. He described in chilling detail how he and everyone he knew were thrown into a nightmare world of Big Brother harassment and surveillance. He claimed his mother was targeted. His girlfriend received nightly visits by men clad in black. "I was in Iceland working with a friend about their constitution's reform. And she saw two men outside of her house on the ground floor in her backyard, meaning that they were on her property inside of a fence. And they—one of them was wearing night vision goggles and watching her sleep," he recounted in a radio interview. "So she just laid in bed in pure terror for the period of time in which they stood there and watched her. And presumably, this is because there was a third person in the house placing a bug or doing something else, and they were keeping watch on her to make sure that if she were to hear something or to get up, they would be able to alert this other person."[84]

He was a great performer and had a knack for giving journalists what they wanted. He spun fantastic stories, and Tor was at the center of them all. Reporters lapped it up. The more exaggerated and heroic his performance, the more attention flowed his way. News articles, radio shows, television appearances, and magazine spreads. The media couldn't get enough.

In December 2010, *Rolling Stone* published a profile of Appelbaum as "the Most Dangerous Man in Cyberspace." The article portrayed him as a fearless techno-anarchist warrior who had dedicated his life to taking down America's evil military-surveillance apparatus, no matter the cost to his own life. It was full of high drama, chronicling Appelbaum's life on the post-WikiLeaks run. Descriptions of barren hideout apartments, Ziploc bags filled with cash from exotic locations, and photos of scantily clad punk girls—presumably Appelbaum's many love interests. "Appelbaum has been off the grid ever since—avoiding airports, friends, strangers and unsecure locations, traveling through the country by car. He's spent the past five years of his life working to protect activists around the world from repressive governments. Now he is on the run from his own," wrote *Rolling Stone* reporter Nathaniel Rich.[85]

His association with WikiLeaks and Assange boosted the Tor Project's public profile and radical credentials. Support and accolades poured in from journalists, privacy organizations, and government watchdogs. The American Civil Liberties Union partnered with Appelbaum on an Internet privacy project, and New York's Whitney Museum—one of the leading modern art museums in the world—invited him for a "Surveillance Teach-In."[86] The Electronic Frontier Foundation gave Tor its Pioneer Award, and Roger Dingledine made it on *Foreign Policy* magazine's list of Top 100 Global Thinkers for protecting "anyone and everyone from the dangers of Big Brother."[87]

As for Tor's deep, ongoing ties to the US government? Well, what of them? To any doubters, Jacob Appelbaum was held up as living, breathing proof of the radical independence of the Tor Project. "If the users or developers he meets worry that Tor's government funding compromises its ideals, there's no one better than Appelbaum to show the group doesn't take orders from the feds," wrote journalist Andy Greenberg in *This Machine Kills Secrets*, a book about WikiLeaks. "Appelbaum's best evidence of Tor's purity from Big Brother's interference, perhaps, is his very public association with WikiLeaks, the American government's least favorite website."

With Julian Assange endorsing Tor, reporters assumed that the US government saw the anonymity nonprofit as a threat. But internal documents obtained through FOIA from the Broadcasting Board of Governors (USAGM), as well as an analysis of Tor's government contracts, paint a different picture. They reveal that Appelbaum and Dingledine worked with Assange on securing WikiLeaks with Tor since late 2008 and that they kept their handlers at the BBG informed about their relationship and even provided information about the inner workings of WikiLeaks's secure submissions system.

"Talked to the WikiLeaks people (Daniel and Julian) about their use of Tor hidden services, and how we can make things better for them," Dingledine wrote in a progress report he sent to the BBG in January 2008. "It turns out they use the hidden service entirely as a way to keep users from screwing up—either it works and they know they're safe or it fails, but either way they don't reveal what they're trying to leak locally. So I'd like to add a new 'secure service' feature that's just like a hidden service but it only makes one hop from the server side rather than three. A more radical design would be for the 'intro point' to be the service itself, so it really would be like an exit enclave."[88] In another progress report sent to the BBG two years later, in February 2010, Dingledine wrote, "Jacob and WikiLeaks people met with policymakers in Iceland to discuss freedom of speech, freedom of press, and that online privacy should be a fundamental right."

No one at the BBG raised any objections. To the contrary, they appeared to be supportive. We do not know if anyone at the BBG forwarded this information to some other government body, but it would not be hard to imagine that information about WikiLeaks' security infrastructure and submission system was of great interest to US intelligence agencies.

Perhaps most telling was that support from the BBG continued even after WikiLeaks began publishing classified government information and Appelbaum became the target of a larger Department of Justice investigation into WikiLeaks. For example, on July 31, 2010, CNET reported that Appelbaum had been detained at the Las Vegas airport and questioned about his relationship with WikiLeaks.[89] News of the detention made headlines around the world, once again highlighting Appelbaum's close ties to Julian Assange. And a week later, Tor's executive director Andrew Lewman, clearly worried that this might affect Tor's funding, emailed Ken Berman at the BBG in the hopes of smoothing things over and answering "any questions you may have about the recent press regarding Jake and WikiLeaks." But Lewman was in for a pleasant surprise: Roger Dingledine had been keeping the folks at the BBG in the loop, and everything seemed to be okay. "Great stuff, thx. Roger answered a number of questions when he met us this week in DC," Berman replied.[90]

Unfortunately, Berman didn't explain in the email what he and Dingledine discussed about Appelbaum and WikiLeaks during their meeting. What we do know is that Tor's association with WikiLeaks produced no real negative impact on Tor's government contracts.[91]

Its 2011 contracts came in without a hitch—$150,000 from the Broadcasting Board of Governors and $227,118 from the State Department.[92] Tor was even able to snag a big chunk of money from the Pentagon: a new $503,706 annual contract from the Space and Naval Warfare Systems Command, an elite information and intelligence unit that houses a top-secret cyber-warfare division.[93] The navy contract was passed through SRI, the old Stanford military contractor that had done counterinsurgency, networking, and chemical weapons work for ARPA back in the 1960s and 1970s. The funds were part of a larger navy "Command, Control, Communications, Computers, Intelligence, Surveillance, and Reconnaissance" program to improve military operations. A year later, Tor would see its government contracts more than double to $2.2 million: $353,000 from the State Department, $876,099 from the US Navy, and $937,800 from the Broadcasting Board of Governors.[94]

When I crunched the numbers, I couldn't help but do a double take. It was incredible. WikiLeaks had scored a direct hit on Tor's government backers, including the Pentagon and State Department. Yet Appelbaum's close partnership with Assange produced no discernable downside.

I guess it makes sense, in a way. WikiLeaks might have embarrassed some parts of the US government, but it also gave America's premier Internet Freedom weapon a major injection of credibility, enhancing its effectiveness and usefulness. It was an opportunity.

Social Media as a Weapon

In 2011, less than a year after WikiLeaks broke onto the world stage, the Middle East and North Africa exploded like a powder keg. Seemingly out of nowhere, huge demonstrations and protests swept through the region. It started in Tunisia, where a poor fruit seller lit himself on fire to protest humiliating harassment and extortion at the hands of the local police. He died from his burns on January 4, triggering a national protest movement against Tunisia's dictatorial president, Zine El Abidine Ben Ali, who had ruled the country for twenty-three years. Within weeks, massive antigovernment protests spread to Egypt, Algeria, Oman, Jordan, Libya, and Syria.

The Arab Spring had arrived.

In Tunisia and Egypt, these protest movements toppled long-standing dictatorships from within. In Libya, opposition forces deposed and savagely killed Muammar Gaddafi, knifing him in the anus, after an extensive bombing campaign from NATO forces. In Syria, protests were met with a brutal crackdown from Bashar Assad's government, and led to a protracted war that would claim hundreds of thousands of lives and trigger the worst refugee crisis in recent history, pulling in Saudi Arabia, Turkey, Israel, the CIA, the Russian Air Force and special operations teams, Al-Qaeda, and ISIL. Arab Spring turned into a long, bloody winter.

The underlying causes of these opposition movements were deep, complex, and varied from country to country. Youth unemployment, corruption, drought and related high food prices, political repression, economic stagnation, and longstanding geopolitical aspirations were just a few of the factors. To a young and digitally savvy crop of State Department officials and foreign policy planners, these political movements had one thing in common: they arose because of the democratizing power of the Internet. They saw social media sites like Facebook, Twitter, and YouTube as democratic multipliers that allowed people to get around official state-controlled information sources and organize political movements quickly and efficiently.

"The Che Guevara of the 21st Century is the network," Alec

Ross, a State Department official in charge of digital policy under Secretary of State Hillary Clinton, gushed in the *NATO Review,* the official magazine of the North Atlantic Treaty Organization.[95] His Che reference smacks of hypocrisy or perhaps ignorance; Che, after all, was executed by Bolivian forces backed by the United States, in particular, by the CIA.

The idea that social media could be weaponized against countries and governments deemed hostile to US interests wasn't a surprise. For years the State Department, in partnership with the Broadcasting Board of Governors (USAGM) and companies like Facebook and Google, had worked to train activists from around the world on how to use Internet tools and social media to organize opposition political movements. Countries in Asia, the Middle East, and Latin America as well as former Soviet states like the Ukraine and Belarus were all on the list. Indeed, the *New York Times* reported that many of the activists who played leading roles in the Arab Spring—from Egypt to Syria to Yemen—had taken part in these training sessions.[96]

"The money spent on these programs was minute compared with efforts led by the Pentagon," reported the *New York Times* in April 2011. "But as American officials and others look back at the uprisings of the Arab Spring, they are seeing that the United States' democracy-building campaigns played a bigger role in fomenting protests than was previously known, with key leaders of the movements having been trained by the Americans in campaigning, organizing through new media tools and monitoring elections." The trainings were politically charged and were seen as a threat by Egypt, Yemen, and Bahrain—all of which lodged complaints with the State Department to stop meddling in their domestic affairs, and even barred US officials from entering their countries.[97]

An Egyptian youth political leader who attended State Department training sessions and then went on to lead protests in Cairo told the *New York Times,* "We learned how to organize and build coalitions. This certainly helped during the revolution." A different youth activist, who had participated in Yemen's uprising, was equally enthusiastic about the State Department social media training: "It helped me very much because I used to think that change only takes place by force and by weapons."

Staff from the Tor Project played a role in some of these trainings, taking part in a series of Arab Blogger sessions in Yemen, Tunisia, Jordan, Lebanon, and Bahrain, where Jacob Appelbaum taught opposition activists how to use Tor to get around government censorship.[98] "Today was fantastic . . . really a fantastic meeting of minds in the Arab world! It's enlightening and humbling to have been invited. I really have to recommend visiting Beirut. Lebanon is an amazing place. Friendly people, good food, intense music, insane taxis," Appelbaum tweeted after an Arab Bloggers training event in 2009, adding: "If you'd like to help Tor please sign up and help translate Tor software into Arabic."[99]

Activists later put the skills taught at these training sessions to use during the Arab Spring, routing around Internet blocks that their governments threw up to prevent them from using social media to organize protests. "There would be no access to Twitter or Facebook in some of these places if you didn't have Tor. All of the sudden, you had all these dissidents exploding under their noses, and then down the road you had a revolution," Nasser Weddady, a prominent Arab Spring activist from Mauritania, later told *Rolling Stone*. Weddady, who had taken part in the Tor Project's training sessions and who had translated a widely circulated guide on how to use the tool into Arabic, credited it with helping keep the Arab Spring uprisings alive. "Tor rendered the government's efforts completely futile. They simply didn't have the know-how to counter that move."[100]

From a higher vantage point, the Tor Project was a wild success. It had matured into a powerful foreign policy tool—a soft-power cyber weapon with multiple uses and benefits. It hid spies and military agents on the Internet, enabling them to carry out their missions without leaving a trace. It was used by the US government as a persuasive regime-change weapon, a digital crowbar that prevented countries from exercising sovereign control over their own Internet infrastructure. Counterintuitively, Tor also emerged as a focal point for antigovernment privacy activists and organizations, a huge cultural success that made Tor that much more effective for its government backers by drawing fans and helping shield the project from scrutiny.

And Tor was just the beginning.

The Arab Spring provided the US government with the confirmation it was looking for. Social media, combined with technologies like Tor, could be tapped to bring huge masses of people onto the streets and could even trigger revolutions. Diplomats in Washington called it "democracy promotion." Critics called it regime change.[101] But it didn't matter what you called it. The US government saw that it could leverage the Internet to sow discord and inflame political instability in countries it considered hostile to US interests. Good or bad, it could weaponize social media and use it for insurgency. And it wanted more.[102]

In the wake of the Arab Spring, the US government directed even more resources to Internet Freedom technologies. The plan was to go beyond the Tor Project and launch all sorts of crypto tools to leverage the power of social media to help foreign activists build political movements and organize protests: encrypted chat apps and ultrasecure operating systems designed to prevent governments from spying on activists, anonymous whistle-blowing platforms that could help expose government corruption, and wireless networks that could be deployed instantaneously anywhere in the world to keep activists connected even if their government turned off the Internet.[103]

Strangely enough, these efforts were about to get a major credibility boost from an unlikely source: an NSA contractor by the name of Edward Snowden.

Strange Alliances

The post-WikiLeaks years were good for the Tor Project. With the government contracts flowing, Roger Dingledine expanded the payroll, adding a dedicated crew of developers and managers who saw their job in messianic terms: to free the Internet of government surveillance.[104]

Jacob Appelbaum, too, was doing well. Claiming that harassment from the US government was too much to bear, he spent most of his time in Berlin in a sort of self-imposed exile. There, he continued to do the job Dingledine had hired him to do. He traveled the world training political activists and persuading techies and hackers to join up as Tor volunteers. He also did various side projects, some of which blurred the line between activism and intelligence gathering. In 2012, he made a trip to Burma, a longtime target of US government regime-change efforts.[105] The purpose of the trip was to probe the country's Internet system from within and collect information on its telecommunications infrastructure, information that was then used to compile a government report for policymakers and "international investors" interested in penetrating Burma's recently deregulated telecom market.[106]

Appelbaum continued to draw a high five-figure salary from Tor, a government contractor funded almost exclusively by military and intelligence grants. But, to the public, he was a real-life superhero on the run from the US surveillance state—now hiding out in Berlin, the nerve center of the global hacker scene known for its nerdy mix of machismo, all-night hackathons, drug use, and partner swapping. He was a member of the Internet Freedom elite, championed by the American Civil Liberties Union and the Electronic Frontier Foundation, given a board seat on eBay founder Pierre Omidyar's Freedom of the Press Foundation, and occupied an advisory role for London's Centre for Investigative Journalism. His fame and rebel status only made his job as Tor's pitchman more effective.

In Berlin, Appelbaum caught another lucky break for the Tor Project. In 2013, his good friend and sometimes-lover Laura Poitras, an American documentary filmmaker who also lived in the German capital in self-imposed exile, was contacted by a mysterious source who told her he had access to the crown jewels of the National Security Agency: documents that would blow America's surveillance apparatus wide open.[107] Poitras tapped Appelbaum's knowledge of Internet systems to come up with a list of questions to vet the possible leaker and to make sure he really was the NSA technician he claimed to be. This source turned out to be Edward Snowden.[108]

From the start, the Tor Project stood at the center of Snowden's story. The leaker's endorsement and promotion introduced the project to a global audience, boosting Tor's worldwide user base from one million to six million almost overnight and injecting it into the heart of a burgeoning privacy movement. In Russia, where the BBG and Dingledine had tried but failed to recruit activists for their Tor deployment plan, use of the software increased from twenty thousand daily connections to somewhere around two hundred thousand.[109]

During a promotional campaign for the Tor Project, Snowden said:

Without Tor, the streets of the Internet become like the streets of a very heavily surveilled city. There are surveillance cameras everywhere, and if the adversary simply takes enough time, they can follow the tapes back and see everything you've done. With Tor, we have private spaces and private lives, where we can choose who we want to associate with and how, without the fear of what that is going to look like if it is abused. The design of the Tor system is structured in such a way that even if the US Government wanted to subvert it, it couldn't.[110]

Snowden didn't talk about Tor's continued government funding, nor did he address an apparent contradiction: why the US government would fund a program that supposedly limited its own power.[111]

Whatever Snowden's private thoughts on the matter, his endorsement gave Tor the highest possible seal of approval. It was like a Hacker's Medal of Valor. With Snowden's backing, no one even thought to question Tor's radical antigovernment bona fides.

To some, Edward Snowden was a hero. To others, he was a traitor who deserved to be executed. Officials at the NSA claimed that he had caused irreparable harm to the security of the country, and every intelligence agency and contractor went on to invest in costly "insider threat" programs designed to spy on employees and make sure that another Edward Snowden would never pop up again. Some called for bringing him back in a black-ops kidnapping; others, like Donald Trump, called for him to be assassinated.[112] Anatoly Kucherena, Snowden's Russian lawyer, claimed that the leaker's life was in danger. "There are real threats to his life out there that actually do exist," he told one reporter.

Indeed, a lot of hate and malice was pointed in Snowden's direction, but to those running the Internet Freedom wing of the US military intelligence apparatus, his embrace of Tor and crypto culture could not have come at a better moment.

In early January 2014, six months after Snowden's leaks, Congress passed the Consolidated Appropriations Act, an omnibus federal spending bill. Tucked into the bill's roughly fifteen hundred pages was a short provision that dedicated $50.5 million to the expansion of the US government's Internet Freedom arsenal. The funds were to be split evenly between the State Department and the Broadcasting Board of Governors.[113]

Although Congress had been providing funds for various anticensorship programs for years, this was the first time that it budgeted money specifically for Internet Freedom. The motivation for this expansion came out of the Arab Spring. The idea was to make sure the US government would maintain its technological advantage in the censorship arms race that began in the early 2000s, but the funds were also going into developing a new generation of tools aimed at leveraging the power of the Internet to help foreign opposition activists organize into cohesive political movements.[114]

The BBG's $25.25 million cut of the cash more than doubled the agency's anticensorship technology budget from the previous year, and the BBG funneled the money into the Open Technology Fund,[115] a new organization it had created within Radio Free Asia to fund Internet Freedom technologies in the wake of the Arab Spring.[116]

Initially launched by the Central Intelligence Agency in 1951 to target China with anticommunist radio broadcasts, Radio Free Asia had been shuttered and relaunched several times over the course of its history.[117] In 1994, after the fall of the Soviet Union, it reappeared

Terminator-like as a private nonprofit corporation wholly controlled and funded by the Broadcasting Board of Governors.[118] Focused on whipping up anticommunist sentiment in North Korea, Vietnam, Laos, Cambodia, Burma, and China, Radio Free Asia played a central role in the US government's anticensorship arms race that had been brewing ever since the BBG began pushing its China broadcasts through the Internet. Radio Free Asia had trouble shedding its covert Cold War tactics.[119] In North Korea, it smuggled in tiny radios and buried cellphones just inside the country's border with China so that its network of informants could report back on conditions inside the country. Following the death of Kim Jong Il in 2011, the radio "kicked into 24/7 emergency mode" to beam nonstop coverage of the death into North Korea in the hopes of triggering a mass uprising. Radio Free Asia executives hoped that, bit by bit, the stream of anticommunist propaganda directed at the country would bring about the collapse of the government.[120]

Now, with the Open Technology Fund (OTF), Radio Free Asia oversaw the funding of America's Internet Freedom programs. To run OTF's day-to-day operations, Radio Free Asia hired Dan Meredith, a young techie who worked at Al-Jazeera in Qatar and who had been involved in the State Department's anticensorship initiatives going back to 2011.[121] With a scruffy beard and messy blond surfer hair, Meredith wasn't a typical stuffy State Department suit. He was fluent in cypherpunk-hacktivist lingo and was very much a part of the grassroots privacy community he sought to woo. In short, he wasn't the kind of person you'd expect to run a government project with major foreign policy implications.

With him at the helm, OTF put a lot of effort on branding. Outwardly, it looked like a grassroots privacy activist organization, not a government agency. It produced hip 8-bit YouTube videos about its mission to use "public funds to support Internet freedom projects" and promote "human rights and open societies." Its web layout constantly changed to reflect the trendiest design standards.

But if OTF appeared scrappy, it was also extremely well connected. The organization was supported by a star-studded team—from best-selling science fiction authors to Silicon Valley executives and celebrated cryptography experts. Its advisory board included big names from the Columbia Journalism School, the Electronic Frontier Foundation, the Ford Foundation, Open Society Foundations, Google, Slack, and Mozilla. Andrew McLaughlin, the former head of Google's public relations team who had brought in Al Gore to talk a California state senator into canceling legislation that would regulate Gmail's email scanning program, was part of the OTF team. So was Cory Doctorow, a best-selling young adult science fiction author whose books about a totalitarian government's surveillance were read and admired by Laura Poitras, Jacob Appelbaum, Roger Dingledine, and Edward Snowden.[122] Doctorow was a huge personality in the crypto movement who could fill giant conference halls at privacy conferences. He publicly endorsed OTF's Internet Freedom mission. "I'm proud to be a volunteer OTF advisor," he tweeted.

From behind this hip and connected exterior, BBG and Radio Free Asia built a vertically integrated incubator for Internet Freedom technologies, pouring millions into projects big and small, including everything from evading censorship to helping political organizing, protests, and movement building. With its deep pockets and its recruitment of big-name privacy activists, the Open Technology Fund didn't just thrust itself into the privacy movement. In many ways, it *was* the privacy movement.

It set up lucrative academic programs and fellowships, paying out $55,000 a year to graduate students, privacy activists, technologists, cryptographers, security researchers, and political scientists to study "the Internet censorship climate in former Soviet states," probe the "technical capacity" of the Great Firewall of China, and track the "use of oppressive spyware command and control servers by repressive governments."[123]

It expanded the reach and speed of the Tor Project network and directed several million dollars to setting up high-bandwidth Tor exit nodes in the Middle East and Southeast Asia, both high-priority regions for US foreign policy.[124] It bankrolled encrypted chat apps, ultrasecure operating systems supposedly impervious to hacking, and next-generation secure email initiatives designed to make it hard for governments to spy on activists' communications. It backed anonymous WikiLeaks-like tools for leakers and whistle-blowers who wanted to expose their government's corruption. It coinvested with the State Department in several "mesh networking" and "Internet-in-a-box" projects designed to keep activists connected even if their government tried turning off local Internet connections.[125] It provided a "secure cloud" infrastructure with server nodes all around the world to host Internet Freedom projects, operated a "legal lab" that offered grantees legal protection in case something came up, and even ran a "Rapid Response Fund" to provide emergency support to Internet Freedom projects that were deemed vital and that required immediate deployment.[126]

The Tor Project remained the best-known privacy app funded by the Open Technology Fund, but it was quickly joined by another: Signal, an encrypted mobile phone messaging app for the iPhone and Android.

Signal was developed by Open Whisper Systems, a for-profit corporation run by Moxie Marlinspike, a tall, lanky cryptographer with a head full of dreadlocks. Marlinspike was an old friend of Jacob Appelbaum, and he played a similar radical game. He remained cryptic about his real name and identity, told stories of being targeted by the FBI, and spent his free time sailing and surfing in Hawaii. He had made a good chunk of money selling his encryption start-up to Twitter and had worked with the State Department on Internet Freedom projects since 2011, but he posed as a feisty anarchist fighting the system. His personal website was called thoughtcrime.org—a reference to George Orwell's *1984*, which seemed a bit tongue-in-cheek given that he was taking big money—nearly $3 million—from Big Brother to develop his privacy app.[127]

Signal was a huge success. Journalists, privacy activists, and cryptographers hailed Signal as an indispensable Internet privacy tool. It was a complement to Tor in the age of mobile phones. While Tor anonymized browsing, Signal encrypted voice calls and text, making it impossible for governments to monitor communication.

Laura Poitras gave it two secure thumbs up as a powerful people's encryption tool and told everyone to use it every day. People at the ACLU claimed that Signal made federal agents weep.[128] The Electronic Frontier Foundation added Signal alongside Tor to its *Surveillance Self-Defense* guide. Fight for the Future, a Silicon Valley–funded privacy activist organization, described Signal and Tor as "NSA-proof" and urged people to use them.

Edward Snowden was the combo's biggest and most famous booster and repeatedly took to Twitter to tell his three million followers that he used Signal and Tor every day, and that they should do the same to protect themselves from government surveillance. "Use Tor. Use Signal," he tweeted out.[129]

With endorsements like these, Signal quickly became the go-to app for political activists around the world. Egypt, Russia, Syria, and even the United States—millions downloaded Signal, and it became the communication app of choice for those who hoped to avoid police surveillance. Feminist collectives, anti–President Donald Trump protesters, communists, anarchists, radical animal rights organizations, Black Lives Matter activists—all flocked to Signal. Many were heeding Snowden's advice: "Organize. Compartmentalize to limit compromise. Encrypt everything, from calls to texts (use Signal as a first step)."[130]

Silicon Valley cashed in on OTF's Internet Freedom spending as well. Facebook incorporated Signal's underlying encryption protocol into WhatsApp, the most popular messaging app in the world. Google followed suit, building Signal encryption into its Allo and Duo text and video messaging apps.[131] It was a smart move because the praise flowed in. "Allo and Duo's new security features, in other words, are Google's baby steps towards a fully-encrypted future, not the sort of bold moves to elevate privacy above profit or politics that some of its competitors have already taken," wrote *Wired*'s Andy Greenberg. "But for a company built on a data collection model that's often fundamentally opposed to privacy, baby steps are better than none at all."

If you stepped back to survey the scene, the entire landscape of this new Internet Freedom privacy movement looked absurd. Cold

War–era organizations spun off from the CIA now funding the global movement against government surveillance? Google and Facebook, companies that ran private surveillance networks and worked hand in hand with the NSA, deploying government-funded privacy tech to protect their users from government surveillance? Privacy activists working with Silicon Valley and the US government to fight government surveillance—and with the support of Edward Snowden himself?

It is very hard to imagine that back in the 1960s student radicals at Harvard and MIT would have ever thought to partner with IBM and the State Department to protest against Pentagon surveillance. If they did, they probably would have been mocked and chased off campus, branded fools or—worse—as some kind of feds. Back then, the lines were clear, but today all these connections are obscured. Most people involved in privacy activism do not know about the US government's ongoing efforts to weaponize the privacy movement, nor do they appreciate Silicon Valley's motives in this fight. Without that knowledge, it is impossible to makes sense of it all. So, talk of government involvement in the privacy space sounds like something cooked up by a paranoiac.

In any event, with support from someone as celebrated as Edward Snowden, few had any reason to question why apps like Signal and Tor existed, or what larger purpose they served. It was easier and simpler to put your trust in app, and to believe in the idea that America still had a healthy civil society, where people could come together to fund tools that countervailed the surveillance power of the state. That suited the sponsors of Internet Freedom just fine.

After Edward Snowden, OTF was triumphant. It didn't mention the leaker by name in its promotional materials, but it profited from the crypto culture he promoted and benefited from his direct endorsement of the crypto tools it financed. It boasted that its partnership with both Silicon Valley and respected privacy activists meant that hundreds of millions of people could use the privacy tools the US government had brought to market. And OTF promised that this was just a start: "By leveraging social network effects, we expect to expand to a billion regular users taking advantage of OTF-supported tools and Internet Freedom technologies by 2015."[132]

False Sense of Security

While accolades for the Tor Project, Signal, and other crypto apps funded by the US government rolled in, a deeper look showed that they were not as secure or as impervious to government penetration as their proponents claimed. Perhaps no story better exemplifies the flaws in impenetrable crypto security than that of Ross Ulbricht, otherwise known as Dread Pirate Roberts, the architect of Silk Road.

After its founding in 2012, Silk Road grew rapidly and appeared to be a place where organized criminals could hide in plain sight—until it wasn't. In October 2013, four months after Edward Snowden came out of hiding and endorsed Tor, a twenty-nine-year-old native Texan by the name of Ross Ulbricht was arrested in a public library in San Francisco. He was accused of being Dread Pirate Roberts and was charged with multiple counts of money laundering, narcotics trafficking, hacking, and, on top of it all, murder.

When his case went to trial a year later, the story of the Tor Project took on a different shade, demonstrating the power of marketing and ideology over reality.

The internal communications and diaries recovered by investigators from Ulbricht's encrypted laptop showed that he believed he was fully protected by Tor. He believed in Tor's claims that were backed up by Edward Snowden and promoted by Jacob Appelbaum. He believed that everything he did in the murkiness of the dark web would have no bearing on him in the real world—he believed it so much that he not only built a massively illegal drug business on top of it but also ordered hits on anyone who threatened his business. His belief in the power of the Tor Project to create a cybernetic island completely impervious to the law persisted even in the face of strong countervailing evidence.

Starting in March 2013, Silk Road was hit with multiple attacks that crashed the Tor hidden server software that enabled it to be on the dark web. Over and over the site's real IP address leaked to the public, a mission-critical failure that could have made it trivial for law enforcement to track down the real identity of Dread Pirate Roberts.[133] Indeed, the attackers not only seemed to know the IP address of the Silk Road servers but also claimed to have hacked the site's user data and demanded that he pay them to keep quiet.

It seemed the party was over. Tor had failed. If it couldn't protect his identity from a group of extortionists, how would it fare against the nearly unlimited resources of federal law enforcement? But Ulbricht still believed. Instead of shutting down Silk Road, he put out a contract with the Hells Angels to whack the extortionists, ultimately paying the motorcycle gang $730,000 to kill six people. "Commissioned hit on blackmailer with angels," he wrote in his diary on March 29, 2013. Three days later, he followed it up with another note: "got word that blackmailer was excuted [sic] / created file upload script."[134] His nonchalance was born out of routine. Earlier that year, he had already paid $80,000 to have a former Silk Road administrator, who he suspected of stealing over $300,000, killed.[135]

Amazingly, just a month before his arrest, Ulbricht was contacted by the creators of Atlantis, one of the many copycat dark web drug stores inspired by Silk Road's success. It was a friendly sort of outreach. They told him that Atlantis was permanently closing up shop because they got word of a major hole in Tor's security, and they implied that he do the same. "I was messaged by one of their team who said they shut down because of an FBI doc leaked to them detailing vulnerabilities in Tor," Ulbricht wrote in his diary. Yet, amazingly, he continued to run his site, confident that it would turn out fine in the end. "Had revelation about the need to eat well, get good sleep, and meditate so I can stay positive and productive," he wrote on September 30. A day later, he was in federal custody.

During his trial, it came out that the FBI and DHS had infiltrated Silk Road almost from the very beginning. A DHS agent had even taken over a senior Silk Road administrator account, which gave federal agents access to the back end of Silk Road's system, a job for which Ulbricht paid the DHS agent $1,000 a week in Bitcoins.[136] Meaning, one of Ulbricht's top lieutenants was a fed, and he had no idea. But it was Silk Road's leaked IP address that ultimately led DHS agents to track Ulbricht's connection to a cafe in San Francisco, and ultimately to him.[137]

Ulbricht confessed to being Dread Pirate Roberts and to setting up Silk Road. After being found guilty of seven felonies, including money laundering, drug trafficking, running a criminal enterprise, and identity fraud, he went from calling for revolution to begging the judge for leniency. "Even now I understand what a terrible mistake I made. I've had my youth, and I know you must take away my middle years, but please leave me my old age. Please leave a small light at the end of the tunnel, an excuse to stay healthy, an excuse to dream of better days ahead, and a chance to redeem myself in the free world before I meet my maker," he said to the court. The judge had no pity. She hit him with a double life sentence without the possibility of parole. And more years may be added to the clock if he is convicted for any of his murders for hire.

The fall of Silk Road pricked Tor's invincibility. Even as Edward Snowden and organizations like the Electronic Frontier Foundation promoted Tor as a powerful tool against the US surveillance state, that very surveillance state was poking Tor full of holes.[138]

In 2014, the FBI along with the DHS and European law enforcement agencies went on the hunt for Silk Road copycat stores, taking down fifty marketplaces hawking everything from drugs to weapons to credit cards to child abuse pornography in an international sweep codenamed Operation Omynous. In 2015, international law enforcement in conjunction with the FBI arrested more than five hundred people linked with Playpen, a notorious child pornography network that ran on the Tor cloud. Seventy-six people were prosecuted in the United States, and nearly three hundred child victims from around the world were rescued from their abusers.[139] These raids were targeted and extremely effective. It seemed that cops knew exactly where to hit and how to do it.

What was going on? How did law enforcement penetrate what was supposed to be ironclad anonymity strong enough to withstand an onslaught by the NSA?

Confirmation was hard to come by, but Tor's Roger Dingledine was convinced that at least some of these stings were using an exploit developed by a group at Carnegie Mellon University in Pennsylvania. Working under a Pentagon contract, researchers had figured out a cheap and easy way to crack Tor's super-secure network with just $3,000 worth of computer equipment.[140] Dingledine accused the researchers of selling this method to the FBI.

"The Tor Project has learned more about last year's attack by Carnegie Mellon researchers on the hidden service subsystem. Apparently these researchers were paid by the FBI to attack hidden services users in a broad sweep, and then sift through their data to find people whom they could accuse of crimes," he lashed out in a blog post in November 2015, saying that he had been told the FBI paid at least $1 million for these services.[141]

It was strange to see Dingledine getting angry about researchers taking money from law enforcement when his own salary was paid almost entirely by military and intelligence-linked contracts. But Dingledine did something that was even stranger. He accused Carnegie Mellon researchers of violating academic standards for ethical research by working with law enforcement. He then announced that the Tor Project would publish guidelines for people who might want to hack or crack Tor for "academic" and "independent research" purposes in the future but do so in an ethical manner by first obtaining consent of the people who were being hacked.

"Research on humans' data is human research. Over the last century, we have made enormous strides in what research we consider ethical to perform on people in other domains," read a draft of this "Ethical Tor Research" guide. "We should make sure that privacy research is at least as ethical as research in other fields." The requirements set forth in this document include sections like: "Only collect data that is acceptable to publish" and "Only collect as much data as is needed: practice data minimization."[142]

Although demands like this make sense in a research context, they were baffling when applied to Tor. After all, Tor and its backers, including Edward Snowden, presented the project as a real-world anonymity tool that could resist the most powerful attackers. If it was so frail that it needed academic researchers to abide by an ethical honor code to avoid deanonymizing users without their consent, how could it hold up to the FBI or NSA or the scores of foreign intelligence agencies from Russia to China to Australia that might want to punch through its anonymity systems?

In 2015, when I first read these statements from the Tor Project, I was shocked. This was nothing less than a veiled admission that Tor was useless at guaranteeing anonymity and that it required attackers to behave "ethically" in order for it to remain secure. It must have come as an even greater shock to the cypherpunk believers like Ross Ulbricht, who trusted Tor to run his highly illegal Internet business and who is now in jail for the rest of his life.

Tor's spat with the researchers at Carnegie Mellon University revealed another confusing dynamic. Whereas one part of the federal government—which included the Pentagon, State Department, and the Broadcasting Board of Governors—funded the ongoing development of the Tor Project, another wing of this same federal government—which included the Pentagon, the FBI, and possibly other agencies—was working just as hard to crack it.

What was going on? Why was the government working at cross-purposes? Did one part simply not know what the other was doing?

Strangely enough, Edward Snowden's NSA documents provided the beginnings of an answer. They showed that multiple NSA programs could punch through Tor's defenses and possibly even uncloak the network's traffic on a "wide scale." They also showed that the spy agency saw Tor as a useful tool that concentrated potential "targets" in one convenient location. [143] In a word, the NSA saw Tor as a honeypot.

In October 2013, the *Washington Post* reported on several of these programs, revealing that the NSA had been working to crack Tor since at least 2006, the same year that Dingledine signed his first contract with the BBG.[144] One of these programs, codenamed EGOTISTI-CALGIRAFFE, was actively used to trace the identity of Al-Qaeda operatives. "One document provided by Snowden included an internal exchange among NSA hackers in which one of them said the agency's Remote Operations Center was capable of targeting anyone who visited an al-Qaeda Web site using Tor."[145] Another set of documents, made public by the *Guardian* that same month, showed that the agency viewed Tor in a positive light. "Critical mass of targets use Tor. Scaring them away might be counterproductive. We will never get 100% but we don't need to provide true IPs for every target every time they use Tor," explained a 2012 NSA presentation.[146] Its point was clear: people with something to hide—whether terrorists, foreign spies, or drug dealers—believed in Tor's promise of anonymity and used the network en masse. By doing so, they proceeded with a false sense of safety, doing things on the network they would never do out in the open, all while helping to mark themselves for further surveillance.[147]

This wasn't surprising. The bigger lesson of Snowden's NSA cache was that almost nothing happened on the Internet without passing through some kind of US government bug. Naturally, popular tools used by the public that promised to obfuscate and hide people's communications were targets regardless of who funded them.

As for the other crypto tools financed by the US government? They suffered similar security and honeypot pitfalls. Take Signal, the encrypted app Edward Snowden said he used every day. Marketed as a secure communication tool for political activists, the app had strange features built in from the very beginning. It required that users link their active mobile phone number and upload their entire address book into Signal's servers—both questionable features of a tool designed to protect political activists from law enforcement in authoritarian countries. In most cases, a person's phone number was effectively that person's identity, tied to a bank account and home address. Meanwhile, a person's address book contained that user's friends, colleagues, fellow political activists, and organizers, virtually the person's entire social network.

Then there was the fact that Signal ran on Amazon's servers, which meant that all its data were available to a partner in the NSA's PRISM surveillance program. Equally problematic, Signal needed Apple and Google to install and run the app on people's mobile phones. Both companies were, and as far as we know still are, partners in PRISM as well. "Google usually has root access to the phone, there's the issue of integrity," writes Sander Venema, a respected developer and secure-technology trainer, in a blog post explaining why he no longer recommends people use Signal for encrypted chat. "Google is still cooperating with the NSA and other intelligence agencies. PRISM is also still a thing. I'm pretty sure that Google could serve a specially modified update or version of Signal to specific targets for surveillance, and they would be none the wiser that they installed malware on their phones."[148]

Equally weird was the way the app was designed to make it easy for anyone monitoring Internet traffic to flag people using Signal to communicate. All that the FBI or, say, Egyptian or Russian security services had to do was watch for the mobile phones that pinged a particular Amazon server used by Signal, and it was trivial to isolate activists from the general smartphone population. So, although the app encrypted the content of people's messages, it also marked them with a flashing red sign: "Follow Me. I Have Something To Hide." (Indeed, activists protesting at the Democratic National Convention in Philadelphia in 2016 told me that they were bewildered by the fact that police seemed to know and anticipate their every move despite their having used Signal to organize.)[149]

Debate about Signal's technical design was moot anyway. Snowden's leaks showed that the NSA had developed tools that could grab everything people did on their smartphones, which presumably included texts sent and received by Signal. In early March 2017, WikiLeaks published a cache of CIA hacking tools that confirmed the inevitable. The agency worked with the NSA as well as other "cyber arms contractors" to develop hacking tools that targeted smartphones, allowing it to bypass the encryption of Signal and any other encrypted chat apps, including Facebook's WhatsApp.[150] "The

CIA's Mobile Devices Branch (MDB) developed numerous attacks to remotely hack and control popular smart phones. Infected phones can be instructed to send the CIA the user's geolocation, audio and text communications as well as covertly activate the phone's camera and microphone," explained a WikiLeaks press release. "These techniques permit the CIA to bypass the encryption of WhatsApp, Signal, Telegram, Wiebo, Confide and Cloackman by hacking the 'smart' phones that they run on and collecting audio and message traffic before encryption is applied."

Disclosure of these hacking tools showed that, in the end, Signal's encryption didn't really matter, not when the CIA and NSA owned the underlying operating system and could grab whatever they wanted before encryption or obfuscation algorithms were applied. This flaw went beyond Signal and applied to every type of encryption technology on every type of consumer computer system. Sure, encryption apps might work against low-level opponents when used by a trained army intelligence analyst like Pvt. Chelsea Manning, who had used Tor while stationed in Iraq to monitor forums used by Sunni insurgents without giving away his identity.[151] They also might work for someone with a high degree of technical savvy—say, a wily hacker like Julian Assange or a spy like Edward Snowden—who can use Signal and Tor combined with other techniques to effectively cover their tracks from the NSA. But, for the average user, these tools provided a false sense of security and offered the opposite of privacy.

The old cypherpunk dream, the idea that regular people could use grassroots encryption tools to carve out cyber islands free of government control, was proving to be just that, a dream.

Crypto War, Who Is It Good For?

Convoluted as the story may be, US government support for Internet Freedom and its underwriting of crypto culture makes perfect sense. The Internet came out of a 1960s military project to develop an information weapon. It was born out of a need to quickly communicate, process data, and control a chaotic world. Today, the network is more than a weapon; it is also a field of battle, a place where vital military and intelligence operations take place. Geopolitical struggle has moved online, and Internet Freedom is a weapon in that fight.

If you take a big-picture view, Silicon Valley's support for Internet Freedom makes sense as well. Companies like Google and Facebook first supported it as a part of a geopolitical business strategy, a way of subtly pressuring countries that closed their networks and markets to Western technology companies. But after Edward Snowden's revelations exposed the industry's rampant private surveillance practices to the public, Internet Freedom offered another powerful benefit.

For years, public opinion has been stacked firmly against Silicon Valley's underlying business model. In poll after poll, a majority of Americans have voiced their opposition to corporate surveillance and have signaled support for increased regulation of the industry.[152] This has always been a deal breaker for Silicon Valley. For many Internet companies, including Google and Facebook, surveillance is *the* business model. It is the base on which their corporate and economic power rests. Disentangle surveillance and profit, and these companies would collapse. Limit data collection, and the companies would see investors flee and their stock prices plummet.

Silicon Valley fears a political solution to privacy. Internet Freedom and crypto offer an acceptable alternative. Tools like Signal and Tor provide a false solution to the privacy problem, focusing people's attention on government surveillance and distracting them from the private spying carried out by the Internet companies they use every day. All the while, crypto tools give people a sense that they're doing something to protect themselves, a feeling of personal empowerment and control. And all those crypto radicals? Well, they just enhance the illusion, heightening the impression of risk and danger. With Signal or Tor installed, using an iPhone or Android suddenly becomes edgy and radical. So instead of pushing for political and democratic solutions to surveillance, we outsource our privacy politics to crypto apps—software made by the very same powerful entities that these apps are supposed to protect us from.

In that sense, Edward Snowden is like the branded face of an Internet consumerism-as-rebellion lifestyle campaign, like the old Apple ad about shattering Big Brother or the Nike spot set to the Beatles' "Revolution." While Internet billionaires like Larry Page, Sergey Brin, and Mark Zuckerberg slam government surveillance, talk up freedom, and embrace Snowden and crypto privacy culture, their companies still cut deals with the Pentagon, work with the NSA and CIA, and continue to track and profile people for profit. It is the same old split-screen marketing trick: the public branding and the behind-the-scenes reality.

Internet Freedom is a win-win for everyone involved—everyone except regular users, who trust their privacy to double-dealing military contractors, while powerful Surveillance Valley corporations continue to build out the old military cybernetic dream of a world where everyone is watched, predicted, and controlled.

Epilogue

Mauthausen, Austria

t is a crisp and sunny morning in late December 2015 when I take a right turn off a small country highway and drive into Mauthausen, a tiny medieval town in northern Austria about thirty-five miles from the border with the Czech Republic. I pass through a cluster of low-slung apartment buildings and continue on, driving through spotless green pastures and pretty little farmsteads.

I park on a hill overlooking the town. Below is the wide Danube River. Clusters of rural homes poke out from the cusp of two soft green hills, smoke lazily wafting out of their chimneys. A small group of cows is out to pasture, and I can hear the periodic braying of a flock of sheep. Out in the distance, the hills recede in layers of hazy green upon green, like the scales of a giant sleeping dragon. The whole scene is framed by the jagged white peaks of the Austrian Alps.

Mauthausen is an idyllic place. Calm, almost magical. Yet I drove here not to enjoy the view but to get close to something I came to fully understand only while writing this book.

Today, computer technology frequently operates unseen, hidden in gadgets, wires, chips, wireless signals, operating systems, and software. We are surrounded by computers and networks, yet we barely notice them. If we think about them at all, we tend to associate them with progress. We rarely stop to think about the dark side of information technology—all the ways it can be used and abused to control

societies, to inflict pain and suffering. Here, in this quiet country setting, stands a forgotten monument to that power: the Mauthausen
Concentration Camp.

Built on a mound above the town, it is amazingly well preserved:
thick stone walls, squat guard towers, a pair of ominous smoke stacks
connected to the camp's gas chamber and crematorium. A few jagged
metal bars stick out of the wall above the camp's enormous gates, rem-
nants of a giant iron Nazi eagle that was torn down immediately after
liberation. It is quiet now, just a few solemn visitors. But in the 1930s,
Mauthausen had been a vital economic engine of Hitler's genocidal
plan to remake Europe and the Soviet Union into his own backyard
utopia. It started out as a granite quarry but quickly grew into the
largest slave labor complex in Nazi Germany, with fifty subcamps that
spanned most of modern-day Austria. Here, hundreds of thousands of
prisoners—mostly European Jews but also Roma, Spaniards, Russians,
Serbs, Slovenes, Germans, Bulgarians, even Cubans—were worked
to death. They refined oil, built fighter aircraft, assembled cannons,
developed rocket technology, and were leased out to private German
businesses. Volkswagen, Siemens, Daimler-Benz, BMW, Bosch—all
benefited from the camp's slave labor pool. Mauthausen, the adminis-
trative nerve center, was centrally directed from Berlin using the latest
in early computer technology: IBM punch card tabulators.

No IBM machines are displayed at Mauthausen today. And,
sadly, the memorial makes no mention of them. But the camp had
several IBM machines working overtime to handle the big churn of
inmates and to make sure there were always enough bodies to perform the necessary work.[1] These machines didn't operate in isolation
but were part of a larger slave labor control-and-accounting system
that stretched across Nazi-occupied Europe, connecting Berlin to
every major concentration and labor camp by punch card, telegraph,
telephone, and human courier. This wasn't the automated type of
computer network system that the Pentagon would begin to build
in the United States just a decade later, but it was an information
network nonetheless: an electromechanical web that fueled and
sustained Nazi Germany's war machine with blazing efficiency.[2] It

extended beyond the labor camps and reached into cities and towns, crunching mountains of genealogical data to track down people with even the barest whiff of Jewish blood or perceived racial impurity in a mad rush to fulfill Adolf Hitler's drive to purify the German people.[3] The IBM machines themselves did not kill people, but they made the Nazi death machine run faster and more efficiently, scouring the population and tracking down victims in ways that would never have been possible without them.

Of course, IBM tabulators didn't start out in this capacity. They were invented in 1890 by a young engineer named Herman Hollerith to help the US Census Bureau count America's growing immigrant population. Fifty years later, Nazi Germany employed the same technology to systematically carry out the Holocaust.

This is, perhaps, a grim note on which to end a book about the Internet. But for me, the story of Mauthausen and IBM carries an important lesson about computer technology. Today, a lot of people still see the Internet as something uniquely special, something uncorrupted by earthly human flaws and sins. To many, progress and goodness are built in to the Internet's genetic code: if left alone to evolve, the network will automatically lead to a better, more progressive world. This belief is embedded deep in our culture, resistant to facts and evidence. To me, Mauthausen is a powerful reminder of how computer technology can't be separated from the culture in which it is developed and used.

As I stood there surveying the idyllic pastoral scene in that horrible place, I thought about my conversation with Stephen Wolff, the National Science Foundation manager who helped privatize the Internet. "There are certainly values built in," he told me. "Whether they're exclusively Western values or not, I couldn't say. There is no culture that I know of that has refused to use the Internet. So, there must be something universal about it. But is it a supra-national entity? No. The Internet is a piece of the world. It's a mirror of the world, but it's a piece of the world at the same time. It's subject to all the ills that the rest of the world is subject to, and participates in the good things as well as the bad, and the bad things as well as the good."[4]

Wolff captures it beautifully. The Internet, and the networked microprocessor technology on which it runs, does not transcend the human world. For good or ill, it is an expression of this world and was invented and is used in ways that reflect the political, economic, and cultural forces and values that dominate society. Today, we live in a troubled world, a world of political disenfranchisement, rampant poverty and inequality, unchecked corporate power, wars that seem to have no end and no purpose, and a runaway privatized military and intelligence complex—and hanging over it all are the prospects of global warming and environmental collapse. We live in bleak times, and the Internet is a reflection of them: run by spies and powerful corporations just as our society is run by them. But it isn't all hopeless.

It's true that the development of computer technology has always been driven by a need to analyze huge amounts of complex data, monitor people, build predictive models of the future, and fight wars. In that sense, surveillance and control are embedded in the DNA of this technology. But not all control is equal. Not all surveillance is bad. Without them, there can be no democratic oversight of society. Ensuring oil refineries comply with pollution regulations, preventing Wall Street fraud, forcing wealthy citizens to pay their fair share of taxes, and monitoring the quality of food, air, and water—none of these would be possible. In that sense, surveillance and control are not problems in and of themselves. How they are used depends on our politics and political culture.

Whatever shape the Internet and computer networks take in the future, it is safe to say that we will be living with this technology for a long time to come. By pretending that the Internet transcends politics and culture, we leave the most malevolent and powerful forces in charge of its built-in potential for surveillance and control. The more we understand and democratize the Internet, the more we can deploy its power in the service of democratic and humanistic values, making it work for the many, not the few.

Acknowledgments

A lot of people helped make this book possible. First is my brother, Eli, who flew out to Los Angeles to push me to first seriously consider putting this project together back in 2014. My beautiful wife, Evgenia, was an incredible help all throughout the process, reading drafts and using her grasp of storytelling and characters to focus the narrative and keep the pages turning. My friends, family, and colleagues have taken time out of their busy schedules to provide support, both intellectual and spiritual: Alexander Zaitchik, Mark Ames, John Dolan, Tim Shorrock, Joe Costello, Boris Levine, and David Golumbia have all helped make me sound smarter and more eloquent than I really am. *Pando Daily*'s Sarah Lacy and Paul Carr were key to the whole project. The reporting that first put me on the scent of the Internet's dark history took place while I was a staffer at *Pando* covering Silicon Valley's for-profit surveillance industry. I miss my time there. I do not think it is possible for a reporter to have better, more supportive editors. Sarah in particular knows all too well the importance of shining a light on Silicon Valley and the lengths to which the tech industry will go to protect its power.

A big thanks to Maria Goldverg (now at Knopf/Vintage) and Benjamin Adams for bringing *Surveillance Valley* to PublicAffairs, as well as Matt Wise (now at Adaptive Studios) and Peter McGuigan at Foundry Media for giving wise counsel every step of the way.

Also key were the good people of the New York Public Library, who gave me a quiet spot in the Frederick Lewis Allen Room in the middle of Manhattan to finish my research and writing.

Last but not least, I want to make a big bow to all the people who supported this book on Kickstarter when it was still just an idea back in the winter of 2014. *Surveillance Valley* would not have happened without their support and trust. Special thanks goes out to Kickstarter backers Carlo Trevisan, Ivor Crotty, Benjamin O'Connor, Michael Oneill of Baycloud Systems, and John Heisel.

Notes

Prologue

1. Ali Winston, "Oakland Surveillance Center Progresses Amid Debate on Privacy, Data Collection," Center for Investigative Reporting, July 18, 2013.

2. Darwin Bond Graham and Ali Winston, "The Real Purpose of Oakland's Surveillance Center," *East Bay Express,* December 18, 2013.

3. Buried among thousands of pages of official Oakland correspondence obtained by an activist through a public records request was a short email thread from October 2013 between Scott Ciabattari, a Google strategic partnership manager, and Renee Domingo, an Oakland official spearheading the DAC project. The emails were short on details but referenced a meeting that had taken place between Ciabattari and Domingo and discussed scheduling a follow-up meeting to find out what kind of Google products could be beneficial to the DAC as well as to Oakland's Emergency Operations Center, an emergency police hub that would be tied to the DAC. "I spoke with our Intern Director of Information Technology, Ahsan Baig, last night and he will provide some potential dates for us to meet with you week after next, to begin the dialogue," Domingo wrote to Ciabattari, cc'ing the Oakland mayor Jean Quan. "He is very interested in seeing some of the demos and products Google has available for our EOC/DAC as well as how the City might partner with Google." She signed off: "I look forward on behalf of the City of Oakland, of working with you and Google." Ciabattari replied, "We are excited to help and I look forward to speaking with you again. . . . Please feel free to contact me anytime." Renee Domingo, email message sent to Scott Ciabattari, "Re: Thank you," October 3, 2013, https://surveillancevalley.com/content/citations/email-thread-between-google-s-scott-ciabattari-and-oakland-officials-about-the-dac-october-2013.jpg.

Chapter 1

1. *Foreign Relations of the United States, 1961–1963, Volume I, Vietnam, 1961*, Document 96, "From June 8 through 25, 1961, a Research and Development Team Headed by William H. Godel . . . " (Washington, DC: US Department of State, Office of the Historian, 1988).

2. *Vegetational Spray Tests in South Vietnam* (US Army Chemical Corps Biological Laboratories, April 1962), http://www.dtic.mil/dtic/tr/fulltext/u2/476961.pdf.

3. Ronald H. Spector, *Advice and Support: The Early Years of the United States Army in Vietnam, 1941–1960* (Washington, DC: Center for Military History, United States Army, 1985).

4. "Vietnam 'Program of Action' by Kennedy Task Force," *New York Times*, July 1, 1971; Mai Elliot, *RAND in Southeast Asia: A History of the Vietnam War Era* (Santa Monica, CA: RAND Corporation, 2010), 33.

5. Judith Perera and Andy Thomas, "This Horrible Natural Experiment," *New Scientist*, April 18, 1985.

6. H. Lindsey Arison III, "Executive Summary: The Herbicidal Warfare Program in Vietnam, 1961–1971," published July 12, 1995, last modified May 1, 1999, http://web.archive.org/web/20061025232940/http://members.cox.net/linarison/orange.html.

7. Donald J. Mrozek, *Air Power and the Ground War in Vietnam* (Maxwell Air Force Base, AL: Air University Press, 1989).

8. "Its goals were to strip the border areas along Cambodia, Laos, and North Vietnam to 'remove protective cover' from Vietcong reinforcements, to defoliate Zone D in the Mekong Delta where the Vietcong had numerous bases, to destroy the manioc groves that the Vietcong used for food, and to destroy the mangrove swamps where the Vietcong hid. Taken together, the two phases of the program would have defoliated 31,250 square miles of jungle—about half the land area of South Vietnam—as well as 1,125 square miles of mangrove swamps and 312 square miles of manioc groves." Mrozek, *Air Power and the Ground War*, 134.

9. Even today, the dioxins that seeped into the soil almost a half century ago continue to cause horrific birth defects. Thousands of Vietnamese infants are born every year with grotesque deformities. Orphanages are full of children suffering from exotic genetic mutations that cause painful conditions such as hydrocephalus, in which the brain fills with fluid and deforms and enlarges a child's head and causes severe brain damage. Ash Anand, "Vietnam's Horrific Legacy: The Children of Agent Orange," News.com.au, May 25, 2015, http://www.news.com.au/world/asia/vietnams-horrific-legacy-the-children-of-agent-orange/news-story/c008ff36ee3e840b005405a55e21a3e1.

10. Yanek Mieczkowski, *Eisenhower's Sputnik Moment: The Race for Space and World Prestige* (Ithaca: NY: Cornell University Press, 2013).

11. Werner von Braun, the former Nazi rocket scientist who got a new lease on life working for the US Army, went on television to warn America that *Sputnik* was a clear sign of impending total domination by the Soviet Union—not only of

earth, but of heaven itself. "I'm convinced that the Russian concept is very clear. They consider the control of space around the Earth very much like, shall we say, the great maritime powers considered the control of the seas in the 16th through the 18th centuries," he said, confident that the *Sputnik* would provide a nice bump to his missile research efforts. *Sputnik Declassified: Top-Secret Documents Rewrite the History of the Famous Satellite and the Early Space Race* (Arlington, VA: PBS, 2007).

12. Ed Creagh, "Nixon Seemed More Concerned over Sputnik Than President," Rome News-Tribune (Associated Press), October 17, 1957, https://surveillance valley.com/content/citations/ed-creagh-nixon-seemed-more-concerned-over -sputnik-than-president-associated-press-17-october-1957.pdf.

13. "The Cleanup Man," *Time*, October 5, 1953.

14. Much of the fine-grained detail about the history of ARPA comes from a previously classified 1975 report that was commissioned by the agency and carried out by Richard J. Barber Associates, *The Advanced Research Projects Agency 1958–1974* (Washington, DC: National Technical Information Service, 1975).

15. Richard J. Barber Associates, *Advanced Research Projects Agency*, II-7.

16. McElroy developed the idea for ARPA in consultation with James R. Killian Jr., the influential president of Massachusetts Institute of Technology and Eisenhower's presidential assistant for science.

17. Katie Hafner and Matthew Lyon, *Where Wizards Stay Up Late: The Origins of the Internet* (New York: Simon & Schuster, 1996).

18. Ibid. The US Chamber of Commerce had proposed something similar to ARPA: "the U.S. Chamber of Commerce had floated the notion of creating a single research-and-development agency for the federal government during congressional hearings months before *Sputnik*. Such talk was in the air." Hafner and Lyon, *Where Wizards Stay Up Late*, 18.

19. President Dwight Eisenhower, State of the Union Address, 1958.

20. Richard J. Barber Associates, *Advanced Research Projects Agency*, I-7.

21. Initially, Roy Johnson wanted to hire Dr. von Braun to be ARPA's first chief scientist. But that would have required relocating his entire team of ex-Nazi rocket scientists to the inner sanctum of the Pentagon. The idea was killed. Instead, Johnson chose Herb York, a respected nuclear scientist who set up an ambitious missiles and nuclear research program for the agency. Hafner and Lyon, *Where Wizards Stay Up Late*, 21.

22. Richard J. Barber Associates, *Advanced Research Projects Agency*, I-8, III-8.

23. Ibid.

24. Parts of this chapter that deal with William Godel's vision of counterinsurgency are largely informed by Annie Jacobsen's *The Pentagon's Brain: An Uncensored History of DARPA, America's Top Secret Military Research Agency* (New York: Back Bay Books, 2016). Other parts come from archival research, memoirs, and declassified ARPA and CIA records. Sharon Weinberger's *The Imagineers of War: The Untold Story of DARPA, the Pentagon Agency That Changed the World* (New York: Alfred A. Knopf, 2017) was also very helpful in filling in some of the finer details

about Godel's life. Both *The Pentagon's Brain* and *The Imagineers of War* are highly recommended as deep histories of ARPA.

25. In State Department documents, William Godel is described as "an expert from the Department of Defense on the techniques and practices of psychological warfare." *Foreign Relations of the United States, 1961–1963, Volume I, Vietnam, 1961, Document 96* (Washington, DC: US Department of State, Office of the Historian, 1988).

26. William Godel's negotiations with North Korea was a delicate issue. Some of the American prisoners had confessed on television to taking part in illegal chemical weapons attacks against North Korea. Godel's job was to cover up the allegations by blaming the whole thing on advanced communist brainwashing techniques, which could reprogram people's minds and make people believe or do anything their captors wanted. Jacobsen, *Pentagon's Brain*, chap. 6, "At the Pentagon, the man tasked with handling the situation was William Godel . . ."

27. The former Nazi asset Ernst Brückner (codename CARPETMAKER) occupied a high office in Germany's Ministry of the Interior. Declassified CIA documents show Godel taking part in an effort to weed out Soviet agents embedded among the mass of German prisoners of war returning from the Soviet Union as well as counseling his CIA asset on how to evade Soviet electronic surveillance inside West Germany. Central Intelligence Agency, FIOA# 51966ec2993294098d509809, Memorandum for the Record: Subject: Meeting with CARPETMAKER, June 27, 1956, https://surveillancevalley.com/content/citations/brueckner-ernst-vol.2-0010-document-number-foia-esdn-crest-51966ec2993294098d50980a.pdf

28. Secretary of Defense Roger M. Kyes, "Memorandum for the Secretaries of the Military Departments, Joint Chiefs of Staff, Assistant Secretaries of Defense, Chairmen of Boards, Committees and Councils, OSD, Assistants to the Secretary of Defense, and Directors of Offices, OSD: Subject: Reorganization—Office of Special Operations, Office of the Secretary of Defense," July 15, 1953, https://surveillancevalley.com/content/citations/subject-reorganization-office-of-special-operations-office-of-the-secretary-of-defense-the-secretary-of-defense-15-july-1953.pdf.

29. Ronald H. Spector, *Advice and Support: The Early Years of the United States Army in Vietnam, 1941–1960* (New York: Free Press, 1985).

30. Jacobsen, *Pentagon's Brain*, chap. 6.

31. Richard J. Barber Associates, *Advanced Research Projects Agency*, 286.

32. Center for the Study of Intelligence, *CIA and the Wars in Southeast Asia 1947–75*, a *Studies in Intelligence* anthology (Washington, DC: Central Intelligence Agency, August 2016), http://web.archive.org/web/20170523094620/https://www.cia.gov/library/center-for-the-study-of-intelligence/csi-publications/books-and-monographs/Anthology-CIA-and-the-Wars-in-Southeast-Asia/pdfs-1/vietnam-anthology-print-version.pdf.

33. Jacobsen, *Pentagon's Brain*, chap. 6.

34. James Bamford, *Body of Secrets: Anatomy of the Ultra-Secret National Security Agency* (New York: Doubleday, 2001), 304.

35. Jacobsen, *Pentagon's Brain,* chap. 6.

36. Richard J. Barber Associates, *Advanced Research Projects Agency,* V-38.

37. Memo, William Godel, Director Policy and Planning Division, ARPA, for Assistant Secretary of Defense, September 15, 1960, quoted in Ronald H. Spector, *Advice and Support,* 351–352.

38. President John F. Kennedy, Special Message to the Congress on the Defense Budget, March 28, 1961.

39. William Godel had access to the inner circle of the Kennedy administration. "Godel's success is not surprising as his assessment of the problem in Southeast Asia closely corresponded to the views of the Kennedy leadership." Richard J. Barber Associates, *Advanced Research Projects Agency,* V-39–V-40.

40. "Vietnam 'Program of Action' by Kennedy Task Force," *New York Times,* July 1, 1971.

41. Eric Pace, "Edward Lansdale Dies at 79; Advisor on Guerrilla Warfare," *New York Times,* February 24, 1987.

42. Weinberger, *Imagineers of War,* chap. 5.

43. Herman S. Wolk, *USAF Plans and Policies: R&D for Southeast Asia, 1965–1967* (Washington, DC: Office of Air Force History, 1969).

44. Project Agile's budget—which started out at $11.3 million in 1962—grew as the war progressed. By 1964, it was $26 million, or one-tenth of ARPA's total budget, according to the Richard J. Barber Associates report.

45. ARPA's Combat Development and Test Center was more than just a technology research and development center. It took part in active counterinsurgency missions, including going out with the 4400th "Jungle Jim" Squadron, a covert special forces counterinsurgency division. *Report on General Taylor's Mission to South Vietnam* (Washington, DC: National Security Council, November 3, 1961), 162.

46. Institute for Defense Analysis, *DARPA Technical Accomplishments: An Historical Review of Selected DARPA Projects,* Vol. I (Washington, DC: Defense Advanced Research Projects Agency, 1990).

47. Richard J. Barber Associates, *Advanced Research Projects Agency,* II-7.

48. Matt Novak, "How the Vietnam War Brought High-Tech Border Surveillance to America," Gizmodo Paleofuture, September 24, 2015, http://paleofuture.gizmodo. com/how-the-vietnam-war-brought-high-tech-border-surveillan-1694647526.

49. Paul N. Edwards, *The Closed World: Computers and the Politics of Discourse in Cold War America* (Cambridge, MA: MIT Press, 1996).

50. *Bugging the Battlefield* (Washington, DC: Department of Defense, 1969), motion picture, https://archive.org/details/gov.archives.arc.4524913.

51. John T. Halliday, *Flying through Midnight: A Pilot's Dramatic Story of His Secret Missions over Laos during the Vietnam War* (New York: Charles Scribner's Sons, 2005).

52. Ibid., 17–18.

53. Edwards, *Closed World,* 4.

54. "These early uses of ground sensors were effective and within a year John Mitchell's Justice Department was seeding a 65-mile experimental stretch of the border with Vietnam-tested acoustic sensors, buried strain-sensitive cables and

infrared detection devices. In 1972, when the test section was fully operational, 128,889 illegal crossers were apprehended and authorities claimed more than 30,000 were netted as a result of the electronic fence. In the fall of 1973 the U.S. Border Patrol and Immigration and Naturalization Service jointly announced plans to expand the fence along the whole 2,000-mile border with the exception of the most inaccessible areas and immediately pledged $1.5 million to start the job. Today electronic sensors are installed at the most active points along the border, but there is some question at the moment whether the whole border will be wired. This situation results largely from the success of the system (although costs have been a factor too). General Leonard F. Chapman Jr., head of the Immigration and Naturalization Service, explained in a 1975 interview in Nation's Business that the sensors work fine but that more than half the alarms go unanswered because the Border Patrol is spread too thin" (Paul Dickerson, *The Electronic Battlefield* [Bloomington: Indiana University Press, 1976]). An excerpt of the book was read into the *Congressional Record.* (*"Surveillance Technology," Joint Hearings before the Subcommittee on Constitutional Rights of the Comm. on the Judiciary and the Special Subcommittee on Science, Technology, and Commerce of the Comm. on Commerce, United States Senate,* 94th Cong., 1st sess. [June 23, September 9 and 10, 1975]).

55. *Foreign Relations of the United States, 1961–1963, Volume I, Vietnam, 1961,* edited by Daniel J. Lawler and Erin R. Mahan (Washington, DC: Government Printing Office, 2010), Document 96, https://history.state.gov/historicaldocuments/frus1961-63v01/d96.

56. Richard J. Barber Associates, *Advanced Research Projects Agency.*

57. *Proceedings of the Symposium "The U.S. Army's Limited-War Mission and Social Science Research," March 26–28, 1962,* edited by William A. Lybrand (Washington, DC: Special Operations Research Office, 1962).

58. Jeffrey Race, *War Comes to Long An: Revolutionary Conflict in a Vietnamese Province* (Berkeley: University of California Press, 2010).

59. The Richard J. Barber Associates report has a great discussion of Godel's pioneering use of data and social science for counterinsurgency: "Despite its hardware and 'hard science' image, ARPA's AGILE leadership—very much reflecting Godel's sensitivity to the 'people' aspects of insurgent warfare—began to undertake studies in Thailand intended to focus on the village and rural atmosphere within which insurgent situations seemed to develop. . . . The MRDC effort, a relatively crude first cut exercise, involved sending a Thai-U.S. team composed of an economist, engineer, forester, anthropologist, and operations analyst to 40 villages in Northeast Thailand. Their report covered physical characteristics, locational and communications data, population and census information, officials and village leadership, villager skills and specialists, migration patterns, and villager responses to perceived 'threats.'" Richard J. Barber Associates, *Advanced Research Projects Agency,* VI-43–VI-44.

60. The RAND Corporation was originally created by the air force in 1946 as Project RAND "to perform a program of study and research on the broad subject of intercontinental warfare, other than surface, with the object of recommending

to the Air Force preferred techniques and instrumentalities for this purpose." US Army Limited-War Mission and Social Science Research symposium, Special Operations Research Office, American University, Washington, DC, June 1962.

61. In *The Imagineers of War,* Sharon Weinberger excavated the previously un-recognized fact that William Godel's ARPA counterinsurgency work in Vietnam played a role in the Strategic Hamlet Initiative. "The Defense Department's in-ternal study of the war, known as the Pentagon Papers, would later claim Rob-ert Thompson, head of the British Advisory Mission, was the one who proposed and persuaded Diem in December 1961 to pursue strategic hamlets," writes Wein-berger. "But by the time Thompson showed up, Godel had already spent months laying the groundwork. Van, the Vietnamese government official who was Godel's traveling companion on his trips in the summer of 1961, made clear who was re-sponsible. 'Only one man helped me and my team to instill the idea [of strategic hamlets] to our government,' Van told American officials investigating Godel in 1964. 'Mr. Godel, and his team'" (chap. 5).

62. Anders Sweetland, *Rallying Potential among the North Vietnamese Armed Forces* (Santa Monica, CA: RAND Corporation, December 1970).

63. Although many of these ARPA studies had the appearance of scientific ob-jectivity, those that produced results that fit preconceived notions or that provided rationales for existing military doctrine got wider play and attention; those that didn't were buried or ignored.

64. *Remote Area Conflict Research and Engineering Semi-annual Report* (Wash-ington, DC: Advanced Research Projects Agency, Project AGILE, July 1–Decem-ber 31, 1963).

65. H. P. Phillips and D. A. Wilson, *Certain Effects of Culture and Social Orga-nization on Internal Security in Thailand* (Santa Monica, CA: RAND Corporation, June 1964).

66. Carolyn Fluehr-Lobban, *Ethics and the Profession of Anthropology: Dialogue for Ethically Conscious Practice* (Lanham, MD: AltaMira Press, 2002), 60–61.

67. Banning Garrett, "The Dominoization of Thailand," *Ramparts,* November 1970, http://www.unz.org/Pub/Ramparts-1970nov-00007.

68. Ibid.

69. Jennifer S. Light, *From Warfare to Welfare: Defense Intellectuals and Urban Problems in Cold War America* (Baltimore, MD: Johns Hopkins University Press, 2005).

70. Take Charles Murray, a young researcher who worked on ARPA's counter-insurgency programs for the American Institutes for Research in Thailand (Eric Wakin, *Anthropology Goes to War: Professional Ethics and Counterinsurgency in Thailand* [Madison, WI: Center for Southeast Asian Studies, 1998]). His expe-rience among the rebellions of Thai peasants marked his thinking for life. He became convinced that the carrot was much less effective than the stick: social programs—things like building roads and health clinics and providing jobs—de-signed to "buy" hearts and minds simply didn't work. But harsh, punitive measures did (Jason DeParle, "Daring Research or 'Social Science Pornography'?: Charles

Murray," *New York Times,* October 9, 1994). He would apply that logic in the United States to the difficult socioeconomic problems faced by black ghettoized communities. Reducing poverty and inner-city crime—these were not problems that could be solved through welfare and social programs. In fact, anything the government did to support and nudge people in the right direction didn't work; they had the opposite effect: they only encouraged the very behavior they were aimed at curbing. So, Murray advised the opposite: harsher prison terms and punitive zero-tolerance measures to deter crime as well as abolishing all government social programs, including food stamps, welfare, and the Social Security pension system ("Prison Called Best Treatment for Juvenile Offenders," Associated Press, November 1, 1979, https://surveillancevalley.com/content/citations /prison-best-treatment-for-juvenile-offenders-associated-press-1-november-1979. png; Charles A. Murray and Louis A. Cox Jr., *Juvenile Corrections and the Chronic Delinquent* [Washington, DC: American Institutes for Research, March 1979]). Today, Murray is a libertarian political scientist and one of the most influential ideological architects of the post-Reagan era. He is best known for *The Bell Curve,* a controversial best seller that promoted racial eugenics theories, claiming among other things that whites and Asians are genetically superior in intelligence to blacks and Latinos. But his most lasting achievement was giving intellectual backing to President Bill Clinton's Personal Responsibility and Work Opportunity Act. Signed into law in 1996, the bill killed traditional federal welfare in America in order to incentivize people to get a job. The law had a specific emphasis on cutting welfare for single mothers as a way to reduce poverty, the idea being that welfare incentivized them to have children, thereby perpetuating poverty. It was a cruel move and, like much of the research tested in Vietnam, was ineffective at achieving its stated goal. Instead of decreasing joblessness and alleviating poverty, these reforms plunged minority communities into even more suffering and impoverishment (Timothy Casey and Laurie Maldonado, *Worst Off—Single Parent Families in the United States* [New York: Legal Momentum, December 2012]).

71. Michael McClintock, *Instruments of Statecraft: U.S. Guerrilla Warfare, Counterinsurgency, and Counter-Terrorism, 1940–1990* (New York: Pantheon Books, 1992), chap. 8.

72. Douglas Valentine, "Dirty Wars and Self-indulgence," *Dissident Voice,* June 7, 2013, http://web.archive.org/web/20170523152813/http://dissidentvoice. org/2013/06/dirty-wars-as-self-indulgence/.

73. Douglas Valentine, *The Phoenix Program* (New York: William Morrow, 1990).

74. Alexander Cockburn and Jeffrey St. Clair, *Whiteout: The CIA, Drugs, and the Press* (New York: Verso Books, 1997). "He may have been involved to some extent with an organization which I think was called Air America. I'm not sure, but it was a CIA operation in Vietnam," said former ARPA director Robert Sproull in a 2006 interview (http://web.archive.org/web/20170523134945/http://www.dod .mil/pubs/foi/Reading_Room/DARPA/15-F-0751_DARPA_Director_Robert _Sproull.pdf).

75. T. Wells, *Wild Man: The Life and Times of Daniel Ellsberg* (New York: Palgrave Macmillan, 2001).

76. Ido Oren, *Our Enemies and US: America's Rivalries and the Making of Political Science* (Ithaca, NY: Cornell University Press, 2002).

77. Barbara Myers, "The Other Conspirator: The Secret Origins of the CIA's Torture Program and the Forgotten Man Who Tried to Expose It," TomDispatch, May 31, 2015, http://www.tomdispatch.com/blog/176004/tomgram %253A_barbara_myers,_the_unknown_whistleblower/.

78. Anthony Russo, "Inside the RAND Corporation and Out: My Story" (photocopy), *Ramparts*, April 1972, http://jfk.hood.edu/Collection/White%20 Materials/White%20Assassination%20Clippings%20Folders/Miscellaneous%20 Folders/Miscellaneous%20Study%20Groups/Misc-SG-045.pdf.

79. Jerry Kline, "Never Talked to Wylie of Money, Godel Says" (photocopy), *Washington Star*, May 1, 1965, https://surveillancevalley.com/content/citations /jerry-klein-never-talked-to-wylie-of-money-godel-says-the-washington-star-1 -may-1965.pdf; Peter S. Diggins, "Godel Tells of Taking $18,000 to Asia and Starting Anti-Guerrilla Center" (photocopy), *Washington Post*, May 15, 1965, https://surveillancevalley.com/content/citations/peter-s.diggins-godel-tells-of -taking-18-000-to-asia-and-starting-anti-guerrilla-center-the-washington-post -15-may-1965.pdf.

80. Weinberger, *Imagineers of War*, chap. 8, "Shortly before 10: 00 p.m., the foreman sent a message to the judge . . . "

Chapter 2

1. President John F. Kennedy, Special Message to the Congress on the Defense Budget, March 28, 1961.

2. A huge problem with radio communication was the deafening engine noise of the aircraft, which made effective communication next to impossible. Lick worked on techniques to counter the noise. Robert M. Fano, *Joseph Carl Robnett Licklider: 1915–1990* (Washington, DC: National Academies Press, 1998).

3. M. Mitchell Waldrop, *The Dream Machine: J.C.R. Licklider and the Revolution That Made Computing Personal* (New York: Viking, 2001).

4. Richard Rhodes, *Arsenals of Folly: The Making of the Nuclear Arms Race* (New York: Alfred A. Knopf, 2007).

5. An amazing Soviet documentary of the test was put together for the personal viewing of Joseph Stalin. It was declassified in the mid-1990s. "Опыт на полигоне № 2. Испытание РДС-1, 1949" ("Experiment on test site No. 2. Testing of RDS-1") (documentary). Most of the information on the details of the nuclear test comes from a three-volume collection of declassified Soviet documents, *Atomic Project of the USSR: Documents and Materials* (Moscow: Fizmatlit, 1998–2009), http://elib .biblioatom.ru/sections/0201/.

6. "Lincoln Laboratory Origins," Lincoln Laboratory, Massachusetts Institute of Technology, https://www.ll.mit.edu/about/History/origins.html.

7. Scott McCartney, *ENIAC: The Triumph and Tragedies of the World's First Computer* (New York: Walker, 1999), 53.

8. Ibid., 54.

9. Jennifer S. Light, "When Computers Were Women," *Technology and Culture* 40, no. 3 (July 1999).

10. "Robot Calculator Knocks Out Figures Like Chain Lightning," *Chicago Tribune*, February 15, 1946.

11. Martin H. Weik, "The ENIAC Story," *Ordnance: The Journal of the Army Ordnance Association*, January–February 1961; McCartney, *ENIAC*, 108.

12. Chief of Research and Development, Department of the Army, *Human Factors Research and Development* (paper presented at the Sixteenth Annual Army Human Factors Research and Development Conference, US Army Defense Center and Fort Bliss, TX, October 1970), http://www.dtic.mil/dtic/tr/fulltext /u2/880537.pdf.

13. Hafner and Lyon, *Where Wizards Stay Up Late*, 30–32; Benj Edwards, "The Never-Before-Told Story of the World's First Computer Art (It's a Sexy Dame)," *The Atlantic*, January 24, 2013.

14. *In Your Defense* (motion picture) (SAGE Programming Agency, US Air Force, 1950).

15. Family interviews and other personal details about Norbert Wiener are informed by the great biography by Flo Conway and Jim Siegelman, *Dark Hero of the Information Age: In Search of Norbert Wiener, the Father of Cybernetics* (New York: Basic Books, 2006).

16. Conway and Siegelman, *Dark Hero of the Information Age,* chap. 1.

17. Norbert Wiener, *The Human Use of Human Beings: Cybernetics and Society* (New York: Doubleday, 1950).

18. Paul N. Edwards, *The Closed World: Computers and the Politics of Discourse in Cold War America* (Cambridge, MA: MIT Press, 1996).

19. Philip Mirowski, *Machine Dreams: Economics Becomes a Cyborg Science* (Cambridge: Cambridge University Press, 2001).

20. For example, cybernetics theory formed the base of Noam Chomsky's work. He rose to fame by redefining the study of linguistics, and helped spark the "cognitive revolution" by positing that human language was produced by what was essentially a specialized language computer module in the human brain—like a sound card plugged into a mother board. He theorized that language could be boiled down to logical expressions, which was the foundation of computer language. His linguistic work at MIT in the 1950s was funded by the army, navy, and air force in large part because the military wanted to develop computer technology that could process human language on the fly in order to analyze intelligence intercepts, to process press reports, and to understand human commands. Chris Knight's *Decoding Chomsky: Science and Revolutionary Politics* (New Haven, CT: Yale University Press, 2016) and David Golumbia's *The Cultural Logic of Computation* (Cambridge, MA: Harvard University Press, 2009) explore this topic in great detail.

21. Edwards, *The Closed World*, 114. Historian Paul Edwards describes this as a *closed world*—"a dome of global technological oversight . . . within which every event was interpreted as part of a titanic struggle between the superpowers" (1). It was a world that broadened the concept of air defense to include all elements of life, a vast computerized system of surveillance and control built by the private sector and deployed and backed up by military power to protect the world from communism.

22. Golumbia, *Cultural Logic of Computation*, 60.

23. "The transfer to this thinking machine. . . . It's a thing that may be very useful to a sane world, but I can't say we're living in one. It is a very dangerous thing socially. If we are going to sell man down the river and replace him, he's going to be a very angry man, and an angry man is a dangerous man," he told the Associated Press in 1949. Hal Boyle, "Writer Claims Machine Gradually Taking Over Duties of Man Until Soon None Will Be Left," *San Bernardino Daily Sun*, April 20, 1949.

24. Wiener, *Human Use of Human Beings*, 189.

25. Interestingly, in the 1950s, the official Soviet position on cybernetics was critical and mirrored Wiener's own denunciations of corporate America's use of cybernetic systems to grab more political and economic power. Here's the entry on cybernetics in the 1954 *Concise Dictionary of Philosophy*, published in the Soviet Union: "Cybernetics: a reactionary pseudoscience that appeared in the U.S.A. after World War II and also spread through other capitalist countries. Cybernetics clearly reflects one of the basic features of the bourgeois worldview—its inhumanity, striving to transform workers into an extension of the machine, into a tool of production, and an instrument of war. At the same time, for cybernetics an imperialistic utopia is characteristic—replacing living, thinking man, fighting for his interests, by a machine, both in industry and in war. The instigators of a new world war use cybernetics in their dirty, practical affairs." Quoted in Benjamin Peters, *How Not to Network a Nation: The Uneasy History of the Soviet Internet* (Cambridge, MA: MIT Press, 2016).

26. Conway and Siegelman, *Dark Hero of the Information Age*, "When his death notice appeared in the Boston Globe, agents in the FBI's Boston Field Office . . ."

27. J. C. R. Licklider, "Man-Computer Symbiosis," *IRE Transactions on Human Factors in Electronics*, March 1960.

28. Hafner and Lyon, *Where Wizards Stay Up Late*, 36.

29. Waldrop, *Dream Machine*, 204.

30. Lick seemed to be channeling a 1960s version of One Laptop per Child, an organization launched in 2005 by Nicholas Negroponte, another member of ARPA's Cambridge Project, to give every poor child in the world a laptop in the belief that lack of access to computers was the impediment to global literacy and education. J. C. R. Licklider, "Motivation and Education through Interaction with Computer-Mediated 'Dynamations,'" MIT Institute Archives and Special Collections, MIT Cambridge Project records, 1970s (exact date uncertain).

31. Richard J. Barber Associates, *Advanced Research Projects Agency*.

32. Waldrop, *Dream Machine*, 203.

33. J. C. R. Licklider, "Man-Computer Symbiosis."

34. Richard J. Barber Associates, *Advanced Research Projects Agency*.

35. *An Interview with J. C. R. Licklider Conducted by William Aspray and Arthur Norberg* (Cambridge, MA: Charles Babbage Institute, October 28, 1988), https://conservancy.umn.edu/bitstream/handle/11299/107436/oh150jcl.pdf.

36. "The objective of this program is to identify and solve problems that arise when a number of digital computers, some of them remote from others, are operated together in a network, and when the information-processing capabilities of a network of computers are distributed among several or many users operating at consoles, some of which are remote from the computers." "ARPA Order No. 471," Advanced Research Projects Agency, April 15, 1963.

37. Thomas A. Sturm, "The Air Force and the World Wide Military Command and Control System 1961–1965" (secret, declassified), USAF Historical Division Liaison Office, August 1966.

38. Janet Abbate, *Inventing the Internet* (Cambridge, MA: MIT Press, 1999), 36.

39. *Interview with J. C. R. Licklider*, 28.

40. A record of the symposium's proceedings shows that Lick's command and control work was considered to be vital to the issue. There was also some discussion about having his division work with Project Agile. "Programs and projects are now being considered by a representative group under the Chairmanship of Dr. Licklider, who will head ARPA programs in Behavioral Sciences and Command and Control. Command and control research involves behavioral scientists and in part meets the recommendations for man-machine systems research outlined in the Smithsonian Report. ARPA may also pursue social science research in Project Agile—its program of research and development in remote area conflict." US Army Limited-War Mission and Social Science Research symposium, Special Operations Research Office, American University, Washington, DC, June 1962.

41. Sharon Weinberger, in *The Imagineers of War*, points out that Project Agile and Command and Control Research were intertwined from the very beginning: "And just a month before Godel traveled to Vietnam, ARPA was handed a new assignment in command and control, which would in less than a decade grow into the ARPANET, the predecessor to the modern Internet. The following year, Godel personally signed off on the first computer-networking study, giving it money from his Vietnam budget." She adds, "DARPA's Vietnam War work and the ARPANET were not two distinct threads but rather pieces of a larger tapestry that held the agency together" (prologue).

42. Richard J. Barber Associates, *Advanced Research Projects Agency*, 303.

43. One example: two contracts issued by Licklider for time-sharing and remote information processing with UCLA and UC Berkeley drew almost $900,000 from Project Agile. "These new contracts put Dr. Licklider $666,000 over his FY 63 program in information processing. This amount plus an additional amount to support another $200,000 prospective new requirement in the month of May has been transferred into his program from AGILE." "ARPA Order No. 471," Advanced Research Projects Agency, April 15, 1963.

44. Robert M. White, "Anthropometric Survey of the Royal Thai Armed Forces," US Army Natick Laboratories, sponsored by Advanced Research Projects Agency, June 1964.

45. "Like its Vietnamese counterpart, this new CDTC would also research and develop techniques and gadgets but with a focus on longer-term counterinsurgency goals, including Licklider's plans for computer-assisted teaching, gaming, and simulation studies." Jacobsen, *Pentagon's Brain*, chap. 9.

46. Geoffrey Austrian, *Herman Hollerith: Forgotten Giant of Information Processing* (New York: Columbia University Press, 1982).

47. Dennis Hodgson, "Ideological Currents and the Interpretation of Demographic Trends: The Case of Francis Amasa Walker," *Journal of the History of the Behavioral Sciences* 28, no. 1 (January 1992): 28–44.

48. North's essay is reprinted by the American Statistical Association: *The History of Statistics: Their Development and Progress in Many Countries* (Boston, MA: American Statistical Association, 1918).

49. Kevin Maney, *The Maverick and His Machine: Thomas Watson, Sr. and the Making of IBM* (New York: Wiley, 2003).

50. A pioneering study explains the role that statistics and early computer technology played in the Holocaust: "It was the use of raw numbers, punch cards, statistical expertise, and identification cards that made it all possible. Every military and labor column existed first as a column of numbers. Every act of extermination was preceded by an act of registration; selection on paper ended with selection on the ramps." Götz Aly and Karl Heinz Roth, *The Nazi Census: Identification and Control in the Third Reich* (Philadelphia: Temple University Press, 2004).

51. Edwin Black, *IBM and the Holocaust: The Strategic Alliance between Nazi Germany and America's Most Powerful Corporation* (New York: Crown, 2001).

52. Robert Sproull, former director of ARPA, stated in an interview that, although ARPA's command and control project did not originate in Project Agile, it overlapped with ARPA's counterinsurgency mission and "may have had some origins." Dr. Robert Sproull, interview commissioned by DARPA, December 7, 2006, http://www.esd.whs.mil/Portals/54/Documents/FOID/Reading%20Room/DARPA/15-F-0751_DARPA_Director_Robert_Sproull.pdf.

53. J. C. R. Licklider, "Memorandum for Members and Affiliates of the Intergalactic Computer Network," Advanced Research Projects Agency, April 25, 1963, Edward A. Feigenbaum Papers collection, Stanford University, https://exhibits.stanford.edu/feigenbaum/catalog/wj409km7108.

54. Abbate, *Inventing the Internet*, 76.

55. Licklider, "Memorandum for Members and Affiliates of the Intergalactic Computer Network."

56. Waldrop, *Dream Machine*, 254, 305.

57. *An Interview with Lawrence G. Roberts, Conducted by Arthur L. Norberg* (San Mateo, CA: Charles Babbage Institute, April 1989), https://conservancy.umn.edu/bitstream/handle/11299/107608/oh159lgr.pdf.

58. Hafner and Lyon, *Where Wizards Stay Up Late*, 48.

59. Abbate, *Inventing the Internet*, 48.

60. *An Interview with Keith Uncapher, Conducted by Arthur L. Norberg* (Minneapolis, MN: Charles Babbage Institute, July 1989), https://conservancy.umn.edu /bitstream/handle/11299/107692/oh174ku.pdf.

61. The smart money was on Raytheon, a major military contractor with deep ties to MIT going back to World War II. But at the last moment, ARPA awarded the IMP contract to Bolt, Beranek and Newman (BBN). Licklider, the man who initiated the ARPANET project, was a partner at BBN. Now his company was awarded a major contract by the very project he had created. It was more than just the money. The contract placed BBN at the center of the next wave of computing: networking. The selection showed the tiny, insular world of public agencies and private contractors that created the Internet. BBN a few decades later became one of the largest Internet service providers in the country.

62. Guy Raz, "'Lo' And Behold: A Communication Revolution," *All Things Considered,* NPR, October 29, 2009.

63. Hafner and Lyon, *Where Wizards Stay Up Late,* 153.

64. Vinton Cerf, interview by Judy O'Neill, April 24, 1990, https://web.archive .org/web/20170104132550/http://americanhistory.si.edu/comphist/vc1.html.

65. Lawrence G. Roberts, "The Evolution of Packet Switching," November 1978, https://web.archive.org/web/20170310205146/http://www.packet.cc/files /ev-packet-sw.html.

66. "250 Jam Harvard Office," *Boston Globe,* September 27, 1969.

67. Victor McElheny, "Sympathy for Protests, but . . . : How MIT Authorities See Student Scene," *Boston Globe,* October 5, 1969.

68. *Project Cam Exposed,* pamphlet 1, 1969, MIT Institute Archives and Special Collections, Cambridge Project.

69. *Project Cambridge Demonstrate,* flier at Harvard, 1969, MIT Institute Archives and Special Collections, Cambridge Project.

70. *Project Cam Exposed,* pamphlet 2, 1969, MIT Institute Archives and Special Collections, Cambridge Project.

71. Judy Kaufman and Bob Park, eds., *The Cambridge Project: Social Science for Social Control* (Cambridge, MA: Imperial City, 1969). Held in MIT Institute Archives and Special Collections, MIT Cambridge Project records.

72. Sasha Issenberg, *The Victory Lab: The Secret Science of Winning Campaigns* (New York: Crown, 2012).

73. Pool's political work was well known by the public at the time. It even inspired a popular 1964 political thriller, *The 480,* by Eugene Burdick, about a dangerous presidential candidate who uses computer simulation technology to manipulate voters and win the election. Jill Lepore, "Politics and the New Machine," *The New Yorker,* November 16, 2015.

74. Joy Rohde, "The Last Stand of the Psychocultural Cold Warriors—Military Contract Research in Vietnam," *Journal of the History of the Behavioral Sciences* 47, no. 3 (2011): 232–250.

75. Ibid., 239.

76. Jennifer S. Light, *From Warfare to Welfare: Defense Intellectuals and Urban Problems in Cold War America* (Baltimore, MD: Johns Hopkins University Press, 2005).

77. Gene Sosin, *Sparks of Liberty: An Insider's Memoir of Radio Liberty* (University Park: Penn State University Press, 1999), 112.

78. Joseph Hanlon, "The Implications of Project Cambridge," *New Scientist and New Science Journal*, February 25, 1971.

79. Joy Rohde, email interview with author, January 9, 2017.

80. Joy Rohde, "Gray Matters: Social Scientists, Military Patronage, and Democracy in the Cold War," *Journal of American History*, June 2009.

81. Joy Rohde, "'The Social Scientists' War': Expertise in a Cold War Nation" (PhD diss., University of Pennsylvania, January 1, 2007). ProQuest AAI3271806. http://repository.upenn.edu/dissertations/AAI3271806. Rohde expanded her dissertation, "'The Social Scientists' War,'" into a full book titled *Armed with Expertise: The Militarization of American Social Science during the Cold War* (Ithaca, NY: Cornell University Press, 2013). Both are great histories of military involvement in social science and the quest to build predictive technologies to manage the world.

82. Howard Margolis, "McNamara Ax Dooms Camelot," *Washington Post*, July 9, 1965.

83. Ellen Herman, *The Romance of American Psychology: Political Culture in the Age of Experts* (Berkeley: University of California Press, 1995).

84. David I. Bruck, "Brass Tacks: The Cambridge Project," *Harvard Crimson*, September 26, 1969.

85. J. C. R. Licklider, "Establishment and Operation of a Program in Computer Analysis and Modeling in the Behavioral Sciences" (2nd draft), December 5, 1968, MIT Institute Archives and Special Collections, MIT Cambridge Project records.

86. "DOW Chemical," Resistance and Revolution: The Anti-Vietnam War Movement at the University of Michigan, University of Michigan History Department, michiganintheworld.history.lsa.umich.edu/antivietnamwar/exhibits/show/exhibit/military_and_the_university/dow_chemical.

87. "Army Experts Sift Rubble for Bombing Clues at U. of Wisconsin Math Center," *New York Times*, August 26, 1970.

88. "Explosion Goes Off on Harvard Campus," *New York Times*, October 14, 1970.

89. Jacobsen, *Pentagon's Brain*, chap. 13, "In America, antiwar protests raged on . . ." Student protests against the ILLIAC-IV quickly devolved into violence: a campus armory and a US Air Force recruiting station were firebombed, and thousands of students protested on campus, smashing windows and breaking into the chancellor's office. The protests put the supercomputer in physical danger, and the university was forced to relocate it across the country to the NASA Ames Research Center, which is today located next door to Google in Mountain View, California.

90. John Markoff, *What the Dormouse Said: How the 60s Counterculture Shaped the Personal Computer* (New York: Viking Adult, 2005).

91. The protests against the Stanford Research Institute were persistent and violent enough that the university regents decided to spin off the Stanford Research Institute as a private entity, hoping to mollify students by officially distancing the university from classified military research.

92. One professor critical of the project recommended that, to placate protesters, all data and research done on Project Cambridge computers be made public. He got a nasty reply from one of the project's original backers at Harvard: "The Department of Justice can arrange with you to do some research on how to keep blacks quiet and when the Cambridge Project has a useful system going, you may utilize that system to do the work you have undertaken. The Cambridge Project will not refuse access to its facilities because it disagrees with your politics," wrote Edward Pattullo, director of Harvard's Center for Behavioral Sciences. "However, if I am doing some work on how to make blacks noisy, also using the Cambridge Project facilities, you and I, individually, have control over the decision on whether or not to share our data." Letter from Edward Pattullo, September 30, 1969, MIT Institute Archives and Special Collections, MIT Cambridge Project records.

93. Judy Kaufman and Bob Park, eds., *The Cambridge Project: Social Science for Social Control* (Cambridge, MA: Imperial City, 1969). Held in MIT Institute Archives and Special Collections, MIT Cambridge Project records.

94. Waldrop, *Dream Machine*, 316.

95. Ibid., 316.

96. "M.I.T.'s March 4: Scientists Discuss Renouncing Military Research," *Science*, March 14, 1969.

97. Robert A. Young, "An Assessment of the Utility of the ARPA Network of Computers for the International Security Affairs Analyst," Defense Advanced Research Projects Agency, September 1, 1973.

Chapter 3

1. Transcripts of Ford Rowan's June 1975 NBC broadcasts were read into the *Congressional Record*. "Surveillance Technology," *Joint Hearings before the Subcommittee on Constitutional Rights of the Comm. on the Judiciary and the Special Subcommittee on Science, Technology, and Commerce of the Comm. on Commerce, US Senate*, 94th Cong., 1st sess. (June 23, September 9 and 10, 1975).

2. Ibid.

3. "That is interesting to me. I had not heard that," Christopher Pyle, a US Army whistleblower and today's leading expert on American military surveillance in the 1970s, told me. "It doesn't terribly surprise me. They often do stuff like that simultaneously. They both shut the system down and transfer the information to other people. But I never found that they had given stuff to ARPA." Christopher Pyle, interview with author, April 2016.

4. Bobby Allyn, "1969: A Year of Bombings," *New York Times*, August 27, 2009.

5. Joan Herbers, "250,000 War Protesters Stage Peaceful Rally in Washington; Militants Stir Clashes Later," *New York Times*, November 16, 1969.

6. Richard Halloran, "An Expert in Counterintelligence," *New York Times*, February 25, 1975.

7. Christopher Pyle, "Vast Army Intelligence Operation Monitors Political Scene," *Hartford Courant*, January 25, 1970 (reprint from *Washington Monthly*).

8. At the symposium, one general remarked on the disparity between the North Vietnamese and the American soldiers in their motivation and willingness to die for the cause and wondered how the army could go about closing that gap. Like others at the conference, he stressed the need to collect more data on the culture and people in places like Vietnam in order to make the army's counterinsurgency ops more effective. So here his concern was in reverse: to understand the enemy so America could make its soldiers just as tough and ready to die for the cause. US Army's Limited-War Mission and Social Science Research symposium, Special Operations Research Office, American University, Washington, DC, June 1962.

9. Comm. on the Judiciary, Subcommittee on Constitutional Rights, Military Surveillance of Civilian Politics: A Report, S. Rep. 93-S7-312 (1973), https://archive.org/stream/Military-Surveillance-Civilian-Politics-1973/MilitarySurveillance CivilianPolitics#page/no/mode/2up.

10. This quote comes from Christopher Pyle's Senate testimony. *Senate Comm. on the Judiciary, Subcommittee on Constitutional Rights, "Federal Data Banks, Computers, and the Bill of Rights: Hearings,"* 92nd Cong., 1st sess., 163 (1971) (statement of Christopher H. Pyle, graduate student at Columbia University).

11. Information on the army's CONUS Intel operation comes mostly from two Senate reports—*Army Surveillance of Civilian Politics: A Documentary Analysis* and *Military Surveillance of Civilian Politics*—released in 1972 and 1973 by a special Senate Subcommittee on Constitutional Rights that was convened by Senator Sam Ervin to investigate Christopher Pyle's revelations.

12. "Persons of Interest," *Life*, March 26, 1971.

13. *"Federal Data Banks, Computers, and the Bill of Rights: Hearings,"* 174 (statement of Christopher Pyle).

14. Ibid.

15. Christopher Pyle, "CONUS Revisited: The Army Covers Up," *Washington Monthly*, July 1970.

16. "Persons of Interest," 22.

17. *"Federal Data Banks, Computers, and the Bill of Rights: Hearings,"* 164 (statement of Christopher Pyle).

18. Ibid.

19. Christopher Pyle, interview with author, April 28, 2016.

20. Frank Donner, *Protectors of Privilege: Red Squads and Police Repression in Urban America* (Berkeley: University of California Press, 1992).

21. John Connolly, "Inside the Shadow CIA," *Spy*, September 1992.

22. Pyle, "Vast Army Intelligence Operation Monitors Political Scene."

23. "Unraveling Data Networks," *ComputerWorld,* November 26, 1975.

24. Joan M. Jensen, *Army Surveillance in America, 1775–1980* (New Haven, CT: Yale University Press, 1991).

25. Daniel R. Kashey, "A Look Inside NCIC," *ComputerWorld,* December 12, 1977.

26. William D. McDowell, "73 Law Enforcement Agencies All Under One Roof," *ComputerWorld,* August 2, 1972.

27. Richard E. Rotman, "GSA Denies 'Secrecy' of Data Bank," *Washington Post,* June 21, 1974.

28. *"Surveillance Technology," Joint Hearings before the Subcommittee on Constitutional Rights of the Comm. on the Judiciary and the Special Subcommittee on Science, Technology, and Commerce of the Comm. on Commerce,* 94th Cong., 1st sess. (June 23, September 9 and 10, 1975).

29. Arthur R. Miller, "The National Data Center and Personal Privacy," *The Atlantic,* November 1967; "Unraveling Data Networks"; Mark Radwin, "Nets Make Reference Data Available in 50 Cities," ComputerWorld, November 26, 1975.

30. Leslie Goff, "1960: Sabre Takes Off," CNN, June 29, 1999.

31. Waldrop, *Dream Machine,* 120.

32. Thomas Petzinger Jr., *Hard Landing: The Epic Contest for Power and Profits That Plunged the Airlines into Chaos* (New York: Times Business, 1995).

33. SABRE could process seventy-five hundred reservations per hour. Not blazing by modern standards, but at the time it was the most sophisticated commercial system of its kind and it quickly became the common platform on which all air booking was done. "By the mid-1960s, Sabre became the largest private, real-time data processing system, second in size only to the US government's system," according to IBM's official history. "Sabre: The First Online Reservation System," IBM, http://www-03.ibm.com/ibm/history/ibm100/us/en/icons/sabre/.

34. "SABRE Press Kit," SABRE, April 29, 2014, http://web.archive.org /web/20170524143915/https://www.sabre.com/files/PressKitUPDATED.4.29.14 .pdf.

35. Steven Lubar, "'Do Not Fold, Spindle or Mutilate': A Cultural History of the Punch Card," *Journal of American Culture,* June 2004.

36. Arthur R. Miller, "The National Data Center and Personal Privacy," *The Atlantic,* November 1967.

37. Lawrence M. Baskir, "Reflections on the Senate Investigation of Army Surveillance," *Indiana Law Journal,* Summer 1974.

38. Rick Perlstein, *Nixonland: The Rise of a President and the Fracturing of America* (New York: Charles Scribner's Sons, 2008); Karl E. Campbel, *Senator Sam Ervin: Last of the Founding Fathers* (Chapel Hill: University of North Carolina Press, 2007).

39. *"Federal Data Banks, Computers and the Bill of Rights. Part I," Senate Comm. on the Judiciary, Subcommittee on Constitutional Rights,* 92nd Cong, 1st sess. (1971).

40. In his opening statement (ibid.), Senator Ervin mentioned that the number of federal government computer systems had increased more than tenfold in a

decade. "In 1959, there were 403 computers in use by the Federal Government. There are now over 5,000. From a total of $464,000 in 1959, we have leaped to a national budget of over $2 million."

41. Richard Halloran, "Senators Hear of Threat of a 'Dossier Dictatorship,'" *New York Times*, February 24, 1971.

42. Baskir, "Reflections on the Senate Investigation of Army Surveillance."

43. Senator Ervin's committee destroyed US Army surveillance files they obtained to protect people's privacy, but the final report on the investigation contained a few anonymized details. An entry on "nationally known civil rights leader" noted that he "has subversive Communist background, and is a sex pervert." An intelligence report on a youth group in Colorado noted that its members engaged in "sex activities of both heterosexual and homosexual varieties."

44. *"Army Surveillance of Civilians: A Documentary Analysis," Subcommittee on Constitutional Rights, Comm. on the Judiciary, US Senate*, 92nd Cong., 2nd sess. (1972), 93.

45. Ibid., v.

46. Senator Ervin's *Army Surveillance of Civilians: A Documentary Analysis* report at multiple points discusses lack of evidence that the army destroyed its surveillance files as well as evidence showing that the data had been deliberately preserved: "Many of the records undoubtedly have been destroyed; many others undoubtedly have been hidden away. . . . On two subsequent occasions it was learned that the Intelligence Command had failed to carry out orders to destroy its computerized files on civilians unaffiliated with the armed forces. . . . The order to destroy the mug books was issued on February 18, 1970, but as of August 26, 1970, less than half had been reported destroyed. . . . At the Counterintelligence Analysis Division this directive was interpreted to permit microfilming of the Compendium before destruction of the office copy was carried out" (v-8). Three years later, Senator Ervin introduced a bill that outlawed domestic military surveillance. The proposed law was supposed to put this issue to rest once and for all, but it was fiercely opposed by the Pentagon. Despite having wide bipartisan support, it never made it past its first reading. By then, public attention had moved on. The army surveillance scandal was old news, eclipsed by the Watergate investigation. Paul J. Scheips, *The Role of Federal Military Forces in Domestic Disorders, 1945–1992* (Washington, DC: Center of Military History of the United States Army, 2012), 398.

47. Christopher Pyle told me that army computers back then were still very rudimentary and could do only the most basic analysis on the surveillance data they contained. "I never came across any information that the computers were able to talk to each other. That was a little too sophisticated for them" (Christopher Pyle, interview with author, April 2016). But that was already changing. ARPA was hard at work building exactly the kind of networked computer database technology that Pyle said the domestic army intelligence program lacked.

48. Transcripts of Ford Rowan's June 1975 NBC broadcasts were read into the *Congressional Record*. "*Surveillance Technology," Joint Hearings Before the Subcommittee on Constitutional Rights*, 4–9.

49. Ford Rowan, interview with author, November 10, 2015.

50. Ford Rowan told me that at the time he aired the story, he was afraid the Pentagon would sue him and NBC and attempt to get him to disclose his anonymous sources. To protect his sources and to protect himself, he wrote their names down on a piece of paper and stuck it in a bank vault. "I ended up footnoting all of those and have the names of all the people I talked with and there was only one copy made. This was back in the days before you had computers to write everything on. So you had a typewriter. I put it in a safe deposit box and gave the key to my editor and in the end six months later he gave me the key back. He said, 'throw it away, as far as I'm concerned.' So I burned the list. Or actually tore it up." Ford Rowan, interview with author, November 10, 2015.

51. Nancy French, a correspondent for *ComputerWorld*, hit up her contacts at MIT, and they confirmed that files on antiwar activists and protesters had indeed been transferred over ARPANET to MIT. French's sources explained that the reason those files were transferred was because MIT, in partnership with Harvard, was developing a special database system for the Pentagon that would handle these surveillance files. One source told French that an army lieutenant colonel had explained that the surveillance data was being sent from the National Security Agency at Fort Mead. "Files were transmitted over the ARPANET to certain parties on a joint MIT-Harvard project who were writing data bank maintenance programs for use on Army surveillance files on civilian antiwar protestors," writes Nancy French. A "data bank maintenance program" in 1970s techie lingo was simply a program that allowed a user to interact with a database, to enter and retrieve data, to search for information, that kind of thing (Nancy French, "Army Files on Citizens Still Not Destroyed," *ComputerWorld*, June 11, 1975). Reporters from MIT's *The Tech* pursued the story, too, looking at allegations that the surveillance files were transferred to ARPA's Project CAM and the MIT Lincoln Laboratory. "Although Defense Department officials testified in 1971 that the program had been terminated and its records destroyed, informed sources—including former military intelligence officers—have told *The Tech* that many of the files were retained. The information, according to intelligence sources, was transferred and stored at the headquarters of the National Security Agency (NSA), at Fort Meade, Maryland. The Army files were transmitted on the ARPANET in about January 1972, sources say, more than two years after the material—and the data banks maintained at the Fort Holabird facility—were ordered destroyed" (Norman D. Sandler and Mike McNamee, "Computers Carried Army Files; MIT Investigation Underway," *The Tech*, April 11, 1975, http://web.archive .org/web/20170530223241/http://tech.mit.edu/V95/PDF/V95-N17.pdf).

52. Ford Rowan, *Technospies* (New York: G. P. Putnam's Sons, 1978), 55.

53. In Senator Tunney's investigation, Pentagon officials made multiple references to the "Cambridge Project." They denied that it was used for surveillance, but this was the MIT center that Rowan identified in his reporting. *"Surveillance Technology," Joint Hearings Before the Subcommittee on Constitutional Rights*, 21, 52.

54. Ibid., 42.

55. *"Department of Defense Appropriations for Fiscal Year 73, Part 1," Subcommittee on DOD Appropriations, Comm. on Appropriations, Senate Comm. on Appropriations* (February 25, 28, March 14, 16, 22–24, May 4, 1972) (testimony of Stephen Lukasik, APRA director, March 14, 1972).

56. In his testimony to the Senate in 1972, Lukasik explains that the AR-PANET was already on its way to being integrated into operational military communications systems including the Worldwide Military Command and Control System (WWMCCS), a global command and control network operated by the Department of Defense. "Now that ARPA has demonstrated the feasibility of distributed network operation, the Defense Communications Agency has ordered three of ARPA's Interface Message Processors so that a prototype ARPANET operation can be established between three of the WWMCCS computers. When this is completed and the network operation has been proven as operationally effective, the WWMCCS network will be expanded to worldwide operation," he said. Ibid.

57. ARPA began developing end-to-end encryption over the ARPANET in 1976. As a report to the Senate explains, this was superior because it did not require physically securing the lines and allowed a general-purpose defense network to be used for both classified and nonclassified tasks. *"Department of Defense Appropriations for FY78 Part 5: Research, Development, Test, and Evaluation," Hearings, Subcommittee of the Comm. on Appropriations,* 95th Cong., 1st sess. (February–March 1977).

58. "The operational defense agencies first became interested in the ARPANET as a model for replacing their existing networks with more advanced technology. The National Security Agency commissioned Bolt, Beranek and Newman to create two smaller versions of the ARPANET for the intelligence community. These were the Community Online Intelligence System ('COINS'), begun around 1972, and the Platform Network, built in the late 1970s. According to Eric Elsam, who managed network projects at BBN's Washington office, both systems provided regular data communications service for intelligence agencies for many years" (Abbate, *Inventing the Internet*). "The most obvious and striking thing that pops out at you while looking at old maps of the ARPANET is that the NSA became a node in the mid-1970s. What does being a node mean? It meant that there was a computer at the NSA that was responsible for routing traffic on the ARPANET. The NSA could connect any computer it wanted to their IMP (the refrigerator-sized modems of the 1960s and 70s) and access the ARPANET and any networks to which it connected" (Matt Novak, "A History of Internet Spying, Part 2," *Gizmodo,* February 20, 2015, http://gizmodo.com/a-history-of-internet-spying-part-2-1686760364).

59. Recently declassified CIA documents show that in 1974 the CIA planned to install ARPANET terminals for its analysts to use. Other declassified CIA files talk about installing terminals as well. *Memorandum: CASCON Report to DCI* (draft), Central Intelligence Agency, January 31, 1974, https://www.cia.gov/library/readingroom/docs/CIA-RDP79M00096A000500010002-6.pdf; an official map

of the ARPANET released in June 1975 lists an NSA node as well as multiple nodes at air force and army bases and military contractors' sites.

60. Stephen J. Lukasik, "Why the Arpanet Was Built," *IEEE Annals of the History of Computing* 33, no. 3 (July–September 2011).

61. Waldrop, *Dream Machine*, 380.

62. Robert Kahn, interviewed by Vinton Cerf, September 30, 2006, http://web .archive.org/web/20170530211316/http://archive.computerhistory.org/resources/access /text/2013/05/102657973-05-01-acc.pdf.

63. ARPA's command and control division was later renamed the Information Processing Technology Office, a more generic name that, whether intentionally or not, masked its military origins.

64. The agency had first-hand experience with the need for this kind of technology. In Vietnam, many battlefield projects relied on data transmission over long distances. There was Igloo White, the ambitious attempt to "bug the battlefield" and detect enemy movement by creating a computer network tied to wireless seismic sensors and microphones along the Ho Chi Minh Trail. Also, multiple ARPA projects worked via remote-controlled helicopters—what we'd now call drones. Several models were being tested in battle by 1968. One model was a submarine hunter-killer launched from navy vessels and equipped with sonar and torpedoes. Another was outfitted for jungle duty with night vision and multiple weapon configurations: Vulcan cannons, missiles, grenade launchers, and cluster bomb dispensers. The drone's real-time video signal was relayed to a mobile control station mounted on an army jeep, and it provided recon information used to call in bomber strikes (F. A. Tietzel, M. R. VanderLind, and J. H. Brown Jr., *Summary of ARPA-ASO, TTO Aerial Platform Programs. Volume 2. Remotely Piloted Helicopters* [Columbia, OH: Battelle, July 1975], http://www.dtic.mil/docs/citations /ADB007793). Early models hunted for submarines; others attacked ground forces, did recon, or worked as hovering antennas for long-distance radio links (*Adverse Effects of Producing Drone Anti-Submarine Helicopters Before Completion of Development and Tests* [Washington, DC: Comptroller of the United States, December 31, 1970]). These drones more or less worked, but they were crude. Their main limitations were short flight times and lack of long-distance control. And, of course, none of them used the ARPANET or any other network because it did not yet exist.

65. Abbate, *Inventing the Internet*, 127–128.

66. Vinton G. Cerf and Robert E. Kahn, "A Protocol for Packet Network Interconnection," *IEEE Transactions on Communications* 22, no. 5 (May 1974).

67. Vinton Cerf, interviewed by Judy O'Neill, April 24, 1990, Charles Babbage Institute.

68. Ibid.

69. *"Department of Defense Appropriations for Fiscal Year 1978, Part 5—Research, Development, Test, and Evaluation,"* 95th Cong., 1st sess. (February 4, 1977–March 18, 1977).

70. For example: in 1973, even as Robert Kahn and Vinton Cerf sketched out the ARPANET 2.0, ARPA director Stephen Lukasik was asking Congress for

$6.5 million to fund an "intelligent systems" program to fulfill the "objective of developing the capability to have computers consider large quantities of complex, real world information and form generalizations and plans based on the totality of information. Progress in these areas is important for the intelligence agencies, especially in intelligence analysis and question-answering systems." Lukasik pointed out: "the tools and techniques to be developed will be available on systems of the ARPA network and therefore will be immediately accessible by the services." *"Department of Defense Appropriations for Fiscal Year 1973, Part 1," Subcommittee on DOD Appropriations, Comm. on Appropriations, Senate Comm. on Appropriations* (February 25, 28, March 14, 16, 22–24, May 4, 1972).

71. Ford Rowan, phone interview with author, November 10, 2015.

Chapter 4

1. Rossetto expanded this quote into a full-blown manifesto in *Wired*'s UK edition: "The most fascinating and powerful people today are not politicians or priests, or generals or pundits, but the vanguard who are integrating digital technologies into their business and personal lives, and causing social changes so profound that their only parallel is probably the discovery of fire."

2. Kevin Kelly, *New Rules for the New Economy: 10 Radical Strategies for a Connected World* (New York: Viking Adult, 1998).

3. Rich Karlgaard and Michael Malone, "City vs. Country: Tom Peters & George Gilder Debate the Impact of Technology on Location," *Forbes ASAP*, February 27, 1995.

4. "Task Force to Focus on Information Revolution," *Deseret (UT) News,* September 15, 1993, http://www.deseretnews.com/article/309821/TASK-FORCE -TO-FOCUS-ON-INFORMATION-REVOLUTION.html.

5. I attempted to interview Stewart Brand for this book, but he declined. "I have to pass," he told me by email on May 28, 2015. "Working too hard on totally other subjects. May your book thrive."

6. Stewart Brand, "SPACEWAR: Frantic Life and Symbolic Death among the Computer Bums," *Rolling Stone,* December 7, 1972.

7. Ibid.

8. Ibid.

9. Ibid.

10. Tom Wolfe, *The Electric Kool-Aid Acid Test* (New York: Farrar, Straus and Giroux, 1968).

11. This chapter was greatly influenced and inspired by Fred Turner's pioneering work on the ties between the military and industrial worlds that spawned the Internet and the hippie culture of the 1960s. Turner is a professor in the Department of Communication at Stanford University. I recommend that anyone who wants a better understanding of the utopian ideas that undergirds so much of our Internet culture today read his fabulous book, *From Counterculture to Cyberculture: Stewart Brand, the Whole Earth Network, and the Rise of Digital Utopianism.* It shows very clearly that what we consider to be new developments are really warmed-over

ideas and notions that originated in the 1960s. Indeed, in that sense, Internet culture is not so different from the rest of American contemporary culture.

12. Quoted in Fred Turner, *From Counterculture to Cyberculture: Stewart Brand, the Whole Earth Network, and the Rise of Digital Utopianism* (Chicago: University of Chicago Press, 2006), 41.

13. John Markoff, *What the Dormouse Said: How the 60s Counterculture Shaped the Personal Computer* (New York: Viking Adult, 2005).

14. Bruce Shlain and Martin A. Lee, *Acid Dreams: The Complete Social History of LSD: The CIA, the Sixties, and Beyond*, rev. ed. (New York: Grove Press, 1994), 155–156.

15. Ibid., 109.

16. Turner, *From Counterculture to Cyberculture*, 4.

17. Ibid.

18. "Steve Jobs' Commencement address," YouTube video, 15:04, June 12, 2005, posted March 7, 2008, https://www.youtube.com/watch?v=UF8uR6Z6KLc.

19. Turner, *From Counterculture to Cyberculture*, 71–72.

20. Adam Curtis, *All Watched Over by Machines of Loving Grace* (London: BBC, 2011), documentary series.

21. The founder of Synergia would go on to lead the Biosphere, a project to create a self-sustaining ecosystem inside a giant glass bowl, which was financed by Edward P. Bass, an oil heir from Texas who had been a member of Synergia in the 1970s. William J. Broad, "As Biosphere Is Sealed, Its Patron Reflects on Life," *New York Times*, September 24, 1991.

22. Quoted in ibid.

23. Ibid.

24. Theresa Hogue, "Cult Survivors Share Experiences," *Corvallis Gazette-Times*, August 4, 2005, https://www.culteducation.com/group/1289-general-information /8651-cult-survivors-share-their-experiences.html.

25. Turner, *From Counterculture to Cyberculture*, 97, 101, 109–111.

26. "The Demo," MouseSite, http://web.stanford.edu/dept/SUL/library/extra4 /sloan/MouseSite/1968Demo.html.

27. Markoff, *What the Dormouse Said*, chap. 5, "From his platform behind the audience . . . "

28. According to Fred Turner's *From Counterculture to Cyberculture*, Engelbart described himself as "very empathetic to the counterculture's notions of community and how that could help with creativity, rationality and how a group works together" (109).

29. Richard Brautigan, "All Watched Over By Machines of Loving Grace," in *All Watched Over by Machines of Loving Grace* (San Francisco: Communication Company, 1967).

30. Quoted in Turner, *From Counterculture to Cyberculture*, 128.

31. "Bio . . . Stewart Brand," The Long Now Foundation, http://sb.longnow.org /SB_homepage/Bio.html.

32. Turner, *From Counterculture to Cyberculture*, 135.

33. Michael Schrage, "Hacking Away at the Future," *Washington Post*, November 18, 1984.

34. *Hackers: Wizards of the Electronic Age* (Arlington, VA: PBS, 1985), short film.

35. Stewart Brand, "Keep Designing," *Whole Earth Review,* May 1985.

36. "The advertisements appeared after a Harris poll, the I.R.S. had begun testing the use of computerized life-style information, such as the types of cars people own, to track down errant taxpayers, while an F.B.I. advisory committee had recommended that the bureau computer system include data on people who, though not charged with wrongdoing, associate with drug traffickers." David Burnham, "The Computer, the Consumer and Privacy," *New York Times,* March 4, 1984.

37. "When I was young, there was an amazing publication called the *Whole Earth Catalog,* which was one of the bibles of my generation. It was created by a fellow named Stewart Brand not far from here in Menlo Park and he brought it to life with his poetic touch. This was in the late 60s, before personal computers and desktop publishing so it was all made with typewriters, scissors, Polaroid cameras. It was sort of like Google in paperback form, 35 years before Google came along. It was idealistic, overflowing with neat tools and great notions. Stewart and his team put out several issues of the *Whole Earth Catalog* and then when it had run its course, they put out a final issue. It was the mid-1970s and I was your age. On the back cover of their final issue was a photograph of an early morning country road. The kind you might find yourself hitchhiking on if you were so adventurous. Beneath it were the words: stay hungry, stay foolish. It was their farewell message as they signed off. Stay hungry, stay foolish. And I have always wished that for myself," said Steve Jobs at a commencement speech he gave at Stanford University in 2005. "Steve Jobs' Commencement address," YouTube video, 15:04, June 12, 2005, posted March 7, 2008, https://www.youtube.com/watch?v=UF8uR6Z6KLc.

38. By some accounts, BZ was deployed in Vietnam to psychologically paralyze North Vietnamese fighters. It was also tested on American soldiers, whose harrowing experiences later inspired the cult classic horror film *Jacob's Ladder.* Bruce Shlain and Martin A. Lee, *Acid Dreams: The Complete Social History of LSD: The CIA, the Sixties, and Beyond,* rev. ed. (New York: Grove Press, 1994).

39. Stephen Wolff, interview with author, October 23, 2015.

40. "That is, it was his role to commercialize the Internet and get the government out of this business. So he did that," Phil Dykstra, a scientist at the Army Research Laboratory, said during a 1996 US Army symposium on the history of the Internet, "50 Years of Army Computing."

41. Stephen Wolff, interview with author, October 23, 2015.

42. Janet Abbate, *Inventing the Internet* (Cambridge, MA: MIT Press, 1999).

43. Karen D. Frazer, *NSFNET: A Partnership for High-Speed Networking* (Ann Arbor, MI: Merit Network, 1996).

44. Waldrop, *Dream Machine,* 463.

45. Mary Linehan, "NSFNET Boost Under Way," *Network World,* December 14, 1987.

46. Mary Petrosky, "NSF T-1 Net Links Schools," *Network World,* March 30, 1987.

47. *America's Investment in the Future* (Arlington, VA: National Science Foundation, 2000), 10, https://www.nsf.gov/about/history/nsf0050/.

48. "Physical Initial NSFNET Topology," Center for Cartographic and Spatial Analysis, Michigan State University, http://internethalloffame.org/sites/default /files/nsfnet_topology.gif. The NSFNET was a civilian academic network, but the entire initiative had heavy military and defense involvement. On a bigger level, most computer science researchers—the principal users of the NSFNET—were funded through military grants. But it was even more specific: many of the network providers were tied to military agencies, contractors, engineers, and key government insiders who had played pivotal roles in developing the ARPANET, and several of the biggest regional network providers were actually run by military contractors, among them CERFNET, which linked universities in Southern California and was operated by a division of General Atomics, a major military contractor based in San Diego and best known today as the US government's premier supplier of drones.

49. Less than a year later, in 1989, the National Science Foundation was already pushing to expand backbone capacity to a T-3 line, which would increase total bandwidth by a factor of 30.

50. Waldrop, *Dream Machine*, 463.

51. Ibid., 463.

52. This chapter's discussion of the privatization process relies on the work of Jay P. Kesan and Rajiv C. Shah, who did an amazing postmortem analysis of the National Science Foundation's privatization of the NSFNET. See: "Fool Us Once Shame on You—Fool Us Twice Shame on Us: What We Can Learn from the Privatizations of the Internet Backbone Network and the Domain Name System," *Washington University Law Review* 79, no. 1 (2001): 91–220.

53. Ellen Messmer, "IBM, MCI and Merit Look to Sign New NSFNET Users," *Network World*, October 1, 1990.

54. The consortium was being paid $9.3 million a year to run the backbone ($9.3 million in 1989 is equivalent to $18.3 million in 2017 dollars). See Kesan and Shah, "Fool Us Once Shame on You," 123.

55. "Although few understood, he meant that the NSF was now buying its NSFNet service as a portion of ANS's private network, rather than paying him to operate the NSF's network," William Schrader, president of NSFNET regional provider PSINET, said in congressional testimony during hearings on the management of the NSFNET. "After the agreements which the NSF had signed creating ANS, and providing it with exclusive commercial access, were released in December of 1991, it was clear that ANS's president was correct, the T3 had been privatized. This occurred without public discussion or disclosure, and was effectively hidden for a year" (*"Management of NSFNET," Hearing Before the Subcommittee on Science of the Comm. on Science, Space, and Technology, US House of Representatives*, 102nd Cong., 2nd sess. [March 12, 1992]). From then on, the NSFNET backbone ran as part of a larger private network owned by MCI and IBM.

56. John Markoff, "Data Network Raises Monopoly Fear," *New York Times*, December 19, 1991.

57. Kesan and Shah, "Fool Us Once Shame on You," 122–123.

58. Ibid. "ANS took advantage of the public in several ways. First, it relied heavily on support from the government. Second, ANS did not find new customers, instead it attempted mainly to convert customers from the government-subsidized regional networks. Finally, ANS's decision to create a for-profit subsidiary raised questions as to ANS's responsibility to the NSFNET and to the public interest. At the time of ANS's creation, it depended on its only customer, the government, for its operating revenue of $9.3 million. . . . In effect, it could be suggested that the federal government funded a competitor to other commercial backbone providers. Some of ANS's national competitors included Sprint and PSI," wrote Kesan and Shah.

59. Kesan and Shah, "Fool Us Once Shame on You," 89. "Might telcos become dominant? Of course there is such a danger. Be careful when you begin to dance with the elephants. But remember if they employ illegal means of increasing market share, we have laws against anti-competitive behavior. I doubt that they would do something questionable and walk away unchallenged," Wolff said in a 1994 interview.

60. "The decisions made by the NSF affected issues such as security, privacy, innovation, and competition. Through these decisions, the NSF essentially regulated the Internet. It is important to note that although the NSF consulted with the affected parties and limited their intervention to broad technical issues, the intervention was not insignificant and did constitute regulation of the Internet." Kesan and Shah, "Fool Us Once Shame on You."

61. Ibid.

62. And despite the danger that a handful of powerful players would dominate an unregulated privatized Internet market, smaller regional networks like PSINET balked at having the government regulate the budding Internet service provider industry. Instead, they pushed for an early version of "net neutrality"—a market-driven self-regulation scheme that would enforce a level playing field among competing Internet service providers. Resolving this conflict was the first real lobbying effort by the newly created Electronic Frontier Foundation. Despite the market power of national carriers like IBM-MCI's ANS to restrict competition, EFF wanted the government to stay out of any overt regulation of the industry. Mitch Kapor, cofounder of EFF, testified before Congress to push for a self-regulatory scheme: "To avoid government involvement, Kapor suggested the use of binding agreements between the commercial backbone networks to interconnect." Ibid.

63. PSINET offered another example of the NSFNET privatization process. It was founded in 1989 by the board of directors of NYSERNET, a regional provider that had been set up in 1986 to connect universities in the New York area to the NSFNET. A few years after setting it up, NYSERNET's directors—led by William Schrader—realized that they could make money by personally buying up the network assets of this federally funded nonprofit and transforming it into a private company that sold commercial services on a network infrastructure subsidized by the federal government. "A year or two after NYSERNet took over it

became apparent to some people that there might be a commercial opportunity in its technology. They proposed to NYSERNet's Board of Directors that they buy the network assets from the corporation and operate it as a for-profit corporation. This commercial spin-off from NYSERNet was called PSINet, formed in 1989," Ben Chi, director of NYSERNET, said in an interview in 2003 ("Talking with Ben Chi of NYSERNet," *Ubiquity* 2003 [September 2003]: article no. 7). From then on, the NSF regional provider NYSERNET bought network services from PSINET, the privatized component of the old NYSERNET, and sold them to the NSFNET (Abbate, *Inventing the Internet*, 197–198). "To provide these services, PSINet bought out NYSERNet's infrastructure. NYSERNet became a broker of network service rather than a provider, buying service from PSINet and selling it to NSF-sponsored users. Since the network infrastructure was no longer directly paid for by the US government, PSINet could also sell its services to business customers for additional profits. PSINet proved to be a successful business venture, and other spinoffs of regional networks quickly followed along the same lines," writes Abbate.

64. Michael Margolis and David Resnick, *Politics as Usual: The Cyberspace Revolution* (Thousand Oaks, CA: Sage Publications, 2000).

65. Stephen Wolff, interview with author, October 23, 2015.

66. Keith Epstein, "The Fall of the House of Schrader," *Washington Post*, April 7, 2001.

67. These budding Internet service providers wanted the government out of the networking business, and soon enough they got their wish. In 1993, after several years of acrimonious spats and conflicts, meetings, and congressional hearings, the National Science Foundation finally addressed the demands of the regional providers by unveiling a new privatized NSFNET design. The original ANSNET backbone would be retired, and multiple market-driven commercial backbones would be allowed to take its place, opening the market to unregulated competition between old NSFNET regional providers and anyone else who wanted to get into the business.

68. Wolff continued: "It was clear to all of us that NSF support for such things [the NSFNET] would not go on forever, and we saw that our job was to compensate for that in the best way that we could. So what we did was to provide for the privatization, that is, to stop funding the network, but at the same time give the money that we had been spending while we still had it, to the regional networks so they could buy the connectivity from the commercial providers." Stephen Wolff, interview with author, October 23, 2015.

69. Consider Al Gore, the Democratic senator from Tennessee. In 1989, a few years before he became vice president of the United States, Senator Gore introduced a bill to finance a program to support the development of a national computer network—which would be developed with federal funds but privatized as soon as "commercial networks can meet the networking needs of American researchers." Gore's bill eventually morphed into the High Performance Computing Act of 1991, which provided $495 million for the creation of a high-bandwidth

fiber-optic educational computer network and expanded funding for computer and networking research. The act led directly to the creation of Mosaic, the first modern web browser created at the University of Illinois and a legend among early computer start-ups. Mosaic started as a government-funded research project but was immediately spun off by members of the University of Illinois research team as a private company called Netscape. Even more important: Senator Gore's bill explicitly called for the privatization of the government-funded NSFNET backbone. During discussions of the bill, Gore repeatedly stressed his intention to support the privatization of the network. Under pressure from telecommunications companies, he had to make it loud and clear that he did not support the government operating a public network—even if the American people had financed its development.

70. Hostility to government regulation of networking ran deep and wide. Even the military scientists and contractors who helped bring the technology into being portrayed government regulations of commercial networks as a slippery slope toward totalitarianism. Ithiel de Sola Pool, the longtime ARPA contractor who worked with J. C. R. Licklider to create counterinsurgency computing technology for the US Army and who dreamed of creating computer systems that could surveil and control entire societies, suddenly took to calling computer networks "technologies of freedom."

71. Steve Behrens, "Inouye Bill Would Reserve Capacity on Infohighway," *Current*, June 20, 1994, https://current.org/wp-content/uploads/archive-site/in/in412 .html.

72. Stephen Wolff, interview with author, October 23, 2015.

73. The law was backed by telephone, cable, and broadcasting companies and had deep bipartisan support, but it was spearheaded by a resurgent Republican Party, which had just won a dual majority in Congress (Dawn Holian, *Wolves in Sheep's Clothing: Telecom Industry Front Groups and Astroturf* [Washington, DC: Common Cause, March 2006]). Leading the charge was House Speaker Newt Gingrich, a Republican congressman from Georgia. His Progress and Freedom Foundation, which was a principal mover and shaker in this deregulatory fervor, was funded by major telephone, cable, and broadcast companies—AT&T, Verizon, Comcast, Time Warner, T-Mobile, Sprint, Clear Channel Communications, and Viacom. According to its mission statement, the organization was set up to promote telecommunications reforms "based on a philosophy of limited government, free markets and individual sovereignty."

74. Here's a roundup of what happened to the NSFNET providers in greater detail: America Online bought up the NFSNET backbone built by the IBM-MCI consortium. Using access to this high-speed national network to outpace competitors like Prodigy and CompuServe, AOL would later end up merging with Time-Warner. The San Francisco Bay Area's BARNET became part of Bolt, Beranek and Newman, J. C. R. Licklider's old firm and an original ARPANET contractor, which itself grew into one of the largest Internet providers in the country and eventually had its networking division absorbed by Verizon (while the rest

of the company went to Raytheon) (Nathan Newman, *Net Loss: Internet Prophets, Private Profits, and the Costs to Community* [University Park: Penn State University Press, 2002]). CERFNET was first bought by Teleport, a large phone company, which was itself bought by AT&T in 1998 (Seth Schiesel, "AT&T to Pay $11.3 Billion for Teleport," *New York Times*, January 9, 1998). PSI went public on the NAS-DAQ in 1995 with an initial valuation of $1 billion, collapsed in the wake of the dot-com bubble, and was snapped up in 2002 by Cogent Communications (Keith Epstein, "The Fall of the House of Schrader," *Washington Post*, April 7, 2001).

75. Timothy B. Lee, "40 Maps That Explain the Internet," Vox, June 2, 2014, https://www.vox.com/a/internet-maps.

76. Neil Weinberg, "Backbone Bullies," *Forbes*, June 12, 2000. The industry would continue to consolidate over the next decade, not just domestically but also internationally. As I write this in 2017, two decades after the Telecommunications Act of 1996 was passed, the US media and telecommunications markets are concentrated in a way that has not been seen for a century: a handful of global, vertically integrated media companies—Verizon, AT&T, Comcast, Charter Communications, Time Warner—own most of the domestic media today, including television and radio networks, film studios, newspapers, and, of course, commercial Internet service providers.

77. "Louis Rossetto Sr., 78, Typesetting Executive," *New York Times*, July 31, 1991.

78. Frank da Cruz, "Columbia University 1968," Columbia University 1968, April 1998, updated May 26, 2016, accessed March 15, 2016, http://www.columbia.edu/cu/computinghistory/1968/.

79. George Keller, "Six Weeks that Shook Morningside," *Columbia College Today*, Spring 1968.

80. Stan Lehr and Louis Rossetto Jr., "The New Right Credo—Libertarianism," *New York Times*, January 10, 1971.

81. Sam Tanenhaus and Jim Rutenberg, "Rand Paul's Mixed Inheritance," *New York Times*, January 25, 2014; Tames Boyd, "From Far Right to Far Left," *New York Times*, December 6, 1970.

82. Louis Rossetto Jr., "Afghan Guerrilla Wants Soviets Out, but Has No Illusions of Victory," *Christian Science Monitor*, October 10, 1985.

83. Gary Wolf, *Wired: A Romance* (New York: Random House, 2003).

84. Ibid.

85. Michael Dobbs, "Negroponte's Time in Honduras at Issue," *Washington Post*, March 21, 2005; Carla Anne Robbins, "Negroponte Has Tricky Mission," Wall Street Journal, April 27, 2004; Scott Shane, "Cables Show Central Negroponte Role in 80's Covert War Against Nicaragua," *New York Times*, April 13, 2005.

86. Stewart Brand, *The Media Lab: Inventing the Future at MIT* (New York: Viking Adult, 1987).

87. "It was our bread and butter for a decade, and I wish it would become again," Nicholas Negroponte said. Brand, *Media Lab*, 163; Edward Fredkin, ed., *Project*

MAC Progress Report IX, July 1971 to July 1972, AD-756689 (Cambridge: Massachusetts Institute of Technology, February 1973), http://www.dtic.mil/dtic/tr/fulltext /u2/756689.pdf; *Project MAC Progress Report III, July 1965 to July 1966*, AD-648346 (Cambridge: Massachusetts Institute of Technology, March 17, 1967), http://www .dtic.mil/dtic/tr/fulltext/u2/648346.pdf.

88. "We came up with the idea of projecting onto video screens sculpted like people's faces and also having the screens swivel a bit—so they could nod, shake their head, turn to each other," Negroponte explained to Stewart Brand in *The Media Lab*. "At my site I'm real and you're plastic and on my right, and at your site you're real and I'm plastic and on your left. If we're talking and looking at each other, and one of the faces across the table interrupts, we would stop and turn toward him" (92).

89. "It was a byproduct of Pentagon interest in the Entebbe hostage-freeing raid of 1973, where the Israeli commandos made a mockup of the airport in the desert and practiced there before trying the real thing" (Brand, *Media Lab*, 141). It was sophisticated for its time, complete with a "season knob" that toggled between different times of the year to show what streets and buildings looked like. It also allowed viewers to walk into buildings and check out what was inside, and even read the menu of a restaurant. "It was the whole town. It let you drive through the place yourself, having a conversation with the chauffeur," explained one the developers of the project (141).

90. Brand, *Media Lab*, 137. "A block slightly askew would be realigned. One substantially dislocated would be placed (straight, of course) in the new position, on the assumption that the gerbils wanted it there. The outcome was a constantly changing architecture that reflected the way the little animals used the place," Negroponte explained.

91. Clients included, according to Brand's *Media Lab*, ABC, NBC, CBS, PBS, HBO, Warner Brothers, 20th Century Fox, and Paramount. IBM, Apple, Hewlett-Packard, Digital Equipment Corporation, Sony, NEC, Mitsubishi, and General Motors were also members, as were major newspapers and news publishing businesses: Time Inc., the *Washington Post*, and the *Boston Globe*.

92. Among other things, DARPA funded lab research on speech recognition technology that promised to identify people by their voices or to visually read their lips from a distance.

93. Todd Hertz, "How Computer Nerds Describe God," *Christianity Today*, November 20, 2002.

94. "*Wired* was meant to be a lifestyle magazine as well as a technology guide," writes John Cassidy in *Dot.Con*, a book about the dot-com bubble. "Sections like 'Fetish' and 'Street Cred' told readers which new gadgets to buy, while 'Idees Forte' and 'Jargon Watch' told them what to think and say." Cassidy, *Dot.Con* (New York: PerfectBound/HarperCollins, 2009), 44.

95. Louis Rossetto, *Wired*, January 1, 1993.

96. Fred Turner writes: "As he told a reporter for *Upside* magazine in 1997, 'The mainstream media is not allowing us to understand what's really happening today

because it's obsessed with telling you, "Well, on the one hand" and "on the other hand"; under conditions of digital revolution, Rossetto believed that a magazine could tell the truth—and achieve distinction—only by 'not being objective.'" Turner, *From Counterculture to Cyberculture,* 2016.

97. The inaugural issue of *Wired* featured a cover story by sci-fi author Bruce Sterling, who was dispatched to profile DARPA's virtual tank battlefield simulator project: a multiplayer online tank game run on a powerful new military ARPANET-like network built just for battle simulations called SIMNET. "The seams between reality and virtuality will be repeatedly and deliberately blurred. Ontology be damned—this is war!" Bruce Sterling, "War Is Virtual Hell," *Wired,* January 1, 1993.

98. Peter Schwartz and Peter Leyden, "The Long Boom: A History of the Future, 1980–2020," *Wired,* July 1, 1997.

99. For more on *Wired*'s embrace of Newt Gingrich and the Republican Right, see Fred Turner's *From Counterculture to Cyberculture.* Here is how he describes the magazine's profile of Gingrich: "In her introduction to the [*Wired* interview with Newt Gingrich], Esther Dyson expressed reservations about Gingrich's social politics, explaining, 'I like his ideals—but not necessarily the people who espouse them. Or the society that will result from them.' But by the end of her interview, the doubts seemed to have washed away. Dyson and Gingrich clearly spoke the same language. . . . Moreover, for regular readers of *Wired,* their encounter came at the end of a long series of articles in which the cybernetic, countercultural, and deregulationist strains of their rhetoric had already been legitimated . . . the notion of business as a source of social change, of digital technology as the tool and symbol of business, and of decentralization as a social ideal were well established in the pages of *Wired,*" he writes. "From here, it took little imagination to guess that perhaps the Republican 'revolution' of 1994 might itself be riding the same 'Third Wave'" (232).

100. David Kline, "Infobahn Warrior," *Wired,* July 1994. "I'll make a commitment to Al Gore, OK? Listen, Al, I know you haven't asked for it, but we'll make a commitment to complete the job by the end of '96. All we need is a little help . . . you know, shoot [FCC Commissioner] Hundt! Don't let him do any more damage, know what I'm saying?" he declared in the interview.

101. "*Wired*—the monthly bible of the 'virtual class'—has uncritically reproduced the views of Newt Gingrich, the extreme-right Republican leader of the House of Representatives, and the Tofflers, who are his close advisors. Ignoring their policies for welfare cutbacks, the magazine is instead mesmerized by their enthusiasm for the libertarian possibilities offered by new information technologies," wrote Richard Barbrook and Andy Cameron in their influential 1995 essay, "The Californian Ideology." Richard Barbrook and Andy Cameron, "The Californian Ideology," *Mute Magazine,* September 1995, http://www.metamute.org/editorial/articles/californian-ideology.

102. The Electronic Frontier Foundation was founded by Lotus Notes creator Mitch Kapor, cattle rancher and Grateful Dead songwriter John Perry Barlow, and early Sun Microsystems employee John Gilmore. It started out with a vague

mission: to defend people's civil liberties on the Internet and to "find a way of preserving the ideology of the 1960s" in the digital era. From its first days, EFF had deep pockets and featured an impressive roster: Stewart Brand and Apple's Steve Wozniak were board members, while press outreach was conducted by Cathy Cook, who had done public relations for Steve Jobs. It did not take long for EFF to find its calling: lobbying Congress on behalf of the budding Internet service providers that came out of the NSFNET network and pushing for a privatized Internet system, where the government stayed pretty much out of the way—"Designing the Future Net" is how EFF's Barlow described it.

103. Mitch Kapor, "Where Is the Digital Highway Really Heading?" *Wired,* March 1, 1993.

104. Joshua Quittner, "The Merry Pranksters Go to Washington," *Wired,* June 1, 1994.

105. "Thanks in part to a confluence of extraordinary economic, technological, and political currents, its technocentric optimism became a central feature of the biggest stock market bubble in American history. Its faith that the Internet constituted a revolution in human affairs legitimated calls for telecommunications deregulation and the dismantling of government entitlement programs elsewhere as well," remarks Fred Turner in *From Counterculture to Cyberculture* while examining *Wired*'s place in the deregulatory and privatization frenzy of the 1990s.

106. John Perry Barlow, "Jack In, Young Pioneer!" (keynote essay for the 1994 *Computerworld* College Edition, August 11, 1994), https://w2.eff.org/Misc /Publications/John_Perry_Barlow/HTML/jack_in_young_pioneer.html.

107. "Louis Rossetto," *Charlie Rose,* season 1996, episode 01.24.96 (Arlington, VA: PBS, January 24, 1996).

108. Brand, "SPACEWAR."

Chapter 5

1. The story of Sergey Brin's search for terrorists in Google's logs comes from *I'm Feeling Lucky: The Confessions of Google Employee Number 59,* an amazing insider account by former Google employee Douglas Edwards. All direct quotes of Edwards in this chapter come from his book.

2. Vivian Marino, "Searching the Web, Searching the Mind," *New York Times,* December 23, 2001.

3. Google engineer Amit Patel, quoted in Steven Levy, *In the Plex: How Google Thinks, Works, and Shapes Our Lives* (New York: Simon & Schuster, 2011), 46.

4. Douglas Edwards, *I'm Feeling Lucky: The Confessions of Google Employee Number 59* (New York: Houghton Mifflin Harcourt, 2011), chap. 16.

5. President George W. Bush, "Remarks on Improving Counterterrorism Intelligence," the American Presidency Project, University of California, Santa Barbara, February 14, 2003, http://www.presidency.ucsb.edu/ws/index.php?pid=62559.

6. "Guantanamo: Facts and Figures," Human Rights Watch, March 30, 2017, https://www.hrw.org/video-photos/interactive/2017/03/30/guantanamo-facts -and-figures.

7. Edwards, *I'm Feeling Lucky,* chaps. 16, 24.

8. Quoted in John Cassidy, *Dot.Con* (New York: PerfectBound/HarperCollins, 2009), 44.

9. Sean Hollister, "Welcome to Googletown," The Verge, February 26, 2014, https://www.theverge.com/2014/2/26/5444030/company-town-how-google-is -taking-over-mountain-view.

10. Richard L. Brand, *The Google Guys: Inside the Brilliant Minds of Google Founders Larry Page and Sergey Brin* (New York: Portfolio, 2011).

11. Marc Seifer, *Wizard: The Life and Times of Nikola Tesla* (New York: Citadel, 1996).

12. John Battelle, *The Search: How Google and Its Rivals Rewrote the Rules of Business and Transformed Our Culture* (New York: Portfolio, 2005).

13. The Advanced Research Projects Agency (ARPA) went through several minor name changes over the years. The last one took place in 1996, when it gained a *D* and became the Defense Advanced Research Projects Agency (DARPA).

14. Aside from founding the university, Stanford's biggest mark on history was *Santa Clara County v. Southern Pacific,* a lawsuit that his railroad took to the Supreme Court and that yielded the infamous decision endowing corporations— legal fictions granted by the state—with all the Constitutional rights of actual people.

15. Michael S. Malone, *The Big Score: The Billion Dollar Story of Silicon Valley* (New York: Doubleday, 1985).

16. Frederick Terman, the influential head of Stanford's engineering department, was the driving force behind the university's engineering might. He had led MIT's Radio Research Laboratory during World War II and stewed in the same rarified corporate-military-academic brew that schooled and brought up many of the personalities who would later head over to ARPA and create the Internet and the modern computer industry. At Stanford, Terman worked hard to re-create that world. Thanks to him, the university carved out the Stanford Industrial Park from hundreds of adjacent acres and invited computer companies to set up shop.

17. Wolfgang Saxon, "William B. Shockley, 79, Creator of Transistor and Theory on Race," *New York Times,* August 14, 1989.

18. The first ARPANET segment that went online in 1969 connected Stanford University to UCLA.

19. Walter Isaacson, *The Innovators: How a Group of Hackers, Geniuses, and Geeks Created the Digital Revolution* (New York: Simon & Schuster, 2014).

20. Scott J. Simon, "Information Architecture for Digital Libraries," *First Monday* 13, no. 12 (December 2008); Digital Libraries Initiative, homepage, National Science Foundation, 1999, http://web.archive.org/web/20000815090028/ http://www.dli2.nsf.gov/; Terry Winograd's Stanford homepage, 1998, http://web. archive.org/web/19981206032336/http://www-pcd.stanford.edu/~winograd/.

21. Stanford University Digital Libraries Project, homepage, Stanford University, 1998, http://web.archive.org/web/19980124140522/http://www-diglib .stanford.edu/diglib/; Human Computer Interaction Group, homepage, Stanford

University, 1998, http://web.archive.org/web/19980126230453/http://www-pcd
.stanford.edu/html/diglibbodyresearch.html.

22. Other universities that took part in the Digital Libraries Initiative include
UCLA, University of California at Santa Barbara, Carnegie Mellon University, University of Illinois at Urbana–Champaign, and University of Michigan.
At Berkeley, researchers searched and analyzed photographs. Carnegie Mellon
University set up the Informedia Project, where researchers focused on getting
computers to automatically understand and transcribe video content, with the goal
of analyzing video broadcasts on the fly—all of which had uses in education and
health care but also "defense intelligence," according to Carnegie Mellon (Informedia Project homepage, Carnegie Mellon University, http://wayback.archive
.org/web/20040602113005/http://www.informedia.cs.cmu.edu:80/). One such
digital library project, which was funded in part by the navy's Space and Naval
Warfare Systems, sought to create searchable databases of foreign media sources
(Multilingual Informedia, Carnegie Mellon University, http://wayback.archive
.org/web/20040603071038/http://www.informedia.cs.cmu.edu:80/mli/index.html).

23. "Lycos was created in May 1994 by CMU's Dr. Michael Mauldin, working
under a grant from the Defense Advanced Research Projects Agency. Like its predecessors, Lycos deployed a spiderlike crawler to index the Web, but it used more
sophisticated mathematical algorithms to determine the meaning of a page and
answer user queries." Battelle, *The Search,* 53.

24. David Hart, "On the Origins of Google," National Science Foundation, August 17, 2004, https://www.nsf.gov/discoveries/disc_summ.jsp?cntn_id=100660.

25. "Page was not a social animal—those who interacted with him often wondered if there were a dash of Asperger's in the mix—and he could unnerve people
by simply not talking," writes Google biographer Steve Levy in *In the Plex,* 11.

26. Interestingly, multiuser dungeon games, or MUDs, emerged, somewhat
unintentionally, from the ARPANET when an ARPA contractor named Will
Crowther developed them in his off time while going through a divorce. Dennis
G. Jerz, "Somewhere Nearby Is Colossal Cave," *Digital Humanities Quarterly* 1, no.
2 (2007).

27. Quoted in Isaacson, *The Innovators,* 452.

28. Brenna McBride, "The Ultimate Search," *College Park Magazine* (University
of Maryland), Spring 2000.

29. Sergey Brin's Home Page, Stanford University, accessed June 11, 2004,
http://www-db.stanford.edu:80/~sergey/.

30. Battelle, *The Search,* 73.

31. John Ince, "The Lost Google Tapes," January 2000, quoted in Walter Isaacson's *The Innovators,* chap. 11.

32. "It's all recursive. It's all a big circle," Larry Page later explained at a computer forum a few years after launching Google. "Navigating Cyberspace," PC
forum held in Scottsdale, AZ, 2001, quoted in Steven Levy's *In the Plex,* 21.

33. John Battelle, "The Birth of Google," *Wired,* August 1, 2005.

34. Ince, "The Lost Google Tapes," quoted in Isaacson, *The Innovators,* chap. 11.

35. Sergey Brin and Larry Page, "The PageRank Citation Ranking: Bringing Order to the Web," Stanford University InfoLab, January 29, 1998, http://ilpubs .stanford.edu:8090/422/1/1999-66.pdf.

36. Steering Committee on the Changing Nature of Telecommunications/ Information Infrastructure, National Research Council, *The Changing Nature of Telecommunications/Information Infrastructure* (Washington, DC: National Academies Press, 1995).

37. David A. Vise, *The Google Story* (New York: Delacorte Press, 2005).

38. Battelle, *The Search*, 62.

39. Levy, *In the Plex*, 47.

40. Ibid., 48.

41. Alex Chitu, "Google in 2000," Google System, December 28, 2007, https:// googlesystem.blogspot.ru/2007/12/google-in-2000.html#gsc.tab=0.

42. Edwards, *I'm Feeling Lucky*, chap. 11.

43. "Google's Revenue Worldwide from 2002 to 2016 (in Billion U.S. Dollars)," Statista, April 11, 2017, https://www.statista.com/statistics/266206/googles -annual-global-revenue/.

44. "Google Advertising Revenue, Billions of Dollars," Vox, accessed July 6, 2017, https://apps.voxmedia.com/at/vox-google-advertising-revenue/.

45. Sergey Brin and Larry Page also understood that Google was going to change—and in fact needed to change—people's expectations of privacy. As Page told Levy: "There's going to be large changes in the world because of all this stuff. . . . People will have to think before when they publish something online, 'This might be here forever associated with me.' Because Google exists." Levy, *In the Plex*, 173.

46. Edwards, *I'm Feeling Lucky*, chap. 24, "To Larry the risks were too high . . . "

47. Ibid., chap. 24.

48. David A. Vise, "Google to Buy 5% of AOL for $1 Billion," *Washington Post*, December 17, 2005.

49. Michael Barbaro and Tom Zeller Jr., "A Face Is Exposed for AOL Searcher No. 4417749," *New York Times*, August 9, 2006.

50. "Gmail Invites Auctioned on eBay," Geek.com, March 5, 2004, https:// www.geek.com/news/gmail-invites-auctioned-on-ebay-556690/.

51. David Pogue, "State of the Art; Google Mail: Virtue Lies in the In-Box," *New York Times*, May 13, 2004.

52. Initially, to placate privacy fears, Google said that it would not combine users' search history with their email data, but the company backtracked on its promise. Today, all Google data—from email, search, and other services—are combined into one profile. Cecilia Kang, "Google Tracks Consumers' Online Activities across Products, and Users Can't Opt Out," *Washington Post*, January 24, 2012.

53. "Thirty-One Privacy and Civil Liberties Organizations Urge Google to Suspend Gmail," Privacy Rights Clearinghouse, April 6, 2004, updated April 19, 2004, https://www.privacyrights.org/blog/thirty-one-privacy-and-civil-liberties -organizations-urge-google-suspend-gmail.

54. Sarah Elton, "Got a Date Friday? Google Knows," *Maclean's* 119, no. 34 (2006): 56.

55. Krishna Bharat, Stephen Lawrence, Mehran Sahami, and Amit Singhal, "Serving Advertisements Using User Request Information and User Information," EP1634206 A4, patent application, Google Inc., June 1, 2004, https://patentscope. wipo.int/search/en/detail.jsf?docId=WO2004111771; Jeffrey Dean, Georges Harik, and Paul Buchheit, "Serving Advertisements Using Information Associated with E-mail," US20040059712 A1, patent application, Google Inc., June 2, 2003, https:// www.google.com/patents/US20040059712.

56. "Testimony of Chris Jay Hoofnagle, Director, Electronic Privacy Information Center West Coast Office, Privacy Risks of E-mail Scanning," California Senate Judiciary Committee, March 15, 2005, http://web.archive.org /web/20170527221053/https://epic.org/privacy/gmail/casjud3.15.05.html.

57. Jeffrey Rosen, "The Year in Ideas; Total Information Awareness," *New York Times*, December 15, 2002.

58. "Testimony of Chris Jay Hoofnagle."

59. "Now, what does information processing technology have to do with surveillance? A great deal? However, to my knowledge very little information processing technology has been researched and developed as surveillance technology per se," Paul Armer, a scientist at Stanford's Center for Advanced Study in the Behavioral Sciences, explained during congressional hearings on surveillance technology in 1976. "Rather, it has been developed with other motives in mind, like improving business data processing or guiding missiles or getting men to the moon. But surveillance is an information-processing task just as much as a payroll application is. If you improve the efficiency of information-processing technology for payrolls, you improve it for surveillance. Often systems that are put up for other reasons . . . can also serve surveillance." *"Surveillance Technology," Joint Hearings Before the Subcommittee on Constitutional Rights of the Comm. on the Judiciary and the Special Subcommittee on Science, Technology, and Commerce of the Comm. on Commerce, United States Senate,* 94th Cong., 1st sess. (June 23, September 9 and 10, 1975).

60. EPIC, the Electronic Privacy Information Center, which emerged as one of Google's fiercest critics, was concerned that Google did not restrict its email surveillance solely to its registered user base but was intercepting and analyzing the private communication of anyone who exchanged email with a Gmail user. As Gmail use skyrocketed, that meant Google was monitoring the email communication of a significant percentage of the world's Internet population. "Gmail violates the privacy rights of non-subscribers. Non-subscribers who e-mail a Gmail user have 'content extraction' performed on their e-mail even though they have not consented to have their communications monitored, nor may they even be aware that their communications are being analyzed," EPIC warned. The organization pointed out that this practice almost certainly violated California wiretapping statutes, which expressly criminalized the interception of electronic communication without consent of all parties involved. Because Google intercepts the private communication of anyone who emails a Gmail user, the company's surveillance reach went beyond just those people who signed up for its service. Gmail Privacy

FAQ, Electronic Privacy Information Center, accessed July 6, 2017, https://epic .org/privacy/gmail/faq.html.

61. "Figueroa Introduces Bill to Stop Google from Secretly 'Oogling' Private E-mails," Senator Liz Figueroa Press Room, April 21, 2004, http://web.archive.org /web/20041010082011/http://democrats.sen.ca.gov/servlet/gov.ca.senate.democrats .pub.members.memDisplayPress?district=sd10&ID=2102.

62. Levy, *In the Plex*, 176.

63. Edwards, *I'm Feeling Lucky*, chap. 8. "'Bastards!' Larry would exclaim when a blogger raised concerns about user privacy. 'Bastards!' they would say about the press, the politicians, or the befuddled users who couldn't grasp the obvious superiority of the technology behind Google's products."

64. Michael Kirk and Mike Wiser, "United States of Secrets (Part One): The Program," directed by Michael Kirk, *Frontline* (Arlington, VA: PBS, May 13, 2014), short film, http://www.pbs.org/wgbh/frontline/film/united-states-of-secrets/.

65. Levy, *In the Plex*, 177.

66. Ibid., 177–178.

67. Pogue, "Google Mail: Virtue Lies in the In-Box."

68. "Google Goes Public," *New York Times*, August 20, 2004. In documents Google filed with the Securities and Exchange Commission prior to its IPO, the company admitted that people's concerns with privacy posed a danger to its business model. "Our business depends on a strong brand, and if we are not able to maintain and enhance our brand, our business and operating results would be harmed," Google warned potential investors. "People have in the past expressed, and may in the future express, objections to aspects of our products. For example, people have raised privacy concerns relating to the ability of our recently announced Gmail email service to match relevant ads to the content of email messages. . . . Aspects of our future products may raise similar public concerns. Publicity regarding such concerns could harm our brand." Final Prospectus, Google, Securities and Exchange Commission, August 18, 2004, 8, https://www.sec.gov /Archives/edgar/data/1288776/000119312504143377/d424b4.htm.

69. Jeff Brantingham, interview with author conducted at University of California, Los Angeles, October 6, 2014.

70. Erik Lewis, George Mohler, P. Jeffrey Brantingham, and Andrea L. Bertozzi, "Self-Exciting Point Process Models of Civilian Deaths in Iraq," US Army Research Office, 2011, http://www.math.ucla.edu/~bertozzi/papers/iraq .pdf; Andrea L. Bertozzi, Laura M. Smith, Matthew S. Keegan, Todd Wittman, and George O. Mohler, "Systems and Methods for Data Fusion Mapping Estimation" (patent application), US Patent and Trademark Office, November 29, 2011, http://web.archive.org/web/20170528111833/http://patft.uspto.gov/netacgi /nph-Parser?Sect2=PTO1&Sect2=HITOFF&p=1&u=/netahtml/PTO/search -bool.html&r=1&f=G&l=50&d=PALL&RefSrch=yes&Query=PN/8938115.

71. George Mohler, "SacBee Online—PredPol Results in Dramatic Crime Reduction," PredPol, October 16, 2013, https://web.archive.org/web /20170528112408/http://www.predpol.com/sacbee-online-predpol-results-in -dramatic-crime-reduction/.

72. Jamiles Lartey, "Predictive Policing Practices Labeled as 'Flawed' by Civil Rights Coalition," *Guardian*, August 31, 2016.

73. David Robinson and Logan Koepke, *Stuck in a Pattern: Early Evidence on "Predictive Policing" and Civil Rights* (Washington, DC: Upturn, August 2016).

74. Julia Angwin, Jeff Larson, Surya Mattu, and Lauren Kirchner, "Machine Bias: There's Software Used across the Country to Predict Future Criminals. And It's Biased against Blacks," ProPublica, May 23, 2016, https://www.propublica.org/article/machine-bias-risk-assessments-in-criminal-sentencing.

75. Darwin Bond-Graham and Ali Winston, two tenacious investigative journalists from the Bay Area, cast serious doubts about PredPol's claims that its predictive analytics lowered crime rates. Their exposé in the *SF Weekly* showed that the company's biggest achievement was its aggressive marketing strategy: forcing police departments that signed up to use their product to promote PredPol in public. Darwin Bond-Graham and Ali Winston, "All Tomorrow's Crimes: The Future of Policing Looks a Lot Like Good Branding," *SF Weekly*, October 30, 2013.

76. Board of Directors, PredPol, March 20, 2014, http://web.archive.org/web/20140320163346/http://www.predpol.com:80/about/board-of-directors-advisors/; David Ignatius, "The CIA as Venture Capitalist," *Washington Post*, September 29, 1999.

77. Fowler had worked in the Clinton administration and had been involved in several Democratic presidential campaigns, including that of Barack Obama. Donnie Fowler, interview with author, May 5, 2014.

78. That's how it decided to create its hit original show *House of Cards*. "In any business, the ability to see into the future is the killer app, and Netflix may be getting close with 'House of Cards,'" reported the *New York Times*. "Netflix, which has 27 million subscribers in the nation and 33 million worldwide, ran the numbers. It already knew that a healthy share had streamed the work of Mr. Fincher, the director of 'The Social Network,' from beginning to end. And films featuring Mr. Spacey had always done well, as had the British version of 'House of Cards.' With those three circles of interest, Netflix was able to find a Venn diagram intersection that suggested that buying the series would be a very good bet on original programming." David Carr, "Giving Viewers What They Want," *New York Times*, February 24, 2013.

79. Jeff Larson, James Glanz, and Andrew W. Lehren, "Spy Agencies Probe Angry Birds and Other Apps for Personal Data," ProPublica, January 27, 2014, https://www.propublica.org/article/spy-agencies-probe-angry-birds-and-other-apps-for-personal-data.

80. Elizabeth Dwoskin, "Pandora Thinks It Knows If You Are a Republican," *Wall Street Journal*, February 13, 2014.

81. One of the early pieces of software eBay used was developed by a law-enforcement contractor called InfoGlide. It expanded when eBay bought PayPal. Tom Fowler, "Infoglide Will Be Ebay's Cop," *Austin Business Journal*, January 7, 2000.

82. Brad Stone, *The Everything Store: Jeff Bezos and the Age of Amazon* (Boston: Little, Brown, 2013); Jennifer Wills, "7 Ways Amazon Uses Big Data to Stalk You," Investopedia, September 7, 2016, http://www.investopedia.com/articles

/insights/090716/7-ways-amazon-uses-big-data-stalk-you-amzn.asp; Greg
Bensinger, "Amazon Wants to Ship Your Package Before You Buy It," *Wall Street
Journal*, January 17, 2014.

83. Hal Bernton and Susan Kelleher, "Amazon Warehouse Jobs Push Workers
to Physical Limit," *Seattle Times*, April 3, 2012.

84. Dan Frommer, "Amazon Web Services Is Approaching a $10 Billion-a-Year
Business," Recode, April 28, 2016, https://www.recode.net/2016/4/28/11586526
/aws-cloud-revenue-growth.

85. Went on a buck-hunting trip with your grandson? A Republican candidate
could target you for gun-rights ads. Belong to an evangelical Bible study group?
Maybe the candidate will show you something about fighting abortion instead.
Facebook allowed politicians to target voters with laser precision on the basis of
information they had never been able to collect before. This profiling system was
so powerful that Barack Obama's 2008 campaign hired Facebook cofounder Chris
Hughes to run its Internet division, and in the end it helped Obama win the presidency. The company had such an impact on the race that pundits took to calling
2008 the "Facebook Election," although now every election is a Facebook election.
"There's a level of precision that doesn't exist in any other medium," Crystal Pat-
terson, a Facebook employee who works with government and politics customers,
told the *New York Times*. "It's getting the right message to the right people at the
right time." Ashley Parker, "Facebook Expands in Politics, and Campaigns Find
Much to Like," *New York Times*, July 29, 2015.

86. By the end of 2016, more than half of American adults logged into Facebook
every day. Robinson Meyer, "Facebook Is America's Favorite Media Product," *The
Atlantic*, November 11, 2016; Alexei Oreskovic, "Facebook Now Gets Almost $20
from Each US and Canadian User, Compared to under $5 at Its IPO," *Business
Insider*, February 1, 2017.

87. "Uber's use of Greyball was recorded on video in late 2014, when Erich England, a code enforcement inspector in Portland, [Oregon,] tried to hail an Uber
car downtown in a sting operation against the company. But unknown to Mr.
England and other authorities, some of the digital cars they saw in the app did not
represent actual vehicles. And the Uber drivers they were able to hail also quickly
canceled. That was because Uber had tagged Mr. England and his colleagues—
essentially Greyballing them as city officials—based on data collected from the
app and in other ways. The company then served up a fake version of the app,
populated with ghost cars, to evade capture." Mike Isaac, "How Uber Deceives
the Authorities Worldwide," *New York Times*, March 3, 2017.

88. Antonio Regalado, "Google's Long, Strange Life-Span Trip," *MIT Technology Review*, December 15, 2016.

89. James Vincent, "99.6 Percent of New Smartphones Run Android or iOS,"
The Verge, February 16, 2017, https://www.theverge.com/2017/2/16/14634656
/android-ios-market-share-blackberry-2016; James Vincent, "Android Is Now
Used by 1.4 Billion People," The Verge, September 29, 2015, https://www.theverge
.com/2015/9/29/9409071/google-android-stats-users-downloads-sales.

90. Ross Miller, "Gmail Now Has 1 Billion Monthly Active Users," The Verge, February 1, 2016, https://www.theverge.com/2016/2/1/10889492 /gmail-1-billion-google-alphabet.

91. Jacob Kastrenakes, "Google Reportedly Accounts for 25 Percent of North American Internet Traffic," The Verge, July 22, 2013, https://www.theverge .com/2013/7/22/4545304/google-represents-quarter-web-traffic-deepfield-analysis.

92. About 87 percent of Google revenue (or about $79.4 billion) came from advertising. Alphabet Inc., "Form 10-K for the Fiscal Year Ended December 31, 2016," https://abc.xyz/investor/pdf/2016_google_annual_report.pdf.

93. Jonathan Taplin, "Is It Time to Break Up Google?" *New York Times,* April 22, 2017; "Google's Revenue Worldwide from 2002 to 2016 (in Billion U.S. Dollars)," Statista, April 11, 2017, https://www.statista.com/statistics /266206/googles-annual-global-revenue/; "Google Advertising Revenue, Billions of Dollars," Vox, accessed January 5, 2017, https://apps.voxmedia.com/at /vox-google-advertising-revenue/.

94. Derek Thompson, "Google's CEO: The Laws Are Written by Lobbyists," *The Atlantic,* October 1, 2010.

95. Par Po Bronson, *The Nudist on the Lateshift and Other Tales of Silicon Valley* (New York: Random House, 1999); Evan Ratliff, "The Whole Earth, Catalogued," *Wired,* July 2007.

96. Avi Bar-Zeev, "Notes on the Origin of Google Earth," Reality Prime, July 24, 2006, http://www.realityprime.com/blog/2006/07/notes-on-the-origin -of-google-earth/.

97. Jerome S. Engel, ed., *Global Clusters of Innovation: Entrepreneurial Engines of Economic Growth Around the World* (Cheltenham, UK: Edward Elger, 2014), 57.

98. John T. Reinert, "In-Q-Tel: The Central Intelligence Agency as Venture Capitalist," *Northwestern Journal of International Law & Business* 33, no. 3 (Spring 2013).

99. David Ignatius, "The CIA as Venture Capitalist," *Washington Post,* September 29, 1999.

100. Tim Shorrock, *Spies for Hire: The Secret World of Intelligence Outsourcing* (New York: Simon & Schuster, 2008).

101. "CIA's Impact on Technology," Central Intelligence Agency, published July 23, 2012, updated February 18, 2014, https://www.cia.gov/about-cia/cia-museum /experience-the-collection/text-version/stories/cias-impact-on-technology.html.

102. Three months after the start of the war, and just four months after investing in Keyhole, In-Q-Tel announced that the company's EarthViewer program was already being put to active use in the Iraq War. "Immediately demonstrating the value of Keyhole's technology to the national security community, [the NGA] used the technology to support United States troops in Iraq," read the In-Q-Tel press release, touting the speed with which Keyhole had been adopted by the military as a measure of In-Q-Tel's investment prowess. "In-Q-Tel Announces Strategic Investment in Keyhole," press release, In-Q-Tel, June 25, 2003, https://www .iqt.org/in-q-tel-announces-strategic-investment-in-keyhole/.

103. "In-Q-Tel invested in Keyhole because it offers government and commercial users a new capability to radically enhance critical decision making. Through its ability to stream very large geospatial datasets over the Internet and private networks, Keyhole has created an entirely new way to interact with earth imagery and feature data," explained Gilman Louie, the In-Q-Tel CEO and former video game entrepreneur famous for being the first person to license Tetris from the Soviet Union and release it in the United States. Ibid.

104. Ratliff, "Whole Earth, Catalogued."

105. Ibid.

106. The transaction continues to exist in a fog of secrecy. My attempts to use a Freedom of Information Act request to force the CIA to divulge the terms of its contract with Google were met with an answer straight out of a Tom Clancy novel. The CIA coolly informed me that it "could not confirm or deny" any of the information I sought. That is: the mere existence or nonexistence of any documents relating to the agency's involvement in the sale of Keyhole to Google is itself a secret. This is what's known as a GLOMAR response, named after the agency's refusal, in the mid-1970s, to confirm or deny the existence of a secret boat called the *Glomar Explorer* built to retrieve a sunken Soviet nuclear submarine. The CIA won't talk about the sale, nor will Google. But there are a few things we do know for certain: in 2005, a year after Google went public, In-Q-Tel sold 5,636 shares of Google stock for $2.18 million—potentially representing the shares it received as part of Google's buyout of Keyhole.

107. John Letzing, "Google, Seeking to Diversify, Looks to Uncle Sam," MarketWatch, March 13, 2008, http://www.marketwatch.com/story/google-seeking -to-diversify-looks-to-government-contracts; Rob Painter's profile, LinkedIn, accessed February 17, 2016, https://www.linkedin.com/in/ripainter.

108. Edwards, *I'm Feeling Lucky,* chap. 26.

109. Some examples: Shannon Sullivan, Head of Defense and Intelligence, Google Enterprise. He graduated from the US Air Force Air University's School of Advanced Air and Space Studies, which prides itself on producing "warrior-scholars." He then served in various signals intelligence capacities in the US Air Force, including overseeing the procurement and acquisition of "command, control, communications, computers, intelligence, surveillance and reconnaissance" technology. After the air force, he took the revolving door into the private sector—first at BEA Systems and then at Oracle. Then there's Jim Young, an enterprise manager on the Google DoD sales team, who came out of the CIA's Directorate of Science and Technology, which functioned as the agency's own ARPA and was responsible for creating In-Q-Tel.

110. In February 2007, Google held a big event at the Ritz-Carlton in McLean, about five miles away from CIA headquarters, to showcase its products and announce its entry into the field. "The search engine giant showed off its ambition yesterday to expand its business with the federal government, kicking off a two-day sales meeting that attracted nearly 200 federal contractors, engineers and uniformed military members eager to learn more about its technology offerings.

Google has ramped up its sales force in the Washington area in the past year to adapt its technology products to the needs of the military, civilian agencies and the intelligence community. Already, agencies use enhanced versions of Google's 3-D mapping product, Google Earth, to display information for the military on the ground in Iraq and to track airplanes that fight forest fires across the country." Sara Kehaulani Goo and Alec Klein, "Google Searches for Government Work," *Washington Post,* February 28, 2007.

iii. Letzing, "Google, Seeking to Diversify."

112. Goo and Klein, "Google Searches for Government Work."

113. "Spy agencies are using Google equipment as the backbone of Intellipedia, a network aimed at helping agents share intelligence. Rather than hoarding information, spies and analysts are being encouraged to post what they learn on a secure online forum where colleagues can read it and add comments," reported the *San Francisco Chronicle.* "Google supplies the computer servers that support the network, as well as the search software that allows users to sift through messages and data." Verne Kopytoff, "Google Has Lots to Do with Intelligence," *San Francisco Chronicle,* March 30, 2008.

114. Shannon Sullivan, "U.S. Army to Cut Costs, Improve Collaboration and Go Mobile with Google Apps," Google Cloud (blog), October 22, 2013, https://cloud.googleblog.com/2013/10/us-army-to-cut-costs-improve.html.

115. "NGA has made a significant investment in Google Earth technology through the GEOINT Visualization Services Program on SECRET and TOP SECRET government networks and throughout the world in support of the National System for Geospatial Expeditionary Architecture," explained the NGA. "The NSG, DoD, and Intelligence Community have made additional investments to support client and application deployment and testing that use the existing Google Earth services provided by NGA." "Geospatial Visualization Enterprise Services," Federal Business Opportunities, August 25, 2010, https://web.archive.org/web/20170528171729/https://www.fbo.gov/index?s=opportunity&mode=form&id=482ab868878ecd0bd81d978216718820&tab=core&tabmode=list.

116. Information on Google's government work comes from my analysis of two government sources: (1) a list of Google contracts from 2003 through 2014 obtained from the Federal Procurement Data System, https://www.fpds.gov (A copy of the saved data set can be obtained here: https://surveillancevalley.com/content/citations/google-contracts-2003–2014-federal-procurement-data-system.csv.) and (2) Google contract data contained in the federal government spending database USAspending.gov, which shows that the company has been involved in 1,934 federal contracts from 2008 through the first half of 2017, both as a prime contractor and a subcontractor, for a total of $224 million. It is important to note that this amount represents only a part of the work Google does for the federal government; the database excludes classified contracts. USAspending.gov, https://www.usaspending.gov/Pages/AdvancedSearch.aspx?k=google.

117. Yasha Levine, "Google Distances Itself from the Pentagon, Stays in Bed with Mercenaries and Intelligence Contractors," *Pando Daily,* March 26, 2014,

https://pando.com/2014/03/26/google-distances-itself-from-the-pentagon
-stays-in-bed-with-mercenaries-and-intelligence-contractors/.

118. Shorrock, *Spies for Hire,* chap. 1, "But whatever one's position on outsourc-ing, there is little doubt that spying for hire has become a way of life in twenty-first-century America . . . "

119. Phil Goldstein, "2017 Budget Boosts IT Spending to $89.9 Billion, Expands U.S. Digital Service," FedTech, February 9, 2016.

120. Google was perfectly suited to succeed as a government and military contractor. Google Search, which originally came out of a DARPA and federal government research program aimed at finding a better way to organize and find information in the chaos of the Internet, is second to none. Naturally, the CIA, NSA, and other federal agencies would want to use it. It was the same with Goo-gle Earth, whose development was carried out under top-secret programs by mil-itary and intelligence agencies. As the company broadened its reach, expanding into email, word processing, databases, cloud hosting, mobile platforms, brows-ers, navigation aids, and cloud-based laptops, military and intelligence agencies bought hardened versions of these tools as well. Indeed, G Suite offers advanced versions of all the collaborative communication tools that J. C. R. Licklider had worked hard to develop as part of his ARPA Command and Control Research program that gave birth to the ARPANET.

121. Ellen Nakashima, "Google to Enlist NSA to Help It Ward Off Cyberat-tacks," *Washington Post,* February 4, 2010.

122. Shane Harris, *@War: The Rise of the Military-Internet Complex* (New York: Eamon Dolan/Houghton Mifflin Harcourt, 2014).

123. "NOAA Announces Agency-Wide Move to Cloud-Based Unified Mes-saging Technology," press release, National Oceanic and Atmospheric Adminis-tration, June 8, 2011, http://www.noaanews.noaa.gov/stories2011/20110609_cloud technology.html.

124. Bill Oates, "Boston Moves 76,000 City Employees, Police, Teachers and Students to the Cloud with Google Apps," Google Cloud (blog), January 6, 2014, https://cloud.googleblog.com/2014/01/boston-moves-76000-city-employees.html.

125. Kirsty Styles, "New York Has Just Opened a Massive Public Spying Net-work," The Next Web, March 22, 2016, https://thenextweb.com/us/2016/03/22 /new-york-just-opened-massive-public-spying-network/#.tnw_1Ahf9OCG.

126. Ron Demeter, "California Selects Pondera Solutions FDaaS as High-Tech Solution to Prevent Unemployment Insurance Fraud," Pondera, October 15, 2014, http://www.prweb.com/releases/2014/10/prweb12249931.htm.

127. Natasha Singer, "How Google Took Over the Classroom," *New York Times,* May 13, 2017.

128. The event was called the "Geospatial Conference of the West" and took place in September 2013.

129. Martha Neil, "Does Using Gmail Put Attorney-Client Privilege at Risk?" *ABA Journal,* October 8, 2014.

130. Google has faced a number of privacy-related investigations and lawsuits over the last decade—for collecting people's WiFi with its Street View vehicles to accusations that it violated wiretapping laws by scanning emails of non-Gmail users without consent. Many of these lawsuits and investigations have focused attention on the company's duplicitousness and evasiveness when talking about privacy and data gathering. For example: a 2016 lawsuit by a group of University of California, Berkeley, alumni and students alleged that the company misled them when it made promises that it would not scan educational account emails, but it turned out that Google had been doing it anyway. The company later promised to stop scanning the emails for "advertising purposes," but the wording of the promise that focused narrowly on "advertising" left the company an opening to nonetheless collect the data for profiling that was not specifically tied to showing ads. At the time of this writing, this lawsuit against Google is still in litigation (Emma Brown, "UC-Berkeley Students Sue Google, Alleging Their Emails Were Illegally Scanned," *Washington Post,* February 1, 2016). In another case, in 2017, Mississippi's attorney general believed he had no other recourse but to take Google to court for the company's answer to basic questions about how it handled data for students who used its Google Classroom products. "Through this lawsuit, we want to know the extent of Google's data mining and marketing of student information to third parties," Jim Hood said. "I don't think there could be any motivation other than greed for a company to deliberately keep secret how it collects and uses student information" (Benjamin Herold, "Mississippi Attorney General Sues Google over Student-Data Privacy," *Education Week,* January 19, 2017).

131. Jack Goldsmith and Tim Wu, *Who Controls the Internet? Illusions of a Borderless World* (New York: Oxford University Press, 2006).

132. Mark Ames, "Team Omidyar, World Police: eBay Puts User Data on a Silver Platter for Law Enforcement," *Pando Daily,* December 14, 2013, https://pando.com/2013/12/14/team-omidar-world-police-ebay-puts-user-data-on-a-silver-platter-for-law-enforcement/.

133. Bill Brenner, "eBay Security Offensive Leads to 3K Arrests Globally," *CSO,* August 6, 2012.

134. Frank Konkel, "The Details About the CIA's Deal with Amazon," *The Atlantic,* July 17, 2014.

135. Even before the CIA deal, Amazon had hundreds of government clients, including military agencies. "There have been more than 600 government agencies worldwide that are using AWS. The Navy has put its non-classified information on AWS and is spending half of what it was spending before. NASA JPL uses it for the Mars Exploration Rover. There's this rover on Mars that is taking pictures and sending them back to JPL to process and assess what else they want pictures of and where they want the rover to go. And that's all done on AWS. The Obama campaign used AWS, and over 18 months built 200 applications. On election day they built a call center, they built an elaborate database to know where their volunteers were, know the neighborhoods where people appeared not to have voted, so they could go knock on doors and get out the vote," Andy

Jassy, head of Amazon Web Services, told *All Things Digital*. "Nine Questions for Andy Jassy, Head of Amazon Web Services," *All Things Digital*, November 8, 2013, https://web.archive.org/web/20170528161820/http://allthingsd.com/20131108/nine-questions-for-andy-jassy-head-of-amazon-web-services/comment-page-1/.

136. Adi Robertson, "Jeff Bezos' Blue Origin Partners with Boeing and Lockheed Martin to Reduce Dependence on Russian Rockets," The Verge, September 17, 2014, https://www.theverge.com/2014/9/17/6328961/jeff-bezos-blue-origin-partners-with-united-launch-alliance-for-new-rocket.

137. Andy Greenberg, "How a 'Deviant' Philosopher Built Palantir, a CIA-Funded Data-Mining Juggernaut," *Forbes*, August 14, 2013.

138. "The genre of people that Cyber Command are working to recruit are fresh out of high school and college. They're going to grow up with Oculus on their head. We want to adapt to provide that kind of interface," an excited DARPA program manager told *Wired* magazine. "You're not in a two-dimensional view, so you can look around the data. You look to your left, look to your right, and see different subnets of information. With the Oculus you have that immersive environment. It's like you're swimming in the internet." Andy Greenberg, "Darpa Turns Oculus into a Weapon for Cyberwar," *Wired*, May 23, 2014.

139. Ellen Nakashima, "With Plan X, Pentagon Seeks to Spread U.S. Military Might to Cyberspace," *Washington Post*, May 30, 2012; "DARPA's Plan X Gives Military Operators a Place to Wage Cyber Warfare," *DoD News*, May 12, 2016.

140. The satellite was launched on September 6, 2008, from Vandenberg Air Force Base, sixty miles north of Santa Barbara, California. The Lockheed Martin missile carrying it into orbit featured a Google logo ("GeoEye-1 Launch," GeoEye Inc., September 6, 2008, https://www.evernote.com/shard/s1/sh/95c0825e-f4ff-4aa1-a006-3fee03b906bb/6762d77427700979). The Lockheed Martin missile carried a 4,300-pound private spy satellite called *GeoEye-1*, a three-way between Google, a satellite military contractor called GeoEye, and the NGA. *GeoEye-1* was a novel venture between the Pentagon and the private sector. Half financed by the government, it was the most accurate commercial imaging satellite on the market. It would provide high-resolution satellite photos for the exclusive use of the NGA, while giving slightly lower quality versions of the same images to Google. "We're commercializing a technology that was once only in the hands of the governments," a GeoEye spokesman told the press. "Just like the internet, just like GPS, just like telecom [were] all invented by the government. And now we are on the front end of the spear that is commercializing this technology" (Brian X. Chen, "Google's Super Satellite Captures First Image," *Wired*, October 8, 2008).

141. John Markoff, "Google Adds to Its Menagerie of Robots," *New York Times*, December 14, 2013; Alex Hern, "Alphabet Sells Off 'BigDog' Robot Maker Boston Dynamics to Softbank," *Guardian*, June 9, 2017.

142. Yasha Levine, "From Russia, with Panic: Cozy Bears, Unsourced Hacks—and a Silicon Valley Shakedown," The Baffler, March 2017, https://thebaffler.com/salvos/from-russia-with-panic-levine.

143. Started as Google Ideas in 2010, it was rebranded as JigSaw in 2016. Eric Schmidt described its mission when announcing the name change. "Jigsaw will be investing in and building technology to expand access to information for the world's most vulnerable populations and to defend against the world's most challenging security threats." Eric Schmidt, "Google Ideas Becomes Jigsaw," @jigsaw, Medium, February 16, 2016.

144. Jared Cohen got his start in foreign policy under President George W. Bush, when he served as an adviser to Secretary of State Condoleezza Rice as part of the State Department's Policy Planning Staff (Christina Larson, "State Department Innovator Goes to Google," Foreign Policy, September 7, 2010, http://foreign policy.com/2010/09/07/state-department-innovator-goes-to-google/). Under Secretary of State Hillary Clinton, Cohen was charged with handling the "21st Century Statecraft" portfolio, figuring out how Silicon Valley and the Internet could be brought to bear on American foreign policy (Jesse Lichtenstein, "Condi's Party Starter," *The New Yorker*, November 5, 2007). Cohen's first big moment in digital diplomacy took place in 2009: a sustained wave of youth protests was taking place in Tehran at the time in response to the country's presidential elections, and Twitter was being used by protesters to organize and coordinate their activities. In the midst of the protests, Twitter announced that it planned to take the site down for scheduled maintenance. The State Department wanted to keep those lines of communication open, hoping that this was finally the mass movement that would topple the Islamic Republic of Iran. Cohen dropped Jack Dorsey, the CEO of Twitter, a note: "It appears Twitter is playing an important role at a crucial time in Iran. Could you keep it going?" Dorsey said sure, and Twitter put its scheduled maintenance on hold while protests in Iran continued. The *New York Times* got wind of this exchange and published a story, writing, "The episode demonstrates the extent to which the administration views social networking as a new arrow in its diplomatic quiver. Secretary of State Hillary Rodham Clinton talks regularly about the power of e-diplomacy, particularly in places where the mass media are repressed" ("Washington Taps into a Potent New Force in Diplomacy," *New York Times*, June 16, 2009).

145. *Fiscal Year 2015 Congressional Budget Request* (Washington, DC: Broadcasting Board of Governors, 2014), https://www.bbg.gov/wp-content/media/2014/03/FY-2015-BBG-Congressional-Budget-Request-FINAL-21-March-2014.pdf; "Google Ideas Develops Citizen Engagement Pilot Project for Somalia," Google Open Source (blog), June 11, 2012, https://opensource.googleblog.com/2012/06/google-ideas-develops-citizen.html. "Google Ideas collaborated with a State Department–funded startup on the development of a VPN proxy network called uProxy that masks the identities of internet users in oppressive countries by swapping their IP addresses with users in the West," according to the Google Transparency Project. "Google's Support for Hillary Clinton," Google Transparency Project, November 28, 2016, http://www.googletransparencyproject.org/articles/googles-support-hillary-clinton.

146. Andy Greenberg, "Google's Clever Plan to Stop Aspiring ISIS Recruits," *Wired*, September 7, 2016; email from Jared Cohen, "Re: Following-up on the digital counter-insurgency," August 13, 2015, WikiLeaks, John Podesta Email Archive.

147. A good roundup of overlap between JigSaw and the State Department was compiled by the Google Transparency Project. "Google's Support for Hillary Clinton," November 28, 2016.

148. Email from Jared Cohen, "Syria," July 25, 2012, WikiLeaks, Hillary Clinton Email Archive. "Please keep close hold, but my team is planning to launch a tool on Sunday that will publicly track and map the defections in Syria and which parts of the government they are coming from . . . which we believe are important in encouraging more to defect and giving confidence to the opposition," Cohen wrote Hillary Clinton's deputy secretary of state William Joseph Burns in a 2012 email.

149. As Julian Assange wryly noted in *When Google Met WikiLeaks*, "If Blackwater/Xe Services/Academi was running a program like [JigSaw], it would draw intense critical scrutiny. But somehow Google gets a free pass." Julian Assange, *When Google Met WikiLeaks* (New York: OR Books, 2014).

150. Yazan al-Saadi, "StratforLeaks: Google Ideas Director Involved in 'Regime Change,'" Al-Akhbar English, March 14, 2012; Doug Bolton, "Google Planned to Help Syria Rebels to Bring Down Assad Regime, Leaked Hillary Clinton Emails Claim," *The Independent*, March 22, 2016, http://www.independent.co.uk /life-style/gadgets-and-tech/news/google-syria-rebels-defection-hillary-clinton -emails-wikileaks-a6946121.html.

151. Fred Burton was referring to information he got from a Google executive about Jared Cohen's plan to visit the United Arab Emirates, Azerbaijan, and Turkey as part of his plan to "engage the Iranian community to better understand the challenges faced by Iranians as part of one of our Google Ideas groups on repressive societies." Burton's email was just one in a series of letters that referred to Jared Cohen and JigSaw (Google Ideas) as possibly engaging in veiled "regime change" operations—from Iran to Egypt, Syria, and Libya. The emails were leaked following the penetration of Stratfor's servers by a group that called itself Anonymous. "On Saturday, hackers who say they are members of the collective known as Anonymous claimed responsibility for crashing the Web site of the group, Stratfor Global Intelligence Service, and pilfering its client list, e-mails and credit card information in an operation they say is intended to steal $1 million for donations to charity," reported the *New York Times* in December 2011. "Hackers Breach the Web Site of Stratfor Global Intelligence," *New York Times*, December 25, 2011.

152. Andy Greenberg, "Inside Google's Internet Justice League and Its AI-Powered War on Trolls," *Wired*, September 19, 2016.

153. Richard Waters, "FT Interview with Google Co-founder and CEO Larry Page," *Financial Times*, October 31, 2014.

154. Eric Schmidt and Jared Cohen saw the role of technology companies as taking over the traditional functions of governments. "Democratic states that have built coalitions of their militaries have the capacity to do the same with their connection technologies. This is not to suggest that connection technologies are going

to transform the world alone. But they offer a new way to exercise the duty to protect citizens around the world," the pair explained in *The New Digital Age,* a book they cowrote. They didn't really see a difference between government and Google. They saw all these parts—entertainment, search, office products, military contracting, fighting terrorism, policing—as part of a bigger whole, working together for mutual benefit. Eric Schmidt and Jared Cohen, *The New Digital Age: Transforming Nations, Businesses, and Our Lives* (New York: Alfred A. Knopf, 2013).

155. Richard Waters, "Google Eyes Better City Life for Billions," *Financial Times,* June 11, 2015.

156. Matt Novak, "Google's Parent Company (Probably) Wants to Build a City from Scratch," Gizmodo, April 5, 2016, http://paleofuture.gizmodo.com /google-s-parent-company-probably-wants-to-build-a-cit-1769181473.

157. Tony Fadell, a former Apple executive and a connected-device guru who works as a personal adviser to Larry Page, sketched one vision of a future where Google's technology benevolently ruled over and mediated everything and everyone in the world. "Tomorrow's Internet will be everywhere and in everything. It will draw on massive amounts of data to augment our own intelligence. And it will help us make better decisions—from avoiding dangerous drug interactions to diagnosing illnesses to deciding when water skiing might not be the best idea. . . . Finally, the Internet of the future will go from doing things *when* we ask to doing things *before* we ask." He then drew on a personal story of how he tore his hamstring while waterskiing to illustrate how a ubiquitous Google could be used to predict and prevent harm. "In the case of my water-skiing accident, my smartphone could have combined existing information . . . to predict that I was considering water skiing, calculate the odds of my getting injured, and advise me against it before I even got in the water. Or, if I was stubborn enough to do it anyway, a computer controlling the boat's throttle could have prevented the engine from pulling me too hard." Who would write the rules and laws in this hyperconnected future? How would people make their voices heard? Who would own all those sensors and controllers embedded in our hamstrings and boats? Fadell didn't address these issues. His vision seemed to take for granted that this new world would be kind and safe. Tony Fadell, "Nest CEO Tony Fadell on the Future of the Internet," *Wall Street Journal,* April 26, 2015.

Chapter 6

1. Glenn Greenwald, Ewen MacAskill, and Laura Poitras, "Edward Snowden: The Whistleblower behind the NSA Surveillance Revelations," *Guardian,* June 11, 2013.

2. Ewen MacAskill, "Edward Snowden, NSA Files Source: 'If They Want to Get You, in Time They Will,'" *Guardian,* June 10, 2013.

3. David T. Z. Mindich, "Lincoln's Surveillance State," *New York Times,* July 5, 2013.

4. "They stressed that the system did not perform any actual surveillance, but rather was designed to use data which had been collected in 'the real world' to help

build predictive models which might warn when civil disturbances were imminent," writes Ford Rowan, the NBC correspondent who broke the ARPANET spying story. Ford Rowan, *Technospies* (New York: G. P. Putnam's Sons, 1978), 55.

5. K. Babe Howell, "Gang Policing: The Post Stop-and-Frisk Justification for Profile-Based Policing," *University of Denver Criminal Law Review* 5 (2015), http://academicworks.cuny.edu/cgi/viewcontent.cgi?article=1067&context=cl_pubs; Ben Popper, "How the NYPD Is Using Social Media to Put Harlem Teens behind Bars," The Verge, December 10, 2014, https://www.theverge.com/2014/12/10/7341077/nypd-harlem-crews-social-media-rikers-prison.

6. "Police in Md. Using Social Media Facial Recognition to Track Suspects," CBS Baltimore, October 19, 2016, http://baltimore.cbslocal.com/2016/10/18/police-in-md-using-social-media-facial-recognition-to-track-suspects/.

7. CI Publishing, homepage, accessed May 1, 2017, https://gumroad.com/cipublishing.

8. From the FBI to the Department of Homeland Security, in one way or another, every federal security agency tapped "open source" Internet data to carry out its mission. For instance, the Department of Homeland Security routinely used social media for investigating people applying for American citizenship. "Narcissistic tendencies in many people fuels a need to have a large group of 'friends' link to their pages and many of these people accept cyber-friends that they don't even know. . . . Once a user posts online, they create a public record and timeline of their activities. In essence, using MySpace and other like sites is akin to doing an unannounced cyber 'site-visit' on petitioners and beneficiaries." "Social Networking Sites and Their Importance to FDN," US Citizenship and Immigration Services, obtained via Freedom of Information Act by EFF, July 2010.

9. "We're looking at YouTube, which carries some unique and honest-to-goodness intelligence," Doug Naquin, director of the Open Source Center, said in 2007. "We're looking at chat rooms and things that didn't exist five years ago, and trying to stay ahead. . . . A lot more is digital, and a lot more is online. It's also a lot more social. Interaction is a much bigger part of media and news than it used to be." *"Remarks by Doug Naquin, Director, Open Source Center,* CIRA Luncheon, 3 October 2007," *Central Intelligence Retirees Association Newsletter* CCCII, no. 4 (Winter 2007), https://fas.org/irp/eprint/naquin.pdf.

10. "Establishment of the DNI Open Source Center," Central Intelligence Agency, November 8, 2005, https://www.cia.gov/news-information/press-releases-statements/press-release-archive-2005/pr11082005.html.

11. Lee Fang, "The CIA Is Investing in Firms That Mine Your Tweets and Instagram Photos," The Intercept, April 14, 2016, https://theintercept.com/2016/04/14/in-undisclosed-cia-investments-social-media-mining-looms-large/.

12. Gerry Smith, "How Police Are Scanning All of Twitter to Detect Terrorist Threats," *Huffington Post,* June 25, 2014, http://www.huffingtonpost.com/2014/06/25/dataminr-mines-twitter-to_n_5507616.html.

13. In 2014, police departments all across the country used it. Indeed, at the same time that Oakland was trying to push through the Domain Awareness

Center, the city's police department purchased a Geofeedia license and used it to monitor protests, including the Black Lives Matter movement. "Social media monitoring is spreading fast and is a powerful example of surveillance technology that can disproportionately impact communities of color," warned the American Civil Liberties Union, which obtained a copy of Geofeedia's marketing materials to law enforcement. "We know for a fact that in Oakland and Baltimore, law enforcement has used Geofeedia to monitor protests." Matt Cagle, "Facebook, Instagram and Twitter Provided Data Access for a Surveillance Product Marketed to Target Activists of Color," ACLU, October 11, 2016, https://www.aclunc.org/blog/facebook-instagram-and-twitter-provided-data-access-surveillance-product-marketed-target.

14. "Usage Overview," Geofeedia (company promotional materials obtained by the ACLU, September 2016).

15. Following the ACLU's exposure of Geofeedia's police contracting work, Facebook and other Internet companies announced that they cut the company off from access to their data. But other similar companies continue to proliferate. "Social Media Surveillance Is Growing in the Wake of Geofeedia's Demise," MuckRock, May 17, 2017, https://www.muckrock.com/news/archives/2017/may/17/social-media-surveillance-growing/.

16. Noah Shachtman, "Air Force's Top Brain Wants a Social Radar to See into Hearts and Minds," *Wired*, January 19, 2012; Mark T. Maybury, "Social Radar for Smart Power," MITRE Corporation, April 2010, https://www.mitre.org/publications/technical-papers/social-radar-for-smart-power. Just like the radar air defense systems, whose ultimate goal is to scramble jets or fire missiles to intercept hostile aircraft before they have time to inflict damage, the Internet-based predictive systems were also aimed at heading off threats. As Mark Maybury, who headed the US Air Force's Social Radar project, explained in 2010: the physical "intercept" component of human radar systems would sometimes be direct physical action—like missile strikes—but at other times it would be social and psychological. Rather than force, it would be a nudge and a push that would guide people in the right direction. "While hard power will always play a key role in warfare, increasingly soft power, the ability to not coerce but to encourage or motivate behavior, will be necessary in the future of our increasingly connected and concentrated global village," he wrote. Maybury, "Social Radar for Smart Power."

17. George I. Seffers, "Decoding the Future for National Security," Signal, December 1, 2015, http://www.afcea.org/content/?q=Article-decoding-future-national-security; "Anticipatory Intelligence," IARPA, accessed April 16, 2017, https://www.iarpa.gov/index.php/about-iarpa/anticipatory-intelligence; Katie Drummond, "Spies Want to Stockpile Your YouTube Clips," *Wired*, June 11, 2010.

18. Noah Shachtman, "Pentagon Forecast: Cloudy, 80% Chance of Riots," *Wired*, September 11, 2007.

19. "It's now being used by various parts of the government. We've had good success at forecasting different types of unrest and different sorts of motivations for that unrest," a Lockheed Martin manager said in 2015. He explained that the

system was constantly evolving and being trained to predict future events in as much detail as possible—not just whether there would be an uprising but also the exact week and the number of people involved. Sandra Jontz, "Data Analytics Programs Help Predict Global Unrest," *Signal,* December 1, 2015, https://www.afcea.org /content/?q=node/15501/.

20. James Risen and Laura Poitras, "N.S.A. Gathers Data on Social Connections of U.S. Citizens," *New York Times,* September 28, 2013. Actually, the NSA mostly sticks to planning and funding, while much of the actual building is done by private military contractors and Silicon Valley itself. Tim Shorrock, "How Private Contractors Have Created a Shadow NSA," *The Nation,* May 27, 2015.

21. David Burnham, "The Silent Power of the N.S.A.," *New York Times,* March 27, 1983.

22. Transcripts of Ford Rowan's June 1975 NBC broadcasts were read into the *Congressional Record.* "*Surveillance Technology,*" *Joint Hearings Before the Subcommittee on Constitutional Rights,* 4–9.

23. Janet Abbate, *Inventing the Internet* (Cambridge, MA: MIT Press, 1999), 134, 234; Matt Novak, "A History of Internet Spying, Part 2," *Gizmodo,* February 20, 2015, http://gizmodo.com/a-history-of-internet-spying-part-2-1686760364.

24. The NSA was also involved in ARPANET development in other ways. For instance: in 1975, the NSA worked with Vinton Cerf on a classified project to design a "fully secured internet system" based on the ARPANET. *Oral History of Vinton (Vint) Cerf, Interviewed by Donald Nielson (*Mountain View, CA: Computer History Museum, November 7, 2007), 20, http://archive.computerhistory.org /resources/access/text/2012/04/102658186-05-01-acc.pdf.

25. The NSA even grabbed users' targeted advertising data—age, gender, household income, marital status, sexual orientation, ethnicity, political alignment—that was being compiled and transmitted by what agency analysts mockingly described as "leaky" mobile apps, including addictive kids' games like Angry Birds. Larson, Glanz, and Lehren, "Spy Agencies Probe Angry Birds."

26. Barton Gellman and Ashkan Soltani, "NSA Infiltrates Links to Yahoo, Google Data Centers Worldwide, Snowden Documents Say," *Washington Post,* October 20, 2013. As the *Washington Post's* Barton Gellman and Ashkan Soltani explained: "The operation to infiltrate data links exploits a fundamental weakness in systems architecture. To guard against data loss and system slowdowns, Google and Yahoo maintain fortresslike data centers across four continents and connect them with thousands of miles of fiber-optic cable. . . . For the data centers to operate effectively, they synchronize large volumes of information about account holders. Yahoo's internal network, for example, sometimes transmits entire e-mail archives—years of messages and attachments—from one data center to another."

27. "NSA Slides Explain the PRISM Data-Collection Program," *Washington Post,* June 6, 2013.

28. Barton Gellman and Laura Poitras, "U.S., British Intelligence Mining Data from Nine U.S. Internet Companies in Broad Secret Program," *Washington Post,* June 7, 2013.

29. Barton Gellman and Todd Lindeman, "Inner Workings of a Top-Secret Spy Program," *Washington Post,* June 29, 2013.

30. Shane Harris, "Meet the Spies Doing the NSA's Dirty Work," *Foreign Policy,* November 21, 2013, http://foreignpolicy.com/2013/11/21/meet-the-spies -doing-the-nsas-dirty-work/.

31. Gellman and Lindeman, "Inner Workings of a Top-Secret Spy Program."

32. Ibid.

33. "NSA Prism Program Slides," *Guardian,* November 1, 2013.

34. Gellman and Poitras, "U.S., British Intelligence Mining."

35. Given the limited set of Snowden documents that have been made public so far, it is not clear whether programs like MUSCULAR and PRISM were ul-timately connected to other advanced Internet monitoring and prediction systems run by the US government—systems like Lockheed Martin's "World-Wide Inte-grated Crisis Early Warning System"—designed to function like advanced warning radar for dangerous human behavior. To date, only a fraction of Snowden's NSA cache has been made public. The full Snowden set is controlled by a single news organization, The Intercept, which is owned by eBay billionaire Pierre Omidyar.

36. Sam Jewler, *Mission Creep-y: Google Is Quietly Becoming One of the Nation's Most Powerful Political Forces While Expanding Its Information-Collection Empire* (Washington, DC: Public Citizen, November 2014), https://www.citizen.org /sites/default/files/google-political-spending-mission-creepy.pdf.

37. "Google CEO Larry Page: NSA Actions Threaten Democracy," YouTube video, 2:27, from CBS This Morning, televised March 20, 2014, https://www.you tube.com/watch?v=IE99DtJmyaA.

38. Claire Cain Miller, "Revelations of N.S.A. Spying Cost U.S. Tech Compa-nies," *New York Times,* March 21, 2014.

39. Ibid.

40. Google Inc., Security and Exchange Commission, Form S-3, August 18, 2005, 12, https://www.sec.gov/Archives/edgar/data/1288776/000119312505170553 /ds3.htm.

41. Joe Mullin, "In 2009, Ed Snowden Said Leakers 'Should Be Shot.' Then He Became One," Ars Technica, June 26, 2013, https://arstechnica.com/tech -policy/2013/06/exclusive-in-2009-ed-snowden-said-leakers-should-be-shot-then -he-became-one/.

42. Edward Snowden, interview with Hubert Siebel on ARD (German television channel), January 26, 2014, transcript at https://edwardsnowden .com/2014/01/27/video-ard-interview-with-edward-snowden/.

43. "Tomgram: Glenn Greenwald, How I Met Edward Snowden," Tom Dispatch, May 13, 2014, http://www.tomdispatch.com/post/175843/tomgram %3A_glenn_greenwald,_how_i_met_edward_snowden/.

44. Glenn Greenwald, Ewen MacAskill, and Laura Poitras, "Edward Snowden: The Whistleblower behind the NSA Surveillance Revelations," *Guardian,* June 11, 2013.

45. Luke Harding, "How Edward Snowden Went from Loyal NSA Contractor to Whistleblower," *Guardian,* February 1, 2014.

46. James Bamford, "Edward Snowden: The Untold Story of the Most Wanted Man in the World," *Wired*, August 13, 2014.

47. Lana Lam, "Snowden Sought Booz Allen Job to Gather Evidence on NSA Surveillance," *South China Morning Post*, June 24, 2013.

48. "Courage finally. Real. Steady. Thoughtful. Transparent. Willing to accept the consequences," the right-wing talk show personality (@glennbeck) tweeted on June 9, 2013, https://twitter.com/glennbeck/status/343816977929867265.

49. Bamford, "Edward Snowden: The Untold Story."

50. Barton Gellman, "Edward Snowden, After Months of NSA Revelations, Says His Mission's Accomplished," *Washington Post*, December 23, 2013.

51. Scott Shane, "Documents on 2012 Drone Strike Detail How Terrorists Are Targeted," *New York Times*, June 24, 2015.

52. Dave Cole, "We Kill People Based on Metadata," *New York Review of Books*, May 10, 2014, http://www.nybooks.com/daily/2014/05/10/we-kill-people-based-metadata/.

53. Micah Lee, "Edward Snowden Explains How to Reclaim Your Privacy," The Intercept, November 12, 2015, https://theintercept.com/2015/11/12/edward-snowden-explains-how-to-reclaim-your-privacy/.

54. Adrian Chen, "The Underground Website Where You Can Buy Any Drug Imaginable," Gawker, June 1, 2011, http://gawker.com/the-underground-website-where-you-can-buy-any-drug-imag-30818160.

55. "5 Things to Know About the Silk Road Trial," *Wall Street Journal*, January 13, 2015.

56. David Golumbia, *The Politics of Bitcoin: Software as Right-Wing Extremism* (Minneapolis: University of Minnesota Press, 2016); Andy Greenberg, *This Machine Kills Secrets: How WikiLeakers, Cypherpunks, and Hacktivists Aim to Free the World's Information* (New York: Dutton, 2012).

57. Timothy C. May, *Crypto Anarchy and Virtual Communities* (December 1994), https://invisiblemolotov.files.wordpress.com/2008/06/crypto_anarchist.pdf.

58. Dread Pirate Roberts, message on the Silk Road Forum, March 20, 2012 *(United States of America v. Ross Ulbricht*, Exhibit 4, filed April 16, 2015).

59. Aaron Sankin, "Searching for a Hitman in the Deep Web," Daily Dot, October 10, 2013, https://www.dailydot.com/crime/deep-web-murder-assassination-contract-killer/.

60. Gary Brecher and Mark Ames, "Interview with Gunnar Hrafn Jonsson," Radio War Nerd, episode 28, April 7, 2016, https://www.patreon.com/posts/radio-war-nerd-7-5106280.

61. To communicate with Sandvik, Snowden used the same anonymous email address—cincinnatus@lavabit.com—that he used a couple of weeks later to unsuccessfully attempt to contact Greenwald. He also provided Sandvik with his full real name and his full real address.

62. Kevin Poulsen, "Snowden's First Move against the NSA Was a Party in Hawaii," *Wired*, May 21, 2014.

63. Michael Isikoff and Michael B. Kelley, "In Exile, Edward Snowden Rakes in Speaking Fees While Hoping for a Pardon," Yahoo! News, August 11, 2016, https://www.yahoo.com/news/edward-snowden-making-most-digital-000000490.html.

64. "Because it's not about the United States, it's not about the NSA, it's not about the Russians, it's not about the Chinese, it's not about the British, it's not about any national government. It's about the world we have, the world we want to live in and the internet, the connections that we want to build between people, between worlds, between every point of presence, in every home, on every phone around the world," he told an auditorium filled with the world's foremost computer and network engineers at a 2015 meeting of the Internet Engineering Task Force in Prague. The audience was filled with the very people who would design the future features of the Internet—academics as well as employees of the most powerful tech companies in the world. "Edward Snowden at IETF93," YouTube video, 56:01, posted by Dev Random, July 28, 2015, https://www.youtube.com/watch?v=oNvsUXBCeVA&feature=youtu.be.

65. Glenn Greenwald, *No Place to Hide: Edward Snowden, the NSA, and the U.S. Surveillance State* (New York: Metropolitan Books, 2014), 24.

66. They posed for a photo at the thirtieth TED event, held in Vancouver, Canada. Chris Anderson (@TEDchris), Twitter post, March 18, 2014, 12:25 pm, http://web.archive.org/web/20170522131119/https:/twitter.com/TEDchris/status/446004368844652545.

67. The Electronic Frontier Foundation described Tor as the digital equivalent of the First Amendment—a tool that was "essential to freedom of expression" on the Internet—and added it to its "Surveillance Self-Defense" privacy toolkit. Fight for the Future, the hip, young Silicon Valley activist group, declared Tor to be "NSA-proof" and recommended that people use it every day. Laura Poitras, director of Citizen Four, the Academy Award–winning documentary on Edward Snowden, endorsed Tor as well. "When I was communicating with Snowden for several months before I met him in Hong Kong, we talked often about the Tor Network and it is something that actually he feels is vital for online privacy and defeating surveillance. It is our only tool to be able to do that," she told an auditorium full of people at a hacker conference in Germany, a giant picture of Edward Snowden projected behind her on stage (Katina, "This Is What a Tor Supporter Looks Like: Laura Poitras," Tor Project [blog], November 23, 2015, https://blog.torproject.org/blog/what-tor-supporter-looks-laura-poitras).

68. Every year Google funds university students to work at Tor during the summer with a stipend of roughly $2,000 a month as part of its "Summer of Code." "Tor: Google Summer of Code 2017," Tor, accessed July 6, 2017, https://www.torproject.org/about/gsoc.html.en; "*Student Stipends*," Google Summer of Code, updated May 5, 2017, https://developers.google.com/open-source/gsoc/help/student-stipends.

69. Alec Muffett, "*1 Million People Use Facebook over Tor*," Facebook, April 22, 2016, https://www.facebook.com/notes/facebook-over-tor/1-million-people-use-facebook-over-tor/865624066877648/.

70. nickm, "This Is What a Tor Supporter Looks Like: Daniel Ellsberg," Tor Project (blog), December 26, 2015, https://blog.torproject.org/blog/what-tor-supporter -looks-daniel-ellsberg.

71. "Q&A Marathon with Jacob Appelbaum and Roger Dingledine," YouTube video, 3:59:35, filmed July 24, 2013, at Technical University of Munich, posted by zerwas2ky, July 31, 2013, https://www.youtube.com/watch?v=c6ja_0X9gyg.

72. "Crypto Party Craze: Australians Learning Encryption to Hide Data from Criminals and Governments as Digital Arms Race Heats Up" blared a 2015 headline on Australia's ABC news. "Crypto parties, where people gather to learn online encryption, are attracting everyone from politicians, to business people, to activists." Margot O'Neill and Brigid Andersen, "Crypto Party Craze: Australians Learning Encryption to Hide Data from Criminals and Governments as Digital Arms Race Heats Up," ABC, updated June 5, 2015, http://www.abc.net.au/news/2015-06-04 /crypto-party-craze:-push-for-privacy-in-the-post-snowden-era/6521408.

73. Jenna Wortham, "Finding Inspiration for Art in the Betrayal of Privacy," *New York Times,* December 27, 2016.

74. Andy Greenberg, "The Artist Using Museums to Amplify Tor's Anonymity Network," *Wired,* April 1, 2016.

75. Paul Carr, "Tor Boss Launches Internal Investigation over Claims Senior Staffer Tried to Smear Pando Reporter," *Pando Daily,* February 7, 2015, https://pando.com/2015/02/07/tor-exec-director-launches-internal-investigation -over-claims-senior-staffer-tried-to-smear-pando-reporter/.

76. Anonymous (@YourAnonNews), Twitter post, November 24, 2014, 11:19 am, https://surveillancevalley.com/content/citations/youranonnews-twitter-24 -november-2014.png.

77. After Edward Snowden appeared on the scene in 2013, Fight for the Future launched several antisurveillance campaigns, including helping organize a big anti-NSA rally in Washington, DC, on October 5, 2013. In the summer of 2014, it launched Reset the Net, which promised to be a global protest campaign to end online surveillance ("Reset the Net: June 5, 2014," Fight for the Future, accessed July 6, 2017, https://www.resetthenet.org/). One of the main tools Reset the Net offered participants as part of its "NSA-proof Privacy Pack": the Tor Project ("June 5th, 2014: Reset the Net," YouTube video, 1:45, posted by Fight for the Future, March 8, 2014, https://www.youtube.com/watch?v=gaH3thsKv20). Fight for the Future is funded by Silicon Valley (Chris Ruen, *Freeloading: How Our Insatiable Appetite for Free Content Starves Creativity* [New York: OR Books, 2012]).

78. "Tor: Google Summer of Code 2017," https://www.torproject.org/about/gsoc .html.en; "Student Stipends," https://developers.google.com/open-source/gsoc /help/student-stipends.

79. Roger Dingledine, curriculum vitae, accessed December 31, 2016, https:// www.freehaven.net/~arma/cv.html.

80. Roger Dingledine, "Free Privacy Enhancing Technologies" (presentation given at Wizards of OS conference, Germany, June 11, 2004).

81. "If you've been able to ignore Pando Daily's 100% non-technical smear campaign against the Tor Project and its developers and supporters, you're lucky," he

wrote on his personal blog. "They also borrow tactics from GamerGate, including making puppet Twitter accounts to harrass [sic] women." Micah Lee, "Fact-Checking Pando's Smears against Tor," Micah Lee's Blog (blog), December 11, 2014, https://micahflee.com/2014/12/fact-checking-pandos-smears-against-tor/.

82. "There are only a few places where funding can't influence the contents of the outcome—maybe fundamental physics, and math, and not much else," wrote Quinn Norton, an influential American journalist who specializes in Internet culture, attempting to explain to me why my thinking about Tor was wrong. Her argument closely echoed that of Micah Lee's. "The math, well known and widely standardized, will work for everyone, or it will not, whoever pays the bills." Quinn Norton, "Clearing the Air around Tor," *Pando Daily*, December 9, 2014, https://pando.com/2014/12/09/clearing-the-air-around-tor/.

83. Here are a few examples of influential privacy personalities telling people to ignore my reporting: "I don't have time for jerks who use that nonsense to service their other agenda. Boring waste of time," Tor developer Jacob Appelbaum tweeted (@ioerror, Twitter post, October 26, 2014, 8:21 am, http://web.archive.org/web/20150623005502/https:/twitter.com/ioerror/status/526393121630740480). Jillian York, director for International Freedom of Expression at the Electronic Frontier Foundation, also counseled her forty-five thousand Twitter followers to ignore my story: "yeah I just don't see the news here," she tweeted. "it seems like only 15 or so people have bothered to tweet the article, so . . . " (@jilliancyork, Twitter post, July 17, 2014, 14:49 am, http://web.archive.org/web/20150623005501/https:/twitter.com/jilliancyork/status/489678221185536000). "I wish all the @torproject conspiracy theorists would just read the damn website," tweeted Morgan Marquis-Boire, former Google security developer and now technologist at The Intercept (@headhntr, Twitter post, July 28, 2014, 5:51 am, http://web.archive.org/web/20150623005513/https:/twitter.com/headhntr/status/493740639927156737).

84. "Meet the Fellows: Chris Soghoian," TechCongress, March 21, 2017, http://web.archive.org/web/20170518163030/https://www.techcongress.io/blog/2017/3/21/meet-the-fellows-chris-soghoian; Christopher Soghoian (@csoghoian), Twitter post, August 5, 2014, 11:43 pm, http://web.archive.org/web/20150623005501/https:/twitter.com/csoghoian/status/496909507390631936.

85. Yasha Levine, "How Leading Tor Developers and Advocates Tried to Smear Me After I Reported Their US Government Ties," *Pando Daily*, November 14, 2014, https://pando.com/2014/11/14/tor-smear/.

86. The Twitter feed of Tor employee Andrea Shepard was awash in insults and homophobic slurs. Here's one as an example, where she says I gagged while performing oral sex on a male colleague: "I presume he gagged while trying to help Mark Ames uncoil his dick." Andre (@puellavulnerata), Twitter post, September 16, 2014, 3:14 pm, http://wayback.archive.org/web/20150623005511/https://mobile.twitter.com/puellavulnerata/status/511956365078589440; Carr, "Tor Boss Launches Internal Investigation over Claims Senior Staffer Tried to Smear Pando Reporter."

87. "I sincerely wonder how high of an activist body count Mark Ames & Yasha Levine will rack up from telling people Tor is a CIA/Koch bros trap," tweeted someone named William Gillis. William Gillis (@rechelon), Twitter post,

November 14, 2014, 8:06 pm, http://web.archive.org/web/20170518171930/https:
/twitter.com/rechelon/status/533471143194152961.

88. The harassment campaign drew condemnation from some quarters of the
privacy movement, but this was a distinct minority. "Given the evidence Levine assembled, his conclusion is unremarkable. But the Tor community has reacted with
anger," wrote privacy technology reporter Stilgherrian on ZDNet. "But I note that
instead of deconstructing Levine's argument, Tor's supporters have merely attacked
him and his motives—at least one even accusing him of working for the CIA."
Stilgherrian, "Tor's Feral Fans Are Its Own Worst Enemy," ZDNet, November
21, 2014, http://www.zdnet.com/article/tors-feral-fans-are-its-own-worst-enemy/.

89. "This article has been amended to remove the claim that Pando journalists were directly involved in a campaign of harassment, which Pando refutes. A
comment from Pando has been added." Tom Fox-Brewster, "Privacy Advocates
Unmask Twitter Troll," Guardian, December 3, 2014.

90. Harry Halpin, "What Is Enlightenment? Google, WikiLeaks, and the Reorganization of the World," *Los Angeles Review of Books*, November 2, 2014.

91. My editor at *Pando Daily*, Paul Carr, addressed the bizarre nature of these
smears. "[The] smear came in early November when a freelance journalist and radical open web advocate called Harry Halpin, writing on the *LA Review of Books*,
casually dropped into a book review the fact that Yasha's reporting had been funded
by the CIA. The only problem with that assertion: It was, and is, a total lie. It was
only after I wrote to the editor of the LARB, pointing out the fact that his publication was guilty of the most egregious defamation against Yasha, and copying
our attorney (the wonderful Roger Myers, who previously defended WikiLeaks),
that the magazine issued a mealy-mouthed retraction and correction, claiming
that the CIA line had been intended as a joke," he wrote (Paul Carr, "It's Time
for Tor Activists to Stop Acting Like the Spies They Claim to Hate," *Pando Daily*,
December 10, 2014, https://pando.com/2014/12/10/its-time-for-tor-activists-to
-stop-acting-like-the-spies-they-claim-to-hate/). "Shockingly, even the Guardian
was briefly fooled into repeating the smears, before issuing a correction over what a
senior editor described as a 'fuck up'" (Paul Carr, "Here We Go. Anonymous Calls
for Attacks against Pando Writers over Our Tor Reporting," *Pando Daily*, December
11, 2014, https://pando.com/2014/12/11/here-we-go-anonymous-calls-for-attacks
-against-pando-writers-over-tor-reporting/).

Chapter 7

1. M. P. Okultra (@okayultra), Twitter post, December 17, 2015, 12:20 p.m.,
http://web.archive.org/web/20170521122643/https:/twitter.com/okayultra/status
/677584177638821888; Khalil Sehnaoui (@sehnaoui), Twitter post, December 18,
2015, 4:52 p.m., http://web.archive.org/web/20170521122706/https:/twitter.com
/sehnaoui/status/678015081301475329.

2. When the privacy community found out I bought tickets and planned to attend the event, they spent days insulting and making veiled threats against me on

Twitter. Much of this was driven by Tor contractor Andrea Shepard, who tweeted out that she would consider my presence at 31c3 conference—a public event attended by thousands of people, including journalists like myself—to be "stalking and aggression" against her personally, and she warned that she would retaliate in "self-defense." At some point on Twitter, she mentioned a hammer and alluded to the fact that drugging my drink would be "liquid-phase hacking." Shepard was not just a random developer attending the conference but an employee of a contractor backed by powerful military and intelligence interests—an organization that I had spent the past year investigating. So I took these threats seriously. I also saw them as a cynical attempt by a Pentagon contractor to escape scrutiny by framing critical investigative journalism as if it was nothing but personal harassment and stalking. Imagine if other powerful private military contractors like Blackwater or Booz Allen made similar claims against reporters? The situation worried Paul Carr, my editor at *Pando*, who grew concerned for my safety and reached out by email to Tor's executive director Shari Steele. "To be clear, Yasha's trip to 32C3 has nothing to do with Ms Shepard (except in so far that she is an employee of Tor) and is part of our continuing coverage on Tor, hacking and surveillance," he wrote on December 19, 2015. "Yasha is entitled to go about his job safely and without threats of violence, especially from paid employees of Tor. My normal next step as Yasha's editor would be to contact police in Berlin to put them on notice of the threat should Ms Shepard or one of her followers decide to act on it. Given the nature of the conference, that's not an ideal way to handle this situation. I'd rather not be responsible for bringing police into a hacker conference. With that in mind, I'm hoping someone at Tor can help. I would be grateful for your prompt assurance that Tor will immediately and completely cease its threats and smears against our reporter." My editor never received an answer from Steele. Andrea (@puellavulnerata), Twitter post, December 18, 2015, 3:43 p.m., https://surveillancevalley.com/content/citations/%40puellavulnerata-twitter-18-december.png; Andrea (@puellavulnerata), Twitter post, December 18, 2015, 4:54 p.m., https://web.archive.org/web/20170808233941/https://twitter.com/puellavulnerata/status/678015551780888580; Andrea (@puellavulnerata*)*, Twitter post, December 19, 2015, 1:03 p.m., https://web.archive.org/web/20170808234142/https://twitter.com/puellavulnerata/status/678168846897934340.

3. Roger Dingledine, Jacob Appelbaum, and Laura Poitras, "State of the Onion," 31c3, December 30, 2014, https://media.ccc.de/v/31c3_-_6251_-_en_-_saal_1_-_201412301400_-_state_of_the_onion_-_jacob_-_arma.

4. Roger Dingledine, Jacob Appelbaum, Mike Perry, Shari Steele, and Alison Macrina, "State of the Onion," 32c3, December 28, 2015, https://media.ccc.de/v/32c3-7307-state_of_the_onion#video.

5. Nicole Perlroth, "Tor Project Confirms Sexual Misconduct Claims against Employee," *New York Times*, July 27, 2016.

6. Jacob Appelbaum's most recent salary information comes from a separation agreement Tor Project sent to him following the sexual harassment allegations, a document that was subsequently leaked to Cryptome.org. "Tor/

Appelbaum Separation Agreement," Cryptome, June 8, 2016, http://web.archive
.org/web/20170521125929/https://cryptome.org/2016/06/tor-appelbaum-separation
.pdf.

7. From 2007 through 2015, the Tor Project received roughly $6.1 million from
the Broadcasting Board of Governors. Yasha Levine, "Notes on Tor Project Funding—Broadcasting Board of Governors," Surveillance Valley, May 2, 2017, https://
surveillancevalley.com/blog/notes-bbg-cia-cutout-funding-of-tor-project.

8. Jacob Appelbaum gave a strange rambling defense of Tor employees taking
money from the Pentagon and said categorically that he would never take CIA
money. That's where he drew the line. Interestingly, as information presented later
in this chapter reveals, Tor gets the bulk of its funding from organizations created by the CIA. "I think it sucks that we take Department of Defense money
sometimes," Appelbaum said in December 2014. "And sometimes I think it's good
when people have the ability to feed themselves and have the ability to have a
home and a family. Now, I don't have those things, really. I mean, I can feed myself. But I don't have a home or a family in the same way, say, the family people
inside of Tor do. And they need to be paid. It is the case that is true. And it raises
questions. I personally would never take CIA money, and I don't think nobody
should. I don't think the CIA should exist." Dingledine, Appelbaum, and Poitras,
"State of the Onion."

9. "People have approached us to do these types of things, and this is a serious
commitment that the whole Tor community gets behind, which is that we will
never ever put in a backdoor," Jacob Appelbaum said in a 2013 talk, relating a story
about how the Department of Justice once tried but failed to get Tor to tap the
network for the federal government. Roger Dingledine and Jacob Appelbaum,
"The Tor Network: We're Living in Interesting Times," 30c3, December 31, 2013,
https://media.ccc.de/v/30C3_-_5423_-_en_-_saal_1_-_201312272030_-_the_tor_
network_-_jacob_-_arma#video&t=0.

10. Paul Syverson, homepage, accessed February 9, 2016, http://www.syverson.org/.

11. Michael Kirk, "Cyberwar!" *Frontline* (Alexandria, VA: PBS, April 24, 2003),
short film.

12. Paul Syverson wrote the *NRL Review* article along with two other cocre-
ators of onion routing, David Goldschlag and Michael Reed, mathematicians and
computer systems researchers working for the US Navy. *NRL Review* was an in-
house navy magazine that showcased all the cool gadgets cooked up by the lab
over the previous year. D. M. Goldschlag, M. G. Reed, and P. F. Syverson, "Internet Communication Resistant to Traffic Analysis," *NRL Review*, April 1997.

13. This last stage of development was funded by both the Office of Naval Research and DARPA under its Fault Tolerant Networks Program. The amount of
the DARPA funding is unknown. "Onion Routing: Brief Selected History," website formerly operated by the Center for High Assurance Computer Systems in the
Information Technology Division of the US Naval Research Lab, 2005, accessed
July 6, 2017, https://www.onion-router.net/History.html.

14. Paul Syverson, email message sent to [tor-talk], "Iran cracks down on

web dissident technology," Tor Project, March 21, 2011, http://web.archive.org /web/20170521144023/https:/lists.torproject.org/pipermail/tor-talk/2011 -March/019868.html.

15. Roger Dingledine, "Tor: An Anonymous Internet Communication System" (presentation made at Panopticon, the 15th Annual Conference on Computers, Freedom & Privacy, Keeping an Eye on the Panopticon: Workshop on Vanishing Anonymity, Seattle, April 12, 2005).

16. Tor was originally an acronym written as TOR, for "The Onion Router," but today just the word "Tor" is used.

17. Roger Dingledine, "Free Privacy Enhancing Technologies" (presentation made at Wizards of OS conference, Germany, June 11, 2004).

18. Funding from DARPA and the Naval Research Laboratory continued through 2004. The navy contract was somewhere around $250,000 a year, according to emails between Roger Dingledine and the Broadcasting Board of Governors. "Onion Routing: Brief Selected History," https://www.onion-router.net /History.html.

19. "We funded Roger Dingledine and Nick Mathewson to work on Tor for a single year from November 2004 through October 2005 for $180,000. We then served as a fiscal sponsor for the project until they got their 501(c)(3) status over the next year or two. During that time, we took in less than $50,000 for the project," EFF's Dave Maass told me by email.

20. Dingledine, "Tor: An Anonymous Internet Communication System."

21. "EFF Joins Forces with Tor Software Project," press release, Electronic Frontier Foundation, December 21, 2004, https://www.eff.org/press/archives/2004/12/21–0.

22. *Wired* magazine called it the "let's-just-wiretap-everyone" bill. Rogier van Bakel, "How Good People Helped Make a Bad Law," *Wired*, February 1, 1999.

23. "Anonymizer.com Launches Kosovo Privacy Project to Protect Online communication in Yugoslavia and Kosovo," press release, Anonymizer, March 26, 1999. EFF partnered with Anonymizer Inc., an early Tor-like commercial anonymous Internet browsing service started by Lance Contrell, a cypherpunk and computer engineer. The Kosovo Privacy Project Anonymizer would go on to do a lot of military and intelligence work, providing Tor-like custom solutions, including anonymous browsing tools and what is known as persona-management software. It is now owned by Ntrepid, which, among other things, in 2011 signed a $2.76 million contract with the Pentagon to provide anonymous/ persona-management software (Nick Fielding and Ian Cobain, "*Revealed: US Spy Operation That Manipulates Social Media,*" *Guardian*, March 17, 2011). Discussion on Anonymizer's intelligence work comes from leaked emails of another intelligence contractor, HBGary, which was hacked by Anonymous (Aaron Barr, "Re: this guy's program is blown?" *email message,* July 1, 2010, https://surveillancevalley.com/content/citations/aaron-barr-aaron%40hbgary .com-re-this-guy-s-program-is-blown-1-july-2010.pdf).

24. John Perry Barlow, "Why Spy?" Forbes.com, October 7, 2002, https://www .forbes.com/asap/2002/1007/042.html.

25. A 2005 *Wired* profile of Tor and Roger Dingledine written by Kim Zetter offered a perfect example of how Tor's military origins and funding were treated in those early years. Although the article discussed Tor's origins as a US Navy project designed to hide spies online, it made no mention of Tor's ongoing military funding and painted Dingledine and his partner Mathewson as independent programmers who had taken a half-baked technology, rebuilt it independently, and released it into the wild. "Tor has been completely rebuilt since the Navy initially designed it in the late' 90s. The EFF has thrown its support behind the project, and its creators are now hopeful they will be able to add servers and attract new users, thus bolstering the system's privacy and security benefits," she wrote. Kim Zetter, "Tor Torches Online Tracking," *Wired*, May 17, 2005.

26. Ken Berman, email message sent to Roger Dingledine, "A roadmap for Tor + IBB," February 8, 2006, https://surveillancevalley.com/content/citations/a-road map-for-tor-ibb-february-08–2006.pdf. All emails between the BBG and employees of the Tor Project quoted in this chapter are taken from documents I obtained through the Freedom of Information Act.

27. Pete Payne, "Tor Protects Anonymous Sources," *Network Computing*, February 5, 2007, http://archive.is/WF1nv.

28. Yasha Levine, "Notes on Tor Project Funding—State Department," Surveillance Valley (blog), March 17, 2015, https://surveillancevalley.com/blog /state-department-funding-tor-project; Yasha Levine, "Notes on Tor Project Funding—The Pentagon," Surveillance Valley (blog), March 2, 2015, https:// surveillancevalley.com/blog/notes-on-pentagon-funding-of-the-tor-project; Yasha Levine, "Notes on Tor Project Funding—Broadcasting Board of Governors," Surveillance Valley (blog), May 2, 2017, https://surveillancevalley.com/blog /notes-bbg-cia-cutout-funding-of-tor-project.

29. A note on word and acronym usage: in the Tor-BBG emails, people sometimes use "International Broadcasting Bureau" or "IBB"—a wing of the BBG—to refer to the BGG. I chose to standardize these references to simply "BBG" or "Broadcasting Board of Governors" for clarity.

30. Ken Berman, email message sent to Roger Dingledine, "Tor + IBB: moving forward," February 24, 2006, https://surveillancevalley.com/content/citations /tor-ibb-moving-forward-24-february-2006-bbg-tor-emails-stack-7.pdf.

31. Bennett Haselton, email message sent to Roger Dingledine, "*Re: Tor + IBB: moving forward*," March 1, 2006, https://surveillancevalley.com/content/citations /email-from-bennett-haselton-to-roger-dingledine-re-tor-ibb-moving-forward -1-march-2006-bbg-tor-emails-stack-7.pdf.

32. Christopher Simpson, *Blowback: America's Recruitment of Nazis and Its Destructive Impact on Our Domestic and Foreign Policy* (New York: Open Road Media, 2014), chap. 7, "The thinking behind this strategy was perhaps best articulated by George F. Kennan, the State Department expert on Soviet affairs . . ."

33. John Lewis Gaddis, *George F. Kennan: An American Life* (New York: Penguin Press, 2011).

34. "The National Security Council, taking cognizance of the vicious covert activities of the USSR, its satellite countries and Communist groups to discredit

and defeat the aims and activities of the United States and other Western powers, has determined that, in the interests of world peace and US national security, the overt foreign activities of the US Government must be supplemented by covert operations. The Central Intelligence Agency is charged by the National Security Council with conducting espionage and counter-espionage operations abroad. It therefore seems desirable, for operational reasons, not to create a new agency for covert operations, but in time of peace to place the responsibility for them within the structure of the Central Intelligence Agency and correlate them with espionage and counter-espionage operations under the over-all control of the Director of Central Intelligence," reads a portion of the directive. "292. National Security Council Directive on Office of Special Projects: *NSC 10/2*," State Department, Office of the Historian, June 18, 1948, https://web.archive.org/web/20170521183859/ https://history.state.gov/historicaldocuments/frus1945-50Intel/d292.

35. Frances Stonor Saunders, *The Cultural Cold War: The CIA and the World of Arts and Letters* (New York: New Press, 2000); Simpson, *Blowback*, chap. 10, "CIA-funded psychological warfare projects employing Eastern European émi-grés became major operations during the 1950s . . . "

36. The US Senate's Church Committee's most thorough investigation of covert operations by American intelligence agencies found that the CIA targeted every segment of society in both Western and Eastern Europe. "This included underwriting most of the French Paix et Liberté movement, paying the bills of the German League for Struggle Against Inhumanity, and financing a half dozen free jurists associations, a variety of European federalist groups, the Congress for Cultural Freedom, magazines, news services, book publishers, and much more," writes historian Christopher Simpson in *Blowback* (chap. 10). Ralph McGehee, a former CIA agent who wrote about his experiences in *Deadly Deceits*, described this effort as more than just rolling back Soviet influence in specific countries. It was an attempt to fight ideas with ideas. "Within the Agency the international organizations division was coordinating an extensive propaganda effort aimed at developing an international anti-communist ideology." Ralph W. McGehee, *Deadly Deceits: My 25 Years in the CIA* (New York: Sheridan Square Press, 1983).

37. Victor Marchetti and John D. Marks, *The CIA and the Cult of Intelligence* (New York: Alfred A. Knopf, 1974); Gene Sosin, *Sparks of Liberty: An Insider's Memoir of Radio Liberty* (University Park: Penn State University Press, 1999). "The facade of a private company was supposed to establish greater credibility for the Radio as an independent voice rather than an official arm of the U.S. communications network," Gene Sosin, a longtime executive of Radio Liberty who worked for military intelligence during World War II, explains in his memoir. "Thus, when Soviet diplomats confronted their American counterparts at international conferences with the accusation that the émigré radio was 'interfering with the internal affairs of the Soviet people,' they were simply informed that it was a private radio station not subject to government control," writes Sosin in Sparks of Liberty. Of course, the CIA wasn't fooling the Soviet government, which had spies crawling all over Europe. More than anything else, the front was meant to hide government involvement from the American people themselves and to keep them in the dark.

The public had no idea these radio stations were CIA projects, and they frequently managed to snare unwitting guests and use them for propaganda purposes—even Martin Luther King Jr. was a guest on the CIA's Radio Liberty news programs. The radio stations were also used as fronts and bases of operation for all sorts of other covert activities. The radio stations themselves—and their antennas—were used as platforms for surveillance and signals intelligence.

38. Simpson, *Blowback,* chap. 10, "RFE/RL recruiters wanted to re-create these governments-in-exile for propaganda use against the USSR . . . "

39. "Worldwide Propaganda Network Built by the C.I.A.," *New York Times,* December 26, 1977. Part of the program included training Chinese journalists at Harvard, according to the *New York Times.*

40. In Latin America, the CIA broadcast through Radio Free Cuba, Radio Swan, and Radio Americas. Some of the stations employed Cuban exiles who had taken part in the failed Bay of Pigs invasion (Joseph B. Treaster, "Cuba Enlivens Radio as U.S. Prepares a Challenge," *New York Times,* August 5, 1984). Indeed, radio programming was frequently used to back up military operations against target countries. The Bay of Pigs was preceded and backed up by propaganda broadcasts calling on Cubans to rise up and overthrow their government. The CIA-backed coup in Guatemala was aided by radio broadcasts, as well, according to Tim Weiner's history of the CIA, *Legacy of Ashes.* "For four weeks, starting on May Day 1954, the CIA had been waging psychological warfare in Guatemala through a pirate radio station called the Voice of Liberation, run by a CIA contract officer, an amateur actor and skilled dramatist named David Atlee Phillips. In a tremendous stroke of luck, the Guatemalan state radio station went off the air in mid-May for a scheduled replacement of its antenna. Phillips snuggled up to its frequency, where listeners looking for the state broadcasts found Radio CIA. Unrest turned to hysteria among the populace as the rebel station sent out shortwave reports of imaginary uprisings and defections and plots to poison wells and conscript children" (Tim Weiner, *Legacy of Ashes: The History of the CIA* [New York: Doubleday, 2007]). These same tactics were later used in Southeast Asia to back up American military operations in Korea and Vietnam.

41. "A Look Back, the National Committee for Free Europe, 1949," Central Intelligence Agency, May 29, 2007, https://www.cia.gov/news-information/featured-story-archive/2007-featured-story-archive/a-look-back.html.

42. Stephen Kotkin, "Sphere of Influence II: What, If Anything, Is the Difference between Fascism and Communism?" IVM Lectures in Human Sciences, Institut für die Wissenschaften vom Menschen, April 19, 2017, http://www.iwm.at/events/event/sphere-of-influence-ii/.

43. "In the Pay of the CIA," *CBS News,* March 13, 1967, https://surveillancevalley.com/content/citations/in-the-pay-of-the-cia-cbs-news-13-march-1967-4-of-5.mp4.

44. Every year the BBG releases a world map with regions and countries where it operates shaded in red—and most of the world is a giant crimson blob: Radio Martí (aimed at Cuba), Radio Farda (aimed at Iran), Radio Sawa (which

broadcasts in Iraq, Lebanon, Libya, Morocco, and Sudan), Radio Azadi (targeting Afghanistan), Radio Free Europe/Radio Liberty (which has tailored broadcasts in over a dozen languages for Russia, Ukraine, Serbia, Azerbaijan, Belarus, Georgia, and Armenia), and Radio Free Asia (which targets China, North Korea, Laos, and Vietnam). RadioFreeEurope/Radio Liberty coverage map, http://web.archive.org/web/20170301215817/http://flashvideo.rferl.org/Flashmapsnew/maps.swf.

45. Nor did the BBG cut ties to the same military and intelligence agencies that supported and sustained it during the Cold War. The National Endowment for Democracy, Freedom House, DARPA, the State Department, and USAID continued to be BBG's close partners. Today, the BBG runs on a $750 million budget provided by Congress, reports to Secretary of State Rex Tillerson, and is managed by a revolving crew of media executives and neoconservative think-tank experts handpicked by the Trump administration. Several sources who work at the BBG tell me that the organization still has spies working under journalistic cover.

46. "Memorandum For: Special Assistant to the President, Subject: International Radio Broadcasting by Radio Free Asia," Central Intelligence Agency, April 1, 1953, https://surveillancevalley.com/content/citations/memorandum-for-special-assistant-to-the-president-subject-international-radio-broadcasting-by-radio-freeasia-cia-1-april-1953.pdf. The United States played a double game with China. It was America's largest trading partner. American companies had eagerly transported their production technology and capacity to China, gutting American manufacturing in pursuit of cheap labor abroad. While American business benefited from China's cheap labor and large market for goods and entertainment, the US government also saw China as a potential adversary that needed to be kept in check.

47. "China's Control of News and Information May Have Worsened SARS Epidemic, Broadcasters Say," Broadcasting Board of Governors, June 5, 2003, https://www.bbg.gov/2003/06/05/chinas-control-of-news-and-information-may-have-worsened-sars-epidemic-broadcasters-say/.

48. Thomas Lum, Patricia Moloney Figliola, and Matthew C. Weed, *China, Internet Freedom, and U.S. Policy* (Washington, DC: Congressional Research Service, July 13, 2012), https://fas.org/sgp/crs/row/R42601.pdf.

49. "Statement of the Broadcasting Board of Governors Before the Congressional-Executive Commission on China: China's Jamming of U.S. International Broadcasting," press release, Broadcasting Board of Governors, December 9, 2002, https://www.bbg.gov/2002/12/09/statement-of-the-broadcasting-board-of-governors-before-the-congressional-executive-commission-on-china/.

50. In 2006, Secretary of State Condoleezza Rice set up the Global Internet Freedom Task Force (GIFT), a top-level "coordination group" that was supposed to "address challenges around the globe to freedom of expression and the free flow of information on the Internet" but instead seemed geared to helping US Internet companies assess business risks in emerging markets.

51. As Shawn Powers and Michael Jablonski write in *The Real Cyberwar:* "Geopolitics often comes veiled in ideological language, at least initially. The State

Department's evolving doctrine of internet freedom, most clearly articulated by Secretary Clinton, is the realization of a broader strategy promoting a particular conception of networked communication that depends on American companies (for example, Amazon, AT&T, Facebook, Google, and Level 3), supports Western norms (such as copyright, advertising-based consumerism, and the like), and promotes Western products. . . . internet policies reflect strategic pursuit of tangible resources. The internet is not only the object of struggle but, in the information age, represents a critical infrastructure for pursuing larger geopolitical goals" (Shawn Powers and Michael Jablonski, *The Real Cyberwar: The Political Economy of Internet Freedom* [Champaign: University of Illinois Press, 2015], 6). The policy was later embraced by Secretary of State Hillary Clinton and expanded into a fleshed-out foreign policy plank of the United States: support for "the freedom to connect—the idea that governments should not prevent people from connecting to the internet, to websites, or to each other" (ibid., 6–9, 180–182).

52. Jennifer Lee, "United States Backs Plan to Help Chinese Evade Government Censorship of Web," *New York Times*, August 30, 2001; Thomas Lum, *Internet Development and Information Control in the People's Republic of China* (Washington, DC: Congressional Research Service, February 10, 2006), https://fas.org/sgp/crs/row/RL33167.pdf; Murray Hiebert, "Counters to Chinese Checkers," *Far Eastern Economic Review*, November 7, 2002.

53. "Who Is Li Hongzhi?" *BBC News*, May 8, 2001, http://news.bbc.co.uk/2/hi/asia-pacific/1223317.stm; William Dowell, "Interview with Li Hongzhi," *Time*, May 10, 1999.

54. "Media Reaction: Secretary Clinton's Speech, U.S.-Japan Relations," diplomatic cable, State Department, January 22, 2010, published by WikiLeaks, https://wikileaks.org/plusd/cables/10BEIJING167_a.html.

55. Ken Berman, email message sent to Roger Dingledine, "A roadmap for Tor + IBB," January 23, 2006, https://surveillancevalley.com/content/citations/a-roadmap-for-tor-ibb-february-08-2006.pdf.

56. Roger Dingledine, email message sent to Ken Berman, "Meeting notes, Jan 11 2008," January 15, 2008, https://surveillancevalley.com/content/citations/meeting-notes-jan-11-2008–15-january-2008.pdf.

57. Roger Dingledine, email message sent to Ken Berman, "(FWD) Re: Tor news," February 12, 2008, https://surveillancevalley.com/content/citations/email-from-roger-dingledine-to-ken-berman-fwd-re-tor-news-12-february-2008-bbg-tor-emails-stack-21.pdf.

58. In 2007, Dingledine wrote his handler at the BBG about a conference where he met "a fellow who works with CIA and State Dept and is working on human rights." In October 2008, Dingledine met with fifty FBI and DOJ agents to talk about Tor. "Keeping FBI informed of (and using!) Tor contributes to project and network sustainability," he wrote to Ken Berman, describing the event. "Most people recognized that Tor has good uses—in fact, some of the agents in the audience told me they use Tor for their work already." Roger Dingledine, email

message sent to Ken Berman, "Notes from ITSG meeting, Oct 22–23," November 22, 2008, https://surveillancevalley.com/content/citations/notes-from-itsg-meeting -oct-22-23-bbg-tor-emails-stack-21.pdf.

59. Roger Dingledine, email message sent to Kelly DeYoe, "IBB notes for Sept," October 10, 2007, https://surveillancevalley.com/content/citations/ibb-notes-for -sept-bbg-tor-emails-stack-21.pdf; Roger Dingledine, email message sent to Ken Berman, "State Dept work on human rights and anonymity?" September 12, 2006, https://surveillancevalley.com/content/citations/state-dept-work-on-human -rights-and-anonymity.pdf; Roger Dingledine, "Tor Development Roadmap, 2008–2011,"Tor Project, September 1, 2008, https://www.torproject.org/press/press kit/2008–12–19-roadmap-full.pdf.

60. Roger Dingledine, email message sent to Ken Berman, "Draft proposal for TLS normalization," October 9, 2007, https://surveillancevalley.com/content /citations/bug-reveal-october-09-2007-bbg-tor-emails-stack-21.pdf. This issue seems to have gone unaddressed for at least four years. Nick Mathewson, "xxx-draft -spec-for-TLS-normalization.txt" [tor-dev], January 31, 2011, https://lists.tor project.org/pipermail/tor-dev/2011-January/001100.html.

61. The amount of funding Tor received from the Cyber-Threat Analytics program is not known. It ran from 2006 through 2008. "Tor: Sponsors," Tor Project, accessed June 24, 2008, http://www.torproject.org/sponsors.html.en.

62. "The Cyber-TA project is currently managed through the U.S. Army Research Laboratory's Army Research Office (ARO) under Research Grant No. W911NF-06-1-0316. . . . In FY05 the Cyber-TA initiative was managed under the guidance of the Disruptive Technology Office (formerly ARDA)." "Welcome to the Cyber-TA Home Page," Cyber-TA, accessed May 18, 2008, http://www.cyber -ta.org.

63. Roger Dingledine, email message sent to Ken Bernman, "IBB/Tor notes for April," May 12, 2008, https://surveillancevalley.com/content/citations/tor-notes -for-april-12-may-2008.pdf.

64. Michael McFaul, *Advancing Democracy Abroad: Why We Should and How We Can* (Lanham, MD: Rowman & Littlefield Publishers, 2009). This arm of the State Department would increasingly oversee the funding of Internet Freedom technologies, emulating the structure of a Silicon Valley venture capitalist firm and "financing as many disparate efforts as possible." Brad Stone, "Aid Urged for Groups Fighting Internet Censors," *New York Times,* January 20, 2010.

65. Greenberg, *This Machine Kills Secrets,* 152–158.

66. Jacob Appelbaum, "The Fountainhead by Ayn Rand," January 12, 2003, accessed February 4, 2005, https://web.archive.org/web/20050204052358/http:// appelbaum.net:80/weblog/index.pl/2003/01/12#thefountainhead.

67. Jake Appelbaum, "Resume," accessed February 8, 2004, http://www .appelbaum.net/.

68. "Interview by Esther Sassaman," September 2005, accessed January 4, 2005, crypto.nsa.org.

69. Lane Hartwell, "So Who Wants to Fuck a Robot," *Wired*, June 10, 2007.

70. These accusations came out in a major way after he was forced out of the Tor Project following an internal investigation of sexual misconduct. For example, here is San Francisco journalist Violet Blue on his time in San Francisco in the mid-2000: "He tried, in a variety of ways and in different situations and parties and events, to convince me to have sex with him. I said no over and over, and as time went by, he became angrier and angrier with me. I was working with an arts organization during those years, and we ended up kicking him out of our machine shop," she wrote. "Jake had sexually targeted a female friend of mine. Her and I going to a large tech party in December; I think it was a Wikimedia party, and Jimmy Wales was there. My friend was feeling hunted by Jake, and early in the party she said he was trying to isolate her, and told me she was scared. She is not a big or strong girl, nor is she loud, and he was trying to convince her to go into a stairwell with him. The convincing turned into trying to pull her away physically, grabbing at her hands." Violet Blue, "'But He Does Good Work,'" Medium, June 15, 2016, https://medium.com/@violetblue/but-he-does-good-work-6710df9d9029.

71. Roger Dingledine, email message sent to Ken Bernman, "IBB/Tor notes for April," May 12, 2008, https://surveillancevalley.com/content/citations/tor-notes-for-april-12-may-2008.pdf.

72. Roger Dingledine, curriculum vitae, accessed March 8, 2008, https://www.freehaven.net/~arma/cv.html.

73. "Mike, Jake, and I talked to Niels Provos, Google's security guy, about how Google search can become more compatible with Tor," wrote Dingledine to his handlers at the BBG. "Niels wants me to come give a talk at Google about Tor, including this issue, to maybe drum up more support for having Google interoperate better with Tor. I think I'm not going to try to squeeze that into my mid November trip, but rather do it a few months after that." Roger Dingledine, email sent to Kelly DeYoe and Ken Berman, "(FWD) Notes from Niels, Google, Tor," November 22, 2008, https://surveillancevalley.com/content/citations/email-from-roger-dingledine-to-bbgs-kelly-deyoe-and-ken-berman-fwd-notes-from-niels-google-tor-22-november-2008.pdf.

74. "Upcoming plans, conferences, and schedules . . . Roger, Jake, and Linus meet with Swedish law enforcement." Andrew Lewman, Executive Director, email message sent to Kelly DeYoe, program officer, BBG, "RE: contract BBG-CON1807S6441," March 10, 2010, https://surveillancevalley.com/content/citations/andrew-lewman-executive-director-to-kelly-deyoe-program-officer-bbg-re-contract-bbgcon1807s6441-10-march-2010-bbg-tor-contract-stack-2.pdf.

75. An example of Roger Dingledine's reports: "One of the best ways we've found for getting new relays is to go to conferences and talk to people in person. There are many thousands of people out there with spare fast network connections and a willingness to help save the world. Our experience is that visiting them in person produces much better results, long-term, than Slashdot articles. . . . The first is in Japan. The second is our first major high bandwidth node in New Zealand."

76. It would be led by Dingledine and Appelbaum. "All around the world there are people teaching other people how to safely use Tor and related applications. This training will be ramping up with projects like iFree, NGO-in-a-box, and the Global Voices seminars. We should help train the trainers about Tor, so they better understand the technology, issues, and tradeoffs and can then do a better job of training the users," wrote Dingledine (Dingledine, "Tor Development Roadmap, 2008–2011"). Their plan to influence journalists in America appeared to be at odds with the US Information and Educational Exchange Act of 1948, known as the Smith-Mundt Act, which forbids the State Department and the Broadcasting Board of Governors funding any effort or organization that seeks to intentionally influence or sway public opinion in the United States (John Schwartz, "Over the Net and Around the Law? U.S. Computer Users Gain Access to Voice of America Broadcasts," *Washington Post*, January 14, 1995).

77. On numerous occasions, Tor employees discussed with BBG ways of influencing press coverage and perception. One example involved EPIC. Andrew Lewman, email message sent to Kelly DeYoe and Roger Dingledine, "EPIC, BBC, Tor, and FOIA," September 10, 2013, https://surveillancevalley.com/content/citations/email-from-andrew-lewman-to-kelly-deyoe-and-roger-dingledine-epic-bbc-tor-and-foia-10-september-2013.pdf.

78. WikiLeaks, email message sent to John Young, "Martha Stewart pgp," Cryptome, January 7, 2007, https://cryptome.org/wikileaks/wikileaks-leak2.htm.

79. Mona Mahmood, Maggie O'Kane, Chavala Madlena, and Teresa Smith, "Revealed: Pentagon's Link to Iraqi Torture Centres," *Guardian*, March 6, 2013.

80. Scott Shane and Andrew W. Lehren, "Leaked Cables Offer Raw Look at U.S. Diplomacy," *New York Times*, November 28, 2010.

81. "Affidavit of Julian Paul Assange," WikiLeaks, September 2, 2013, https://wikileaks.org/IMG/html/Affidavit_of_Julian_Assange.html.

82. "In late 2010, when Assange seemed to be on the brink of long-term jail awaiting questioning for alleged sex crimes, one WikiLeaks staffer told me he hoped Appelbaum might even be the favored successor to Assange in WikiLeaks' hierarchy." Greenberg, *This Machine Kills Secrets*.

83. Nathaniel Rich, "The American WikiLeaks Hacker," *Rolling Stone*, December 1, 2010.

84. Amy Goodman, "Part 2: Daniel Ellsberg and Jacob Appelbaum on the NDAA, WikiLeaks and Unconstitutional Surveillance," Democracy Now, February 6, 2013, https://www.democracynow.org/2013/2/6/part_2_daniel_ellsberg_and_jacob_appelbaum_on_the_ndaa_wikileaks_and_unconstitutional_surveillance.

85. Rich, "American WikiLeaks Hacker."

86. The American Civil Liberties Union partnered with Tor ("Privacy Groups Announce Developer Challenge for Mobile Apps," press release, ACLU of Northern California, February 4, 2011, https://www.aclunc.org/news/privacy-groups-announce-developer-challenge-mobile-apps). Teach-in at Whitney Museum featuring "Jacob Appelbaum, computer security researcher, privacy advocate, hacker, and human rights activist" ("Laura Poitras: Surveillance Teach-In," Whitney

Museum, April 20, 2012, http://web.archive.org/web/20170521210801/http://whitney.org/Events/LauraPoitrasObservationAndTrust).

87. "The FP Top 100 Global Thinkers," *Foreign Policy*, November 26, 2012.

88. Roger Dingledine, email message sent to Kelly DeYoe, "contract BBGCON1807S6441," January 10, 2008, https://surveillancevalley.com/content/citations/BBGCON1807S6441-bbg-tor-contract-stack-9.pdf?1488563621.

89. Elinor Mills, "Researcher Detained at U.S. Border, Questioned about WikiLeaks," CNET, July 31, 2010, https://www.cnet.com/news/researcher-detained-at-u-s-border-questioned-about-wikileaks/.

90. Andrew Lewman, email message sent to Ken Berman, "July Monthly Report from Tor," August 10, 2010.

91. Despite telling people he was being hunted by the US government, Jacob Appelbaum visited the BBG's offices in Washington, DC, in 2011. Andrew Lewman, email message sent to Ken Berman and Kelly DeYoe, "RE: Tor Contract," October 18, 2011, https://surveillancevalley.com/content/citations/email-from-tor-executive-director-andrew-lewman-to-bbgs-ken-berman-and-kelly-deyoe-re-tor-contract-18-october-2011-bbg-tor-emails-stack-8.pdf.

92. Levine, "Notes on Tor Project Funding—Broadcasting Board of Governors." Actually, the State Department funding took a dip in 2011 from the $913,000 that came in in 2010. It's not clear why the funding decreased, but it was just temporary, and previous funding levels were restored just two years later. In 2013, State Department funding amounted to $882,312 (Levine, *"Notes on Tor Project Funding—State Department"*). Meanwhile, Tor Pentagon funding continued to go up: $503,706 in 2011 and $876,099 in 2012 (Levine, "Notes on Tor Project Funding—the Pentagon").

93. "IRS Form 990," Tor Project Inc., 2011, https://surveillancevalley.com/content/citations/2011-tor-project-form-990.pdf; "Navy Command, Control, Communications, Computers, Intelligence, Surveillance, and Reconnaissance Program Information," Catalog of Federal Assistance, accessed July 6, 2017, https://www.cfda.gov/?s=program&mode=form&tab=step1&id=e957455dd32744ebfc0f3ec8a9c18683. The Space and Naval Warfare Systems Command, known as SPAWAR, is headquartered in Sand Diego and staffed by nearly eight thousand people all over the world. It engages in everything from intelligence gathering to satellite communications networks and nuclear weapons targeting systems. SPAWAR also houses a secret offensive cyber unit that wages electronic war against foreign adversaries. As one SPAWAR spokesman put it: "We're on every continent, including Antarctica. We're on the oceans, below the seas, in the air and in space." SPAWAR's objective was to maintain full-spectrum information dominance—not just for itself but also for the rest of the intelligence and military community. It seemed Tor helped it fulfill its mission.

94. "Office of Management and Budget Data Collection Form," Tor Project Inc., 2011, https://surveillancevalley.com/content/citations/2011-tor-project-dcf.pdf. Because Tor's Broadcasting Board of Governors funding is distributed across several subsidiary organizations, including Radio Free Asia and the Open Technology Fund, and because public accounting of the funds is not uniform or complete, it

can be difficult to pin down the exact amount of money it gets from this agency (Levine, "Notes on Tor Project Funding—Broadcasting Board of Governors.")

95. Alec Ross, "Social Media: Cause, Effect and Response," *NATO Review*, 2011, http://web.archive.org/web/20160914003415/http://www.nato.int/docu /review/2011/Social_Medias/21st-century-statecraft/EN/index.htm.

96. Ron Nixon, "U.S. Groups Helped Nurture Arab Uprisings," *New York Times*, April 14, 2011. In the lead-up to the Arab Spring, in 2008, the State Department teamed with Facebook, Google, MTV, and other corporate partners to launch the Alliance of Youth Movements Summit, billed as an event that would "Bring Together Global Youth Groups, Tech Experts to Find Best Ways to Use Digital Media to Promote Freedom and Justice, Counter Violence, Extremism and Oppression." This effort was launched by Alec Ross and his State Department colleague Jared Cohen, who would later head up Google's JigSaw think tank, but similar training sessions took place almost every year. "Announcement on Alliance of Youth Movements Summit, December 3–5: Summit Brings Youth Groups, Tech Experts Together to Promote Freedom," US Department of State press release, America.gov, November 18, 2008, http://web.archive.org /web/20090306184954/http://www.america.gov/st/texttrans-english/2008 /November/20081120122321eaifaso.3440363.html.

97. Agence France-Presse estimated the US government spent $76 million from 2007 through 2011 on programs focusing on "online freedom." Rob Lever, "Online Freedom? There'll be an App for That," AFP News, June 12, 2012, https://sg.news .yahoo.com/online-freedom-app-coming-185419926.html.

98. "Jacob Appelbaum Presents Tor at Arab Bloggers Workshop 2009," Global Voices, December 9, 2009; Andrew Lewman, email message sent to Kelly DeYoe, "RE: contract BBGCON1807S6441," November 8, 2011, https://surveillancevalley .com/content/citations/email-from-andrew-lewman-executive-director-to-kelly -deyoe-program-officer-bbg-re-contract-bbgcon1807s6441-8-november-2011 -bbg-tor-contract-stack-5.pdf; Roger Dingledine, "Trip Report, Arab Bloggers Meeting, Oct 3–7," Tor Project (blog), October 16, 2011, https://blog.torproject .org/blog/trip-report-arab-bloggers-meeting-oct-3-7. Tor's Middle East trainings began in 2009. In December of that year, Jacob Appelbaum did a big tour of the Middle East before heading to the end-of-the-year activist blowout at the Chaos Computer Club conference in Berlin. A monthly activity report filed by Tor with the BBG shows that Jacob met with journalists from Al Jazeera in Qatar and trained a group of activists in Amman, Jordan. The highlight of the trip was a training session at the Arab Bloggers Conference in Beirut. Andrew Lewman, email message sent to Kelly DeYoe, "BBGCON1807S644."

99. Jacob Appelbaum (@ioerror), Twitter posts, December 9-11, 2009, https:// twitter.com/ioerror/status/6502200803, https://twitter.com/ioerror/status /6572987080; Jacob Appelbaum (@ioerror), Twitter post, 8:18am, December 9, 2009, https://twitter.com/ioerror/status/6500619633.

100. David Kushner, "The Darknet: Is the Government Destroying 'the Wild West of the Internet'?" *Rolling Stone*, October 22, 2015.

101. Some inside critics involved with the Broadcasting Board of Governors admitted that promotion of Internet Freedom technologies was part of a much bigger US government project to leverage the Internet as a foreign policy weapon. Jillian York, an employee of the Electronic Frontier Foundation who worked as an adviser to the BBG, minced no words: "I do fundamentally believe that the State Department's 'Internet freedom agenda' is at heart an agenda of regime change, and have made no secret of that opinion," she wrote on her blog in 2015. Jillian C. York, "There Are Other Funding Options Than the USG," February 6, 2015, http://jilliancyork.com/2015/02/06/there-are-other-funding-options-than-the-usg/.

102. Mary Beth Sheridan, "U.S. Warns against Blocking Social Media, Elevates Internet Freedom Policies," *Washington Post*, January 28, 2011.

103. James Glanz and John Markoff, "U.S. Underwrites Internet Detour Around Censors," *New York Times*, June 12, 2011.

104. Tor also began funding multiple high-bandwidth nodes across Europe, Canada, and the United States to speed up the network and keep up with increasing user numbers. Tor even specifically hired a person to expand the so-called independent Tor node network, with funds provided by Tor: "We've hired a dedicated relay community manager. Moritz Bartl of Torservers.net is now responsible for maintaining relationships with relay operators, finding new ISPs for hosting exit relays, and growing the Tor network. . . . We're working on finding partners in Africa and Asia for diversity," wrote Dingledine in a December 2012 report. "We signed a Memorandum of Understanding with the Wau Holland Stiftung organization in Germany to reimburse exit relays located in the European Union," he wrote in a February 2013 update (Dingledine, "April 18–May 17 2013 Progress Report for BBG Contract 50-D-11-0061," Tor Project [blog], 2013, https://surveillancevalley.com/content/citations/bbg-tor-contract-stack-6.pdf). Interesting to note that Dingledine worried that funding Tor nodes could classify Tor as an Internet service provider, which would force it to install a legally mandated FBI surveillance tap. "We are in final discussions about the Tor network and legal aspects of running a funded relay under US laws," he wrote his handlers at the BBG in 2012. "The main concern here is not falling under the definition of Internet Service Provider or telecommunications carrier which would subject Tor to CALEA compliance regulations." CALEA was the legally mandated FBI surveillance tap that every network provider had to install. Ibid.

105. Burma was a curious place for American antisurveillance activists funded by a CIA spinoff to travel to, considering that it has long been a target of US regime change campaigns. In fact, the guru of pro-Western "color revolutions" (Sheryl Gay Stolberg, "Shy U.S. Intellectual Created Playbook Used in a Revolution," *New York Times*, February 16, 2011), Gene Sharp, wrote his famous guide to nonviolent revolutions, *From Dictatorship to Democracy*, initially as an insurgency guide for Burma's opposition movement to help the US overthrow the military junta in the late 1980s. Sharp had crossed into Burma illegally to train opposition activists there—all under the protection and sponsorship of the US government and one Colonel. Robert Helvey, a military intelligence officer (Ruaridh Arrow, *How to Start a Revolution*, documentary film, September 18, 2011). Helvey later played a central role in training Otpor student activists in Serbia, who helped overthrow

Serbian president Slobodan Milosevic ("Interview: Col. Robert Helvey," *A Force More Powerful*, January 29, 2001, http://www.aforcemorepowerful.org/films/bdd /story/otpor/robert-helvey.php).

106. *Internet Access and Openness: Myanmar 2012* (Washington, DC: Open Technology Fund and Radio Free Asia, February 2013), https://www.opentech.fund /files/reports/otf_myanmar_access_openness_public.pdf.

107. Laura Poitras, *Risk*, documentary film, May 2016.

108. "The NSA and Its Willing Helpers," Spiegel Online, July 8, 2013, http://www .spiegel.de/international/world/interview-with-whistleblower-edward-snowden -on-global-spying-a-910006.html.

109. Patrick Howell O'Neill, "Tor Now Reaches 200,000 Users in Russia," Daily Dot, June 18, 2014, https://www.dailydot.com/news/russia-tor-users-censorship/.

110. mikeperry, "This Is What a Tor Supporter Looks Like: Edward Snowden," Tor Project (blog), December 30, 2015, https://blog.torproject.org/blog/what -tor-supporter-looks-edward-snowden.

111. While Edward Snowden stayed quiet regarding US government backing of Tor, the government continued funding it. In 2014, Tor financial disclosures revealed that government contracts added up to $2.3 million, or roughly 90 percent of its discosed budget for that year. The Pentagon, State Department, and Broadcasting Board of Governors each contributed roughly a third of that sum. "2014 IRS Form 990, State of MA Form PC, and Independent Audit Results," Tor Project Inc., 2014, http://web. archive.org/web/20170508113258/https://www.torproject.org/about/findoc /2014-TorProject-combined-Form990_PC_Audit_Results.pdf.

112. Joe Mullin, "Trump's Pick for CIA Director Has Called for Snowden's Execution," Ars Technica, November 18, 2016, https://arstechnica.com/tech-policy/2016/11 /trumps-pick-for-cia-director-has-called-for-snowdens-execution/.

113. Dan "Blah" Meredith, "Update from Congress: More Funds for Internet Freedom Than Ever Before," Open Technology Fund, January 19, 2014, https:// www.opentech.fund/article/update-congress-more-funds-internet-freedom-ever.

114. The law stipulated that the money be used to maintain "the United States Government's technological advantage" in the censorship arms race that had been brewing ever since the Broadcasting Board of Governors began pushing its China broadcasts through the Internet, specifying that the funds be prioritized for countries considered to be "important to the national interests of the United States." The law also was very clear that these tools were meant to subvert the sovereign control of the Internet in targeted countries—what it described as countering "the development of repressive Internet-related laws and regulations." In Washington-speak, that meant that authoritarian allies that heavily censored their Internet such as Saudi Arabia and the United Arab Emirates were off-limits for Internet Freedom. Consolidated Appropriations Act, 2014, Pub. L. No. 113-76, Global Internet Freedom, Sec. 7080, January 15, 2014.

115. Adam Lynn, "OTF Sees Significant Increase in Budget for 2014," Open Technology Fund, April 17, 2014, https://www.opentech.fund/article/otf-sees -significant-increase-budget-2014; *Internet Anti-Censorship Fact Sheet* (Wash-

ington, DC: Broadcasting Board of Governors, May 2013), https://www.bbg.gov/wp-content/media/2013/05/Anti-Censorship-Fact-Sheet-May-2013.pdf.

116. The Open Technology fund, which was launched after the Arab Spring in 2012, was initially called Freedom2Connect. "Radio Free Asia's next generation freedom2connect program is designed to ensure secure communication tools exist for millions of individuals whose online interactions are being monitored or obstructed by repressive governments. Through support of research, development, and implementation of globally-accessible secure communications..." (Freedom2Connect, Radio Free Asia, accessed June 20, 2012, http://web.archive.org/web/20120620231727/http://f2c.rfa.org:80/index.html). The State Department also set up a "venture-capital-style" unit in Washington, DC, that paired career foreign policy operatives with young, hip techies and put them to work cooking up all sorts of gadgets that leveraged the power of social networks. One initiative, which the *New York Times* described as an "operation out of a spy novel" staffed with "young entrepreneurs who look as if they could be in a garage band," involved the creation of something called "Internet in a suitcase"—a device that could be smuggled into a country and unpacked to provide an instant wireless Internet network that would be shared by any device with a WiFi connection and then linked to the rest of the world. The point was to undercut the ability of foreign governments to stop opposition movements by turning off the Internet. Then–Secretary of State Hillary Clinton made projects like this the central plank of her Internet Freedom policy. To her, this was not about regime change but about helping people around the world talk to one another. "We see more and more people around the globe using the Internet, mobile phones and other technologies to make their voices heard as they protest against injustice and seek to realize their aspirations," she told the *New York Times*. "So we're focused on helping them do that, on helping them talk to each other, to their communities, to their governments and to the world." Glanz and Markoff, "U.S. Underwrites Internet Detour."

117. The first version of Radio Free Asia shuttered in 1955, after the agency realized that the Chinese were too poor to own radios and that no one was listening to its broadcasts ("Worldwide Propaganda Network Built by the C.I.A.," *New York Times*, December 26, 1977). A second-generation Radio Free Asia appeared a decade later, this time funded through even murkier organizations with ties to the government of South Korea, the Rev. Sun-Myung Moon's Unification Church, and the Central Intelligence Agency (SAC, San Francisco, "Memorandum to Director, FBI, Subject: *Moon Sun-Myung*, IS—Korea," October 6, 1975, https://surveillancevalley.com/content/citations/moon-sun-myung-fbi-6-october-1975.pdf). Through the 1960s, Radio Free Asia served as a psychological operations component of the Vietnam War. According to the FBI, it "produced anti-communist programs in Washington and beamed them into China, North Korea and North Vietnam" (Scott Armstrong and Charles R. Babcock, "Ex-Director Informs on KCIA Action," *Washington Post*, May 6, 1977). It enjoyed high-level support from within the first Nixon administration and even featured Congressman Gerald

Ford on its board (Robert Parry, "Dark Side of Rev. Moon: Truth, Legend & Lies," Consortium, 1997, https://www.consortiumnews.com/archive/moon4.html). But this version of Radio Free Asia also shut down after being investigated by the Justice Department as part of a larger probe into South Korean government attempts to influence American public opinion to keep the US military engaged against North Korea (Investigation of Korean-American Relations: Report of the Subcommittee on International Organizations of the Comm. on International Relations,' H.R. Rep. [October 31, 1978], https://archive.org/stream/InvestigationOfKorean AmericanRelations/Investigation%20of%20Korean-American%20Relations#page /no/mode/2up).

118. Radio Free Asia was created by Congress and managed and funded by the Broadcasting Board of Governors, but it was also organized as a private nonprofit. This curious structure shielded Radio Free Asia from public accountability, allowing it to claim exemption from the Freedom of Information Act. The private, opaque structure reminded me that during the Cold War, the CIA funneled money to its global propaganda radio station network through private foundations, cutouts designed to hide the agency's involvement. Radio Free Asia seemed to be involved in a similar tradition. I found this out the hard way when I tried to request records from Radio Free Asia and was told that it was exempt from this federal law.

119. "Just as the enormously successful Radio Free Europe and Radio Liberty have retired from the Cold War business, Radio Free Asia has picked up the fight halfway around the world," declared syndicated columnist Georgie Anne Geyer, calling the radio station an "enemy of tyranny." Georgie Anne Geyer, "Enemy of Tyranny," Universal Press Syndicate, January 17, 1997, https://surveillance valley.com/content/citations/georgie-anne-geyer-enemy-of-tyranny-universal -press-syndicate-17-january-1997.png.

120. "FY 2013 Budget Request," Broadcasting Board of Governors, 2012, https:// www.bbg.gov/wp-content/media/2012/02/FY-2013-BBG-Congressional-Budget -Request-FINAL-2-9-12-Small.pdf; James Brooke, "Threats and Responses: Airwaves; Infiltrators of North Korea: Tiny Radios," *New York Times,* March 3, 2003; Glanz and Markoff, "U.S. Underwrites Internet Detour."

121. Dan "Blah" Meredith, "Something About Me," accessed May 2, 2017, https://danblah.com/.

122. "This Is Open Technology Fund—Advisory Council," Open Technology Fund, accessed May 2, 2017, https://www.opentech.fund/about/people/advisory -council.html.

123. OTF programs attracted participants from all over the world: North and South America, Europe, Asia, Africa. They called themselves various names: technologists, researchers, cryptographers, political scientists, and activists. Many of them looked hip and edgy, wore piercings, had funky hairdos and dreads, and swore online like sailors. OTF-sponsored activists talked the language of social justice—of fighting for freedom and defending the powerless—but their projects lined up with US foreign policy objectives. China, Iran, Russia, and Belarus

would pop up in these projects, whereas authoritarian allies of the United States such as Saudi Arabia and United Arab Emirates were conspicuously absent. "Fellows," Open Technology Fund, accessed May 7, 2017, https://www.opentech .fund/about/people/fellows.html.

124. The Tor Project received over $1 million from OTF to pay for security audits and traffic analysis tools and to set up fast Tor exit nodes in the Middle East and Southeast Asia. Yasha Levine, email message sent to Dan Meredith, "Media Request: OTF & Tor," February 9, 2015, https://surveillancevalley.com/content /citations/email-from-yasha-levine-to-dan-meredith-media-request-otf-tor-9 -february-2015.png.

125. Among the tools funded by OTF: a radical anarchist collective called RiseUp used a special secure email and VPN system designed for activists that received over $1 million from the OTF ("LEAP Encryption Access Project," Open Technology Fund, accessed May 22, 2017, https://www.opentech.fund/project /leap-encryption-access-project); a WikiLeaks whistleblowing alternative called GlobaLeaks, endorsed by Tor's Jacob Appelbaum, received nearly $350,000. The platform was used by a variety of organizations in line with the State Department's regime-change operations around the world: from right-wing portals that asked for the evidence of Hugo Chavez's corruption in Venezuela to the leaks submission systems of a Tunisian group set up to help Internet organizing during the Arab Spring ("GlobaLeaks," Open Technology Fund, accessed May 22, 2017, https:// www.opentech.fund/project/globaleaks). Qubes OS, a secure operating system, received $570,000 ("Qubes OS," Open Technology Fund, accessed May 22, 2017, https://www.opentech.fund/project/qubes-os). There are several dozen other projects and fellowships. For more information, see OTF's website: https://www .opentech.fund.

126. "We really quickly found out that a lot of developers that were trying to access places close to censorship, if they wanted really good service, they needed to go through Amazon—which has servers in the United States, couple of places in Europe and Japan and Hong Kong. We pushed a cloud close to these areas in places . . . we can put nodes and servers in places say like Turkey and know that it's probably not going to get raided if people are doing things that are in trouble in other places," Dan Meredith explained during in a 2014 BBG board meeting. "We give our tools in-kind access to this so they can get really really close so that they don't have to send a proposal to us every time with system administration or engineering costs. We save money paying thirty different projects for exactly the same thing, we invest in it one time and they get access to it. We contract it with these good folks to keep it maintained and updated and it saves everybody money" ("BBG Board Meeting, Part 4," April 11, 2014, https://archive.org/details /BBGBoardMeeting04112014). Countries where OTF funds were deployed for "digital emergencies" included Iran, Azerbaijan, Vietnam, Myanmar, and Tibet ("Results," Open Technology Fund, accessed May 7, 2017, https://www.opentech. fund/results).

127. Danny Yadron, "Moxie Marlinspike: The Coder Who Encrypted Your Texts," *Wall Street Journal*, July 9, 2015. "Open Whisper Systems," Open Technology Fund, accessed September 26, 2017, https://www.opentech.fund/project/open-whisper-systems.

128. "Every time someone downloads Signal and makes their first encrypted call, FBI Director Jim Comey cries. True fact." Chris Soghoian (@csoghoian), Twitter post, November 2, 2015, 3;14 p.m., https://twitter.com/csoghoian/status/661320586115858432.

129. Edward Snowden (@Snowden), Twitter post, September 21, 2016, 6:50 a.m., https://twitter.com/snowden/status/778592275144314884; Edward Snowden (@Snowden), Twitter post, November 2, 2015, 2:46 p.m., https://twitter.com/snowden/status/661313394906161152.

130. Edward Snowden (@Snowden), Twitter post, October 12, 2015, 5:05 p.m., https://twitter.com/snowden/status/653723172953583617?lang=en.

131. moxie, "Open Whisper Systems Partners with Google on End-to-End Encryption for Allo," Open Whisper Systems (blog), May 18, 2016, https://whispersystems.org/blog/allo/. Google also entered into a partnership with the Open Technology Fund on a privacy project called Simply Secure, which promised to make privacy and encryption easy to use for even the most technically incompetent user.

132. *2014 Annual Report* (Washington, DC: Open Technology Fund, 2014), https://www.opentech.fund/sites/default/files/attachments/otf_fy2014_annualreport.pdf. Also: "With increasingly restrictive regulations in a growing number of nation-states, and a sharp rise in sophisticated attacks against the people and organizations who support a more civil and democratic society, the need for OTF support is greater than ever. That same year saw a tightening of censorship in Russia, Southern Africa, Latin America, Southeast Asia, and China."

133. "Someone knew the real IP. I assumed they obtained it by becoming a guard node. So, I migrated to a new server and set up private guard nodes. There was significant downtime and someone has mentioned that they discovered the IP via a leak from lighttpd," wrote Ulbricht in his diary on March 25. "Attack continues. No word from attacker. Site is open, but occasionally tor crashes and has to be restarted," he wrote on May 2. "Ulbricht Log," *United States of America v. Ross William Ulbricht*, Case 15-1815, Document 121–1, SA-38 through SA-42, June 17, 2016.

134. Andy Greenberg, "Read the Transcript of Silk Road's Boss Ordering 5 Assassinations," *Wired*, February 2, 2015; "Ulbricht Log," Document 121–1, SA-38 through SA-42. After a user told Dread Pirate Roberts (aka Ross Ulbricht) he had hacked Silk Road and obtained contact details for every user of the site, and threatened to leak the information unless he was paid off, Dread Pirate Roberts talked to the Hells Angels—a major supplier of drugs for Silk Road—and put out several hits. This information came out during a federal trial that showed in the end Dread Pirate Roberts paid the Hells Angels $730,000 to kill a total of six people (the blackmailer and the blackmailer's associates), although it is not clear whether those murders were actually carried out.

The founder of Silk Road did approve and pay for the murders; some journalists speculate that it was actually a ruse to extort money from him. See: Joe Mullin, "The Hitman Scam: Dread Pirate Roberts' Bizarre Murder-for-Hire Attempts," Ars Technica, February 9, 2015, https://arstechnica.com/tech-policy/2015/02/the-hitman-scam-dread-pirate-roberts-bizarre-murder-for-hire-attempts/.

135. The system administrator, Curtis Green, was never actually killed. He was busted by the police and turned into an informant. His death was staged for Ulbricht's benefit. "Dread Pirate Roberts believed Green had stolen money from Silk Road. Green worked closely with Carl Mark Force, a Drug Enforcement Administration agent, who masqueraded as a hitman. He pretended to murder Green and even sent Roberts staged photos of the hit. Federal law enforcement and prosecutors argue that Ulbricht was the one who ordered the hit." Howell O'Neill, "Silk Road Murder-for-Hire Target Is Writing a Memoir," Daily Dot, June 21, 2016, https://www.dailydot.com/layer8/curtis-green-silk-road-memoir/.

136. Sarah Jeong, "The DHS Agent Who Infiltrated Silk Road to Take Down Its Kingpin," *Forbes*, January 14, 2015.

137. Joshuah Bearman, "The Untold Story of Silk Road, Part 2: The Fall," *Wired*, June 2015.

138. It's not clear whether Julian Assange's support was what gave Dread Pirate Roberts the confidence to use Tor to build Silk Road, but the young programmer began developing the site almost at the same time WikiLeaks became an international sensation.

139. "Child-Porn Website Creator Accidentally Reveals IP Address, Leading to 870 Arrests," ABC News, May 6, 2017, http://www.abc.net.au/news/2017-05-06/playpen-child-porn-site-creator-steven-chase-sentenced/8502626.

140. Joseph Cox, "Confirmed: Carnegie Mellon University Attacked Tor, Was Subpoenaed by Feds," Motherboard Vice, February 24, 2016, https://motherboard.vice.com/en_us/article/d7yp5a/carnegie-mellon-university-attacked-tor-was-subpoenaed-by-feds.

141. Roger Dingledine, "Did the FBI Pay a University to Attack Tor Users?" Tor Project (blog), November 11, 2015, https://blog.torproject.org/blog/did-fbi-pay-university-attack-tor-users.

142. "Ethical Tor Research: Guidelines," Tor Project, November 11, 2015, http://web.archive.org/web/20170506125847/https://blog.torproject.org/blog/ethical-tor-research-guidelines.

143. "Tor Stinks," National Security Agency top-secret presentation, June 2012, first released by the *Guardian*, https://surveillancevalley.com/content/citations/tor-stinks-national-security-agency-top-secret-june-2012.pdf.

144. Barton Gellman, Craig Timberg, and Steven Rich, "Files Show NSA Targeted Tor Encrypted Network," *Washington Post*, October 5, 2013.

145. This *Washington Post* article, published on October 5, 2013, just four days after Ulbricht's arrest in San Francisco, added that techniques developed by the NSA were being used by federal law enforcement to target dark web sites like Silk Road.

146. "Tor Stinks," 23.

147. The 2012 "Tor Stinks" NSA presentation also revealed that the NSA, along with the British spy agency GCHQ and other partners, ran multiple Tor nodes in order to control as much of the network as possible. Although the document omits the exact number of nodes run by the NSA and its partners, the author plainly indicates that the agency was interested in running more. This was an important detail that promoters of Tor were loath to discuss. Despite Tor's claims of having thousands of nodes that made up the parallel network, the network was engineered in a way that routed traffic through nodes with the largest bandwidth. As a result, the vast bulk of Tor's connection ran through a handful of the fastest and most dependable servers. Fifty relays handled about 80 percent of the traffic, whereas just five relays handled 30 percent (Roger Dingledine, email message, "[tor-relays] Call for discussion: turning funding into more exit relays," July 23, 2012, http://web.archive.org/web/20170502103740/https://lists.torproject.org/piper mail/tor-relays/2012-July/001433.html). Running fifty Tor nodes doesn't seem too difficult to do for any of the world's intelligence agencies—whether American, German, British, Russian, Chinese, or Iranian. Hell, if you're an intelligence agency, there's no reason not to run a Tor node. As Snowden's documents showed, both the NSA and GCHQ ran such nodes.

148. Sander Venema, "Why I Won't Recommend Signal Anymore," November 5, 2016, https://sandervenema.ch/.

149. Yasha Levine, "#J20, Signal, Spies and the Cult of Crypto," Surveillance Valley (blog), January 14, 2017, https://surveillancevalley.com/blog /thoughts-on-activists-and-the-cult-of-crypto.

150. "Vault 7: CIA Hacking Tools Revealed," WikiLeaks, March 7, 2017, https://wikileaks.org/ciav7p1/.

151. It later emerged during the trial of Chelsea Manning that the army private used Tor during his work in Iraq. "Tor is a system intended to provide anonymity online. The software routes internet traffic through a network of servers and other Tor clients in order to conceal the users location and identity. I was familiar with Tor and had it previously installed on a computer to anonymously monitor the social media website of militia groups operating within central Iraq," he said during trial. Micah Lee, "Bradley Manning's Statement Shows that US Intelligence Analysts Are Trained in Using Tor," Micah Lee's Blog, March 12, 2013, https://micahflee .com/2013/03/bradley-mannings-statement-shows-that-us-intelligence-analysts -are-trained-in-using-tor/.

152. In 2010, 70 percent of people polled by Gallup said they were against the tracking of online behavior for advertising (Lymari Morales, "U.S. Internet Users Ready to Limit Online Tracking for Ads," Gallup, December 21, 2010, http:// www.gallup.com/poll/145337/internet-users-ready-limit-online-tracking-ads .aspx). In another poll a few years later, 68 percent believed current privacy laws did not do enough to protect people online (Lee Rainie, Sara Kiesler, Ruogu Kang, and Mary Madden, "Anonymity, Privacy, and Security Online," Pew Research Center, September 5, 2013, http://www.pewinternet.org/2013/09/05 /anonymity-privacy-and-security-online/).

Epilogue

1. D. M. Luebke and S. Milton, "Locating the Victim: An Overview of Census-Taking, Tabulation Technology and Persecution in Nazi Germany," *IEEE Annals of the History of Computing* 16, no. 3 (Autumn/Fall 1994): 35.

2. Edwin Black, *IBM and the Holocaust: The Strategic Alliance between Nazi Germany and America's Most Powerful Corporation* (New York: Crown, 2001).

3. Götz Aly and Karl Heinz Roth, *The Nazi Census: Identification and Control in the Third Reich* (Philadelphia: Temple University Press, 2004).

4. Stephen Wolff, telephone interview with author, October 23, 2015

Index

Evgenia Kovda

Yasha Levine is a Russian-born American investigative journalist and a founding editor of *The eXiled*. His work has been published in *The Baffler*, *Pando Daily*, *Wired*, *The Nation*, *Penthouse*, and many others. He and his wife, Evgenia, split their time between New York and St. Petersburg, Russia.